The Films of Edgar G. Ulmer

Edited by
Bernd Herzogenrath

THE SCARECROW PRESS, INC.
Lanham • Maryland • Toronto • Plymouth, UK

SCARECROW PRESS, INC.

Published in the United States of America
by Scarecrow Press, Inc.
A wholly owned subsidiary of
The Rowman & Littlefield Publishing Group, Inc.
4501 Forbes Boulevard, Suite 200, Lanham, Maryland 20706
www.scarecrowpress.com

Estover Road
Plymouth PL6 7PY
United Kingdom

British Library Cataloguing in Publication Information Available

Library of Congress Cataloging-in-Publication Data

The films of Edgar G. Ulmer / Bernd Herzogenrath [editor].
p. cm.
Includes bibliographical references and index.
ISBN 978-0-8108-6700-0 (pbk. : alk. paper) — ISBN 978-0-8108-6736-9 (ebook)
1. Ulmer, Edgar G. (Edgar George), 1904–1972—Criticism and interpretation. I. Herzogenrath, Bernd, 1964–.
PN1998.3.U46F55 2009
791.4302'32092—dc22 [B] 2008051365

∞™ The paper used in this publication meets the minimum requirements of American National Standard for Information Sciences—Permanence of Paper for Printed Library Materials, ANSI/NISO Z39.48-1992.
Manufactured in the United States of America.

To the Memory of Edgar G. Ulmer

* * *

For Arianné
For Olomouc

Contents

Foreword

Arianné Ulmer Cipes, the Edgar G. Ulmer Preservation Corp.

I was delighted to learn that Professor Bernd Herzogenrath was compiling an anthology of works about my father for publication by Scarecrow Press. He has and continues to have my full cooperation and authorization. More than ten years ago, as my mother, Shirley Kassler Ulmer, began to decline with age, we felt it essential to start the process of preserving the works of Ulmer. We then established a nonprofit public benefit corporation, the Edgar G. Ulmer Preservation Corporation.

Thanks to the hard work and dedication of many, especially Michael Friend, Michael Pogorzelski, and Howard Prouty, we now have a large collection of 35 mm and 16 mm prints and negatives at the Academy of Motion Picture Arts and Sciences Film Archive in Hollywood, in addition to various other worldwide archives. All paper, photographic, and family memoirs are held at the Herrick Library of the academy. We presently have ongoing projects to preserve additional films. Hopefully, new interest stimulated by many festivals will help raise the necessary funds from donors to achieve these goals. In 2006 we coproduced with Mischief Films a documentary, *Edgar G. Ulmer—The Man Off-Screen* (dir. Michael Palm), distributed by Kino Video/DVD in the United States. I would also like to thank David Kalat of *All Day Entertainment*, who has written many articles on Ulmer and distributed seven DVDs of Ulmer productions.

Aside from the obvious preservation of the actual films, it is the written materials, books and articles, that are truly precious. These guarantee that future generations will know the details and facts regarding the films of Edgar G. Ulmer. This year Bill Krohn, an undaunted pioneer in resurrecting the works of Ulmer, published a definitive piece on *The Naked Dawn* in the

French Revue Cinema 013 of *Esthetic and History of Cinema*, Spring 2007. The British Film Institute published Noah Isenberg's book *Detour* in 2008, a detailed analysis of this iconic film. He is presently working on *Perennial Detour: The Cinema of Edgar G. Ulmer*, the Ulmer family authorized biography. Naturally, but for the limits of time and space, I would also thank each of the many contributors to the written materials that have been created in recent years.

I wish to express my profound gratitude to Professor Bernd Herzogenrath, who has recently been the moving force for the collection of Ulmer aficionados throughout the world. His establishment of the Ulmerfest 2006 at Palacký University in Olomouc, Czech Republic (Ulmer's birthplace) made it possible to finally gather these contributors.

It is my fondest desire that you both enjoy and be inspired by this book, as you become more acquainted with the films of Edgar G. Ulmer.

"Talent Obliges"—Edgar G. Ulmer

Foreword

Out of Nothing

Peter Bogdanovich

Edgar G. Ulmer had been a kind of legendary underground figure for years when I decided to look him up early in 1970. He was recovering from a stroke that had for a while deprived him of speech and the power in his legs, but he had struggled back and by the time I met him he had only a slight limp and minor difficulties with words. His recovery was as much a miracle against heavy odds as some of his best pictures. And nobody had ever made good pictures faster or for less money than Edgar Ulmer. What he could do with nothing (occasionally in the script department as well) remains an object lesson for those directors, myself included, who complain about tight budgets and schedules. Edgar rarely had more than six days for a feature! That he could also communicate a strong visual style and personality with the meager means usually available to him is close to miraculous. But he did—and more than once—making poverty-row classics like the ultimate one-dark-night-as-I-was-driving picture, *Detour*, or that mystical Karloff-Lugosi thriller, *The Black Cat*. These and the dense psychological melodramas *Ruthless* and *The Naked Dawn*, as well as John Carradine's *Bluebeard*, are just the first that come to mind.

Though nearly seventy, he was anything but an invalid in mind or body, was involved in several projects, was full of time and advice for students, and was generous to me with his energy. He had humor and passion and a kind of demonic charm. Of course, Hollywood exploited him—he was too quick, too smart. If he could turn out quality as fast as he did, why give him more time? Generally, the industry has always preferred "faster" to "better." The acting

Kindly reprinted with permission from Peter Bogdanovich, *Who the Devil Made It: Conversations with Legendary Film Directors*, New York: Ballantine Books, 1998, 558–604.

and the execution may not always have been as brilliant as the basic conception, but often this was all Ulmer could get: with such grueling schedules, degrees of compromise are allowed. Edgar went from the Olympian heights of picture making to the absolute lower depths. As assistant to the incomparable German F. W. Murnau on his three most important and influential films—*The Last Laugh*, *Sunrise*, and *Tabu*—Ulmer was there at the heart and soul of the best that pictures can offer; thirty years later, when things were really rough, Ulmer had to direct a Z-budget nudie. In 1929, he was closely involved as codirector on a project (*People on Sunday*) that marked the debut in pictures for Billy Wilder (writer), Fred Zinnemann (assistant photographer), and Eugen Schüfftan (photographer); Robert Siodmak codirected. These four became superstars while Ulmer always had to scrape by, often doing the most oddball, fly-by-night movies—for a Yiddish organization, say, or a Ukrainian committee. Somehow Edgar seemed never to lose his excitement or enthusiasm, no matter how lowly the work: he found ways to make things interesting; everything that might be considered a hindrance by most was a challenging test for him. Of course, he could experiment—no one really cared what he did if he stayed within budget. Experimenting is what Ulmer loved; he took wild risks all the time, and always landed on his feet.

We had three interview sessions—during which I met his beloved wife and collaborator, Shirley Castle Ulmer, and their picture-wise daughter, Arianné—and then my work on a film took me away for almost a year. We had covered his early days in Germany and America and much of his career into the late forties, leaving another couple of decades to go. We spoke several times on the phone, but before we could meet again to finish our talks, another stroke paralyzed him. He never walked nor spoke again, though he could understand everything that was said to him, responding with a nod or shake of his head. That must have only made it worse for such an active man. I never saw him again. He died a year later.

The interviews did seem to be the only ones of any length that have survived. They were originally published in somewhat different form in Jonas Mekas's *Film Culture* in 1974; that version was reprinted in Todd McCarthy's excellent anthology, *Kings of the Bs* (1975), now out of print. Since his death, Shirley Ulmer and I have conspired a couple of times to try to get new versions done of some of Edgar's work; this year a remake is being planned of one of his little-known Yiddish comedies, which I was approached to direct.

What I remember most about Edgar is his extraordinarily intense passion for pictures and the process of making them. There was such exuberance and joy in his telling of the most outrageous or difficult, loony or surreal aspects of making pictures, especially ones with virtually no money and no professionals—like those amazing Ukrainian productions—that the good-natured obsession he had with pictures was obvious. Did he have a tendency to exaggerate—as some have accused him of? Don't most people? Certainly the movies are a fabulist's paradise, because anything *is* possible. Didn't Edgar have to prove that with nearly every picture? Ulmer was a child of theater and of the movies in their childhood, and he never lost his innocent wonder at the challenge and magic of the medium.

Acknowledgments

Thank you, Claudia, for all your love and support during all these years.

I would like to thank the good people at Scarecrow for this opportunity; plus a big THANX! to Janna Wanagas for her great help.

I have dedicated this book to Olomouc, the Moravian town where Ulmer was born, but what I *really* mean is that I dedicate this to my Olomouc friends Jana Kynclová, Matthew Sweney, and Bob Hýsek, and to all the coffee-girls of past, present, and future . . .

A sincere and heartfelt "Díky!" goes out to Andrea Konstankiewicz of Tara Fuki. You know why.

Introduction

Necessary Detours—Putting the Ulmer Back into Ulmermouc

Bernd Herzogenrath

Edgar G. Ulmer was the "King of Poverty Row," a director who the French *nouvelle vague* regarded as an auteur, a filmmaker whose individual voice and handwriting stands out, a maker of *independent movies* before that category even existed. Undeservedly almost forgotten, Ulmer was rediscovered in the 1950s by the French critics of *Cahiers du cinéma* and in the early 1970s by some young American directors who were interested in the history of film, the dimly-lit side streets of the Hollywood mainstream, and Ulmer's particular brand of filmmaking. As François Truffaut put it, watching Ulmer's films, "we see him behind every image and feel we know him intimately when the lights go back on" (156).

But who was Edgar G. Ulmer? A confidence man? A genius? A jack of all trades? The curious circumstance that Ulmer legend and Ulmer fact are somewhat conjoined twins that cannot be separated makes the issue of the Ulmer identity an exciting question. Stefan Grissemann, in his excellent and much-welcomed biography of Ulmer, often talks about Ulmer as a "phantom," a kind of "man who wasn't there."[1]

According to Ulmer himself, it all started in Vienna, the city of his birth . . . and here, the legend already takes over . . .

Vienna—the mere mention of this city evokes ideas of culture and decadence, contrasting images of high and low art, glamor and vice. That's what Ulmer might also have thought when he gave Vienna as his place of birth in his interviews with Truffaut and *Cahiers du cinéma*. However, as cosmopolitan as it may sound, it's the stuff of legend, of a self-propelled legend, to be sure. Edgar Georg Ulmer was the son of Henriette Ulmer, née Edels, from Vienna, and Siegfried Ulmer, a Jewish socialist and wine merchant from Ivanovice na Hané in the present-day Czech Republic. On September 17, 1904, Ulmer was born in Olomouc (then Olmütz) in the Czech Republic—and *not* in Vienna—because the Ulmer family was living there at the family property of Siegfried Ulmer's grandparents. Though he left Olomouc when he was still young and was to work in Vienna (for example, with Max Reinhardt at the Theater an der Josefstadt), Ulmer was not to return to Vienna until the 1950s, as he was too scared to return to what he thought was a ruined city "probably full of murderers," as he put it in a private letter.

After years of communicating with officials and consulting archives in the Czech Republic, I was able to locate Ulmer's birthplace in Olomouc. Because of his Jewish background, his family papers were not held in the Olomouc City Archives but collected centrally in Prague. It was there, in the vaults of the Národní Archiv (National Archives), that I finally struck paydirt and discovered Ulmer's birth certificate, with all the necessary details. It revealed that Edgar G. Ulmer was born in Olmütz in "Resselgasse 1, Ort Neugasse." That was his address in 1904—today, the address reads "Resslova 1," in the part of town known as "Nová ulice." If you go there today, you will find two memorial plaques created by the Olomouc artist Bohumil Teplý—a large one

Figure I.1. Ulmer's birth home in Olomouc, Czech Republic. Courtesy of Bernd Herzogenrath.

commemorating the birth of Olomouc's famous son, and a smaller one commemorating the discoverer, yours truly.[2]

Speaking of "Olomouc's famous son": In 2006, when the idea for this memorial plaque was brought before the city council in Olomouc, the people in charge first thought it was a hoax . . . a double hoax, even. They (1) had never heard of Ulmer, and (2) wouldn't believe that such a famous director had been born in their small city. "Yes, Virginia, there is an Edgar G. Ulmer" is one reaction that springs to mind. One also thinks of Freud's famous "kettle logic," from his *Interpretation of Dreams*:

> [A man was] charged by one of his neighbors with having given him back a borrowed kettle in a damaged condition. The defendant asserted, first, that he had given it back undamaged; secondly, that the kettle had a hole in it when he borrowed it; and thirdly, that he had never borrowed the kettle from his neighbor at all. (152–53)

It should be noted that Freud was born in Příjbor, North Moravia, not far from Olomouc. Edmund Husserl also was born a stone's throw away, in Prostějov. Ludwig Wittgenstein attended military school in Olomouc. So Ulmer was in illustrious company, and, far from being provincial, northern Moravia can be considered the cradle of modernism.

This reaction on the part of the officials is also quite fitting, I argue, for a man and artist whose life and work can be characterized by one word (which also is the title of one of his most famous movies)—*Detour*. There was nothing smooth about Ulmer's life, ever. Nor was there anything smooth about his art, which both in its totality and its individual contributions never forms a Keatsean "well-wrought urn," but is more of a postmodern pastiche, a nomadic patchwork of non sequiturs—and it's all the fresher and more enjoyable for that. Not an urn, but always a turn—a detour at every instant, darting sideways on every level.

As Gilles Deleuze has stated in a commentary, not on filmmaking, but on art and writing, "There are no straight lines . . . [Art] is the set of *necessary detours* that are created in each case to reveal the life in things" (*Essays Critical and Clinical*, 2, my emphasis). And in his *Cinema* books, which unfortunately do not take notice of Ulmer, Deleuze comments on the important effect that low-budget moviemaking had on the invention and creation of new cinematic images. "Economic constraints undoubtedly gave rise to flashes of inspiration and images dreamed up with a view to economy could have universal repercussions" (162), Deleuze writes, and he concludes that "we can often see the B movie as an active center of experimentation and creation" (163). True—and in the case of Ulmer criticism, this should also put a stop to speculations about what masterpieces Ulmer, the auteur, would have created if only he'd had the money. Perhaps Ulmer's films are great *because* of these restrictions, not *despite* them. In this way, Ulmer can be seen as the Silver Surfer, brilliantly riding the waves of turbulence. Working on the edge of chaos, far from equilibrium, far from Hollywood's rich tables, he uses this turbulence as a source of artistic creation. Ulmer may have been born with a plastic spoon in his mouth; but with this plastic spoon, he could make magic.

This anthology attempts to shed some light on this magic, on the "Ulmer touch," and on these necessary detours that reveal the life in things.[3] After a head start with Peter Bogdanovich's well-known "Out of Nothing," the introduction to his interviews with Ulmer (which is reprinted here from *Who The Devil Made It* with the author's kind permission), Noah Isenberg's essay, surveying a range of exemplary films directed by Ulmer, seeks to explore the striking tendency in Ulmer to address the vexing question of home and homelessness in his work, as well as in his personal writings. "Permanent Vacation: Home and Homelessness in the Life and Work of Edgar G. Ulmer" examines the tendency as a phenomenon related to a specific cultural-historical moment and an individual career trajectory, while extrapolating from the case of Ulmer larger conclusions with regard to the position of exiled European artists and filmmakers in America. Isenberg mainly focuses on the aesthetic dimensions of Ulmer's films—some of them, such as *The Black Cat* (1934) and *Detour* (1945), rather well known, others more of an independent and underground nature—while Ulmer's biography, a life marked by constant displacement, figures with considerable prominence in his discussion.

Ulmer's sustained engagement with American mass culture and European art cinema is an engagement riddled with idiosyncrasy and contradiction, as he frequently drew on elements of both traditions in depicting home (familiarity, identification, belonging) and homelessness (rupture, disorientation, despair). For Ulmer, the two poles tend to remain aesthetically interwoven—inextricably bound up together in his life story—and in productive, if also painful, dialogue with each other, rather than in simple binary opposition.

It is this constant feeling of "not belonging" that may have urged Ulmer into exploring visions of shared traditions. In his chapter "The Search for Community," John Belton explores the utopian aspects of Ulmer's Yiddish films of the 1930s, distinguishing them from the director's more dystopian film noirs of the 1940s and 1950s. Drawing on Fredric Jameson's distinctions between works of mass and folk culture, the chapter argues that films such as *Green Fields*, *The Light Ahead*, *The Singing Blacksmith*, and *American Matchmaker* are products of an organic social group and share a common language and references to a common cultural tradition. These (and other) Yiddish films draw on and appeal to a traditional folklore and body of cultural practices that provide a common heritage for this unique ethnic group. Just as important is the fact that these works are produced and consumed within this common social group; they are created by members of this community for other members of that same community (rather than by one social group for another, as is often the case with white-produced race films).

A completely dystopian vision (of a community as Satanist sect) drives Ulmer's *The Black Cat* (1934). As discussed by Herbert Schwaab in his chapter "On the Graveyards of Europe: The Horror of Modernism in *The Black Cat*," this is a film which belongs to a cycle of classic horror films from the beginning of the sound-film era. Among films such as *Frankenstein*, *Dracula*, *Dr. Jekyll and Mr. Hyde*, and *The Mummy*, *The Black Cat* is unique for its set design, which is strongly influenced by modernist architecture and art deco. Whereas most horror films relied on an unspecific Englishness of old "gothic" castles and ghost houses, Ulmer's human monsters haunt a stylish world of white walls with clear geometric lines and abstract and minimalist ornaments. Making clear references to the traumatic experience of World War I, especially in one scene in which the camera roams aimlessly and elegantly through the vaults of a former fortress, the film could be read as a weird reflection on modernism. It foreshadows cinematic techniques used in the European art cinema decades later, for example the tracking shots in Alain Resnais' *Hiroshima mon amour* and *La guerre est finie*. Ulmer's film seems to blame modernism as the source of moral decay, the same way Pier Paolo Pasolini blames abstract art as the source for cruelty and fascism in *Salo,* another masterpiece of art cinema.

Schwaab focuses on the following questions: Is it possible to draw a line from a preclassical Hollywood horror film to the postclassical modernism of art film? And to what purposes is Ulmer using the modernist architecture and stylistic devices such as tracking camera shots, expressionistic decor, and synthetic editing in the style of Eisenstein? Schwaab argues that Ulmer's modernism and highly conscious use of style are ambiguous and allow for no final statement on the meaning of the film. But this might also explain why the film remains an object of incessant fascination for cinephiles and film scholars. Its "failed" modernism, Schwaab claims, gives us beautiful and significant moments, in which the cinematic devices such as the tracking camera are set free from the narration to leave a deep impression on the film's viewers.

D. J. Turner, in his chapter "From Nine to Nine," presents the facts surrounding the genesis, shooting, and eventual release in Great Britain of what must now be the least known and least seen of all the films in Ulmer's eclectic oeuvre. It was made in Canada, set in Canada, and produced by a company incorporated in Canada at the behest of a company (Universal) that had, according to all accounts, blackballed Ulmer in Hollywood. Turner, apart from locating and restoring the original nitrate negative, has established that the print released in Britain was twelve minutes longer than the version now extant. He tries to extract some meaning from the muddled plot of this modest thriller shot in just nine days and delivered for registration under the British quota act just five weeks after the end of shooting. Turner has found records of the London trade show that took place one week after registration. Those present, according to the reviewer for *Kinematograph Weekly*, recognized the continuity problems; he gave it a very poor notice, adding that the film "got the bird" at the trade show. Thanks to his British schooling, Turner has confirmed that this term has a decidedly negative connotation and the film was most likely met with hoots of derision.

Jonathan Skolnik, in his chapter "Exile on 125th Street: African Americans, Germans, and Jews in *Moon over Harlem*," presents Ulmer's foray into the world of black-cast filmmaking. *Moon over Harlem*, in this respect, is unique among his "ethnic" productions of the 1930s. Skolnik gives new information about the film's genesis and reception, as well as a discussion of archival evidence of Ulmer's conflict with industry censors (the Hays office) over the film. Skolnik interprets *Moon over Harlem* as being emblematic of the complex identity of a German-Jewish refugee from Nazi racism in urban America during the segregation era. Seen against the background of black/Jewish tensions in Depression-era Harlem, Skolnik argues, Ulmer's aesthetic choices as a director take on new meaning.

Together with *Moon Over Harlem*, Ulmer's four Yiddish films—*Grine Felder* (*Green Fields*, 1937), *Yankl der Shmid* (*Yankl the Blacksmith*, 1938), *Di Klyatshe* (*The Light Ahead*, 1939), and *Amerikaner Shadkhn* (*American Matchmaker*, 1940)—constitute Ulmer's "ethnic oeuvre," which is generally treated as an anomalous interlude in a career more noted for his canonical film noirs. Ulmer's checkered relationship to his Jewishness—marrying and becoming an Episcopalian, remarrying a Jew and reconverting—also makes him an unlikely candidate for spearheading a so-called "golden age" of Yiddish cinema. But Ulmer's relationship to Hollywood, to his Jewishness, to his Weimar-era background, and to his status as a European refugee in America are precisely what make his Yiddish-language films so fascinating. Indeed, as Vincent Brook argues in his chapter "Forging the 'New Jew': Ulmer's Yiddish Films," Ulmer's "double exile—from mainstream American culture as well as from his Austro-German homeland—coupled with his prodigal return to Jewishness, made him an ideal conduit and catalyst for the Yiddish film revival."

The key thematic strand in Ulmer's Yiddish films is the concept of the "New Jew." In *Grine Felder* and *Yankl der Shmid*, the concept is articulated through a dialectical exchange between two Jewish archetypes, the *yeshive bokher* (religious-school student) and the *musklyid* (Muscle Jew). In *Di Klyatshe* and *Amerikaner Shadkhn*, the Old World *shrayber* (writer) and New World matchmaker carry the torch for the New Jew. Each film proposes the urgent need for forging a New Jew in the wake of the demise of eastern European Jewry. Taken as a body of work, the films indeed can be seen as a stepping-stone for his more famous films to come, but not merely due to Ulmer's growing aesthetic affinity for a darkly expressionist cinematic style. On a more fundamental level, his Yiddish-language work bears witness to Ulmer's growing existential awareness of what it meant "to be or not to be" a Jew.

In his Oscar-winning *Annie Hall* (made in 1977), Woody Allen closes his reflection on human relationships with the following joke: "A man complains to his psychiatrist that his brother-in-law thinks he's a chicken. When the doctor suggests putting him in a mental institution, the man claims: 'I would like to but we need the eggs.'" This joke displays a paradox typical not only for the "Jewish neurosis," but also for the two movies that Miriam Strube analyzes in her chapter "When You Get to the Fork, Take It: From Ulmer's Yiddish Cinema to Woody Allen." Strube argues that in Ulmer's fourth and final Yiddish film, *Amerikaner Shadkhn* (made in 1940), some of Allen's central themes are anticipated: existential issues, such as questions of Jewish ambivalence and feelings of differentness from and similarities to WASP society; intellectual approaches to life; urban settings; neurotic insecurities and, in connection with this, the interest in, but also suspicion of, Freudian psychoanalysis as a means to a better understanding of human thinking and behavior; and, last but not least, problematic gender relations.

Woody Allen is certainly the leading director who focuses on the figure of the Jewish neurotic. However, as Strube shows, all the essentials of this figure can already be found in Ulmer's *Amerikaner Shadkhn*: the feeling of in-betweenness, the absence of Judaism but presence of a Jewish sensibility, the humor, the self-reflexivity, the troubled relationship to women, and the assimilation and Americanization of Jewish identity into a non-Jewish lifestyle.

In his 1943 movie *Isle of Forgotten Sins*, Ulmer, along with composer-conductor Leo Erdody, shapes a dreamy South Seas adventure into a meditation on the universal philosophical themes developed in Richard Wagner's four-part music drama *Der Ring des Nibelungen*. (See chapter 8, "A World Destroyed By Gold: Shared Allegories of Capital in Wagner's *Ring* and Ulmer's *Isle of Forgotten Sins*," in this book.) Ulmer expresses these concerns with liberal quotations of Wagnerian leitmotifs woven into the movie's almost constant underscoring. Andrew Repasky McElhinney contextualizes Ulmer in a line of theatrical geniuses beginning with Buchner and continuing with Brecht, while exploring Wagner's and Ulmer's shared allegories of modern capital (i.e., gold), where wealth can only be achieved by renouncing love/nature.

From fatal allegories (and allegories of fate), we proceed to Ulmer's classic film about fate—*Detour*. And woman proves to be most fatal here—the femme fatale has been recognized as one of the iconic representations of the qualities of the film noir. Based on the premise that the general characteristics of the film noir are linked to the visual style, Alena Smiešková's chapter on "Ulmer and the Noir Femme Fatale" focuses on three dissimilar representations of the femme fatale in Ulmer's films. Hedy Lamarr, Ann Savage, and Barbara Payton portray the elusive and subversive women dislocated from the traditional family definition. Smiešková's chapter examines two aspects of Ulmer's films, the aesthetic and historical aspects. In terms of the aesthetics, the argument goes back to the Kantian idea of the sublime, as it has been reinterpreted by Jean-François Lyotard in connection with the unpresentable and unrepresentable in contemporary art. Thus, she interprets Ulmer's noir femme fatale as a construct where physical presentations of beauty reflect the abstract concepts that elude the figuration, such as evil, fate, and truth. The chapter focuses on the visual and stylistic nuances that Ulmer employs in order to find the physical figuration of the unpresentable—that is, lighting, editing, camera angle, and rhetoric. It also examines the history of Ulmer's particular film-noir strategies in correspondence with the changing tradition of American film after World War II. *Strange Woman* (1946), *Detour* (1945), and *Murder Is My Beat* (1955) convey forbidden themes, where corruption and despair can be the norm. They thus represent an aberration from a classical understanding of American character, and create familiar settings populated by unfamiliar characters. The ephemeral qualities of noir femmes fatales converge with the social context "in transition," and their identities foreground fluctuating identities on the borderline between the past and the present. Both of these aspects contribute to the genuine poetics of Ulmer's films and anticipate the changing poetics of American film in general, for example the revival of noir films in the '80s and '90s.

Ulmer has become increasingly recognized as an auteurist filmmaker: a true artist schooled in German expressionism and a maverick exiled from Hollywood because he couldn't play nice, who set his mind to no-budget marvels imbued with unique vision and a bleak worldview so consistent as to be a fingerprint for the man himself. Here, they say, was a director with a style recognizable even in the grubbiest of cheapies. And with "they say," David Kalat is referring to himself, as he is as much to blame as anyone for allowing this myth to calcify.

In his chapter "*Detour*'s Detour," Kalat focuses on one of Ulmer's most celebrated films, a legend among fans of film noir. "Noirest of the noir," says Jeff Ulmer. "May be the greatest achievement in B-movie making in history," says Jeffery Anderson. "Edgar G. Ulmer's masterpiece," says Glenn Erickson.

"His unquestioned masterpiece," says Gary Morris. "No one who has seen it has easily forgotten it," adds Roger Ebert. Not bad for a 67-minute quickie cobbled together in two weeks on a budget of just $25,000.

Detour tells the story of an embittered artist who struggles to make ends meet and is forced to make compromises that gradually wear away his soul. A wicked combination of poor decisions and cruel fate push the poor sap into a spiral of self-destruction that is riveting to behold. Critics with an eye for such things see it as a fable of Ulmer's own life, somewhere between a personal manifesto and a secret confession.

Of course, the story was not his. It was adapted from Martin Goldsmith's novel, and adapted by Goldsmith himself, at that. Other filmmakers would be inspired by Ulmer's film and reference it in their own work—none so ostentatiously as Wade Williams, who took the son of *Detour*'s star and cast him in a curious remake-cum-homage in 1992, using the same car that Ulmer used in the original (which was Ulmer's own car).

Thanks to these variant routes, detours all, Kalat claims, *Detour* offers an opportunity to retroactively "see" Ulmer's contribution. By comparing the extant film to the source novel by Martin Goldsmith and the Wade Williams cover version, one can filter out Ulmer's personality as it expressed itself through the material. Where his choices differ from theirs, we can spot the outlines of his shadow.

Hugh S. Manon's chapter on "Fantasy and Failure in *Strange Illusion*" advances a psychoanalytic account of Ulmer's 1945 film. *Strange Illusion* is a major work in the Ulmer oeuvre, but a film about which very little substantial work has been done. At times cartoonish, the "perfect crime" plot discovered by the film's young protagonist Paul Cartwright (Jimmy Lydon) can be understood as a *fantasy*, as defined by French psychoanalyst Jacques Lacan—not a dream of satisfaction, but a framework of lack through which the subject learns how to desire. Likening the film to David Lynch's *Mulholland Drive* (2001) and other contemporary films in which the audience fails to recognize that the narrative is not objectively "real," Manon argues that *Strange Illusion* is most radical in neither confirming nor denying that the events on screen actually occur. In a strong sense, then, the only objectively "real" portions of the film are the two dream sequences that open and close the film; everything else is, to a greater or lesser degree, a fantasy in which Paul grapples with his identity as a being of desire.

The strongest indication the film provides concerning its status as fantasy, according to Manon, comes in Ulmer's various manipulations of film form—stylistic flourishes that are at times stunning in their willingness to reveal the cheapness of the film's "Poverty Row" production. By foregrounding the flaws inherent in-low budget production—for instance, the film's out-of-kilter use of rear-projection screens—Ulmer subtly suggests that what Paul sees is not objective evidence concerning the guilt of the film's alleged villain, but rather a barrier to the attainment of his object of desire. It is only by imagining a brilliant criminal case, and then solving it, that Paul can align his desire with that of his deceased father (a gifted criminologist), thus reconstituting his world as a domain of insidious criminals and innocents in need of protection. Manon claims the final shot of the film makes it clear that Paul, having passed through the fantasy, is now free to pursue his desire in the same sort of heterosexual union that his father once enjoyed.

According to Bill Krohn, Ulmer's films of the '50s and '60s are his most personal and his least well known, for the same reason. The Yiddish films of the '30s have been preserved and studied by specialists in Yiddish cinema; the Producers Releasing Corporation films of the '40s are treasured by fans of B cinema. But in these films and in *The Black Cat*, which carries on the tradition of Universal horror, Ulmer is masked by the very cultural elements that have drawn interest to the films for reasons extrinsic to him. In the '50s, however, Krohn claims in his chapter on "The Naked Filmmaker," the mask falls, so that we can get a clearer view of the filmmaker's very own concerns—religious (Gnosticism), cultural (the influence of Murnau), political (the feminism of *Babes in Bagdad* and *Loves of Three Queens*), and formal (the modernist inventions of *Murder Is My Beat* and *Daughter of Dr. Jekyll*).

Referring back to Belton's account of an Ulmer in search of a community, the issue of "solidarity" might also have been one of Ulmer's "very own" concerns in the '50s. Reynold Humphries focuses on the question of solidarity in his chapter on "The Political and Ideological Subtexts of *The Naked Dawn*." In this film from 1955, two Mexican bandits steal merchandise from a train stationed in a border town. One is shot, and the other stumbles onto a farm belonging to a young Mexican couple. Visibly attracted to the wife, the bandit nevertheless chooses to undertake the social and moral education of the husband. Having been paid for the merchandise, which he had stolen at the request of a corrupt U.S. official, he steals the rest of the official's money when the latter tries to cheat him, then spends much of it lavishly during a night that he and the husband spend in a cantina.

However, the husband, tired of poverty, considers that money must be saved and not spent, and plans to kill the bandit in order to live better. His wife turns against him and abandons him for the bandit. They turn back when the U.S. official shows up and tries to kill the husband, and the bandit is killed saving him. Husband and wife are reunited.

Summed up thus, *The Naked Dawn* sounds distinctly banal, yet it is not. Instead, the script (by blacklisted writer Julian Zimet) is a most subtle and thoughtful deconstruction of a whole panoply of clichés—thematic and narrative—which adds up to a denunciation of conservative values based on individualism (the bandit is a disappointed revolutionary), the fetishization of money and property, and the submission of women (the loving husband orders his wife around and beats her up). More than this is at stake, however. In its portrayal of loyalty and betrayal (the bandit stands by his dying companion, whereas the husband is ready to kill the bandit as he sleeps), *The Naked Dawn*, Humphries argues, cunningly raises the question of solidarity during the hearings held in Hollywood in 1951–1952 by the House Committee on Un-American Activities. The script avoids suggesting that a fictional character is based on a real-life one. Rather, it sketches in the conditions under which sticking by a friend on the one hand, or knifing him in the back on the other hand, both came to be seen as "natural" reactions to an extreme situation, depending on the values being defended. The film comes down unambiguously on the side of loyalty, Humphries claims, although the road to that conclusion is fraught with pitfalls.

Beyond the Time Barrier (1959) also presents another "sketching of conditions," another "test lab," in Dr. Ulmer's '60s filmmaking. What happens when an Air Force test pilot falls through a rabbit hole in time and finds himself trapped in Ulmer's strange web of deceit and design? When a film threatens to take on an actual shape? Robert Skotak's chapter "A Grave New World: Cast and Crew on the Making of *Beyond the Time Barrier*" is an attempt to explain exactly this.

Aside from William Cameron Menzies's *Things to Come* (1936) and *Invaders from Mars* (1953), few science fiction films aspired so overtly to exploit design and scheme. This was more often the realm of horror cinema (e.g., *The Cabinet of Dr. Caligari*, *Son of Frankenstein*, Ulmer's own *Black Cat*). Fewer directors yet traded on dialogues between geometric structure and dramatic patterns. Armed with a desperately inadequate $125,000 to stage this "spectacle of the world of tomorrow" (so said the ads), and a mere ten days of shooting far from Hollywood's handy resources, Ulmer set out to impress style and substance on what might have otherwise quickly devolved into pure melodramatic throwaway. Largely ignored, and seldom and incorrectly commented upon, *Beyond the Time Barrier* is a film whose minor miracles pop up as a welcome reprieve on an obstacle course of low-budget pitfalls. Skotak's chapter is a first (and first-class) insider look at this film. Recalled through chats with the auteur's on-set collaborators and observers, it is an attempt to lend insight to Ulmer's process of development and execution, to correct misinformation, and, ultimately, to reveal his creative interplay with cast and crew.

Skotak's chapter draws extensively on interviews he conducted between 1976 and 2008 with various *Time Barrier* alumni, such as Robert Clarke, Arianné Ulmer Cipes, Shirley Ulmer, and Arthur Pierce, thus providing one of the most extensive primary-source glimpses behind an Ulmer film to date.

An Ulmer film of the '60s, *The Amazing Transparent Man* might appear, at first sight, to be the work of a director well past his prime, of an ailing talent which has seen better days and indeed better budgets. Yet, as Alec Charles argues in "Invisibility and Insight: The Unerasable Trace of *The Amazing Transparent Man*," it is a film whose subject matter and style deconstruct such superficial appearances, and, as such, it merits a further, and a deeper, look.

The Amazing Transparent Man was released in the same year that Alfred Hitchcock's *Psycho* was unleashed upon the world, and it shares with Hitchcock's masterpiece not only a coincidence of setting and plotting, but also an interest in similar cultural and psychological themes, an interest whose depth and complexity perhaps seem at odds with its primary subject matter—the tale of a criminal mastermind who plans to create an army of invisible men. The film is able to exploit its budgetary disadvantages in ways which may speak not so much of a cinematic naiveté as of a level of textual irony almost reminiscent of the self-conscious dramatic devices of Bertolt Brecht. Furthermore, Charles claims, Ulmer's film constructs itself around a web of filmic and literary allusions which invoke, alongside references to the director's own earlier work, not only such classics of horror cinema and fiction as *The Invisible Man* and *Frankenstein*, but also various versions of the myth of Faust.

Through its exploration of these different manifestations of the stereotypically insane and overreaching scientist, and of the psychological factors which may motivate such figures, Ulmer's film comes to address its central moral concern: the subject of the Holocaust—and, specifically, how the Holocaust performed by the Third Reich might be reenacted, two decades on, in the proliferation and employment of weapons of mass destruction by the opposing superpowers of the (then-contemporary) cold war. *The Amazing Transparent Man* suggests that its central moral dilemma—the defining problem of its period—can only be successfully resolved through reconciliation and forgiveness; and, while its message may appear dated, clumsy, and sentimental, its sincerity and its urgency can hardly be dismissed. As a document of its times, and as a moral and cultural meditation upon those times, *The Amazing Transparent Man* may therefore be seen not only as a text of historical interest, but also as one of ongoing and increasing relevance to a world facing continuing questions over the control and use of such apocalyptic armaments.

This collection finishes with two "goodies," or extras. First, there is Tom Weaver's interview with Shirley Ulmer, conducted in 1998, which reveals many insights into "the Man." Then there is Ulmer in his own words: in an interview with Bernard Eisenschitz and Jean-Claude Romer for *Midi-Minuit Fantastique* in 1965, Ulmer talks about some of his American heroes and inspirations—Tod Browning, James Whale, Bela Lugosi, and Boris Karloff. For the first time, this document is available in an English translation.

For Truffaut, commenting on *The Naked Dawn* as one of those movies that were important to him, Ulmer's films "were made with joy; every shot shows a love of cinema, and pleasure in working in it" (156). And it is time to return the joy, the love that Ulmer's work continues to give to us.

Ulmer was "a Ulysses of cinema, who wasn't destined to return home, but who, on his long voyage through various genres and film cultures, spanned the entire spectrum: cool modernity alongside lascivious speculation, cheap trash beside classic virtuosity," the German film critic Bert Rebhandl writes (as quoted in the press kit of Michael Palm's wonderful documentary *Edgar G. Ulmer: The Man Off-Screen*, Kino Video). Finally, Ulysses Ulmer *has* returned home, has returned home to his place of birth.

"The lights go out, but the films continue . . ."

NOTES

1. For a detailed biography of Ulmer, see the meticulously researched book by Stefan Grissemann.
2. The memorial plaque was unveiled in a small ceremony on occasion of the Ulmerfest in Olomouc in 2006, a three-day conference which I organized as an almost natural consequence of my discovery of Ulmer's birthplace there. For info about the Ulmerfest 2006, see www.uni-koeln.de/phil-fak/englisch/abteilungen/berressem/herzogenrath/ulmer/index.htm (last accessed 4 August 2008).
3. For another recent anthology on Ulmer, see Bernd Herzogenrath, ed., *Edgar G. Ulmer: Essays on the King of the Bs* (Jefferson, N.C.: McFarland, 2009).

BIBLIOGRAPHY

Deleuze, Gilles. *Cinema 1: The Movement-Image*, trans. Hugh Tomlinson and B. Habberjam (Minneapolis: University of Minnesota Press, 1986).

———. *Essays Critical and Clinical*, trans. Daniel W. Smith and Michael A. Greco (Minneapolis: University of Minnesota Press, 1997).

Freud, Sigmund. *The Interpretation of Dreams*, trans. and ed. James Strachey (New York: Avon Books, 1980).

Grissemann, Stefan. *Mann im Schatten: Der Filmemacher Edgar G. Ulmer* (Vienna: Paul Zsolnay Verlag, 2003).

Schwaab, Herbert. "On the Graveyards of Europe: The Horror of Modernism in *The Black Cat*," chapter 3 in the current book, *The Films of Edgar G. Ulmer* (Lanham, Md.: Scarecrow Press, 2009).

Truffaut, François. "Edgar Ulmer: *The Naked Dawn*," in *The Films in My Life*, trans. Leonard Mayhew (New York: Simon and Schuster, 1978), 155–56.

1

Permanent Vacation

Home and Homelessness in the Life and Work of Edgar G. Ulmer

Noah Isenberg

> Dwelling, in the proper sense, is now impossible. The traditional residences we grew up in have grown intolerable; each trait of comfort in them is paid for with a betrayal of knowledge, each vestige of shelter with the musty pact of family interests. (Theodor W. Adorno, *Minima Moralia*)

> All I need is a brief glimpse, an opening in the midst of an incongruous landscape, a glint of lights in the fog, the dialogue of two passersby meeting in a crowd, and I think that, setting out from there, I will put together, piece by piece, the perfect city, made of fragments mixed with the rest, of instants separated by intervals . . . discontinuous in space and time, now scattered, now more condensed. (Italo Calvino, *Invisible Cities*)

I

Writing in her preface to the catalog published in conjunction with the Edgar G. Ulmer retrospective, held at the 1997 Edinburgh Film Festival, curator Lizzie Francke observes how the Austrian-born director and so-called "wandering émigré" once tellingly remarked, "There are no nationalities, the only home you have is the motion picture set" (148). For Ulmer, who was born in 1904 in Olmütz (Olomouc), in the provinces of the Austro-Hungarian Empire, a multinational designation which no longer existed by the time he was in his teens, the question

This chapter originally appeared in Sabine Eckmann and Lutz Koepnick, eds., *Caught By Politics: Hitler Exiles and American Visual Culture in the 1930s and 1940s* (New York: Palgrave Macmillan, 2007), 175–94. I wish to express grateful acknowledgment to Palgrave Macmillan for permission to reprint the essay.

of home and nationality not only began, but also remained, an elusive one. He personally witnessed the mass migrations prompted by two world wars—the first landing him in foster care in Uppsala, Sweden, after his father's death in Austrian uniform in 1916, and the second sealing his fate to remain, at least temporarily, among the many refugees from Hitler's Europe who decamped from Berlin and Vienna for Southern California in the 1930s and 1940s. And in his career of some thirty-five years as a director, he returned to the basic theme of displacement with a near-obsessive frequency. The lack of permanence or firm footing that might link his subjects to a stable location—a city, a community, a nation—is something Ulmer explores in his best-known works, including *The Black Cat* (1934), *Detour* (1945), and *Ruthless* (1948), as well as in his lesser-known films: his ethnic pictures directed in and around New York City during the mid- to late 1930s; his eleven-film cycle of B movies shot at Producers Releasing Corporation (PRC), the Poverty Row studio where, from 1942 to 1946, Ulmer earned a reputation as one of the pioneers of low-budget independent filmmaking; and his later films, many of which were shot in Europe in the 1950s and 1960s, and all of which were made outside the industry norms and standards of Hollywood.

Unlike the more illustrious career paths of his filmmaker contemporaries Billy Wilder, Robert Siodmak, or Fred Zinnemann (all three of whom collaborated with Ulmer on their legendary 1929 production of *Menschen am Sonntag* [*People on Sunday*]), the trajectory of Ulmer's film career never quite brought him the recognition he undoubtedly sought. Instead, he often took on unconventional projects—both out of necessity and by choice—that kept him from the spotlight of American and European cinema. As John Belton has argued, "Ulmer occupies an unknown, uncharted, and apparently invisible space on the margins of cinema history" ("Cinema Maudit" 150).[1] In what follows, I wish to examine the life and career path of Ulmer, in an effort to widen the scope of analysis in the research on exiled artists and filmmakers. Despite Ulmer's enigmatic career, the story that emerges here is one that may shed further light onto some of the received wisdom concerning German exiles and that may, in turn, complicate our understanding not only of Ulmer but of the vicissitudes of exile and émigré culture in general. Attempting to combine biographical sources with formal film analysis, the structure of my examination will follow several of the key detours that Ulmer's life and career took.[2] It will thus move among the cities and sites, real and imagined, that he inhabited and reflected in his work.

II

Although Ulmer was born in the provinces, his family moved back to Vienna soon after his birth. Like many artists before and after him, Ulmer felt the need to claim Vienna as his true birthplace, and, in doing so, he declared a profound attachment—emotional, cultural, and otherwise—to the much-heralded city. By the eve of the Great War, just as Ulmer was approaching his tenth birthday, a catchy tune entitled "Wien, du Stadt meiner Träume" ("Vienna, You are the City of My Dreams"), written by Rudolf Sieczynski, was making the rounds in the Imperial capital and becoming a worldwide hit. Its refrain goes as follows:

> Wien, Wien, nur Du allein
> Sollst stets die Stadt meiner Träume sein
> Dort wo die alten Häuser stehn,
> Dort wo die lieblichen Mädchen gehn . . .
>
> (Vienna, Vienna, none but you,
> Can be the city of my dreams come true
> Here, where the dear old houses loom,
> Where I for lovely young girls swoon) (cited in Morton 185–86)

As Ulmer's first metropolitan experience, Vienna certainly attained the status of "city of dreams," and he continued to treat it as such long after he left it behind, first for Sweden; then for Berlin, where he went in order to work on Max Reinhardt's stage productions; and, later still, for New York and Hollywood, whence he eventually returned to Europe. For Ulmer, the memories and fantasies of Vienna were always recalled in a musical and aesthetic register. Consider, for instance, the opening paragraphs of his incomplete novel *Beyond the Boundary*—an elliptical, highly fragmentary, and blatantly autobiographical work—which he signed and dated "Hollywood, 1935":

> It is quiet in the large dark room. The dawn hasn't broken yet. The presence of sleeping humans is obvious. The window is open and past the snow-covered ledge, streams in the cold winter air. It gets quite cold in Vienna in the winter.
>
> The window looks out upon a back yard. Fore-shortened in perspective, one feels the back wall of the other house alongside. And opposite that bleak back wall, in "L" form runs a wing, housing the servant- and kitchen-quarters. Beyond that . . . the skyline of Vienna.
>
> It's futile to describe it. Listen to Schubert, Johan Strauss, to Mozart and Hayden, and you will feel the strange substance of sentimentality, charm . . . the Spanish court-ceremonial and the Wienerwald . . .The Danube. (Ulmer 1–2)

The novel follows its protagonist George (Ulmer's middle name) through the streets of the war-torn capital, from the breadlines to the brothels, and chronicles George's coming of age—the traumatic death of his father (the work is dedicated to Siegfried Ulmer, "one of many thousands who died in the First World War"), his sexual awakening in adolescence at the hands of a local prostitute, and the final departure from his maternal home. Although the work is far from first-rate in terms of its overall literary quality, it does offer something in the way of substance concerning Ulmer's cultural sensibility, a sensibility that would be translated—never completely, often only in traces—in his cinematic output. Indeed the sounds of Vienna, not to mention the "ghostlike" figures and "shadows" that populate Ulmer's novel, would continue to crop up in his aural and visual lexicon. As the German film critic Frieda Grafe once put it in her reevaluation of Austrian film history, "Vienna was a reservoir of dreams"; or, as she remarks further in the same essay, "Austrian film history is a phantasm, because it is not tied to a fixed place; its cinema is a kind of film without a specific space" (Grafe 227).

From the very beginning, film in Austria was necessarily international, with well-trodden paths leading to Berlin, Paris, and, somewhat later, also to Hollywood (see Sannwald). It should perhaps come as no surprise, then, that the Viennese-born or, in Ulmer's case, Viennese-trained film directors were particularly adroit fabulists when it came to dreaming up their pasts in the film world of Hollywood, the factory of dreams. Erich von Stroheim would take on the self-avowed air of Prussian aristocracy, Billy Wilder the identity of a former gigolo, and Ulmer (the persona, that is) a wunderkind from Reinhardt's renowned drama school; each of these roles, and there were of course many more, would offer a new identity to the displaced émigré in need of a quick makeover, especially one that might bring more work. "The secret affinity that existed between Hollywood on one side and Vienna or Paris on the other," writes Thomas Elsaesser, "was that they were societies of the spectacle, cities of make-believe and of the show. The decadence of the Hapsburg monarchy was in some ways the pervasive sense of impersonation, of pretending to be in possession of values and status that relied for credibility not on substance but on convincing performance, on persuading others to take an appearance for reality" ("Ethnicity" 112).

As was the case with most German and Austrian filmmakers of his generation, Ulmer learned much of his trade in the theater. And like these other directors (F. W. Murnau, Otto Preminger, William Dieterle, et al.), he eventually made his way to Max Reinhardt. Even if his only official credit working with the Reinhardt stage was as a set designer, together with Rochus Gliese, for the acclaimed 1928 Berlin production of Ferdinand Bruckner's *Die Verbrecher* (*The Criminals*; see Huesmann, and also Preminger), he clearly identified himself, both professionally and aesthetically, with the theater, and he asserted his deep-seated ties to the great impresario. A calling card from the 1920s makes this assertion most apparent: it lists Ulmer's title as *Regissseur* (director) and *Ausstattungschef* (head of design) for the Reinhardt stage, and also gives Vienna, Berlin, and New York as his cities of operation, an early gesture toward the cosmopolitan identity he embraced until his death. When Ulmer set sail for New York, in spring of 1924, the staging of Reinhardt's *Das Mirakel* (*The Miracle*) at New York's Century Theatre was well underway. Ulmer himself claimed to have been involved in the stage design, and he described his first trip to New York, at the age of nineteen, as one that had been arranged by the Schildkrauts, the father-and-son acting duo Rudolf and Joseph, with whom Ulmer had spent a formative phase of his late youth in Vienna. Indeed, Rudolf Schildkraut, like Fritz Feld, was part of the original cast of *The Miracle* that traveled to New York with the show. As his record from Ellis Island indicates, Ulmer traveled on the *SS President Roosevelt* and arrived in New York Harbor on 12 April 1924, almost four months after the play's premiere.[3] It is, however, fully conceivable that Ulmer had a hand, perhaps as one of the many designers or simply one of the roughly seven hundred people said to have been enlisted, in the play's highly successful ten-month run. (Feld, a principal actor in the Reinhardt production, and a player in several of Ulmer's pictures, attests to this fact in his eulogy to Ulmer from October 1972. See Young, and also Feld.)

In his extensive interview with Peter Bogdanovich, Ulmer comments on his initial experiences in New York City: "When I came to New York the first time, Reinhardt hired Schildkraut, who had worked for him in Europe, to play in *The Miracle*. And I was taken down to Second Avenue, and met the Jewish Art Theatre, which had some tremendous actors—Muni Weisenfreund [Paul Muni], Jacob Adler, Maurice Schwartz—it was something which didn't exist elsewhere in all of New York . . . It was a second Broadway down there" (Bogdanovich 577–78). This early contact with the thriving Yiddish stage on New York's Lower East Side may have inspired Ulmer, over a decade later, to direct the Yiddish films he completed in the late 1930s. His childhood friend Joseph Schildkraut, who had already arrived in New York in August 1920, writes in his memoir, *My Father and I*: "My first impression of New York was mixed, more confusing than exhilarating. The skyline, the harbor, the piers, the crowd—all these were exactly as I had seen them in paintings and photographs. Reality was merely copying art" (Schildkraut 114). It is rather ironic that Schildkraut should find this relationship between art and reality in the New World, when in numerous cases émigrés found themselves engaged in the process of imitating reality—or what, in the New World, was taken for reality—in their art, even an imagined reality of the Old World left behind. Perhaps for Ulmer the main attraction of New York was the fact that there were so many fellow émigrés in his midst, many of them artists, actors, directors, and crew members, who drew on their pasts as a means of communicating with their new audience. In Ulmer's case, it was often his European training, the true extent of which he occasionally embellished, that linked him to other émigrés working in the United States.

In 1926–1927, Ulmer joined forces with German-born Rochus Gliese in set design at Fox studios, assisting F. W. Murnau, also a former Reinhardt pupil, on his Hollywood debut, *Sunrise*. Ulmer, who was already in Hollywood working in the art department at Universal and churning out two-reel westerns on the side, considered Gliese "[his] partner, a fantastic designer and camera builder" (Bogdanovich 568). Gliese, whose set design for *Sunrise* earned him an Oscar nomination, had worked on several early German film productions, including the second Golem film, *Der Golem und die Tänzerin* (*The Golem and the Dancer*, 1917), which he directed. For Ulmer, the significance of *Sunrise*, one of the greatest pictures Murnau ever made and, in Ulmer's words, "the *only* picture Murnau himself counted" (Bogdanovich 565), cannot be underestimated. The film, which blends European and American styles from the *Straßenfilm* to the early Hollywood melodrama, pits traditional life in the provinces against the big city. The blissful harmony—or dreadful tedium—of family life between man (George O'Brian) and woman (Janet Gaynor) in the country is interrupted, much as in a classical horror film, by the intrusion of an outsider, the Woman from the City (Margaret Livingston). Murnau casts these two worlds in stark opposition, opening the film with a brilliant montage (à la Ruttmann's *Berlin: Die Sinfonie der Großstadt*) and having the city woman lure away the man of the country, indulging him in fantasies of urban decadence. In such scenes as the man and city woman imagining the city, or the man and wife having their photo taken during their later visit to the city, the film can be viewed, as Lucy Fischer asserts, "as a self-reflexive text which, provisionally, identifies the cinema with the metropolitan" (40). One might add to this equation the European city which seems to symbolize the cosmopolitan sensibility par excellence, a sensibility Murnau frequently incorporated into his work, as Ulmer did later.

In order to achieve this most effectively, Murnau had to rely on high-quality production design, much of it pioneered in Weimar Germany, as a means of depicting the separate worlds. As Lotte Eisner remarks, "Gliese [and, by extension, Ulmer working with him] had created every kind of landscape, from fields and meadows, through an industrial area and the sparse gardens of the suburbs to the city itself" (180). The ostensible lessons that Ulmer learned while working with Murnau—not merely in terms of design, but also in terms of handling his characters and themes—would stick. One can indeed see shades of Murnau in several of Ulmer's subsequent films. As late as 1955, in his Mexican Western shot in Technicolor, *The Naked Dawn*, the rural-urban dialectic is played out again in a new light. The film is, according to the trenchant interpretation by Belton, "a reworking of Murnau's

Sunrise—Santiago, with the lure of money for the husband and tales of exotic Vera Cruz for the wife, taking the part of Murnau's Woman from the City" ("Edgar G. Ulmer" 342). Not only does the film present a plausible "reworking," but it also picks up on several of Ulmer's own stock themes: the false promise of material wealth; the romantic wanderings of a lonely hero; and the struggle to remain loyal to a more noble, if less profitable, calling. In a critical moment, the film shows the husband (Eugene Iglesias) falling prey to the venal impulses of a modern man, a man who is willing to forsake his seemingly perfect home—and his beautiful wife (Betta St. John)—for financial gain, thus contrasting him in striking terms with the homeless renegade Santiago (Arthur Kennedy), who has no deep connection to the money he acquires and therefore does not allow himself to be alienated by its material worth.

Just as Ulmer saw himself as belonging to the "Romantic" and "art-possessed" directors, as opposed to the "group [for] whom theatre and film was a business" (Bogdanovich 566), so too his characters often confront the clash between those higher pursuits—be they artistic, philosophical, or even theological—and base material concerns, between art and commerce. From the

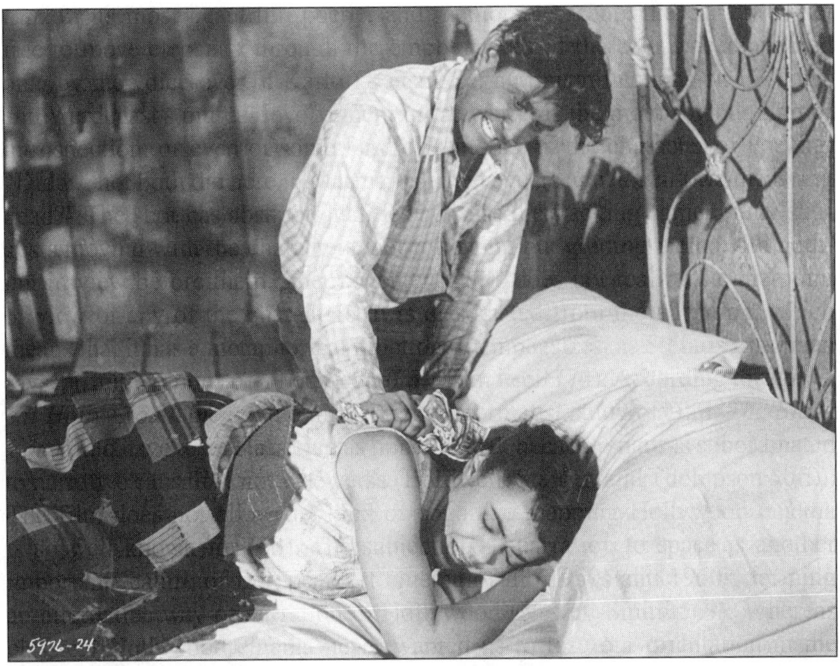

Figure 1.1. Production still from *The Naked Dawn* (1955). Courtesy of Jerry Ohlinger's Movie Material Store, Inc.

beginning of his American career to his final pictures made in Europe, this dialectical tension remained palpable both on and off the set.

III

Ulmer's American directorial debut, or, more precisely, his big-studio debut, took place a good three decades before *The Naked Dawn*. The 1934 production of *The Black Cat* lies at the heart of the famed Universal horror cycle, which starts with *Dracula* and *Frankenstein*, both from 1931, and ends with *Son of Frankenstein* (1939). The film offers a fascinating glimpse into the world of an émigré filmmaker negotiating American financial and aesthetic constraints. With Bela Lugosi and Boris Karloff in leading roles—the first of seven pictures in which they would star opposite each other—it is a film that represents the rich interplay between European art cinema and the Hollywood blockbuster, between reflections of exile and those of home. The film opens with images of transit: a European railway station, packages and luggage, train officials and passengers. Aboard the Orient Express is a newlywed, patently American couple, the mystery-thriller writer Peter Alison (David Manners) and his young bride Joan (Jacqueline Wells), bound for a luxury resort in the Carpathian mountains (a familiar destination for viewers of early German horror as the home of Murnau's *Nosferatu*). The honeymooners, shown affectionately in their cheery, brightly lit compartment, soon face an intruder, Dr. Vitus Werdegast (Lugosi), who in fact does become a guest, as his name—in German, literally "I shall be a guest"—tells us. His jarring screen presence disrupts the harmonious moment shared by the Alisons. Werdegast immediately finds himself enraptured by the sight of Joan, which Ulmer captures in several revealing point-of-view shots—a foreboding sign of what's to come. (Lugosi's role in *The Black Cat* was very much colored by his memorable performance in *Dracula*.) The remainder of the film pivots on two levels: the tale of the European returnee (Werdegast), who accompanies his American guests to the original site of his wartime trauma—the same location where former general and engineer Hjalmar Poelzig (Karloff) has constructed his spectacular compound; and the face-off between Werdegast and Poelzig, which includes a few notable flourishes of gruesome sadism, bondage, and revenge along with the requisite American happy end.

In keeping with the American horror genre, *The Black Cat* adheres to the boilerplate plotlines of murder and deception. Unlike its counterparts, however, it introduces two important elements to the genre: a score that showcases European, largely German and Austrian, classical music (Brahms, Schubert,

Figure 1.2. Production still from *The Black Cat* (1934). Courtesy of Jerry Ohlinger's Movie Material Store, Inc.

and Beethoven); and a high-modernist aesthetic that informs the overall design of the film. The clean lines, luminous interiors, and sleek, minimalist decor all replicate the taste of 1920s Berlin, Vienna, Paris, and Amsterdam.

As Ulmer claims, somewhat boastfully, in his interview with Bogdanovich, the film was "very much out of my Bauhaus period" (Bogdanovich 576). Once again, in an effort to have his name associated with some of the most venerable artistic figures, movements, and institutions, Ulmer's inflated appraisal should be considered a bold indicator of the highly self-conscious approach to making a film which would deliberately evoke the style of a period in which Ulmer had little part. Jim Hoberman's memorable phrase, riffing on the famous title of Kracauer's history of Weimar cinema, still rings true: "From Caligari to Hitler in one lurid package" ("Low and Behold").

On the set, Ulmer worked together with British-born designer Charles Hall, producing what Donald Albrecht, in his book *Designing Dreams: Modern Architecture in the Movies*, has pronounced an "architectural tour de force" (100–101). Albrecht credits Ulmer with the construction of Poelzig's elaborate compound, the space in which Ulmer's implicit nod to his former home, that is, to the European high-modernist aesthetic cultivated in his choice of design, comes into direct conflict with the homeless characters that languish within it: Werdegast, the Alisons, even the preserved bodies of former inhabitants. Despite the fact that the film's supposed location is far removed from an urban world, the highly stylized interiors suggest something more out of the European metropolis than out of the provincial hinterland.

Ulmer's playful adaptation of early German cinematic style in *The Black Cat* manifests itself in a variety of ways. His dramatic use of light and shadow throughout the film evokes a hallmark, by now nearly clichéd, of German expressionism. There are also narrative strategies that appear to be holdovers from the silent era: for example, when Poelzig lies down in bed, he reads the *Rites of Lucifer* (like *Book of Vampires* in *Nosferatu*—indeed, the affinities with *Nosferatu* and, more broadly, with Murnau proliferate throughout). However, some of Ulmer's references to Weimar cinema resemble more of an inside joke among German and Austrian émigrés than a genuine homage: in using the name Poelzig, and making the character an engineer at that, it is impossible to miss the allusion to renowned German architect Hans Poelzig, who designed the sets for Paul Wegener's 1920 *Golem* film and who also built one of Berlin's most celebrated theaters, the Grosses Schauspielhaus. As for the sadistic personality of Poelzig, Paul Mandell has argued that the figure was based on Fritz Lang, who was widely considered to be a tyrannical director (see Mandell 36). The sets, Ulmer suggested to Bogdanovitch, were inspired by conversations with Gustav Meyrink, the Prague novelist who wrote his own rendition of *The Golem*, on which Wegener's film of 1920 was partly based, and who had allegedly considered writing a play set in a French military fortress from World War I (Bogdanovich 576).

Although *The Black Cat* was by all counts a commercial success, ending the year as Universal's top-grossing picture of 1934, Ulmer's days as a Hollywood studio director were numbered. While working on the film, he met his wife-to-be Shirley Castle (neé Kassler), a script supervisor and screenwriter, who at the time was still married to studio boss Carl Laemmle's nephew Max Alexander. Their liaison immediately branded Ulmer persona non grata in the powerful Laemmle's domain, a stronghold that reached far into other studio dynasties. In the words of Bill Krohn, Ulmer was "blackballed not for politics, but for love" (61). The rejection made Ulmer a different kind of "exile" in Hollywood; unlike one by national policy, it was a banishment from a new home and from the world in which he once saw great potential to flourish. Ulmer and his wife became, in Shirley's words, "Hollywood outcasts."[4] They were soon forced to seek work elsewhere, in markets outside of Southern California.

IV

After completing a B-class Western, *Thunder over Texas* (1934), and shooting a cheap thriller in Montreal, *From Nine to Nine* (1936), Ulmer set up shop in New York, where he would direct, among other projects, four feature-length Yiddish pictures, ranging from the pastoral *Grine Felder* (*Green Fields*, 1937) and the gloomy *Fishke der Krumer* (*The Light Ahead*, 1939) to his self-consciously urbane *Amerikaner Shadkhn* (*American Matchmaker*, 1940). Almost a sequel to *The Light Ahead*, which chronicles the dilemmas faced by a town's two social pariahs who flee the world of the shtetl in search of a better life in the city, *American Matchmaker* brings us directly to the world of the metropolis—not Odessa, as in *The Light Ahead*, but New York—and introduces us to the different roles that Yiddish-speaking Jews occupy there. As Krohn has suggested, *American Matchmaker* might indeed be viewed as a "comedy in which we see what became of Fishke and Hodl's descendents in the city" (64). The film's protagonist Leo Fuchs, regarded at the time as the "Yiddish Fred Astaire," plays the upwardly mobile, highly successful, assimilated businessman Nat Silver, who in the process of continuing to climb the social ladder of New York City in the late 1930s takes on a career makeover ("human relations," or what is sardonically called "human relishes") and changes his name from Silver to Gold (see Hoberman, *Bridge of Light* 317). The film opens inside a sumptuously designed apartment on Central Park West—an address where Ulmer himself once lived with his wife—where the bachelor party of Nat Silver is underway.

The elegant setting, lavish design, mannerism, and style of the opening sequence conjure a milieu that is anything but specifically Jewish. The only thing that marks the film as Jewish, as critics have observed, is the fact that Yiddish is spoken; and even that is highly Americanized, and urbanized, with continuous references to contemporary idiomatic phrases and expressions evocative of street-savvy sophistication (see, e.g., Forman; Goldberg). "The big city, as it's portrayed," asserts Stefan Grissemann, "is still more of a village than a jungle, a very manageable small world in which the Jewish community, almost as if there were no other religions or social groups in New York City, effortlessly sticks together" (143). There are, however, running gags within the story line of the film which explicitly address the issue of assimilation—for example, the faux-English butler (Yudel Dubinsky) who insists on speaking a Yiddishized British English, or the other characters' constant use of American slang to pepper their speech. Moreover, the transformation of the film's protagonist, from "Silver" to "Gold," as it were, entails a complete embrace of secular, urban American culture. Hoberman calls attention to the fact that this was the only one of the four Yiddish pictures Ulmer directed in which he was also partly responsible for the script, which he cowrote with his wife and his Viennese cousin Gustav Heimo (né Horowitz), and that the film might be seen as a personal response to the dilemmas of Jewish assimilation in an urban setting, a dilemma with which Ulmer undoubtedly had some familiarity, having grown up in Vienna during the first decades of the twentieth century. For Hoberman, the character of Nat Gold represents the "bridge between the hapless Menakhem Mendl [the famed *luftmentsh* of Sholem Aleichem's stories] and the neurotic heroes of Woody Allen" (*Bridge of Light* 321).

In terms of Ulmer's career development, the film fits into an extended phase of directing pictures aimed at minority audiences. Around the same time that he shot his Yiddish pictures, Ulmer was at work on a series of shorts commissioned by the Brooklyn-based National Tuberculosis and Health Association, among them *Let My People Live* (1939), a plea for disease prevention among African Americans filmed at the all-black Tuskegee Institute in Alabama. During that year Ulmer and Shirley also teamed up again with cousin Gustav, along with Shirley's brother Fred (as assistant director) and her father Peter (as associate producer), to make the musical drama *Moon over Harlem* (1939). Catering to a target audience of African American cinemagoers, the film takes the viewer into the inner world of the famed neighborhood, "black Manhattan," as the film's hero Bob (Carl Gough) calls it: a world of gangsters and mob control—populated by characters from rival gangs, with names like Dollar Bill and Wall Street—but also one of an aspiring middle class, represented by Bob and his like-minded girlfriend Sue (Ozinetta Wilcox)—both of whom seek to overcome adversity and triumph in the city, just as Nat Silver does in *American Matchmaker*. For them, it is less cultural assimilation than class assimilation—certainly a fraught issue in Nat Silver's quest as well—that stands in the way of their dreams of success. They must invent a new home in a hostile urban world beset by violence, poverty, and other social maladies, a collective pursuit in which countless characters from Ulmer's film repertoire engage themselves. Finally, there is, on a less overt level, a shared plight or an analogous state of exile from the dominant culture that links the black characters on the screen to the displaced émigrés on the set.[5] This may indeed help to explain Ulmer's choice of direction as well as his input on the story. And it may give further meaning, albeit merely symbolic in nature, to the general experience of homelessness, or estrangement from one's birthplace, as treated in Ulmer's films.

V

Another narrative thread in which Ulmer seems to play out a kind of European-American dialogue is the recurrent battle between art and consumerist mass culture in his films. Never quite striking a preachy, didactic, or doctrinaire tone, he frequently pits aesthetic compromise against material or professional payoff. For instance, in his low-budget melodrama *Jive Junction* (1943), he draws on the musical talent of émigré composer Leo Erdody—with whom he collaborated on many occasions during the PRC years—to tell the story of young Peter Crane (Dickie Moore), a classically trained pianist and self-proclaimed "lover of music," who finds himself drawn into the big-band jazz scene at Clinton High School. Early on in the film, Ulmer has the viewer catch precious glimpses of Peter listening to his father's favorite composers (strictly of the European variety, from Brahms to Schubert)—as we quickly learn, Peter's father, like Ulmer's own father, has died on the battlefront—before he heads down the path toward mainstream pop music played at juke joints like Jive Junction. The underlying conflict of the film, then, is not merely musical, but generational, especially when Peter has to turn to his former mentor at the conservatory, the so-called "Maestro" (played by Viennese-born Frederick Feher), to help procure instruments for the school band's big performance broadcast on live radio. The Maestro's final words, as he accompanies Peter to the performance, express both the ambivalence of the film's story line and that of its director: "It's noisy . . . but beautiful . . . maybe."

Ulmer's preoccupation with jazz culture and a kind of urban social anxiety carried on throughout the 1940s. Arguably his most famous film, *Detour* (1945) is filtered through the pained, edgy noir voice-over of downtrodden nightclub pianist Al Roberts (Tom Neal), a man whose dreams, musical and otherwise, are ultimately shattered. Toward the beginning of the film, as Al remembers his past while seated in a roadside diner somewhere in Nevada, we witness him dismissing the encouragement of his singer girlfriend Sue (Claudia Drake), who tells Al that he'll make it to Carnegie Hall someday. We soon discover that Sue is leaving behind her job, Al, and the New York nightclub in which they work, to try her luck in Hollywood; she travels alone. But as soon as Al gets an unexpected tip of $10, after playing a classical-jazz medley (from Brahms to boogie-woogie), he immediately calls Sue and announces his plans to join her in Los Angeles.

The path from New York to Los Angeles, graphically shown in a series of stock shots of telephone operators, traveling phone lines, and finally a map, fuses with the melody of "I Can't Believe You're in Love with Me," the same song that first summons up Al's memory at the diner and that links him and Sue. Al's desperation to get to Los Angeles (by "train, plane, bus, magic carpet . . . I'll get there if I have to crawl, if I have to travel by pogo stick") may mirror in unexpected ways Ulmer's own desire to make it in Hollywood, a desire he expressed rather passionately in several letters from the early 1940s, after having held out in New York for so long. However, the fact that Sue is working as a "hash slinger," and has not broken into the trade, does not bode well. As Ulmer once remarked, in his interview with Bogdanovich, "I did not want to be ground up in the Hollywood hash machine" (592). In this case, then, the big city (Los Angeles) possesses at least two very different symbolic functions: it is a place of flight for those who are left homeless, where Al—after he becomes implicated in murder on his fateful trek to the West Coast—believes he'll be able to find anonymity ("In a small town I might be noticed, but in a city I should be safe enough"); it is, however, also a place that can, and will, eventually drive people into the ground. Nearly the entire film encompasses Al's restless wanderings, his total lack of refuge, and the frenetic pace that propels him through an inhospitable world.[6]

Just as Krohn claims that we might understand *American Matchmaker* as a kind of postscript to *The Light Ahead*, so too we may consider *Carnegie Hall* (1947)—or at least the rather corny story line of the film—a happy-end sequel to *Detour*. In other words, this is the story of what could have happened to Al Roberts, had he made it to the big leagues. In the film, Tony Salerno Jr. (William Prince) pursues a similar path to Al's, moving freely in the world of urban musical culture, from classical to jazz; but he, unlike Al, succeeds in the end. He makes it in spite of the fact his mother, who works her way up from janitor of Carnegie Hall (which, after all, is what Al, in his self-deprecating fit in *Detour*, tells Sue should be his proper role) to a high-level office worker, castigates the turn from high to low art. As the American musicologist Erik Ulman has recently noted, "it is tempting to read Ulmer's own situation into these films, as an artist who descended from Murnau and Reinhardt to the depths of PRC, with Tony as a kind of wish fulfillment of finding artistic validity . . . in commercial culture" (Ulman). Ulmer, for his part, was rather dismissive of the story line of the film, and would have preferred to have made a documentary—"to have the Hall speak," as he put it—featuring the same virtuoso performances (Artur Rubinstein, Jascha Heifitz, Bruno Walter, Fritz Reiner, Artur Rodzinski) without the canned narrative. In his interview with Bogdanovich, he asks: "What are you going to do after Rubinstein plays Chopin?" (Bogdanovich 599).

To Ulmer, whose first passion—even before theater and cinema—was music, Carnegie Hall represented a mythical place, a sacred shrine or Golden Temple that embodied the best that an advanced metropolitan culture could offer. (He makes passing reference to it, as the quintessential marker of success, not only in *Detour*, but also in *Her Sister's Secret* [1946], when the toddler Billy is banging the keys on his toy piano and Bill Sr. quips, "Skipper, we have a long way before Carnegie Hall.") Like the name Max Reinhardt, Carnegie Hall possessed household recognition; it was a name to be venerated, one that carried enormous cultural cachet, and a name with which Ulmer was all too happy to be associated. As he had done half a decade before, in *Jive Junction*, Ulmer fashions the maestro as something of a savior, a figure who transcends the prosaic concerns of everyday life and deals with things on a higher plane. At numerous junctures in the film, Ulmer has the conductor shot from an extreme low angle, thereby endowing his character with a larger-than-life aura. Perhaps even more significant, in terms of Ulmer's career trajectory, *Carnegie Hall* represents another film in which he, as director, is able to revisit a lost world—complete with the resonant chords of Old Vienna and the luminaries who, not unlike Ulmer, migrated to the New World.

VI

Ulmer's fellow Austrian émigré and screenwriter Salka Viertel notes in her memoirs, *The Kindness of Strangers,* how she and presumably many others in her shoes were hoping for the opportunity to retrace their steps to the world they had left behind. "In those first years in California [in the early 1930s]," she writes, "I don't think I met anyone who had been born or raised there. The actors and writers, especially those from the East, were transitory, having come to make money and to get out as soon as possible. I also was counting the days till our return to Europe" (143). After struggling to keep afloat in Hollywood throughout much of the 1940s, Ulmer finally severed ties to the American B studios—with his major four-year, eleven-film stint at PRC having come to an unceremonious end in 1946—and made his way across the Atlantic, where he eventually became involved in a variety of eclectic productions. These began with *I Pirati di Capri* (*Pirates of Capri*, 1949), his Italian swashbuckler starring Luis Hayward (a regular in Ulmer's ensemble), and led up to the Danziger Brothers' Spanish production of *Muchachas de Bagdad* (*Babes in Bagdad*, 1951); Ulmer's garish Italian Technicolor fantasy film *L'Atlantide* (*Journey beneath the Desert*, 1961); and his final picture, *Sette contro la morte* (*The Cavern*, 1965), a gripping wartime drama shot in the mountains of Italy and Yugoslavia. These churned-out movies have been largely forgotten—some for good reason—by film history.

Grissemann has recently suggested that Ulmer's career reached its "official" apex in the years 1947–1948, after the release of *Carnegie Hall*, and that essentially, with a few exceptions, his career went downhill from that moment onward. "Assignments became ever more irregular," Grissemann asserts, "and he had to consider working outside of the country, overseas" (253–54). He attributes this development to Ulmer's reputation as a "cheap" director, a filmmaker who plumbed the depths of Poverty Row, and to the fact that he hadn't worked at A-list studios since his first (and only) picture for Universal,

The Black Cat, in 1934. After his relatively stable and successful run at PRC in the early to middle 1940s, Ulmer was essentially left unmoored, stripped of any residual ties to a studio, independent or otherwise. As Grissemann puts it, in his pithy summation, "Independence can hurt."

After pursuing several untenable ideas, including a remake of Leni Riefenstahl's *Das blaue Licht* (*The Blue Light*, 1932), and after the American B-picture industry had lost its steam, Ulmer found himself committed to producer Victor Pahlen, in late summer 1948, on an Italian coproduction *Pirates of Capri*. The Pahlen project brought him back to Europe, where he initially hoped to thrive in a nascent industry away from Hollywood. What it also did, however, was make him even more aware of his lack of success on the other side of the Atlantic and his increasing alienation from that world. As he writes on 13 October 1948 from Rome: "I am of course very lonesome, they tell me life is very beautiful in Rome; I'd rather be home in King's Road [i.e., just above Sunset Boulevard, in Hollywood, where the Ulmers had a house at the time]."[7] Ulmer's conception of home became complicated during his years abroad; he may, at times, have thought of himself as a citizen of the world, but he also encountered an acute and recurrent sense of homelessness while living in Europe, signing a postcard mailed from Belgrade in 1956 as the "Wandering Minstrel."

Ironic as it may seem, Ulmer, who never managed to lay roots in Hollywood, yearned even more for a second calling there after he returned to Europe. During the early 1940s, before he began his stint at PRC, he had expressed similar hopes of landing work at one of the big studios. In 1941, in a letter to his wife Shirley dated 1 July on Hollywood Plaza Hotel stationery, Ulmer writes: "The prayer has worked. Sweetest I am so excited I hardly can hold the pen in my hand. I just returned from Paramount. Sherle, they have not forgotten. Sherle, I am as good as signed with Paramount. Producer—director—good God! Sweets we are home again and on the way." He then proceeds to assert, repeating what the studio bosses have presumably told him: "Well, Ulmer, I am sold on you 1,000% . . . You are going to be one of the big men on the lot. Dearest, I hardly could keep from crying out. So seven years [1934–1941] I had to suffer and starve. I nearly sold you out, you, [the] picture business, my family, myself. Oh, I am so excited I hardly can think."[8] In the last lines of the letter, Ulmer announces the two pictures he hopes to shoot for Paramount: first, an idea called *Beggar on Horseback*, based on the Broadway comedy, a parody of German expressionist drama, written by George S. Kaufman; and second, a remake of *The Blue Angel*, starring Veronica Lake. Neither of the two pictures ever panned out, and Ulmer's fantasy of becoming a redeemed and celebrated studio director at Paramount remained just that: a fantasy.

After his return to Europe, several years later, these unfulfilled desires resurfaced. As much as he tried to reinvent himself abroad—even taking on the title of Dr. Ulmer during his brief tenure as a producer at the Munich-based Eichberg Film Company in the 1950s—he often looked back to Hollywood. For example, following the shoot of *Pirates of Capri*, Ulmer writes from Rome that he keeps humming Cole Porter's "Just biding my time." And, not long after, in a letter to Shirley from 4 May 1951, he spells out his predicament: "In plain English, I need a job in Hollywood pronto . . . I need a job quick *at home* in Hollywood [emphasis added]."[9] During this period of intense disenchantment, Ulmer writes frequently to his agent, the Viennese-born Ilse Lahn of the Paul Kohner Agency (known for representing a host of émigré filmmakers, from Billy Wilder to Erich von Stroheim), urging her to assist him in securing work in America. In a letter of 25 August 1951, he writes to Lahn from Barcelona:

> I cannot tell you how lonesome I am for Hollywood, and if it would be not be for Shirley and Arianné [his daughter] I surely would have chucked the whole think [*sic*] and be on my way home. I can only repeat again and again "You can only make pictures in Hollywood and nowhere else." By that I mean make them and don't work yourself into a state where everything borders on heart failure. Undoubtedly we are spoiled. A sun ark [*sic*] becomes something awfully precious when you leave the shores of the U.S.A.[10]

Unlike 1930s émigré directors in Hollywood (e.g., Walter Reisch), who conjured up an "imaginary homeland" in their work, Ulmer's personal writings from the 1950s and 1960s seem to rely on the notion of a fantasy Hollywood, a world which, when regarded from his stilted, desperate vantage point, is stripped of all the imperfections he knew so well (see Elsaesser, *Weimar Cinema*; Rushdie).

As several critics have noted, Ulmer's films often feature characters without a fixed abode, who are given to unexpected and frequent movement and who experience a similar kind of transience to what Ulmer himself experienced in his early and later years. French filmmaker Bertrand Tavernier has said of Ulmer's characters, "They are always wandering."[11] This is true of his figures from the ethnic films of the 1930s and of Al Roberts from *Detour*, as well as being true of similar kinds of uprooted and estranged characters from his later work. As for Ulmer's personal predicament during the 1950s, he goes so far as to liken himself to "a dog in search of a place to find peace," and his own restlessness elicits deeper reflection both on and off the screen. In a letter of 5 October 1953, following yet another ill-fated project (this time *Loves of Three Queens* [1954], starring Hedy Lamarr), he writes to Lahn from Rome:

> Just a quick note with real news. Sad! But news. Hedy unfortunately is completely out of hand and I am unable to cope with her. She refuses direction. Therefore to avoid another "Babes in Bagdad" I have resigned from the picture. I have finished "Genevieve," but "Helene" and "Josephine" must be done by somebody else. The little self-respect I still have I cannot and will not lose . . . So I am at liberty and willing to make a picture from the first of November on. But only in Hollywood. I've got my fill of wandering.[12]

Even though Shirley may have felt, as she formulated it in a letter to her husband of 4 February 1961, that "home is where you are and where we are working,"[13] Ulmer himself did not seem, ultimately, to have shared this same view. The constant movement, the near nomadism of his later years in Europe, left him distraught and eager for just one final return—even if, in the end, it meant that his filmmaking career would come to a close. Writing to his agent from Paris in autumn 1961, he notes in a rueful key: "Shirley and I are desperately lonely and very, very homesick. It has been a long haul in Europe for both of us."[14] The romance of a wandering hero, while perhaps seductive in film and in fiction, lost its allure over time. That is perhaps the true point at which exile (the idea) and exile (the reality) part ways.

NOTES

1. See also Belton's early study, *Howard Hawks, Frank Borzage, Edgar G. Ulmer* (New York: A. S. Barnes, 1974).

2. For a more thorough exploration of this line of inquiry, see my "Perennial Detour."

3. The database available at www.ellisisland.org contains Ulmer's passenger record from 12 April 1924, with his place of residence given as "Wein [*sic*], Austria" and his ethnicity as "Austria Hebrew."

4. See Tom Weaver's interview with Shirley Ulmer in this volume. According to Shirley Ulmer, "We were told that we'd never work in Hollywood again. He couldn't get a job—that's why we went back to New York."

5. On the greater significance of African American characters in the films of exiled directors, see Kaes.

6. One can, indeed, read the film as a compelling allegory of exile. For further analysis along these same lines, see my "Perennial Detour," 15–19. See also my book-length treatment of the film, *Detour*.

7. Unpublished letter of 13 October 1948, Edgar G. Ulmer to Ilse Lahn, Paul Kohner Archive, Box 4.3-88/14-6 (EGU to PK 1948–1955), Berlin Filmmuseum.

8. Unpublished letter of 1 July 1941, Edgar G. Ulmer to Shirley Ulmer, Edgar G. Ulmer Collection, Margaret Herrick Library, Academy of Motion Picture Arts and Sciences, Beverly Hills, Calif.

9. Unpublished letter of 4 May 1951, Edgar G. Ulmer to Shirley Ulmer, Edgar G. Ulmer Collection, Margaret Herrick Library, Academy of Motion Picture Arts and Sciences, Beverly Hills, Calif.

10. Unpublished letter of 25 August 1951, Edgar G. Ulmer to Ilse Lahn, Paul Kohner Archive, Box 4.3-88/14-6 (EGU to PK 1948–1955), Berlin Filmmuseum.

11. Bertrand Tavernier, unpublished interview by Michael Henry Wilson, 7 November 1997, Paris, 62.

12. Unpublished letter of 5 October 1953, Edgar G. Ulmer to Ilse Lahn, Paul Kohner Archive, Box 4.3-88/14-6 (EGU to PK 1948–1955), Berlin Filmmuseum.

13. Unpublished letter of 4 February 1961, Shirley Ulmer to Edgar G. Ulmer, Edgar G. Ulmer Collection, Margaret Herrick Library, Academy of Motion Picture Arts and Sciences, Beverly Hills, Calif.

14. Unpublished letter of 5 October 1961, Edgar G. Ulmer to Ilse Lahn, Paul Kohner Archive, Box 4.3-88/14-6 (EGU to PK 1948–1955), Berlin Filmmuseum.

BIBLIOGRAPHY

Albrecht, Donald. *Designing Dreams: Modern Architecture and the Movies* (New York: Harper and Row, 1986).

Belton, John. "Cinema Maudit," in *Retrospective* (Edinburgh: Edinburgh Film Festival, 1997), 149–50.

———. "Edgar G. Ulmer (1900[*sic*]–1972)," in *American Directors*, Vol. 1, ed. Jean-Pierre Coursodon with Pierre Sauvage (New York: McGraw-Hill, 1983), 339–47.

Bogdanovich, Peter. "Edgar G. Ulmer: An Interview," *Film Culture* 58–60 (1974), reprinted in *Who the Devil Made It: Conversations with Legendary Film Directors* (New York: Ballantine, 1998), 558–604.

Eisner, Lotte. *Murnau* (Berkeley: University of California Press, 1973).

Elsaesser, Thomas. "Ethnicity, Authenticity, and Exile: A Counterfeit Trade? German Filmmakers in Hollywood," in *Home, Exile, Homeland: Film, Media, and the Politics of Place*, ed. Hamid Naficy (New York: Routledge, 1999), 97–123.

———. *Weimar Cinema and After: Germany's Historical Imaginary* (New York: Routledge, 2000).

Feld, Fritz. "In Memoriam of Edgar Ulmer" (unpublished ms), 3 October 1972.

Fischer, Lucy. *Sunrise* (London: BFI, 1998).

Forman, Betty Yetta. "From *The American Shadchan* [*sic*] to *Annie Hall*: The Life and Legacy of Yiddish Film in America," *National Jewish Monthly*, November 1977, 4–13.

Francke, Lizzie. "Edgar G. Ulmer," in *Retrospective* (Edinburgh: Edinburgh Film Festival, 1997), 148.

Goldberg, Judith N. *Laughter through Tears: The Yiddish Cinema* (Madison, NJ: Farleigh Dickinson University Press, 1982).

Grafe, Frieda. "Wiener Beiträge zu einer wahren Geschichte des Kinos," in *Aufbruch ins Ungewisse: Österreichische Filmschaffende in der Emigration vor 1945*, ed. Christian Cargnelli and Michael Omasta (Vienna: Wespennest, 1993), 227–43.

Grissemann, Stefan. *Mann im Schatten: Der Filmemacher Edgar G. Ulmer* (Vienna: Zsolnay, 2003).

Hoberman, J. *Bridge of Light: Yiddish Film between Two Worlds* (New York: Museum of Modern Art, 1991).

———. "Low and Behold," *Village Voice*, 17 November 1998.

Huesmann, Heinrich. *Welttheater Reinhardt* (Munich: Prestel 1983).

Isenberg, Noah. *Detour* (London: BFI, 2008).

———. "Perennial Detour: The Cinema of Edgar G. Ulmer and the Experience of Exile," *Cinema Journal* 43, no. 2 (Winter 2004): 3–25.

Kaes, Anton. "A Stranger in the House: Fritz Lang's *Fury* and the Cinema of Exile," *New German Critique* 89 (Spring–Summer 2003): 35–58.

Krohn, Bill. "King of the Bs," *Film Comment* 19, no. 4 (July–August 1983): 60–64.

Mandell, Paul. "Edgar Ulmer and *The Black Cat*," *American Cinematographer*, October 1984, 34–47.

Morton, Frederic. *Thunder at Twilight: Vienna 1913/14* (New York: Da Capo, 2001).

Preminger, Otto. "An Interview," in *Max Reinhardt 1873–1973*, ed. George Wellwarth and Alfred Brooks (Binghamton, N.Y.: Max Reinhardt Archive, 1973), 109–11.

Rushdie, Salman. *Imaginary Homelands* (London: Granta Books, 1991).

Sannwald, Daniela. "Metropolis: Die Wien-Berlin-Achse im deutschen Film der 10er und 20er Jahre," *Elektische Schatten: Beiträge zur Österreichischen Stummfilmgeschichte*, ed. Francesco Bono et al. (Vienna: Filmarchiv Austria, 1999), 139–48.

Schildkraut, Joseph. *My Father and I* (New York: Viking, 1959).

Ulman, Erik. "Edgar G. Ulmer," *Senses of Cinema*, at www.sensesofcinema.com/contents/directors/03/ulmer.html (accessed 3 March 2003).

Ulmer, Edgar G. "Beyond the Boundary" (unpublished ms).

Viertel, Salka. *The Kindness of Strangers: A Theatrical Life; Vienna, Berlin, Hollywood* (New York: Holt, Rinehart and Winston, 1969).

Young, Stark. "The Miracle," *New York Times*, November 9, 1924.

2

The Search for Community

John Belton

In "Reification and Utopia in Mass Culture," Fredric Jameson describes social life within late capitalism as "reified" and "atomized," lacking the cohesiveness of "authentic collective life" (140). The status of the individual within mass culture is one of fragmentation and alienation. The individual is cut adrift from traditional institutions such as community and family that once provided a sense of one's place within a larger collectivity. This alienation constitutes one of the "fundamental social anxieties" (141) that lie at the heart of mass culture. Jameson argues that these anxieties find expression in works of mass culture but do so in such a way that they are ultimately managed or repressed. Jameson's examples, *Jaws* and *The Godfather*, repress social and political anxieties "by the narrative construction of imaginary resolutions and by the projection of an optical illusion of social harmony" (141).

As works of mass culture, noir films give a remarkably powerful expression of social, political, and sexual anxieties. If mainstream Hollywood films manage or repress those anxieties, film noir exposes and exploits them, with often only minimal management of them. Film noir emerges as an exception to Jameson's thesis—but an exception that nonetheless proves the rule. One could argue, for example, that a film like Edgar G. Ulmer's *Detour* (1945) stages anxieties about marriage and the liberated, new woman of postwar America. Sue's reluctance to marry Al and her decision to pursue her career thousands of miles away pose initial threats that he subsequently attempts to handle by hitchhiking across the country to join her. But along the way, he encounters Sue's opposite image (and, ironically, his own mirror image) in the form of Vera, the film's femme fatale. Vera is so independent that she lacks any connection with the world around her.

She has no family, friends, home, or profession. Sue's reluctance to marry is nightmarishly reversed with Vera, who *forces* Al to play the role of her husband when they get to Los Angeles. The anxieties embodied in Vera are resolved through her accidental death, a resolution familiar to film noir. The threat that Al himself poses to the social order as homeless, nameless outcast and criminal is, in turn, resolved with his arrest in the final scene. Thus the film "contains" the anxieties it unleashes.

As Tag Gallagher has persuasively argued, all of Ulmer's films are morality plays, focusing on the moral failures of their heroes and/or heroines, who suffer for the choices they make or fail to make (2 of 29). In this sense, then, *Detour* reaffirms the social order. As Robert Warshow notes of the gangster film, the tragic fate of the gangster acts out and manages our fantasies. We, like the gangster, desire to succeed and abhor failure. But individual success—for the gangster, at least—inevitably culminates in death. The gangster pays for success with his life. As Warshow writes,

> This is our intolerable dilemma: that failure is a kind of death and success is evil and dangerous, is—ultimately—impossible. The effect of the gangster film is to embody this dilemma in the person of the gangster and resolve it by his death. The dilemma is resolved because it is his death, not ours. We are safe for the moment, we can acquiesce in our failure, we can choose to fail. (133)

We are reconciled to failure, to the ultimate unattainability of success. If the gangster film explores the tragedy of success, *Detour* explores the tragedy of failure in the form of a moral lesson, its characters serving as cautionary exemplars to guide our own choices and behaviors. In this sense, even a bleak film like *Detour* manages the "social and political anxieties and fantasies" that Jameson finds in every "mass cultural text."

Ulmer's most critically celebrated films tend to be his "Hollywood" features—*The Black Cat* (1934), *Bluebeard* (1944), *Strange Illusion* (1945), *Detour* (1945), *The Strange Woman* (1946), *Ruthless* (1948), *The Naked Dawn* (1955), and *The Cavern* (1965). All of these films speak to the alienated state of the individual in mass culture. It is true that none of these films projects the utopian, "optical illusion of social harmony" that characterizes the mass cultural texts described by Jameson. Indeed, Ulmer's exposure and exploitation of social and political anxieties might be viewed as politically progressive, as critiques of late capitalist mass culture. His central characters are proletarian tough guys, or maybe not-so-tough guys like Al Roberts in *Detour*. Roberts spouts the tough-guy lingo and adopts the hard-boiled attitude of pulp fiction, but he becomes so entangled in his cynical philosophy of life that he becomes solipsistic to an extreme and lacks any sense of a concern for the social.

Like Vendig in *Ruthless*, Jenny Hager in *The Strange Woman* climbs out of poverty on the backs of those around her, but she remains steadfastly sympathetic to the poor, feeding and housing them, doctoring them when they are sick, and attempting to close down the grog houses that condemn them (like her father) to alcoholism and wasted lives. Even if there is a streak of misogyny in her representation, Jenny is nonetheless seen as a product of a social and cultural system in which men have all the money and power, and she understands, even as a child, that the only way in which she can obtain this power is through men. Vendig, on the other hand, is a study in class betrayal. The *Ruthless* script, written by blacklisted writer Alvah Bessie, documents the way in which capitalism has corrupted the film's hero. A *New York Times* review of the film noted that "the authors have built a financial pirate of titanic proportions; a man so possessed by avarice and so cruelly cold and inhuman that he assumes a degree of monstrousness unrelated to reality." Mistaking a radical critique of American capitalism for a failed attempt at "realism," the *Times* proved itself to be totally clueless as to the intentions of the film.

Exceptions to this rule serve largely to confirm it. The Count of Monte Cristo and his wife, in the film which bears her name, struggle on behalf of disenfranchised French workers against the corrupt aristocracy and the bureaucracy that supports them. In *The Pirates of Capri*, Count Amalfi, chief adviser to the Queen, subverts the interests of his own class and, in Gary Morris's words, leads a "proletarian revolt against an increasingly cruel Neapolitan aristocracy" (2 of 5).

Gallagher likens Ulmer's films to morality plays, tracing this aspect of his work back to his Jesuit education as a child. If we understand Ulmer as a secular moralist, rather than as a Jesuit-educated Jewish allegoricist, it's possible to see his films in terms of moral struggle. But the struggle is not a struggle for the soul or for salvation, as it is in Murnau. Rather it's a struggle within the self, a struggle within the field of one's contradictory desires, a struggle against one's weaknesses, a struggle with the essential nature of one's character. In other words, Ulmer's morality plays are not religious; they are behavioral. And the behaviors that drive them reflect the reification and commodification of late capitalist mass culture. His central characters remain victims of the individualistic desires, fantasies, and dreams generated by mass culture. *The Strange Woman* would seem to be a morality play of the religious sort. Its climax presents its heroine with her own self-image, described in the words of a frontier evangelist preacher. Turning from a female sinner on display at the front of the chapel to the good women of Bangor, the preacher asks, "Which of you has taken a man from her sister?" as we watch Jenny, who stole her husband from her best friend, squirm in her seat. Ulmer cuts to a close-up of Jenny as the preacher denounces female lust. The preacher's logic becomes more and more psychotic—beauty makes women evil; evil will necessarily reveal itself; evil cannot propagate itself—there will be no sons to mourn for you, the preacher says, looking at Jenny, who is unable to bear children. "The lips of a strange woman drip honey and her mouth is smoother than oil. But her end is as bitter as wormwood; sharp as a two-edged sword." The preacher's sustained religious fanaticism emerges as a kind of crazy truth—a staging of the heroine's own conflicts over her prior behavior. Though this "truth" is given religious form, it is a truth about the nature of the heroine's self-knowledge, not about the state of her soul.

In *Detour*, Roberts struggles with his knowledge of his own weaknesses—thus the defensive mechanism of the tough-guy, hard-boiled facade. Sue, at the Break o' Dawn Club in New York, bolsters his self-image, promising that his talent at the piano will get him into Carnegie Hall. "Yeah," he replies, "as a janitor." Characteristically, he demolishes any idealized image of himself. When Sue suddenly tells him that she's decided to go alone to Los Angeles to seek a career for herself, she tacitly acknowledges what we've sensed already—that Al is a loser and that she'd be better off without him. And she takes any positive self-image he might have with her. Al's journey can be seen as a last-ditch attempt to reconstruct his shattered self-image by reacquiring Sue as his mirror. Minutes before Haskell dies, Roberts fantasizes Sue singing *their* song, "I Can't Believe That You're in Love with Me," in the rearview mirror of Haskell's car. Though idealized in the mirror, Sue is or is about to be behind him—she's in the past, something he has left behind on his journey to nowhere. He winds up with Vera instead. Vera is, of course, better matched to Roberts than Sue ever was. Vera is a more accurate mirror for him. As she tells him, "We're both alike, both born in the same gutter." Every bit as tough and cynical as he is (if not more), Vera, dying slowly of consumption, becomes Roberts's true mirror, reflecting back the hopelessness and sense of fatality that are essential to his nature.

If being with Sue was "a little like working in Heaven," being with Vera is clearly more like being in Hell. But it is a Hell of his own making, the result of his own unconscious self-destructiveness. What else would you call it when a man in a stolen car, wearing the clothes of a man he accidentally killed and carrying over $750 of the dead man's money, decides to pick up a female hitchhiker? At any rate, Roberts gets to L.A.; but instead of marrying Sue, he becomes trapped in a nightmarish inversion of that—he is forced into a marriage of convenience with Vera, locked into a two-room honeymoon apartment with her.

Roberts gets to Vera through Haskell. Haskell is Roberts's physical double; even Vera remarks that they look alike—enough for Roberts to take Haskell's place in her inheritance scheme, without arousing suspicion. The resemblance gives concrete form to Roberts's weakened self-image. He would rather be somebody else, anybody else—even a womanizing, small-time bookie like Haskell—than be himself. He would rather be dead than Al Roberts. So he becomes Haskell and leaves himself—in the form of Haskell's body, now dressed in Roberts's clothes and bearing his ID—lying dead in a roadside ravine.

In this morality play, Roberts confronts mirrors of himself. They range from Sue to Vera, and each is a bit truer to his own self-image. In killing Vera, the last personification of his virtues and vices, he is left without any identity whatsoever. His journey is, as one of my former students put it, "a story of self-actualization." He finally realizes the essential lack that has always been at the core of his being.

The irony, for Roberts and other Ulmer characters, is that they can never escape who they are. Roberts has become locked in a pattern of behavior that he semi-realizes is self-destructive, but he is too weak to do anything other than be carried by the momentum of his own inertia toward self-annihilation. Roberts, Jenny, and others battle their inner weaknesses even as they resign themselves to them. What is so hypnotic about the moral struggle that certain characters in Ulmer films undergo is the oscillating movement that propels them in an endless back-and-forth cycle between desire and doubt. An inability to resolve this movement constitutes their moral dilemma.

What remains to be resolved in the portrait of Ulmer that I am presenting here is the precise nature of the relationship between his social and moral visions. The answer to this question lies, I think, in Jameson's notion of the alienation of the individual within late capitalism and the desire for that individual to reclaim membership in an authentic, but no longer attainable, "folk" community. It's possible to understand Jenny Hager's genuine dedication to the poor in *Strange Woman* as a feature of her social alienation and an aspect of her desire for community. Her alienation, however, is realized in bourgeois terms—her quasi-psychotic quest for male power and the moral struggles she undergoes in an attempt to find a place for herself within an oppressive, patriarchal social structure.

Al Roberts, on the other hand, has no obvious commitment to the world from which he comes and enjoys an alienation for which there is no hypothetical solution. His goal is the restoration of an idealized past with Sue, not with any preindustrialist, agrarian, folk community. His moral struggle is clearly a product of his social alienation, but the film refuses to provide an alternative social space with which he might identify. In *Detour*, there is no possibility for a return to a precapitalist paradise. Its characters are condemned to live, or rather die, in a world where money rules. But even if it is the only thing of value, it can't buy what Roberts wants. It is only a piece of paper, crawling with germs.

To some extent, Ulmer's last film, *The Cavern*, provides a solution to the problem that has plagued his earlier characters. The film creates a community of alienated characters, forcing the community to come into being by sealing its characters off in a cave together. The film's biblical overtones, communicated through the General's reading of "Genesis," are accompanied by a series of shots which show the various entrapped characters in their individual isolation, listening as a fragmented collective to the words he says aloud. Mimicking the story of "Genesis" itself, the scene depicts the creation of a new social and moral order. But this preindustrial, pastoral order is still a prison of sorts. And it is undermined, like Poelzig's house in *The Black Cat*, with dynamite. The explosion of this world, set off by the very character who read "Genesis" aloud, sends its surviving characters back out into the world but also into a less-than-perfect social order, where one supposes that their alienation will return with a vengeance.

In his essay, Jameson opposes "the mass cultural text" to what he refers to as "popular . . . folk art of the past" (134). Folk art was "the 'organic' expression of . . . distinct social communities or castes" (134). If, as Jameson acknowledges, modernist authors such as Gertrude Stein lack "a unified social group with its own cultural specificity" and thus write for themselves and for strangers rather than for an organic community, works of folk art enjoy an authenticity that works of modernism or of mass culture do not. "The only authentic cultural production today," writes Jameson,

> has seemed to be that which can draw on the collective experience of marginal pockets of the social life of the world system: black literature and blues, British working-class rock, women's literature, gay literature, the *roman quebecois*, the literature of the Third World; and this production is possible only to the degree to which these forms of collective life or collective solidarity have not yet been fully penetrated by the market and by the commodity system (140).

Jameson might well have included Yiddish literature and film in his list of folk cultural texts. These works possess the necessary characteristics that define them as the product of an organic social group—a common language and references to a common cultural tradition. Much as Gaelic embodies aspects of Irish identity that elude Irish English, so Yiddish serves as source of ethnic and cultural identity for Jews in opposition to more official, national languages within which the Yiddish-speaking population lives, such as Russian, Polish, German, or English. At the same time, Yiddish literature (theater, novels, short stories, poems, and oral works) and film draw on and appeal to a traditional folklore and body of cultural practices that provide a common heritage for this unique ethnic group. Just as important is the fact that these works are produced and consumed within this common social group; they are created by members of this community for other members of that same community (rather than by one social group for another, as is often the case with white-produced race films; indeed, Ulmer's race film, *Moon over Harlem* [1939], lacks the ethnic authenticity of those directed by African American filmmakers such as Oscar Micheaux or Spencer Williams). As Jameson suggests, folk art involves "an aesthetic 'contract' between a cultural producer and a certain homogeneous class or group public: they drew their vitality from the social and collective status . . . of the situation of aesthetic production and consumption" (136).

The group of Ulmer films discussed earlier—his "classics"—represent only Ulmer's most familiar work. Ulmer also directed four Yiddish films—*Green Fields* (1937), *The Singing Blacksmith* (1938), *The Light Ahead* (1939), and *American Matchmaker* (1940). Though Ulmer himself did not speak Yiddish (Hoberman 247), he was Jewish and was an associate of members of the Yiddish theater. In other words, though something of an outsider, he quickly became involved with a cohesive group of writers, producers, actors, and other members of the Jewish Art Theater on the Lower East Side of Manhattan. Ulmer's four Yiddish films reveal a radically different social vision—one that illustrates Jameson's argument about folk art. The notion of community found in these films is diametrically opposed to that found in Ulmer's film noirs. The films depict a viable ethnic collectivity, ranging from entirely Jewish communities in films set in the shtetl (*The Singing Blacksmith*, *The Light Ahead*) and rural farmland (*Green Fields*), to primarily Jewish communities in contemporary urban areas (*American Matchmaker*). Though the narratives feature conflict among the films' various characters, that conflict belies a more profound sense of common purpose and community that ties the characters together. *Green Fields*, based on a Yiddish play by Peretz Hirschbein (who also wrote the screenplay), provides an excellent example of this.

The narrative trajectory of the film takes the central character, Levi Yitskhok—a rabbinical student—from an urban yeshiva where he seems to have lost his way (he falls asleep at his studies while his two colleagues study through the night) to a rural farm where he becomes the houseguest of a Jewish peasant family. The last scene of the film has him become part of the family; in the last shot, he walks off into the distance with the farmer's daughter, Tsine, whose hand in marriage he has requested.

The script frames his journey as a search for truth. His fellow students note that "some hidden force drives him to leave us." Levi is vaguely dissatisfied with his spiritual state. His colleagues describe him as "restless." For them, study leads to peace of mind, but not for Levi.

Elements of traditional folktales involving quests structure the film, as can be seen in the film's use of night and day scenes. The only night scene in the film occurs in the yeshiva at the start. The only time we see Levi asleep also occurs in this scene. As he opens the door to leave on his journey, a shaft of sunlight enters and shines on him; it's a deliberate visual effect on Ulmer's part—it is even marked by a continuity error at the start of the shot, in that the synchronization of the shaft of light and the opening of the door is imperfect. This light, of course, symbolizes the light of truth. The dialogue with the other students makes this clear. They explain to him that he need not go out into the world: "The light of truth is everywhere," they insist. "You need not search for it." Levi replies, "The light of truth is everywhere. But one must still search for it." The search takes him from the all-male, urban, enclosed world of the yeshiva to a world of nature. It takes him from a world of students to one of family and community—the family of David-Noich and the community of this family and a neighboring family (Elkone, Gitl, and Sterna).

The journey is presented as a movement through nature. A medium close-up of Levi walking is superimposed over a montage of shots of fields, meadows, and fruit trees. Levi is initially detached from nature—the image of his face is superimposed over shots of the landscape that technically exclude him. This is the first of several montages of nature and farming. The montage ends with Levi's encounter with David-Noich's youngest son, the boy Avrom-Yankov, an encounter which begins Levi's new course of instruction on farming, rural life, and nature.

The film begins with an emblematic shot of the communal harvesting of a field of hay. (The film was released by a company called Collective Film Producers and was codirected by Ulmer and Jacob Ben-Ami; J. Hoberman describes the collective as having "progressive" politics, 247). In this shot (which reappears later), a group of women rake hay in the foreground while men lift hay with pitchforks onto a hay wagon in the background. It is to this image that the film moves. The image evokes all the positive values of community and nature. It looks back to a preindustrial, agrarian paradise unspoiled by the forces of modernity.

This Edenic paradise is associated with the "true Jews" that Levi seeks. Levi is presented as a wandering Jew in search of "true Jews." In answer to questions about his journey and where he is going, he explains, "I'll stop wherever I find true Jews." When Avrom-Yankov points out where he and his family live, Ulmer interjects another nature montage, dissolving from long shots of trees in a grove and fruit trees in blossom to a medium-close shot of a plow (followed by a pair of male feet) digging furrows in a field, and a pair of women planting rows of potatoes in a plowed field.

The theme of "nature" is extended through notions of "naturalness." Though the two families of farmers are seen as having various cycles of melodramatic interaction, peppered by quarrels and making up after quarrels, these cycles are presented as natural—as part of the everyday give and take of communal life in rural areas. Thus the resolution of the separated lovers plotline involving Hersh-ber and Sterna climaxes with Hersh-ber's emotional outbreak—actual anger at Elkone, Sterna's father, for standing in their way—to which Elkone responds positively, as if he has been waiting for an open, demonstrative act of quarrelling so that they could set things right. Levi is cast as a voyeuristic outsider to all this; he scrupulously avoids any involvement in the families' quarrels. His gestures differ dramatically from those of the people around him. He seems disaffected and distant. He almost never looks those he converses with directly in the eye, but constantly looks off in a state of semi-self-absorption. His hands nervously stroke the lapels of his coat jacket or play with buttons on his coat, illustrating his self-containment. His progress through the film is from isolation and alienation to contact and community, a progress that begins with his contact with the boy, Avrom-Yankov, and culminates with his encounter with Tsine, who immodestly kisses him. As in a fairy tale, her kiss seems to awaken him from his self-absorption and leads to his union with her. They walk off, hand in hand, in the final shot—the most natural presentation of him in the film. Levi has found his place within this community, an event signaled by the pastoral nature of this final shot, which frames him and his bride-to-be through the handles of a plow that rests in the foreground. Though the two families quarrel over social protocols (the proper behavior of their children, proprietorship over Levi as honored houseguest), they recognize one another as "good Jews," assist one another at harvests, and oversee the marriage of their children to one another, making two families one within an unseen but implicitly larger, Jewish community of farmers.

The world in which *Green Fields* is set bears no temporal or spatial marks that could identify it. Its world appears to be preindustrial, agrarian, and possibly eastern European. We see a horse-drawn cart, a plow, a thatched-roof cottage, simple peasant clothing, and bare feet. We see no automobiles, tractors, electric lights, telephones, or other machinery of modernity. This is the spatial and temporal landscape of the folk tale. *The Singing Blacksmith* somewhat resembles this world, though it is set in a rural shtetl rather than on a farm. The most sophisticated machinery that we can see consists of a traditional blacksmith's forge and the tools of his trade (a pair of bellows, an anvil, a steel mallet). The world of the film is the space of the small village in which it is set — the simple streets through which characters walk and the cozy interiors (taverns, sewing rooms, parlors) in which they interact. Ulmer populates this village with various tradesmen and working-class types—the blacksmith, a cart driver, seamstresses, two matchmakers—as well as members of the "better," merchant class. In the very first scene, when Yankel is apprenticed to the old blacksmith, Yankel's father, Simcha, explains that his son had unreasonably wanted to "go to the gymnasium with the aristocrats" but that he thought his son was better suited for manual labor. The film explores class difference through the blacksmith Yankel's marriage to the orphaned daughter of a merchant, contrasting his energy, vitality, and sensuality to her sensitive and somewhat sickly reserve. The matchmaker laughs at Yankel's insistence that she arrange a match between him and Tamara, the niece of the wealthy Reb Aaron. Later, Yankel apologizes to Tamara, noting that her former friends no longer visit her because she married a lowly blacksmith. But class difference is not the source of dramatic conflict. The class dynamics of the shtetl seem to easily accommodate Yankel's potentially transgressive marriage. Rather, it is Yankel's lack of seriousness in his attitude toward life that emerges as the source of narrative disturbance. Yankel is initially presented as cool and indifferent to those around him. When the blacksmith who trained Yankel hands over his business to him and retires, he tells Yankel about his life, his hopes, and his frustrations. He reminisces about his dead wife and child. Yankel listens but eats while doing so and does not seem to care. After the old man refers to his dead son buried in the village graveyard, Yankel unemotionally notes that "we all end up there eventually."

Yankel's father asked the blacksmith to teach his son the trade of the smithy but also to make him "virtuous." The blacksmith agrees to the former but not to the latter. Yankel's chief virtues as an adult appear to reside in his delight in leisure-time activities—in drinking, singing, dancing, and womanizing. After a montage sequence in which Yankel's apprenticeship as a blacksmith is linked to the changing cycles of nature (tree branches heavy with ice and snow followed by fruit trees in blossom), he inherits the smithy and is not seen at work again until a scene shortly before he first sees Tamara, when he sings the "Strike the Hammer" song. When a matchmaker tells Yankel he should have a wife, he replies, "Why do I need stale bread when I can get fresh rolls?" We have already seen Yankel taking girls to the woods, where he seduces them, and flirting with Rivke, a girl promised in marriage to another. The appearance of Tamara transforms Yankel from a self-indulgent, pleasure-seeking wastrel into a "mensch." He now has a goal—Tamara—which he pursues doggedly. He drags the matchmaker with him to her house and forces her to propose the match. He confesses to Tamara that, after meeting her, he felt ashamed of himself, referring to his reputation as a womanizer.

As with Levi in *Green Fields*, Yankel moves from alienation to engagement as he discovers the importance of family and community. Unlike Levi, Yankel is introduced as a full-fledged member of this village. His father and the old blacksmith engage in ritualistic bargaining as they negotiate the arrangement for his apprenticeship, which they then celebrate with a drink. The blacksmith then gives the young Yankel his first drink, bringing him into the ritual. Rituals associated with work give way to those associated with play. Musical sequences show Yankel singing and dancing in spaces where the villagers gather after work. But his relationship to this communal life of the village is presented in terms of the pursuit of his own desires—his series of affairs with young village women. The narrative's central conflict hinges on Yankel's moral dilemma. His encounter with Tamara makes him realize the emptiness of his existence. His marriage with her and the birth of his son emerge as redemptive acts. But his past comes back to haunt him in the form of Rivke, who leaves her husband and attempts to take Yankel away from his wife and child. In one of the film's most erotic moments, a drunken Yankel stokes the fire in the forge as Rivke pumps the bellows. They kiss, and the fire flames up. Having given in to temptation, Yankel is again ashamed of himself and cannot face Tamara. He wanders the streets of the village and encounters the lonely old blacksmith, who advises him to go back to his wife. As in *Sunrise*, a film which seems to be a model for the melodramatic story of the husband, wife, and other woman told here, Rivke is expelled and husband and wife are reunited. The final shot of the film is the equivalent of Murnau's sunrise—a shot of the baby in its crib, the beginning of a new life in a world of new possibilities. Family and community are made whole again. Yankel has finally become "virtuous" through the agency of his redemptive/forgiving wife and the morally regenerative aura of his newborn son.

The quasi-utopian vision of life depicted in *Green Fields* is complicated somewhat by the more complex and diverse representation of village life in *The Singing Blacksmith*. In both films, the depiction of the Jewish community is not without a certain ambivalence, traceable, no doubt, to the source materials on which the films are based. The negative aspects (neighborly jealousy and contention in *Green Fields*; class difference and moral flaws in *Singing Blacksmith*) are counterbalanced by the positive virtues of a family and community that have withstood the trials and tribulations of life and found happiness in one another. Critics have tended to view *The Light Ahead* as a film that is highly critical of the Jewish community within which the story is set. The town of Glupsk (literally "Foolstown") is presented as provincial, superstitious, and corrupt. "Glubsk is still firmly in the Middle Ages," writes Hoberman. "The life of the town is depicted as miserable and degrading, religion shown to be self-serving and hypocritical—even the dietary laws have been perverted by commerce" (302). Yet the character who occupies the film's moral center, bookseller Reb Mendele, understands these flaws within the culture to be features that define Jewish life. For him the lives of Jews are characterized by "all the calamities, adversities, hardships, curses, troubles, afflictions, miseries, [and] disasters." It is "always the same old story" that befalls his people. He continues, "every village has its rich, its paupers . . . its wise men, scholars, fools, ignoramuses . . . its stirrers of pots, its leading citizens . . . its innocent lambs and insolent ruffians." Glupsk is such a village.

For David Desser, Yiddish culture is a "mélange of conflicting intellectual and emotional ideas and ideals born of Jewish hope and pain in the cities and *shtetls* of Eastern Europe, now gone forever" (40). From the vantage point of the late 1930s and the imminent Nazi takeover of Poland (and as conveyed in Desser's 1990s perspective), there is an understandable nostalgia within Yiddish culture for even the negative aspects of Jewish life. In fact, Reb Mendele repeatedly rhapsodizes about Jewish resilience, invoking "Jewish people . . . with their eternal hope and belief in a better dawn." It is his optimism about the future that oversees the trials and tribulations of the film's young hero and heroine. In short, the film's critique of community takes place within the context of a larger optimism about its abilities to survive and improve.

If *Singing Blacksmith* invokes the narrative pattern of *Sunrise*, *The Light Ahead* draws on that film's universalized character types and its expressionistic set design. Ulmer's film resembles a folk tale in its broad strokes, in its essentialization of its central characters—a poor, lame boy (Fishke) and a poor, blind girl (Hodel) who are both orphans. The expressive stylization of Murnau and Borzage (*Street Angel*, *Seventh Heaven*) is visible in the Caligariesque set design of the village, with its angled streets and stucco-faced houses. The sets contribute to the somewhat gothic, fairy-tale quality of the film's urban spaces. This setting provides the backdrop for an unusual romantic melodrama in which lovers, unable to marry because of their poverty, are subsequently *forced* to marry in observance of a bizarre cultural practice designed to atone for the violation of religious protocols. The traditional marriage that concludes the conventional fairly tale thus takes on a somber cast, preliminary to a happier ending when the couple escapes this grim fate and flees to a more promising future in another city.

The film's hopefulness resides, in part, in its discursive strategies and rhetorical shifts. It appears to establish a series of thematic antinomies which it then qualifies and rethinks. The narrow-minded, medieval, closed community of Glupsk is opposed to the more open-minded, culturally progressive city of Odessa. It is to Odessa that Fishke travels in the film's opening scene, in his flight from unhappiness in Glupsk. The past and tradition are opposed to the present and modernization. Rural town is opposed to urban center. City is contrasted with country; irrationality with rationality. Superstition informs the beliefs and behaviors of the citizens of Glupsk, who blame the outbreak of a cholera epidemic on the violation of the Sabbath by a group of girls who have gone for a swim in the town's polluted river. Though the town desperately needs to embrace modern science in the form of doctors and a hospital, it attempts to deal with the cholera epidemic through superstitious ceremony—by marrying its two poorest citizens at nighttime in a graveyard.

The reworking of these antinomies begins in the very first scene, when Mendele insists that Fishke should not go off alone (i.e., without Hodel) to the larger, more modern metropolis of Odessa because he would be lonely in the big anonymous city. Mendele reminds Fishke that he has a place within the community in Glupsk. Even though the city is petty and corrupt, it nonetheless gives meaning and substance to his life. Yet at the end of the film, Mendele engineers Fishke and Hodel's departure to Odessa, where they can establish themselves anew and escape their identities as Glupsk's "cholera bride and cholera groom." An uncertain future becomes more promising than the curse of the past, articulated in the language of disease ("cholera").

Mendele oversees the film's action with a benign optimism—combining acceptance and forgiveness with a forward-looking belief that life can be wonderful. This moral dynamic is conveyed in the opening scene, when a potential argument swiftly turns into a friendly encounter between two men, Mendele and Reb Alter, whose horse has eaten Mendele's hay. From formerly riding in separate carts, they now ride together. The natural setting—the sequence is located at the edge of a clearing outside of town—frames the encounter and encourages its peaceful resolution. Here, four of the film's social outcasts (Mendele, Alter, Isaak, and Fishke) form a little group of fellow Israelites within the peace and beauty of the pastoral landscape. Mendele speaks of "Nature in all of its glory" and Ulmer pans away to reveal a verdant meadow. Mendele breathes deeply and extols the quality of the air. He refers to the countryside as "paradise."

The town of Glupsk itself is set against this pastoral world as a space of quarrels and misunderstandings, hypocrisy, and superstition, as well as friendship and love. Hodel and Gitel are genuinely friends, as we see in their first encounter in the street. Dropke, the old woman with whom Hodel lives, seems initially somewhat mercenary and harsh in her relations with Hodel. She encourages her to exploit her blindness by becoming a beggar, a suggestion which Hodel adamantly refuses. But Dropke does seem to care about Hodel's fate, and, by the end of their argument, she seems genuinely sorry for what she has said and for making Hodel cry.

Though the narrative tends to focus on the romantic couple and their vicissitudes, it constantly digresses to portray the life of the community as well. This is done through Mendele's interactions with the town's inhabitants. There's a scene with a rabbinical student who complains to his friend that there are only six days in the week and that he has "no Thursday." This is a reference to the custom of *esn teg* or "eating days" and means that he has no host family to invite him to dinner on Thursdays. Mendele listens to his tale and then offers him money so that he can eat. Later, there's a scene between Mendele and a childless woman. Mendele is selling prayer books and she asks him if he has any prayers for childless women. He offers her one and, unable to read herself, she asks him to read it aloud, weeps a bit, and then walks off without buying the prayer. Neither of these scenes advances the central narrative, but both scenes give the film's depiction of community texture and depth.

The opposition between nature and culture is not absolute but remains important. Only by getting outside of the village are characters able to see its values and its limitations. Mendele's wisdom seems to derive not only from his association with books but from his status as an outsider. His wandering has put him in contact with the beauties of nature—with the world outside of town. Nature within Glupsk has become polluted by the town; the filthy river is the source of a cholera epidemic that literally plagues the community. Similarly, the town has imposed a rigid, unnatural class structure that discriminates against those at the bottom (Fishke and Hodel), relegating them to an economic and social prison of sorts. The religious elders control the community economically and socially. The town coffers contain 100,000 rubles, but the elders refuse to use these funds to build a hospital, preferring to support prayer groups. The wife of the chief elder enforces social regulations, denouncing the girls for bathing on the Sabbath and forcing Fishke and Hodel to marry in the graveyard in order to assuage God's wrath.

The folk aspects of the story lie in its attempts to depict the trials and tribulations of the Jewish people in the figures of Fishke and Hodel. Fishke and Hodel describe themselves as "cursed," not only because of their physical afflictions but also because of the way in which events seem to frustrate their hopes and desires for the future. Even their wish to one day marry has a twisted and unwanted fulfillment. They are "cursed" as "the cholera bride and cholera groom." But within the larger darkness of the film, there is the promise of a new day. The screenplay introduces metaphors from nature to depict this hope. In one scene, Fishke describes to Hodel how the moon lights up the night. In another, Gitel gives a flower to Hodel to touch. She describes the flower and notes that its petals are closed at night but that they will open up when the sun rises, adding that "people are that way too." Again, Murnau's *Sunrise* would seem to be a source for these metaphors. At the end of the film, Fishke and Hodel are driven to the clearing outside of town seen at the beginning of the film. Mendele suggests that they will be cured of their lameness and blindness in Odessa, and the couple walk off, hand in hand, up a hill into the countryside. Those once cursed will find cures. Though the Jewish people live in hardship, they will surely endure and ultimately triumph over it.

The central character of *American Matchmaker* is also "cursed." Nat Silver has inherited his Uncle Shya's bad luck with women. Each of Nat's eight engagements has been broken off at the last minute. So Nat does what his uncle did—he becomes a matchmaker, or *shadchen*, and devotes himself to making other people happy. In doing this, Nat establishes a bond of sorts between his identity as a successful New York garment manufacturer and the European past of his extended family. More important, he finds a new identity for himself through a revival of Jewish tradition. He becomes a matchmaker. But Nat is not quite a traditional matchmaker. He doesn't wear a derby and a raincoat like his matchmaking colleagues in the Bronx. He wears an elegant tuxedo. The sign on his door does not read "Matchmaker," or "*Shadchen*," but "Advisor in Human Relations." (Morris, his comic sidekick and butler, is unfamiliar with the Latinate term "relations" and asks what "human relishes" are.) And he attempts to take matchmaking to a new level, introducing modern techniques such as psychological profiling. His staff includes a secretary, a psychiatrist, a doctor, a lawyer, and a rabbi. As Morris quips, Nat uses all sorts of "modern *shadchen*ology" in his business. Nat becomes a vehicle for staging the adaptation of traditional, Old World customs to the New World.

In many respects, *American Matchmaker* differs from Ulmer's other Yiddish films—primarily in its spatial and temporal setting of 1940s New York City. It begins with a montage of urban settings at night—bridges, skyscrapers, automobiles—and takes us to Nat's tastefully furnished apartment on Central Park West, where a bachelor party is in progress (attended by Nat and five of his manufacturer friends, all wearing tuxedos). Later in the film, Ulmer inserts another montage of urban nightlife, featuring neon signs advertising consumer products (Chevrolet, Planters, Coca-Cola), movie-theater marquees, a busy bar, and a crowded restaurant. This montage answers the first and introduces Judith Aarons, who will become Nat's love interest. Two scenes later, we return to Nat's apartment for the first time since he became a matchmaker, and we see him dine at home with Judith. The lack created by the last scene set in Nat's apartment, when he agreed to break off his engagement with Shirley (so that she and her childhood sweetheart could marry), is liquidated in this scene when Nat tells Judith why he became a matchmaker (his failures with women) and sets in motion a series of events that will lead to their marriage. The logic of the narrative suggests that only by reestablishing connections with folk traditions can modern Jews find true happiness.

What is also striking about the film in terms of Ulmer's earlier Yiddish films is the presence of English phrases and expressions among the Yiddish-language dialogue. Nat's sister Elvie betrays her Americanization in her dialogue, which is 50 percent English. At his bachelor party, Nat's butler, Morris, speaks English to the guests, who joke with him about his refusal to speak Yiddish. The English-only dialogue is clearly an attempt to observe social propriety; in more intimate conversations with Nat and his maid, Morris speaks Yiddish (sprinkled with English words and phrases). As with the tradition of the matchmaker, which has been modernized, so the language of Yiddish has incorporated new, non-Yiddish expressions like "okay" and "nice."

When Nat's mother tells him about his uncle Shya, she says, "He thought by helping others he might help himself." She tells Nat that he resembles his uncle in every way. Nat responds, "Incredible—but this is America, not Europe." She answers, "Family characteristics know no boundaries. They travel across oceans . . . over mountains." This is the message of the film—cultural traditions, like family characteristics, know no boundaries. They have migrated with the Jewish people from Europe to the United States and have found new vitality and energy in new, more modern forms.

Shortly after making *American Matchmaker*, his last Yiddish film, Ulmer took a job in Los Angeles at Producers Releasing Corporation (PRC), rejoining his former colleague Seymour Nebenzal (producer of *People on Sunday*), who had become an investor in the company. The heyday of Yiddish film in Poland and the United States was over, and only a few Yiddish-language films were ever made after 1945. Though PRC was only a marginal studio within the larger production system of Hollywood, it still made films for a mass audience. Like Gertrude Stein, Ulmer was relegated to making films "for himself" and "for strangers." His films were no longer produced and consumed within an organic, ethnic collectivity. In the context of his career as a whole, his four Yiddish films stand out for the optimism of their social vision. They were inhabited by characters who shared a common language, culture, and tradition unique to them as a people, within the multicultural mass publics that dominated cultural production and consumption in the first half of the twentieth century. These films provide a representation of a cohesive social group that Ulmer's subsequent films insistently yearn for, like an amnesiac for a forgotten identity. They represent a social fantasy that speaks to the deepest desires of the alienated individual in contemporary mass culture.

Author's note: I want to thank Sharon Pucker Rivo of the National Center for Jewish Film at Brandeis University for loaning me video copies of *Green Fields* and *The Light Ahead*, and Jeffrey Shandler for his help with *esn teg*.

BIBLIOGRAPHY

Desser, David. Review of *Bridge of Light: Yiddish Film between Two Worlds*, by J. Hoberman, *Film Quarterly* 47, no. 1 (Autumn 1993): 40–42.

Gallagher, Tag. "All Lost in Wonder," at www.latrobe.edu.au/screeningthepast/firstrelease/fr0301/tgafr12a.htm (accessed 30 October 2002).

Hoberman, J. *Bridge of Light: Yiddish Film between Two Worlds* (New York: Museum of Modern Art, 1991).

Jameson, Fredric. "Reification and Utopia in Mass Culture," *Social Text* 1 (Winter 1979): 130–48.

Morris, Gary. "Unmistakably Ulmer: *The Pirates of Capri* on DVD," at www.brightlights.com/32/piratesofcapri.html (accessed 30 October 2002).

T.M.P., *New York Times*, 4 September 1948.

Warshow, Robert. *The Immediate Experience: Movies, Comics, Theatre and Other Aspects of Popular Culture* (New York: Doubleday, 1962).

3

On the Graveyards of Europe

The Horror of Modernism in *The Black Cat*

Herbert Schwaab

In his last film *Salò, or the 120 Days of Sodom*, from 1975, Pier Paolo Pasolini claims that there is a connection between modern art and acts of violence which take place in a modern version of a ghost house. The paintings of Leger, Feininger, and the cubist artists look down with indifference on the victims and their tormentors (Minas 65). The paintings become passive bystanders to what happens inside a northern Italian *palazzo* in the last days of World War II. Pasolini expresses his deep ambivalence about the emancipative power of modern art. The visual style of this film emphasizes the condition of voyeurism, as if Pasolini were questioning himself as a filmmaker at the sight of the real horror of moral decay and fascism (66).

Ulmer's *The Black Cat*, from 1934, belongs to a cycle of classic horror films from the beginning of the sound-film era. Amongs films such as *Frankenstein, Dracula, Dr. Jekyll and Mr. Hyde*, and *The Mummy, The Black Cat* is unique in terms of its set design, which is strongly influenced by modernist architecture and art deco. Whereas most horror films of the era rely on an unspecific Englishness showing old gothic castles and ghost houses, Ulmer's human monsters haunt a "new" and stylish world of white walls, with clear geometric lines and abstract ornaments. The film is also unique in referring directly to the sociopolitical reality in the aftermath of the First World War. The house is built on the remnants of Fort Marmaros, next to a gigantic graveyard left behind by the war in Hungary. Its destruction by the Russian army is the result of Hjalmar Poelzig's treachery in war. Poelzig, one of the film's main characters, has returned to the scene of the crime as the architect and owner of the house.

The film is very short and very strange: within its 65 minutes, it offers us Satanism, extreme sadism, erratic characters, highly self-conscious dialogues mocking themselves, a score of classical music (very often used contrapuntally), implausible actions, the celebration of a Black Mass, visual elegance, the adaptation of German expressionism, and a camera set free from the constraints of narration to move through the interiors of this house. Its heterogeneity and exaggerations sometimes lend the film a quality of campiness, as Noah Isenberg has noticed (7). The excessiveness and unevenness in style, narration, and acting turn the film into an irritating art object. It is for this reason that the film remains a challenge and enigma for cinephiles and film scholars. This is why one tends to "overread" the film, wanting to attribute meaning to it. And this may offer an excuse for the fact that Pasolini's film came into my mind in relation to Ulmer's film, and that I felt encouraged to interpret the film as a weird reflection on modernism. Both are about the horrors of modernism. However, Pasolini's intellectual approach to filmmaking sets him miles apart from Ulmer's work in Hollywood cinema. *The Black Cat* was the first (and for a long time the only) major work of a then-thirty-year-old film director with artistic ambitions and some training in European culture. Due to his untimely death, *Salò* has often been regarded as Pasolini's epitaph, a highly conceptual work resuming the long-lasting quarrel with film, art theory, and culture undertaken by one of Italy's most important intellectual figures of the 1960s and 1970s. As Ulmer's approach to filmmaking lacks this theoretical depth, it is to be argued whether the film deserves to be read as a reflection on the relationship between modernism and inhumanity. The close examination of the relationship between Ulmer's film and modernism that follows here can be read as testing the limits of such projections onto a film text.

To find an answer to the question of whether *The Black Cat* can be read as a piece of intellectual cinema, let us first have a look at the film's content: On their honeymoon through eastern Europe, Peter and Joan Alison meet the mysterious Dr. Vitus Werdegast, Hungary's most famous psychiatrist, played by Bela Lugosi. Following a road accident, the three become uninvited guests of a man who happens to be Werdegast's rival, Hjalmar Poelzig. Werdegast wants to take revenge on Poelzig, who eighteen years earlier, during World War I, not only betrayed his own troops and sold them to the Russians—which led to Werdegast's fifteen-year imprisonment in Kurgal—but also took his beloved wife from him. A well-known architect (named after real-life Austrian architect Hans Poelzig), Poelzig has returned to the battleground and has built a modern home on a hill next to Europe's biggest graveyard. The house is built on top of the basement of the former fortress. This enables a particular structure, which John Belton refers to as a demonic inversion of the surface logic and clarity of Poelzig's house, lying beneath it (154). Poelzig receives his guests, including his rival, with some reservations, but he soon plans to use Joan Alison, who rests to recover from the accident, for a Black Mass—because Poelzig is a Satanist as well as a modernist. In the ensuing events "the house becomes a new battleground, the space in which the two European 'monsters' vie for power and control over their American prey" (Isenberg 6). Peter Alison is held captive in the cellar. At the same time, devil worshippers from all over the country gather to celebrate a Satanist ritual, with Werdegast interfering in the last moment to rescue Joan. Werdegast, having discovered the night before that Poelzig had not only married his daughter but had also killed her, plans to take revenge by skinning him alive. But before finishing his business, he is accidentally shot by Peter. In the moment of his own death, he lets the American couple escape and pushes a red button that causes the still-mined building to explode. The film ends with Peter and Joan taking a train to Vienna.

Art is indeed a subject, not only of Ulmer's film, but also of many readings of *The Black Cat.* In his own words, in the famous interview with Peter Bogdanovich, Ulmer labels the film as a horror picture in the style of Caligari, a film "very much out of my Bauhaus period" (575–76). Bill Krohn stresses the references to Murnau's *Nosferatu*, making us aware of its sources in romanticism: "the myths of Expressionism are made new by being married to the private mythology of Poe, with Karloff playing the doomed artist figure—a fusion of American and European strains of Romantic extremism" (61). That Poelzig is an artist who, in Werdegast's words, built his "masterpiece of construction on top of the masterpiece of destruction" is one of the few clear references to the character created by Karloff, whose performance gives Poelzig an air of dandyism. Every spoken word and every little gesture is delivered with the highest restraint. Karloff moves his body like a robot and talks as if he were reciting poetry. One could add that Poelzig's attitude is the consequence of repression, the product of a sublimation of the horrors of war and the crimes he committed: Satanism and aestheticism could be seen as a relapse into the inhumanities suffered during the war. But we could also regard his "perverted" modernism as the prime source of his evilness.

The film remains ambivalent about this, and this ambivalence is possibly grounded in Ulmer's in-betweenness, his being lost between two worlds, which, according to Isenberg, becomes apparent in this film:

> *The Black Cat* offers a fascinating glimpse into the world of an émigré filmmaker negotiating American financial and aesthetic constraints . . . the film represents the rich interplay between European art cinema and Hollywood camp, between the undistinguished horrors of war and their psychosexual counterparts, between reflections of exile and those of home. (5)

In this sense, Poelzig becomes some kind of alter ego of Ulmer, as he creates an aesthetic realm in which all the conflicts between old and new, tradition and modernity, come literally to the surface in his stylish mannerism. The house stands in for a void of modernism, its ambition to end all old and to begin anew, to leave everything behind. Contradicting the modernist project to bring enlightenment to its purpose and to overcome human limitation, Poelzig's debased modernism creates monstrosities. The film is at the heart of the ambivalence of modernism. It is some kind of horror-film version of Adorno and Horkheimer's groundbreaking study *Dialectic of Enlightenment*. Written ten years later under similar conditions of exile, *Dialectic of Enlightenment* is based on comparable premises about the contradictions of civilization, modernity, mass culture, freedom, and totalitarianism, and the differences between Europe and America.[1]

But not only is Ulmer stuck between two worlds, *The Black Cat* itself is the product of a period of transition in film history and style. The film belongs to the cinema before the code, and before Hollywood established its classical mode of sound-film narration, which was to become the norm of all cinematic storytelling. Following film scholar Richard Maltby, the Production Code (or Hays Code), a system of self-censorship which was introduced in 1934, was helpful in creating a style and a mode of narration that avoided being too offensive or attracting only a small part of the audience. Hollywood's principal product—entertainment—had to be accessible to all (446). *The Black Cat* has, in fact, some kind of 'raw sensationalism' (Isenberg 8) that Hollywood cinema preferred not to display in the years following. This led to the decline of the horror-film genre in the late 1930s. The films became excluded from the ranks of A movies, and most of the major studios stopped producing them.

The code helped to define the visual style and the forms of narration in classical Hollywood cinema (Maltby 448). Classical Hollywood cinema began to create the norm against whose background European modernism began to take shape in the late 1950s. But sound films made before 1934, and I count *The Black Cat* among them, do have glimpses of modernism because they were falling out of the system of classical storytelling. None of the films of the early 1930s was truly subversive. The good had to win and the bad had to be punished in the end. However, the films were often more surrealistic,[2] they dealt with more daring subjects and social critique (the Warner Brothers' gangster films),[3] and they offered more violence.[4] *The Black Cat* shares its "uniqueness" with many other films, and many of the film's peculiarities have to be credited to the specific conditions of a period of transition.

The stylistic and narrative digressions of *The Black Cat* and other films of this period stimulate the imagination of cinephilia in a similar way to Ulmer's B movies of the 1940s and 1950s. As some kind of outsider cinema, the films do not wholly belong to the classical Hollywood cinema, and they tend to offer digressions. At the same time, readings of Ulmer's films which are based on the concepts of auteur theory, for example Belton's,[5] are eager to evoke the homogeneity of style and narration, and the logic of Ulmer's aesthetic decisions. Ulmer himself supported this view, for example by referring to his films as "morality plays" (Moullet and Tarvernier 10), claiming intellectual depth for his films. But as by-products of specific historical and aesthetic conditions, the films don't really allow such readings. The films' lack of closure is one of the main reasons why they are so well loved. Cinephilia is based on the capacity to imagine things. The love for a film, especially in horror and B movies, is a love for moments; it can even be satisfied by still photographs. Before there were DVDs, cinephiles all over the world had nothing to look at but still photographs printed in film books, but they developed a capacity to fill in the gigantic gaps with the remembrance of films they had never seen.[6] In reading *The Black Cat,* we should keep in mind how much our imagination is inspired by memorable moments of the film, and not by a closed film text being read from beginning to end. Watching a film may give us the occasion to watch some memorable moments in it.

Let us have a closer look at the visual and narrative oddities of *The Black Cat.* In its most beautiful, poetic, and memorable scene, the camera is set free to move elegantly through the empty spaces of the cellar, accompanied only by the voice-over of Karloff's character and his reflections on Poelzig's and Werdegast's mutual involvement in the war. It is the most obvious sign of introspection, or even of some kind of remorse, in the character of Poelzig: "Did we not both die here in Marmaros fifteen years ago? Aren't we the living dead?" The shot has abstract qualities because the tracking camera only suggests moving with the characters, not following but guiding them, with nothing in view before them. The movement itself does not really take the point of view of any of the characters. It is dissociated from the narration, which means that it has a metaphorical function. It emphasizes, as Stefan Grisseman says, an autonomous point of view of the film itself (74). According to *Classical Hollywood Cinema*, the influential neoformalist study of film, *The Black Cat* would have to be classified as nonclassical, because space is subordinated to narrative causality, not vice versa (Bordwell, Staiger, and Thompson 50ff.). The film does not allow the kind of cognitive mapping Hollywood cinema is so well known for (53). The subjection of narration to space is another important feature of European art cinema of the 1950s and 1960s, forming an alternative way of narration to Hollywood (Nowell-Smith 569). Whereas classical Hollywood cinema never wanted us to lose our orientation in the space created by a film, we simply feel lost in modernist films, as well as in Ulmer's precode horror film.

The digression from the path of conventional cinema—which was caused by the specific conditions of the cinema before the code—enables Erik Ulman to notice a relation between this scene and a film by the pioneer of intellectual cinema, Alain Resnais: "[That the] camera detaches itself from the action to roam through the underground passages prefigures the elegant and ghostly fluency of Alain Resnais' *L'Année dernière à Marienbad* (1961)." A similar thought came into my mind just before I read Ulman's text, which was published in the online magazine *Senses of Cinema*. I take this as a proof that it is possible to read *The Black Cat* along the lines of our experiences with modern cinema of the 1950s and 1960s. But I don't agree with Ulman on his choice of example. There are some similarities with *Marienbad*, whose nameless characters move like zombies through a haunted world of illusions and unreliable memories, in what has the air of a horror film. But *Marienbad*'s abstractness, which avoids placement in a specific period and locale, doesn't allow references to specific historic and political events. This is why the sequence reminds me rather of *Hiroshima mon amour* (1959). The quasi-philosophical voice-over of Karloff's character has some resemblance with the two characters' voices underlying the shots in the film in which they tell the parallel story lines of their lives in occupied France and in Japan facing nuclear horror. *Hiroshima* is a film about the traumatic memory of war. The camera is signifying the forces of memory, and it learns to move in order to cope with that trauma. It is often argued that Resnais' autonomous tracking camera aimed to create the visual equivalent for the dynamics of thinking and remembering, searching for modes to represent the way the human mind works.[7]

In *The Black Cat*, whose ambitions differ from those of Resnais' intellectual cinema in significant ways, the tracking shot builds the emotional center of the film, but it nevertheless remains somehow isolated in it. Poelzig seems to show real grief over the death of his wife and some understanding for the sorrow-ridden Werdegast. In this moment, Poelzig's voice-over does not wholly inhabit the same diegetic world as the other voices in the film. For a brief moment, the film turns over to the realm of intellectual cinema and becomes a counterpart to Resnais' *Hiroshima*. In another scene, in which Poelzig sees Joan Alison for the first time, the similarities become even more apparent, as two subsequent tracking shots from slightly altered standpoints moving toward Poelzig are combined. This form of repetition is a technique used by Resnais, especially in *La guerre est finie* (1965), another film obsessed with war and remembrance.[8] That Ulmer's film may find some resonance in Resnais' work proves that it is possible to read the film along the lines of modernism. But what does it have to say about the interplay of progress and regression, or about the connection between abstract art and Satanism?

The movements add an almost-pure visual pleasure to the film that can be used for many ends. Camera movements engage the viewer immediately with the image. The development of the steadicam and the advent of digital cinema have led to films such as Gus van Sant's *Elephant* (2003) and Sokurov's *Russian Ark* (2002), films that are entirely based on endlessly extended tracking shots. *Elephant* is a visual essay on the Columbine High School massacre, and its reflection on beauty and death pays tribute to the young people killed in the traumatic incident. *Russian Ark* is dedicated to the remembrance of things lost. The tracking camera is on a time travel through the long walks of the Leningrad Hermitage. Both films use camera movements to create an immediate emotional response in the viewer. There may be a similar emotional or even redemptive force involved in the camera moving through the vaults of the fortress in *The Black Cat.* The camera movement is a mode of communication: the films want to get to their audiences. But at the same time, tracking shots have always been a staple of horror films, from Rouben Mamoulian's *Dr. Jekyll and Mr. Hyde* (1931) to Stanley Kubrick's *The Shining* (1980).[9] In these cases tracking shots are not used for communication; they are used to signify horror, violence, and human suffering. Whenever the camera moves too much it is as if the camera were guiding us to unknown territory, which is possibly one way of causing horror for us. Being the emotional center of the film—the moment, from which my reading of the film takes its strongest impulses—the tracking shot in the cellar remains ambivalent because an autonomously moving camera almost automatically has connotations of horror.

The ambiguity of the film is further stressed in another memorable scene with visual attractions, the celebration of the Black Mass. It is a dynamic, rhythmic, extremely well-composed and well-paced sequence, but its visual beauty has not been made to signify something outside of the film. Satanism may lead us to the extreme limits of art for art's sake or to horror for horror's sake, but there is always a certain hollowness involved in Satanism. And the film itself doesn't make any attempts to offer us a plausible explanation for how and why Poelzig turned to Satanism. Ulmer even seems to mock Satanism. Grissemann refers to the parody of a family idyll in the scene in which Poelzig reads some lines in a Satanist book before lying down next to his wife to sleep (77). It may prove to be the case that Satanism feels like an element that has been added to the film, an element that is disconnected from the film's narration and its characters. The claustrophobic atmosphere of the film, a world reduced to only a few interiors and characters, comes under attack as this world is unnecessarily crowded with all the unknown people attending the Black Mass. After this scene the film hurries, not really convincingly, to its climax. The self-destruction of the two human monsters in a giant explosion is quite plausible and inevitable: Europe's troubled history, embodied in the two characters, has to be left behind. But the heroine's screaming is rather unmotivated, and Vitus is shot accidentally by the supposed American hero. In its first fifty minutes, the film carefully creates an atmosphere of sorrow, doom, haunted memories, and aestheticism, but in the last ten minutes the tone of the film has apparently changed. This heterogeneity proves that the film is made up of individual moments.

But this possibly unintended unevenness of the film gives it a specific quality. Isenberg points us to the campiness of *The Black Cat*, which is most apparent in the dialogues; in Lugosi's overacting and melodramatic gestures, which contrast with Karloff's extremely controlled robotic acting; the melodramatic or ironic quality of all the memorable lines; and the blurring of boundaries between high and low, Europe and America, war trauma and repressed sexual desires (5). Isenberg defines *camp*—referring to Susan Sontag's famous text "Notes on Camp"—as "seriousness that fails" (8). Ulmer becomes campy because he is too ambitious. *The Black Cat* is obsessed with art and Ulmer wants to put as much as possible into the film —a mixture of expressionism (something in the style of Caligari), some Bauhaus, and the music of the composers he admired so much. Camp is not intended; it is art, mostly popular art, running wild. Following Sontag, it should be added that camp escapes auctorial control; it is art without authors, or great art coming from minor artists. Camp is situated beyond the realms of high-cultural connoisseurship. Sontag clearly connects camp to marginalized members of society, to minorities and subcultures, who are excluded from high culture. They therefore create their own canon of beloved works by reading them against the grain of commonly held aesthetic values. In this way the unintended "bricolage" aesthetics of camp becomes a form of resistance and protest against art and society (Sontag).

As a form of protest, all the campy moments of *The Black Cat* can also be read as theatrical or melodramatic. The gestures and words of the characters, but also the movements of the camera and other elements of the visual style, are aspects of an excessive mode of expression, of an excessive want to communicate with the viewer, a foregrounding of the telling of the story and not the told. Peter Brooks traces the sources of melodrama back to a crisis of communication in the nineteenth century, resulting from the alienation caused by the secularization and transformations of modern society: The melodramatic mode is a "desire to express all" (2). In his book on the classical Hollywood melodrama, film philosopher Stanley Cavell, whose work is based on the philosophy of ordinary language, defines the melodramatic condition as an expression of our general estrangement from the means of language and communication (42). It is the desire to communicate, under conditions in which one is deprived of the words to express oneself satisfyingly.[10] With their raw and pure sensationalism, the horror films seem to be exclusively interested in the titillation of their audience. But in a genre that often shows traces of melodrama[11]—in being concerned with finding modes of expression for things which can't be expressed, in this case the horrors of World War I—the tracking shots become a mode of communication based on a desire to "express all," or to find words when the conditions of language have been lost. But although the horror film's raw sensationalism can be used for such a purpose, Ulmer himself didn't seem to like the genre.

Ulmer's contempt for the horror film becomes surprisingly apparent in his attitude toward the European art cinema of the late 1950s and early 1960s. In an interview with Luc Moullet and Bertrand Tavernier for the *Cahiers du cinéma*, he expresses his dislike for Jean-Luc Godard's *Á bout de souffle* (1959), which he finds ugly, shocking, and disgusting: it's "comme dans un film d'horreur" (12). Does he seal the fate of *The Black Cat* in his condemnation of Godard's masterpiece of modern art cinema as a "horror film"? Would Ulmer himself exclude *The Black Cat* from the high ranks of art because he had nothing but contempt for the genre? Did he himself finally come to the conclusion that there was a problematic relation between modernism and horror? Of course, Ulmer has never been a reliable source of information about his own life and work. Regarding himself as an artist, he invented stories and events to confirm this view. But contradictory remarks about his works are as much the product of his ambivalence toward art and Hollywood as they are the product of the ambivalence of modernism itself: films such as *A bout de souffle* or even *Salo* are melodramatic, excessive, and overambitious. They have some kind of "raw sensationalism" because they want to communicate with their audiences; they want to signify what no longer can be signified within conventional modes of representation. There are no clear-cut boundaries between popular and art cinema, between horror films and European art cinema. Popular culture itself could be regarded as a contributor to modernism. Film critic J. Hoberman's concept of "vulgar modernism" points us to a modernism that operates out of the hybridity of popular culture itself:

> There is a particular sensibility that is the vulgar equivalent of modernism itself. By this I mean a popular, ironic, somewhat dehumanized mode reflexively concerned with the specific properties of its medium or the conditions of its making. (33)

Hoberman refers to the self-referential moments of film comedies such as the 1941 *Helzapoppin,* to *Mad* magazine's highly self-reflexive relation with popular culture, and to the pioneering efforts of TV comedian and "avant-garde artist" Ernie Kovacs. That Godard learns from a filmmaker such as Frank Tashlin proves that the boundaries between high and low tumble down (36).[12] Another proof for the close link between popular culture and art cinema can be found in Joan Hawkin's essay on the "canons" and cultural hierarchies of trash cinema. In mail-order catalogs for lovers of trash cinema, masterpieces of European art cinema such as Godard's *Weekend* (1967) find themselves on the same pages with films such as *The Yeti and the Werewolf* (1975). Hawkins takes this as an opportunity to shed some light on an aspect "generally overlooked or repressed in cultural analysis, namely, the degree to which high culture trades on the same images, tropes, and themes which characterize low culture" (15). This brings out the horror-film qualities of *Salò*. The film's advertising in such a catalog simply leaves out any information about Pasolini's intentions to point us to the sources of fascism and sadism, and refers to the film with the helpful description "left audiences gaggling" (16). Amos Vogel's important book *Film as Subversive Art* offers another example of transcending the boundaries between high and low. Popular films, B movies, experimental and avant-garde cinema, and classic art and European art cinema are all given the same attention as films that attack capitalist society and shake our beliefs and convictions (Vogel).

All this may prove that modernism itself is ambivalent and contradictory. The narration and the visual style of *The Black Cat* are deeply rooted in this ambivalence. This means that there isn't any closure. The film can be read on more than one level. It cannot be reduced to the stylish architecture and the "art for art's sake" mentality of Poelzig and his inhuman, detached approach to life. It also involves the more progressive forces of Dr. Werdegast, Hungary's greatest psychiatrist (that is, before he is totally driven out of his mind). Michael Henry Wilson refers to the subversiveness of "the metaphysical perversity of a quasi-experimental" film (251), but I doubt that the film really is shockingly subversive. Does the film answer the question of whether Poelzig's degeneration can be traced back to his attitude toward modernism? The film may be subversive in enabling us to raise such questions, but it is too hybrid, too uneven, too campy to really answer such questions. It should not be read as if there were an intended subversiveness. As a film which, according to Raul Ruiz, "breaks up into a series of situations, each with a life of its own" (cited in Ulman), it is a film dominated by significant moments, and the tracking shots in the cellar possibly belong to the set of moments we remember most.

Within this text I cannot offer a real conclusion to the questions asked. My chapter runs the risk of becoming a B movie itself. As homage to *The Black Cat*, I hurry toward the climax of my paper. I will not credit all the confusion of this text to *The Black Cat*, but I will attribute some of it to the film. It is not an organic work of art answering all our questions. If we have a unified view of *The Black Cat*, we may assume that the two European monsters have to be destroyed in a huge explosion: doomed Europe has to be left behind. But what really becomes erased from the film, at least in my memory of it, is the "new world" represented by the undistinguished American couple: who cares who they are and what happens to them? We might say that Europe carries the film aesthetically: expressionism and the art of silent cinema bring the film to its unique existence, not Hollywood's classical mode of narration, which came into existence in the years following *The Black Cat.* But is there any moral to be drawn from that? I think not. The film offers moments of intensive reflections on the fates of its two main characters. But I wish the film would go on like this and really turn into a modernist film and not a horror movie. I wish the film would carry us away on an endlessly extended tracking shot. I wish Poelzig were not a Satanist, and I wish Werdegast did not attempt to skin his rival alive. I wish I could care for these characters the way I care for the characters in *Green Fields,* a true piece of outsider cinema made not more than three years after *The Black Cat*. Both films are indebted to European culture, but *Green Fields* creates a more convincing representation of the interrelation of past and present. Its realistic, vivid, and authentic portrayal of Yiddish life causes a deep feeling of loss and longing for a world far away and long gone. Of course, *The Black Cat* is visually more interesting, but its use of style often refers to nothing outside its claustrophobic narrative realm. The visual beauty of one of the most spectacular camera movements in Hollywood cinema, and the philosophical depth of Poelzig's comment that they were both killed in Marmaros, are wasted within the conventions of the narrative concerns of a precode horror movie. But as the memory of this scene dominates my imagination of *The Black Cat*, and since all my memories and all my knowledge of films turn out to be based on moments—who cares?

NOTES

1. See also "Ulmer and Culture," Bernd Herzogenrath's excellent reading of *The Black Cat*, which is based on Freud's notion of culture, but which also refers to Adorno and Horkheimer and the dark side of modernism and enlightenment. He shows very convincingly how the film can be read as structured around the concepts of culture and cult. Identifying similar motives in Ulmers's *Bluebeard*, which was made ten years later and which also deals with the subject of horror and European culture, he claims that Ulmer knew exactly what he was doing. This results in a more conclusive reading of the Satanist ritual at the end of *The Black Cat* than the one that will be offered here. Bernd Herzogenrath, "Ulmer and Culture," in *Edgar G. Ulmer: King of Poverty Row*, ed. Bernd Herzogenrath (Jefferson, N.C.: McFarland, 2009), 23–38.

2. Before the Marx Brothers were tamed in the postcode years at MGM, they made five surrealistic and anarchic comedies for Paramount. Also, *Million Dollar Legs* (1932) with W. C. Fields, a bizarre comedy about the inhabitants of the republic of Klopstockia joining the Los Angeles Olympic tournament to raise money for their bankrupt state, offers many surrealist moments.

3. William A. Wellman's *Wild Boys of the Road* (1932) is a good example of a precode film by the Warner Brothers studios. The film deals with the Depression and with teenagers leaving home because their parents can no longer nourish them. They roam the streets of the United States in a desperate search for work and money. The film offers social critique and is unique for its realistic and sensitive portrayal of adolescence.

4. *King Kong* (1933) had to be recut for its redistribution in the late 1930s, leaving out the scenes in which the giant ape devoured humans. Much of the overt sadism of the original version was toned down. See Ronald Haver, *David O. Selznick's Hollywood*, 112.

5. John Belton's pioneering work as a film scholar and historian was strongly influenced by the auteur theory and its notion that films can be read as expressions of the individual personalities of their creators. The theory was imported from France to the United States in the 1960s by Andrew Sarris and his book *The American Cinema.* As "auteur theory forced attention to what was really happening in a lot of films" (Caughie 12), it created a new form of criticism that was helpful for the establishment of film studies at universities. But as a regression into romanticist concepts of art and authorship, the theory had its limitations (11). Although film studies began to emancipate itself from this anachronistic discourse, finding new paradigms to follow (e.g., semiotics, psychoanalysis), auteur theory did not vanish, but became one of the dominant modes of practicing film criticism (15).

6. William K. Everson's important book on the classical Hollywood horror films demonstrates the capacity and need for imagination in the early days of film studies. Everson's pioneering effort in film history very often has to refer to films never seen, but he attempts to evaluate these films on the basis of film stills, production notices, and reviews. See William K. Everson, *Classics of the Horror Film.*

7. For film philosopher Gilles Deleuze, Resnais creates "a cinema of the brain" (206). In his monography on Resnais, James Monaco speaks of a truism of Resnais' intellectualism, denying that his films are a cold and abstract "cinema of the brain" (3). The later works of Resnais indeed show the more playful, nonintellectual side of his way of creating films; this becomes apparent in the neomusical *On connaît la chanson* (1997) and its indebtedness to popular culture.

8. In *La guerre est finie* the repetition of camera movements and shots is used to signify the state of mind of a member of the Spanish resistance on the verge of his decision to return to Spain from his exile in France. In *The Black Cat*, the repetition of the tracking shots doesn't seem to be intended, but it remains an important element of the peculiar visual style of the film and its digressions.

9. *Dr. Jekyll and Mr. Hyde* begins with an extended subjective tracking shot seen with the eyes of Dr. Jekyll: we have to wait until his arrival at the university, where he gives a lecture, to actually see the character for the first time. *The Shining*, from Stanley Kubrick, is one of the first horror films (but not the last) to use the steadicam.

10. Cavell describes the melodramatic condition with the following words: "It is like searching for the power of a word when the conditions of language have been lost" (42). He interprets the manner of performance of the melodrama's female protagonist as an alternative mode of existence within a society that denies her existence and represses her voice.

11. James Whale's *Bride of Frankenstein* (1935) offers a good example of the melodramatic qualities of horror films. Melodrama deals with the negative condition of denial of acknowledgement by others. The human monster desperately seeks acknowledgement as a human being, which will only be granted for a brief stay with a blind hermit.

12. Hollywood film director Frank Tashlin, who made some very inspiring comedies and film parodies with Dean Martin and Jerry Lewis, was adored by the critics of the *Cahiers du cinéma*. Tashlin was one of the first artists who acknowledged the indebtedness of film to popular and mass culture.

BIBLIOGRAPHY

Adorno, Theodor, and Max Horkheimer. *Dialectic of Enlightenment* (New York: Continuum, 1987).

Arnold, Frank. "Before the Code: Hollywood 1929–1934," *Epd-Film*, January 1997, 24–36.

Belton, John. *The Hollywood Professionals,* Vol. 3, *Howard Hawks, Frank Borzage, Edgar G. Ulmer* (London: Tantivy Press, 1974), 149–80.

Bogdanovich, Peter. "Edgar G. Ulmer: An Interview," *Film Culture* 58–60 (1974), reprinted in *Who the Devil Made It: Conversations with Legendary Film Directors* (New York: Ballantine, 1998), 558–604.

Bordwell, David, Janet Staiger, and Kristin Thompson. *Classical Hollywood Cinema: Film, Style and Mode of Production to 1960* (New York: Columbia University Press, 1985).

Brooks, Peter. *The Melodramatic Imagination: Balzac, Henry James, Melodrama, and the Mode of Excess* (New Haven: Yale University Press, 1976).

Caughie, John, ed. *Theories of Authorship* (London: Routledge, 1981).

Cavell, Stanley. *Contesting Tears: The Hollywood Melodrama of the Unknown Woman* (Chicago: University of Chicago Press, 1996).

Deleuze, Gilles. *Cinema 2: The Time-Image*, trans. Hugh Tomlinson and R. Galeta (London: Athlone Press, 2000).

Everson, William K. *Classics of the Horror Film* (Secaucus, N.J.: Citadel Books, 1974).

Gallagher, Tag. "All Lost in Wonder," at www.latrobe.edu.au/screeningthepast/firstrelease/fr0301/tgafr12a.htm (accessed 3 March 2008).

Grisseman, Stefan. *Mann im Schatten: Der Filmemacher Edgar G. Ulmer* (Vienna: Paul Zsolnay Verlag, 2003).

Haver, Ronald. *David O. Selznick's Hollywood* (Munich: Rogner und Bernhard, 1981).

Hawkins, Joan. "Sleaze Mania: Euro-Trash and High Art," *Film Quarterly,* Winter 1999, 15–29.

Herzogenrath, Bernd. "Ulmer and Culture," in *Edgar G. Ulmer: King of Poverty Row*, ed. Bernd Herzogenrath, 23–38 (Jefferson, N.C.: McFarland, 2009).

Hoberman, J. *Vulgar Modernism: Writing on Movies and Other Media* (Philadelphia: Temple University Press, 1991).

Isenberg, Noah. "Perennial Detour: The Cinema of Edgar G. Ulmer and the Experience of Exile," *Cinema Journal* 43, no. 2 (Spring 2004): 3–25.

Krohn, Bill. "King of the B's," *Film Comment*, July–August 1983, 60–64.

Maltby, Richard. "A Brief Romantic Interlude: Dick and Jane Go to 3 1/2 Seconds of the Classical Hollywood Cinema," in *Post-Theory: Reconstructing Film Studies*, ed., David Bordwell and Noël Carroll (Madison: University of Wisconsin Press, 1996), 434–59.

Minas, Günther. "Ein Fresko auf einer großen Wand: Die Bedeutung der Malerei für die Filmarbeit Pasolinis," in *Kraft der Vergangenheit: Zu Motiven der Filme von Pier Paolo Pasolini*, ed. Christoph Klimke (Frankfurt: Fischer, 1988), 51–69.

Monaco, James. *Alain Resnais: The Rôle of Imagination* (New York: Oxford University Press, 1978).

Moullet, Luc, and Bertrand Tavernier. "Entretien avec Edgar G. Ulmer," *Cahiers du cinéma* 21, no. 122 (August 1961): 1–16.

Nowell-Smith, Geoffrey. "Art Cinema," in *The Oxford History of World Cinema*, ed. Geoffrey Nowell-Smith (Oxford: Oxford University Press, 1996), 567–75.

Sontag, Susan. *Against Interpretation, and other Essays* (New York: Farrar, Straus and Giroux, 1966).

Ulman, Erik. "Edgar G. Ulmer," *Senses of Cinema*, at www.sensesofcinema.com/contents/directors/03/ulmer.html (accessed 3 March 2008).

Vogel, Amos. *Film as Subversive Art* (New York: Random House, 1974).

Wilson, Michael Henry. "Edgar G. Ulmer: 'Let There Be Light,'" in *Divine Apparizioni*: *Cinegrafie*, Vol. 12 (Ancona: Transeuropa, 1999), 249–55.

4

From Nine to Nine

D. J. Turner

Shot in Canada in nine days in February 1936 for a Canadian company, *From Nine to Nine* is possibly the rarest and also one of the least appreciated of Edgar Ulmer's films. It was intended for distribution in the United Kingdom by Universal in partial fulfillment of that company's distribution obligations under Britain's quota laws.

The British government had enacted the Cinematograph Films Act 1927 in a bid to resuscitate the United Kingdom's ailing film industry and encourage British film production. Enacted for a ten-year period, it set rising quotas for distributors and exhibitors. They were required to distribute and show, respectively, a modest percentage of British product. For the purposes of the act, films produced anywhere in the British empire were eligible, and this opened the door to production of "quota" films in Canada.

The result of the act was a deluge of very low budget films, contemptuously dubbed "Quota Quickies," which were the object of much denigration. Some, however, were actually better than many American-made B films; and these British B films, on which the likes of Michael Powell and David Lean cut their teeth, are now undergoing critical reevaluation, a process that is providing some interesting discoveries as well as substance for a number of equally interesting books.[1]

To make *From Nine to Nine*, Coronet Pictures, Ltd., a company incorporated in the province of Quebec, rented the recently constructed, then state-of-the-art studios of Associated Screen News in Montreal. The only shooting outside the studio was done in Montreal's Mount Royal Hotel. The crew was comprised almost entirely of Montrealers: James W. Campbell (production manager), Harold Peberdy (designs), Fred Govan (art director, Donald Govan on the print), Alfred Jacquemin (photography), Robert Martin (assistant cameraman), Maurice Metzger (sound), and Ross Pitt-Taylor (editor, Phillip Taylor on the print), all employees of Associated Screen News. As usual, Shirley Ulmer acted as script assistant, but only for the start of shooting. She was in a Montreal hospital having her appendix removed. Local actors Alexander Frazer, Julian Gray, George A. Temple, Frederick Dodds Slade, Gerald Rowan, Alex Michael, and Cecil Nichol made up half of the cast. To complete the cast, Ulmer brought in actors from the New York stage, among them Miriam Battista, Doris Covert, Eugene Sigaloff, and Arthur Stenning. To head them all he hired former American serial queen Ruth Roland; another established American film actor, Roland Drew; and Kenneth Duncan, who was a writer, a Canadian, and also an established film actor.[2]

One of the working titles for *From Nine to Nine* was "Death Strikes Again," but the original script was called "The Man with the Umbrella" for reasons that become evident when the film is viewed—except that it's a woman who wields the brolly. The title *From Nine to Nine* has nothing to do with the

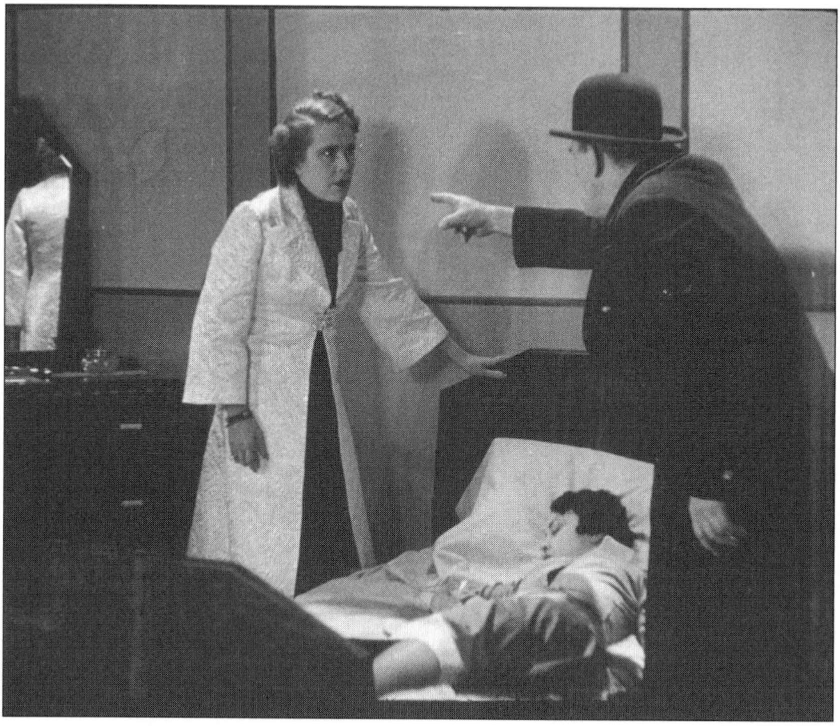

Figure 4.1. Ruth Roland (Cornelia Du Play), Miriam Battista (Toinette, the maid, dead on the bed), and Arthur Stenning (Detective Sgt. Williams, pointing).

film. However, Bill Krohn has drawn my attention, via Lotte Eisner, to the fact that in 1927 F. W. Murnau planned to make a film of this title based on a popular book by Leo Perutz. First published in 1918 in German, the book was translated into English and published in 1926 as *From Nine to Nine*. Perhaps Ulmer remembered the project from his time working with Murnau, liked the title, and decided to use it. An homage, perhaps.

From Nine to Nine was intended for release in the United Kingdom as part of Universal's quota compliance. But why would Universal, the very company that had allegedly banished him from Hollywood after *The Black Cat*, hire Ulmer? The genesis of the project is difficult to ascertain, but in his "Past Service Record," a document that Ulmer personally established (from memory) in 1969, Ulmer wrote that he was "sent to New York from Hollywood at the request of Universal's New York quota film producer to then make a picture in Canada." Note that he wrote "sent." For his next feature, *Natalka Poltavka*, Ulmer wrote, "brought to New York from Hollywood" and not "sent." Is it possible he was still under contract to Universal at the start of 1936?[3]

Besides the mention by Ulmer in his "Past Service Record" and the film's submission to the British Board of Film Censors by Universal, there is little to connect Universal to the production. On the credits of the existing material, New York–based independent producer William Steiner, who would later distribute the film in the United States (if the cumulative title list in the *Film Daily Year Book* is correct), is credited as associate producer. There is no producer credit and no mention of Universal.

On 18 February 1936, both English- and French-language newspapers in Montreal accorded some attention to the shoot. While Léon Franque, film chronicler in *La Presse*, sniffed, "The film will show nothing of Montréal and have no publicity value for the city," he did offer one interesting piece of intelligence: all the scenes had been rehearsed ahead of time in order that shooting should be over ten days hence. The *Montreal Daily Star* claimed their reporter had caught Ruth Roland in a taxi as she left the Mount Royal Hotel for the studio for the first day's shooting. The film was described as a thriller, tentatively titled "Death Strikes Again" or "From Nine to Nine." Miss Roland told the *Star* reporter, "We hope to create a character that I can keep using in other motion pictures to be made here." Franque mentioned that there were five more films to come. Was this really the plan, or had Roland been strung a line? In either case, this would be Ruth Roland's last film.

Film Daily had mentioned earlier in the month that Ulmer and company had left New York by train for Montreal with, among others, Len S. Kennedy, who was to act as assistant supervisor.

From Nine to Nine was a considerable change of pace for Ulmer after *Damaged Lives* and *The Black Cat*, not to mention *Thunder over Texas*, and he seems to have been having fun with this modest tale of jewel thieves, murder, and blackmail. He allows Roland to overact till there's no scenery left to chew and throws in comic relief on top of comic relief. Roland's parrot endlessly squawks, "Trouble, nothing but trouble" (the director's commentary?) when not suggesting it is time for cocktails, and a bumbling comic detective is thrown in for good measure.

The plot is a little difficult to follow, possibly because twelve minutes would seem to be missing from the extant U.S. release version—though the reviewer for the *Kinematograph Weekly* had some problems with the continuity in what was presumably the longer version.[4] If indeed it is minus twelve minutes, this could explain some of the continuity issues in the film in its extant form. This presents a bit of a mystery in that this nitrate negative is a camera original, complete with splices. But perhaps the bigger mystery is why anyone would have gone to the trouble of cutting it at all.

The plot is as follows: In a snowy Montreal, a chauffeur with a French accent and a magnificent raccoon coat delivers a message to the home of wealthy jeweler Balsac. A snooty butler (Alexander Frazer) reminds him bluntly of the existence of a servants' entrance, then tells him he may wait where he is (after instructing him to remove his cap). The chauffeur complies in silence. Balsac (Julian Gray) is in the middle of telling his daughter's suitor, John Sommerset (Kenneth Duncan), that, far from getting engaged, they must break off their relationship, even if Sommerset is secretary to the governor-general.[5] Balsac declines at first to read the message. When he does finally elect to read the note, he abruptly takes his leave and enters the waiting car. The chauffeur, meanwhile, has pilfered a few cigars. Outside, a man asks two policemen for a light. (Though the film is clearly set in Montreal, the policemen wear the familiar uniform of the British bobby, complete with the distinctive helmet, a garb never worn by the Montreal police force.) The man's accent could be from the Balkans or the Scottish Highlands. This is our introduction to Ivanov (George A. Temple).

To the sound of sirens we discover Balsac in the now-abandoned car, a bullet through his head. Inspector Vernon (Roland Drew) of the Criminal Investigation Division (CID) informs Balsac's daughter Yvonne (Doris Covert) of her father's demise and sends Williams (Arthur Stenning), a bumbling detective, to interview the servants. After establishing that the daughter is not aware of her father having any enemies, Vernon dismisses the young couple. Once alone, he helps himself to a generous belt of Balsac's scotch. At headquarters, Vernon interviews the butler but learns nothing. The butler, back at the house, opens a safe to remove jewels and documents. A waiting intruder whose face we never see strangles the butler and heaves his body out of the window. Vernon now interviews Ivanov, who claims to be the lover of the maid, Toinette (Miriam Battista), and also claims to be employed at the Mount Royal Hotel. Toinette corroborates his story.

Cornelia Du Play (Ruth Roland), a longtime acquaintance of Balsac, shows up at his office, conveniently located in the Mount Royal Hotel, and asks to see his latest acquisition, the extremely valuable Lavretsky collection of precious stones. After she has upset a tray of gems, a particularly precious specimen is found to be missing. Vernon, who just happens to be in the building, is summoned; but Du Play is released after only a perfunctory search.

Sommerset receives a blackmail letter: someone has discovered that when Balsac married Yvonne's mother, his first wife was still alive—a fact unknown to Balsac. Yvonne is thus the issue of a bigamous marriage. The ubiquitous Toinette eavesdrops at every possible opportunity. International jewel thief Schubin (Eugene Sigaloff) and his wife Gruschenka are also in the hotel. Toinette enters their room to accuse them of double-crossing her and her partner Ivanov, complaining that the blackmail plot was not part of their agreed plan. Knowing that Schubin shot Balsac and that Ivanov killed the but-

Figure 4.2. Ruth Roland (Cornelia Du Play), Roland Drew (Inspector Vernon), and Kenneth Duncan (John Sommerset).

ler, Toinette threatens to turn state's evidence to save herself. The impulsive Gruschenka shoots Toinette.

The pair take her body to Du Play's room in the Mount Royal Hotel and dump it on the bed while Miss Du Play, oblivious to the deposit, sings in her bath. Williams comes in to arrest Miss Du Play but she knocks him out with a flatiron. Meanwhile, Sommerset makes his way to a dingy café, bearing an envelope containing money provided by Vernon, which is intended for the blackmailers. There a waitress instructs him to go to a flower shop located (where else?) in the Mount Royal Hotel. Du Play meanwhile heads to Schubin's room and proposes to buy the now slightly depleted Lavretsky collection. Ivanov arrives, followed by the police, and is chased onto the roof, where he is shot. Schubin and Gruschenka are arrested, along with Du Play; but Du Play is quickly released when it is revealed that she is a private investigator working for an American agency (the Jewellers' Protective Association).

The screenplay and dialogue were written by Kenneth Duncan based on an original story by Edgar Ulmer and Shirley Ulmer. If the story is both routine and ramshackle and some of the acting amateurish, the camera work is good, and Ulmer manages to touch on some interesting points. The film is unusual for what is in large part an American production in that it makes no attempt to hide the fact that it is set in Canada. Indeed, it rather insists on it, playing up differences, real or simply introduced as plot devices, between Canadian and U.S. practices. While playing on these differences it also touches on Canada's social-class differences, as well as the English/French divide of that era in Montreal: the butler with his British accent lording it over the chauffeur with his French accent; the chauffeur pilfering a fistful of cigars; the CID inspector talking down to everyone and then, in his turn, pilfering a glass of scotch. Though the film is set in Montreal many of the accents are British, or imitations of British accents, rather than Canadian. This is to some extent appropriate, given that most immigrants at that time were from the British Isles (fleeing the scourge of the Quota Quickie, perhaps). As Bill Krohn so astutely observes in his article on Ulmer, "King of the B's," in *Film Comment*, Ulmer uses "the conventions of the fake-English detective story to paint a subtly corrosive portrait of Canadian society" (62).[6]

Improbably, all the protagonists live or work in the Mount Royal Hotel. Mention of this venerable establishment, where some of the film was shot, is repeated until it begins to look like a send up of product placement. Probably the producers paid nothing for the use of this plush setting.[7] Meanwhile, back at the studio, the sets, built on the new Northern Electric Wide Range–equipped sound stage, bear a striking similarity to the art deco sets of *The Black Cat*.[8] There is no evidence that the film was ever shown in Canada (Ontario provincial censors have no record of it being submitted, and Quebec censorship records of the period have been destroyed); but according to *Kinematograph Weekly*, after being trade shown on 2 April 1936, just six weeks after the end of shooting, it was set for release on 17 August 1936 in the United Kingdom (see supplement iv).

Though registered under the act on 31 March by Universal, it would be released by General Film Distributors, Ltd.[9] No American reviews have been found for *From Nine to Nine*. It was passed without cuts by the New York State censor in 1937, and distribution was attributed to Emerson Pict. Corp., a company that does not seem to exist. (See New York State censorship file #32376, box #501). *Film Daily* did not review it, but it is mentioned in the cumulative title list in the *Film Daily Year Book*, with William Steiner as the distributor, starting with the 1937 issue.

One rarely finds lost films by actively looking for them. One stumbles over them, there are chance encounters, or they find you. If you are lucky. My recovery of *From Nine to Nine*, begun in 1975, deviated little from the pattern I have outlined. I first contacted Universal in Los Angeles, London, and Canada, looking for the film, and I drew a blank. Then, in 1981, I mentioned it to Bill Krohn, who told me it was in the American Film Institute's list of holdings. I had gone through the AFI list from A to Z . . . and missed it. So much for actively looking!

Low on its list of priorities, the AFI agreed to send its holdings on this title to Canada. Six reels of original picture neg and five reels of sound track arrived: there was no sound for reel 2. I had a safety print struck immediately, and then I began the search for the missing ten minutes of sound. Fortunately, 16 mm prints had been made in the late '30s for rental libraries—by the '70s a thing of the past—so I began to trawl private collectors, a notoriously secretive tribe. I made slow progress. Bill Everson told me, tantalizingly, that he had given away two prints. One had gone to the Cinémathèque Française, he claimed, but the Cinémathèque professed no knowledge of it. The other print he had sent to a collector in Paris, but my efforts to access this print came to nought. Then, in 1998, at the invitation of Bruce Goldstein, I presented the film (with reel 2 still mute) at Film Forum in New York. After the projection and subsequent Q&A, a member of the audience came to me and asked why there was no sound on reel 2. I explained the situation and described my search for a print. To my surprise and delight he told me there was someone in the audience who had a 16 mm print. That was when I first met Richard Crane, a veteran New York collector with a vast collection of rare films. Mr. Crane very generously agreed, there and then, to let me lift the missing sound from his print. The process would take another four years; but finally reel 2 would have sound, some twenty years after I'd begun my search. And the 75-minute version? Keep watching the skies.

NOTES

1. Among the best books are *Quota Quickies: The Birth of the British "B" Film*, by Steve Chibnall; *A Chorus of Raspberries*, by David Sutton; and *The Unknown 1930s*, by Jeffrey Richards.

2. Formed in Montreal in 1920 as Associated Screen News of Canada, Ltd. (a branch of Associated Screen News in New York), the company was reincorporated as Associated Screen News, Ltd., in 1926. It operated until 1956.

3. Ulmer made *Natalka Poltavka*, a Ukrainian-language feature based on the operetta by Ivan Kotlyarevsky, for Vasile Avramenko. Shooting began in September 1936, in the Biograph Studio in the Bronx, N.Y., and continued on location at Flemington, N.J.

4. The print passed by the British Board of Film Censors on March 27, 1936, ran 74 minutes 41 seconds. The extant nitrate negative runs only 62 minutes 26 seconds.

5. The governor-general was the king's representative in the colony. This office still exists today.

6. Krohn's original title was "Ulmer without Tears." "King of the B's" was a title furnished by *Film Comment*.

7. In 1922, when it was built, this 1,000-room hotel was the largest in the British Empire.

8. Totally owned by Bell Telephone, Northern Electric was the Canadian equivalent of Western Electric in the U.S.

9. In May, at the time Carl Laemmle—Ulmer's nemesis—was ousted from Universal, General Film Distributors acquired a 25-percent interest in the reorganized Universal, and C. M. Woolf, a director of General Film, joined the board of the new Universal. General Film henceforth released Universal product in England.

BIBLIOGRAPHY

Kinematograph Weekly, August 6, 1936, Supplement iv.
Krohn, Bill. "King of the B's," *Film Comment* 19, no. 4 (July–August 1983): 60–64.

5

Exile on 125th Street

African Americans, Germans, and Jews in *Moon over Harlem*

Jonathan Skolnik

Moon over Harlem (1939) occupies a unique place within Edgar Ulmer's "ethnic intermezzo"[1] in the 1930s. The story of Ulmer's turn to niche-audience filmmaking is well known: after his affair with Shirley Kassler (who at the time was married to a nephew of Carl Laemmele) damaged his relations with major Hollywood studio executives, Ulmer moved in 1935 to New York, where he directed a series of foreign language and "race" films, turning rural New Jersey into a location for Yiddish *shtetlach* and Ukrainian farms; he also directed several health-education films that targeted minority communities (see Grissemann 99–158). Ulmer's foray into the world of black-cast/black-audience feature filmmaking, however, opened up a deeper political and social register in his work. As a rare white director of films for African Americans in the segregation era, Ulmer entered into a direct confrontation with the contradictions of Jewish identity within an American culture shaped by racism and racial division.

Polemical debates about the specific role of "Jewish" Hollywood in the objectification and exploitation of other minorities, especially African Americans, have colored the scholarly investigation of ethnicity and film production in America from the advent of sound film through the end of Jim Crow.[2] Yet beyond the thunder of accusation, *mea culpa*, or denial, there remains the striking fact that the "separate cinema"[3] to which blacks were relegated in the segregation era also allowed for and, in many cases, depended upon some degree of creative and financial interaction between African Americans and whites (including a heavy overrepresentation of Jewish Americans) at the margins of the American social system. Were these interactions a positive collaboration which subverted racial boundaries, or did they amount to cynical opportunism, or even exploitation? What interests me is not a search for a simplistic answer to this complex cultural nexus—there is none—but rather the fact that cultural products themselves, in this case the films, often reflect upon these very questions, the condition of their production. The 1965 film *The Pawnbroker*, which focuses on a German-Jewish Holocaust survivor in Harlem, is a vivid example of this kind of film. In the following, I want to bring these perspectives to bear on *Moon over Harlem,* the major black-audience production directed by the German-Jewish refugee Edgar G. Ulmer.

German-Jewish refugees from the Nazified film industry occupied a paradoxical place in American society: in exile from Nazi racism, they were also "white" in segregation-era America, immigrant outsiders in a new land, and *German* Jews in an American-Jewish cultural landscape (and, indeed, a Hollywood business climate) where Eastern European Jews were just as likely to dominate. In the larger project from which this chapter is taken, I examine the specific role of German-Jewish directors (Fritz Lang, Josef von Sternberg, Otto Preminger, and many others) in exploring *American* racial dilemmas.[4] What is important to remember here, in the context of my analysis of *Moon over Harlem*, is that Ulmer's foray into "race" film is not unique. Indeed, another German-Jewish immigrant, Arthur Dreifuss, was a major director of black-cast films in the 1930s and 1940s. Due to space considerations, I cannot offer a comparative analysis here; but in my discussion of *Moon over Harlem* I wish to take issue with the general claim made by film historian Thomas Cripps that the black-cast productions of Dreifuss, Ulmer, the Goldberg brothers, and others subject African American film to the "B-picture assembly line" (Cripps 40–41). Instead, I would like to show how Edgar Ulmer helps push to the breaking point the conventions of what Cripps calls the black-cast "genre film."

The plot of *Moon over Harlem* is intricate: Minnie (Cora Green), a widow who works hard as a housekeeper in a posh hotel and nightclub, marries Dollar Bill (Bud Harris), a smooth-talking ne'er-do-well. Minnie's daughter Sue (Izenetta Wilcox) attends college and goes out with Bob (Earl Gough), a well-spoken idealist who dreams of cleansing Harlem of corruption and gangsters like Dollar Bill. When Minnie walks in on Dollar Bill trying to rape Sue, she throws her daughter out. Sue becomes a nightclub performer, and the famous jazz clarinetist Sidney Bechet makes a cameo appearance. Dollar Bill is under pressure from white gangsters who want to take over Harlem, as well as from Bob, who mobilizes Sue's idealist college friends to dissuade honest Harlemites from paying protection money. Bullets fly, and Dollar Bill and Minnie are killed. After the funeral of her mother, Sue and Bob stare dreamily at the "moon over Harlem."

In his interview with Peter Bogdanovich, Ulmer claims the film was shot in four days on a budget of only $8,000 (the dancers were paid a pittance), and that he was brought in only after the film had been cast, invited by Donald Heywood.[5] While research on the genesis of *Moon over Harlem* is far from complete, there may indeed be a degree of self-mythologizing on the part of Ulmer as to his "quick and dirty" filmmaking. Ulmer's plans for a Harlem film seem to date from as early as November 1937. According to an article in the *Chicago Defender*, a major African American newspaper, Ulmer had contracted to direct a film by Mathew Mathews, to be titled "Blues in My Heart."[6] Mathews was identified as a playwright previously honored by the Academy of Dramatic Arts, Donald Heywood was mentioned as the composer, and Alec Lovejoy was listed as an actor. The production company was named as "Kinotrage [*sic*] Pictures." The company never existed, and the name was likely a typo of "Kinotage," suggesting a venture planned by a German-speaker, that is, Ulmer himself. In January 1939, the paper mentioned that Cora Green would play the female lead in "Moon over Harlem," and on 4 February further casting choices were announced.[7] (The title "Moon over Harlem," by the way, was probably derived from the popular 1932 song "Underneath a Harlem Moon," by Mack Gordon [the pen name of Warsaw-born Morris Gittler]; the painter William H. Johnson used *Moon over Harlem* as the title for a work about the 1943 Harlem riot, referencing both song and film—a fine example of allegedly inauthentic popular culture becoming an authentic tradition. See figure 5.1.

The 4 February *Defender* article also mentioned that work had begun at Lido Studios, on 146th Street and Seventh Avenue; the reporter detailed his excitement over the impressive technical outfitting of the studio. On 11 February, the paper reported that shooting continued at the Lido Ballroom.

Ulmer's film project generated considerable excitement in the African American press. On 25 March 1939 the *Defender* reported that the film was ready and remarked that "it has a good chance to set a new high in major Race productions."[8] By 29 April, however, the film had not yet been released, and the newspaper's critic was impatient, as were the actors: "What Has Happened to *Moon over Harlem*?" asked the headline.[9] Some actors complained that they had not been paid. Others (perhaps the same ones) hoped the film would be released soon: "They feel that the film is one of the best ever made, expertly directed and firmly handled." On 17 June, the paper reported on the film's dressy premiere at the Regent. But on 29 July, the *Defender* sounded a note of disappointment: star Bud Harris planned a lawsuit because Million Dollar Pictures had sold distribution rights to Alfred Sack, and Harris did not expect the return he had been promised. The film itself was warmly received by the *Defender* and praised by other black newspapers such as the *New York Age*: *Moon over Harlem* was not just an excellent "race" film, but an excellent film.[10]

Figure 5.1. William H. Johnson, "Moon over Harlem" (ca. 1943–1944). Reprinted with permission from the National Humanities Center.

The film begins as the credits roll over stylized drawings of dressed-to-impress African American dancers and Donald Heywood's soundtrack—which wavers between lyrical, melodic jazz and agitated hurried phrases. The music continues as the scene shifts to a nighttime panorama of a glitzy urban boulevard. As we recognize notable Harlem landmarks in the bright lights of 125th Street—the Apollo Theater, Blumstein's department store, the Alhambra nightclub and another one called "the Plantation"—we notice how Ulmer's camera revisits Blumstein's and lingers in front of Ludwig Bauman's clothing shop.

By dwelling on names that are both German and Jewish, Ulmer references his own identity as a Jew in exile from Nazi Germany. As Ulmer zeros in on the Jewish-owned businesses in the 1930s black metropolis, he alludes perhaps to his own complex role as a white director of a black-cast film, projecting himself onto the cityscape: he is now both an integral part of the Harlem landscape and a privileged outsider at the intersection of capitalism, race, and 125th Street. Jewish-owned stores, particularly Blumstein's, had been the target of an angry "Don't Buy Where You Can't Work" campaign in the early 1930s, and many Jewish business had been attacked in the 1935 Harlem riot.[11]

If names like "Blumstein" or "Ludwig Bauman" can function in the film as a kind of hidden "signature" for Ulmer as the film's author, it is because they stand for a concrete historical and economic presence that subsumes rather than erases Ulmer's own name—the business establishment. For the characters in Ulmer's black-cast film, this cannot be the case. They (the men, that is) are often known only by nicknames: the gangster is "Dollar Bill," the black theater owner is "Broadway," and the underground banker is "Wall Street." The names are ironic references to the corridors of cultural and economic power from which African Americans were marginalized in 1930s New York.[12]

Ulmer's most striking disruption of the conventions of black-audience entertainment cinema concerns the casting choices. As Cripps, Edward Mapp, and other film historians have pointed out, black-cast films reflected the widespread skin-tone prejudices within the black community: the heroes were light-skinned, with dark-skinned African American actors cast as villains or bystanders. In *Moon over Harlem*, these conventions are exaggerated to the point that they seem to be called into question. To start with, some of the very first conversations in the film (at the wedding of Minnie and Dollar Bill) are discussions of skin tone among the guests, which raises the issue as

Figure 5.2. Bud Harris as "Dollar Bill." Courtesy of the Edgar G. Ulmer Preservation Corp.

Figure 5.3. Dollar Bill and the prostitute. Courtesy of the Edgar G. Ulmer Preservation Corp.

a question for the film. The villain, Dollar Bill, is conventionally dark skinned (figure 5.2) and is a vicious, manipulative character.

Yet *Moon over Harlem* never descends into pure melodrama because Dollar Bill has the positive qualities of an antihero: he is bold and unafraid of the white mob moving in to Harlem. One of his henchmen (ironically an extremely short "comic" actor) quips, "Dollar, you make us all feel more like men." In general, *Moon over Harlem* walks a fine line between drama and satire in its use of exaggeration: the dark-skinned villains are *extremely* dark, and the well-spoken Bob is always a notch *too* well spoken. (Bob prefaces an invitation to cut a cake with a speech beginning "in defense of my reputation.")

In fact, the film's casting choices caused significant problems with the censors. In one scene, Dollar Bill consorts with a prostitute (figure 5.3), a black woman who is so light-skinned that the Hays office assumed she was white and threatened to block the film in June 1939 for portraying sexual relationships between the races in defiance of the code.[13]

In comparison with the Hays office files on other black-cast films of the era, this level of objection and intervention was highly unusual. At most, other films were lightly chastised for risqué dialogue or dress, or for not showing strongly enough the consequences of gambling or crime—but never for openly challenging race laws and social conventions of the segregation era. Although Ulmer claims in the above-mentioned interview with Bogdanovich that *Moon over Harlem* was cast before he became involved, the records show that he took it upon himself to intervene in person with the censorship office over this matter—which was resolved amicably. My sense from the censorship files is that no other black-cast director would have risked jeopardizing his work with such a provocation, and that Ulmer and his collaborators took a chance and got away with it.

Moon over Harlem is also unique as a black-cast film for including rare white characters. In fact, there are two. One, a bartender, is from a stock-footage clip, probably an advertisement that Ulmer used either for fun or to economize (figure 5.4).

The effect, however, is to give a visual dimension to the sense of a poor art, which depends more on human talent than slick technique; it concretizes a sense of estrangement from the glossy world of advertising, the world of the powerful which is by definition circumscribed for a ghetto art. The other white character depicted in *Moon over Harlem* is the downtown gangster boss who barks orders to an unusually deferent Dollar Bill. Tellingly, the

Figure 5.4. The Bartender. Courtesy of the Edgar G. Ulmer Preservation Corp.

Figure 5.5. The Neck. Courtesy of the Edgar G. Ulmer Preservation Corp.

white mobster is only pictured from behind: a bulging, muscular neck and hat (figure 5.5).

By reversing the gaze of conventional cinema, power relations are thematized, indeed exposed. To return to my qualification of Cripps's description of the white director's handling of black actors in this era as the "B-movie assembly-line": this may indeed be true of Ulmer's work. Yet I would argue that in his case it may be a compliment. Ulmer's ability to use limited resources to create a powerful poor art that simultaneously undermines the conventions of a marginalized "entertainment" genre for political effect is here a virtue.

NOTES

1. This is Noah Isenberg's apt coinage. See Isenberg, "Perennial Detour," 9.

2. See Michael Rogin, *Blackface/White Noise: Jewish Immigrants and the Hollywood Melting Pot* (Berkeley: University of California Press, 1996); Joel Rosenberg, "Rogin's Noise: The Alleged Historical Crimes of *The Jazz Singer*," *Prooftexts* 22, nos. 1–2 (Winter–Spring 2002): 221–39; Harold Brackman, "The Attack on 'Jewish Hollywood': A Chapter in the History of Modern American Anti-Semitism," *Modern Judaism* 20, no.

1 (2000): 1–19; and, most recently, Patrick McGilligan, *Oscar Michaux: The Great and Only* (New York: Harper Collins, 2007), 257–81.

3. For a history of black-audience productions and their relation to Hollywood productions during Jim Crow and the Hays code era, see Edward Mapp and John Kisch, *A Separate Cinema* (New York: Farrar, Straus, and Giroux, 1992); and Thomas Cripps, *Slow Fade to Black: The Negro in American Film, 1900–1942* (New York: Oxford University Press, 1977).

4. See my forthcoming book, "*Two must have got hanged together . . .": African Americans and German Jews in Hollywood, 1932–1965.*

5. Peter Bogdanovich, "Edgar G. Ulmer: An Interview," *Film Culture* 58–60 (1974): 189–234.

6. "Dorothee Codozoe Selected to Head New Harlem Film," *Chicago Defender*, 13 November 1937, 19.

7. "Ted Yates Covers New York Town," *Chicago Defender*, 28 January 1939, 17, col. 3; and "Bud Harris to Take Lead in New Film," *Chicago Defender*, 4 February 1939, 18, col. 4. Note the nice pun "take lead," which gives away the fate of Harris's character in the story.

8. "*Moon over Harlem* Ready to Screen," *Chicago Defender*, 25 March 1939, 18, col. 3.

9. "What Has Happened to *Moon over Harlem*?" *Chicago Defender*, 29 April 1939, 1.

10. Excerpts from two reviews are in Clarence Taylor, *The Black Churches of Brooklyn* (New York: Columbia University Press, 1994), 74–75.

11. See Cheryl Lynn Greenberg, *"Or Does It Explode?" Black Harlem in the Great Depression* (New York: Oxford University Press, 1991), especially 114–39; Larry A. Greene, "Harlem: The Depression Years; Leadership and Social Conditions," *Afro-Americans in New York Life and History* 17 (July 1993); Isabel Boiko Price, "The Black Response to Anti-Semitism: Negroes and Jews in New York, 1880 to World War II" (PhD diss., University of New Mexico, 1973), especially 177–339; and Mark Naison, *Communists in Harlem during the Depression* (New York: Grove Press, 1983).

12. I am grateful to Edward Mapp (City University of New York) for this insight, conveyed in a conversation at the film series "German Exiles Confront Race in America," which I organized at the University of Maryland in 2003.

13. See the letter of 1 June 1939 from the Production Codes Administration to Mr. G. Harris, secretary, Mercury Film Laboratories, New York. "Moon over Harlem" file, MPAA/PCA records, the Margaret Herrick Library of the Academy of Motion Picture Arts and Sciences, Los Angeles. I would like to thank the academy (how many times does a professor get to say *that*?) for access to the archive.

BIBLIOGRAPHY

Cripps, Thomas. *Black Film as Genre* (Indianapolis: Indiana University Press, 1978).

Grissemann, Stefan. *Mann im Schatten: Der Filmemacher Edgar G. Ulmer* (Vienna: Paul Zsolnay Verlag, 2003).

Isenberg, Noah. "Perennial Detour: The Cinema of Edgar G. Ulmer and the Experience of Exile," *Cinema Journal* 43, no. 2 (Winter 2004): 3–25.

Taylor, Clarence. *The Black Churches of Brooklyn* (New York: Columbia University Press, 1994).

6

Forging the "New Jew"

Ulmer's Yiddish Films

Vincent Brook

At first glance, Edgar G. Ulmer would seem an unlikely candidate, cinematically and ethno-religiously, to spearhead a "golden age" of Yiddish film in America. Yet together with the Polish American director Joseph Green, the Austrian American Ulmer would play a pivotal role in the late-1930s rejuvenation of Yiddish cinema, with four films: *Grine Felder* (*Green Fields*, 1937); *Yankl der Shmid* (*Yankl the Blacksmith*, aka *The Singing Blacksmith*, 1938); *Di Klyatshe* (*The Old Mare*, aka *Fishke der Krumer* [Fishke the Cripple], aka *The Light Ahead*, 1939); and *Amerikaner Shadkhn* (*American Matchmaker*, 1940; Hoberman 7). This small but impressive body of work, however, is generally treated by historians as an anomalous interlude in Ulmer's career—between his early-Weimar and late-Hollywood periods—when it is discussed at all. Rather, his prominent place in film history has been secured by his work as set designer on F. W. Murnau's *The Last Laugh* (1924) and other German expressionist classics; his subsequent canonical film noirs (*Detour*, 1945; *The Strange Woman*, 1945; and *Ruthless*, 1947); and a dark, low-budget Western, *The Naked Dawn* (1954).

As for the ethno-religious aspect, Ulmer's problematic relation to his Jewishness is rivaled among European émigré directors only by that of Fritz Lang. Lang, born to a Jewish mother who converted to Catholicism, steadfastly denied his Jewishness; yet he was forced to flee Nazi Germany because of his Jewish lineage and was regarded not only by the Nazis but by the entire émigré community as a Jew (Gunning). Ulmer's Jewish approach-avoidance syndrome is even more complex and convoluted. Born in 1904 in Olomouc, Moravia, he was raised from infancy in Vienna by his Jewish parents. However, due to a staunchly secular upbringing, he claims not even to have been cognizant of his Jewish heritage until, upon admittance to a Jesuit school as an exceptional student, he learned of the *Numerus Klauses*—the 4-percent quota on Jewish enrollment (Bogdanovich 577). His Jewish identity was literally imprinted on him shortly after World War I, when, following his father's death on the battlefield, he was sent to a home for war orphans in Uppsala, Sweden, where he was made to wear a Jewish star on his clothing. Although the marker was intended to identify the wearer as a needy child and was not necessarily a sign of Jew-hatred, its negative associations could hardly have failed to rub off on a sensitive fourteen-year-old who had almost been barred from school on account of his Jewishness and who, consciously Jewish or not, had been exposed since childhood to Vienna's notoriously anti-Semitic climate (Grissemann 26; Ulmer Cipes).

Ulmer would largely be spared the effects of Austrian anti-Semitism upon his return to Vienna in 1920, largely because he did not remain in Vienna for any extended period of time. Upon joining Max Reinhardt's theater academy in Vienna as an actor/art director in training, he traveled back and forth between Vienna and Berlin, where he was surrounded by Jews, of course, but of a determinedly cosmopolitan variety (Ulmer Cipes). He also began, as was the wont in Austro-German cultural circles, to move freely between the theater and film media. In film this entailed, according to Ulmer, set construction (uncredited) on the cream of early Weimar cinema, including *The Cabinet of Dr. Caligari* (1920), *The Golem* (1920), and *Die Nibelungen* (1921; Bogdanovich 561–63).[1] In theater it meant, still as a teenager, traveling with Reinhardt to New York and Los Angeles for the 1923 touring production of *The Miracle*. For the remainder of the decade, Ulmer would divide his time between Hollywood and Berlin, and, on his last American sojourn, would cause a further rent in his Jewish identity. Quite remarkably, for the future director of landmark Yiddish films, Ulmer not only married Josephine Warner, an American Episcopalian, but himself converted to Episcopalianism.

As with Lang, of course, Ulmer's conversion provided no immunization against Nazism. Thus, even before completion of the fabled *Menschen am Sonntag* (*People on Sunday*, 1929), with its who's who of soon-to-be Jewish-émigré filmmakers (besides Ulmer, Robert Siodmak, Billy Wilder, Fred Zinnemann, Eugen Schüfftan, and Seymour Nebenzahl), Ulmer emigrated permanently to the United States in 1929. The refugee experience, reinforced through contact with the burgeoning refugee community in Los Angeles, including attendance at Salka Viertel's weekly salons, no doubt laid the groundwork for Ulmer's rapprochement with his Jewishness (Ulmer Cipes). But it was a Hollywood romance that played the decisive role in his return to his hereditary roots. A seeming up-and-comer following the success of the Universal horror feature *The Black Cat* (1934), Ulmer would be "blackballed not for politics but for love" when he became involved with a Jewish script supervisor, Shirley Kassler Alexander (Krohn 61). Ulmer was divorced from Josephine by then, but Shirley was still married to Max Alexander, a nephew of Universal chieftain Carl Laemmle. By the time Shirley obtained her divorce and a reconverted Ulmer married her in a Jewish ceremony in New York City in 1935, a pall had been cast over his Hollywood career that would last nearly a decade.

Hollywood's loss, however, was Yiddish cinema's gain. Indeed, I would argue that Ulmer's double exile—from mainstream American culture as well as from his Austro-German homeland—coupled with his prodigal return to Jewishness, made him an ideal conduit and catalyst for the Yiddish film revival.

PHASING INTO YIDDISH FILM

Ulmer's entry into the world of Yiddish cinema coincides with what J. Hoberman terms the fourth phase of Yiddish-language film (7). Although New York *myusik hols* (music halls) had already begun showing movies in the pre-Nickelodeon days, the Jewish press tended to deride the first "flickers" as a "goyish" form of lowbrow entertainment that "symbolized the loss of *yiddishkeit* [Jewishness] in the New World" (Thissen 29). With cinema constructed as the "low Other," Yiddish vaudeville, which previously had been relegated to the bottom rung of the cultural ladder, was redefined as a respectable theatrical tradition and elevated to middlebrow status, while the already legitimated Yiddish stage "maintained its status as a highbrow institution" (29). Not surprisingly, then, the first phase of Yiddish film production (1911–1917), unlike the movies in general, emerged not in New York (or Hollywood) but in Russia and Poland (mainly Warsaw, then a part of Russia). Ironically, however, just as Adolph Zukor, the head of Famous Players (later Paramount) and himself a Hungarian-Jewish immigrant, would raise mainstream movies' stature by filming leading stage actors in classic plays, Yiddish cinema's cultural cachet would grow through the filming of Yiddish theater, and with the New York Yiddish stage providing much of the material (Hoberman 6).

During Yiddish film's second phase (1917–1928), Austria joined Poland and the newly formed Soviet Union as a production center, and Jewish novelists (e.g., Sholem Aleichem, Isaac Babel, Joseph Opatoshu, Harry Seckler) joined playwrights as the prime suppliers of source material. The films, like their sources, reflected "various vanguard tendencies—Symbolism, expressionism, Futurism, communism—even when concerned with the Jewish past" (Hoberman 6). The advent of the sound era ushered in the third phase (1929–1935), and while it heralded New York City's arrival as an industrial hub (the first Yiddish-language talkie was filmed in New York in 1929), the films—"everything from canned vaudeville acts and displays of cantorial virtuosity to Biblical pageants, dubbed silent films, and political documentaries"—were generally undistinguished (6).

Yiddish cinema "reached its zenith" during the fourth phase (1936–1941; Hoberman 7). Spurred by a renaissance of the Polish movie industry in 1935 and the Spanish and French popular front movements, this phase flourished in Europe during a brief eighteen-month period: from Germany's annexation of Austria in March 1937, through the Nazi-Soviet invasion of Poland in September 1939 that signaled the start of World War II and brought Polish-Yiddish film production to a halt. U.S. production continued until the attack on Pearl Harbor and America's entry into the war in late 1941 (7).[2]

Besides Ulmer's deepening interest in Jewishness (his own and that of the Jewish people)—induced by his exilic status, his new Jewish wife, and the "Jew York City" environment—other factors, in his background and that of Yiddish film, made his involvement with this subcultural form far from counterintuitive, but rather a natural fit. Ulmer, after all, had cut his cinematic teeth on some of the classics of German expressionist cinema, including, if we can believe his claim, the first Expressionist (with a capital "E") works, *The Cabinet of Dr. Caligari* and *The Golem*.[3] In addition to demonstrating links between certain expressionist thematic elements (extreme states of consciousness, a dystopian worldview, and the supernatural) and the prophetic and mystical strands in Judaism, *The Golem* is based on a Jewish folk tale of a humanoid monster conjured by a medieval eastern European rabbi, which not only predates Mary Shelley's classic horror story but also provides the basic premise for *Caligari* (itself cowritten by the Jewish Carl Mayer and directed by the Jewish Robert Wiene). Moreover, the 1920 version of *The Golem*, which was a remake of a 1914 German film of the same name, would be remade again in France by Julian Duvivier and released in New York in a Yiddish-language version in 1937, the year of Ulmer's first Yiddish film.

An even more profound conflation of German expressionism and Jewish concerns can be found in S. Ansky's play *Der Dibek* (*The Dybbuk*). One of the "postwar masterpieces of the high modernist cultural canon," bracketed with *Caligari* and *The Golem* "as an example of popular expressionism," *Der Dibek* was first staged in New York in 1921 and, more significantly for our purposes, in Berlin around the same time by Ulmer's mentor, Max Reinhardt (Hoberman 60). Regarded as a prime example of "Chasidic grotesque" or "Chasidic gothic," this period tale of female possession by evil spirits "infuses a specifically Jewish sense of the uncanny" with a Freudian-inflected "sexual content" (280). The 1937 film version, directed in Poland by Michal Waszynski, was one of thc three biggest international hits of the fourth phase of Yiddish film, the others being Joseph Green's *Yidl mitn Fidl* (*Yiddle* [little Jew] *with the Fiddle*, 1936) and Ulmer's *Grine Felder*. And, together with Green's and Ulmer's films, it represented the high point of the Golden Age.

GRINE FELDER AND *YANKL DER SHMID*: *YESHIVE BOKHERIM* AND *MUSKLYIDN*

A *yeshive bokher* is a young, male religious-school student training to become a Talmudic scholar or a rabbi. *Musklyid* is Yiddish for *Muskeljude* (muscle Jew), a German term coined by early Zionist leader Max Nordau, as a rhetorical counter to the anti-Semitic weakling stereotype and a model for the strong, tough, "New Jew" Nordau believed to be a prerequisite for the establishment of a viable Jewish state. As archetypes, the *yeshive bokher* and *musklyid* are polar opposites, physically, psychologically, and ideologically.

The *yeshive bokher* is a physically frail, mild-mannered, somewhat effeminate figure who, in his departure from, if not outright rejection of, Western standards of masculinity, has been viewed, historically and as a cultural construct, in three main ways: from the conventional gentile perspective, as an embarrassment and a figure of scorn; from the Orthodox Jewish perspective, as an exemplar of an honored religious and scholarly tradition; and, most recently, from the queer perspective, as a progressive alternative to heteronormativity (Boyarin). The *musklyid*, befitting his construction as an anti–*yeshive bokher*, is everything his "nerdy" cousin is not: a virile man's man given to bodily pleasures, labor in the fields and factories, and engaging the world vigorously and with supreme self-confidence.

The ideological tension between the two types—the religious student stuck in the past versus the man of nature geared to the future—responded to the socialist strand within Zionism and the break-up of shtetl life in eastern Europe. These political and demographic trends infused the historical moment of the early 1920s, when Peretz Hirschbein's play *Grine Felder*, on which Ulmer's film was based, was written and first produced. By the time of the film's release in 1937, these forces had been strengthened and exacerbated by the formation of the Popular Front on the one hand and the advance of fascism on the other. Hirschbein's genius was to meld past and future through an idealized vision of eastern European life that emphasized its kinship with, rather than resistance to, the emergence of the New Jew.

The precredits image of Ulmer's *Grine Felder*, repeated at a key turning point in the body of the film, emblematizes this syncretic fusion. Redolent of socialist-realist images of peasants joyfully working the fields, a group of men and women robustly reap the harvest on a resplendent, sunny day, to the accompaniment of heroic music. The first diegetic image both starkly contrasts with this idyllic, somewhat derivative composition and shows Ulmer's auteurist hand. Two *yeshive bokherim* davening in prayer in the shadows of a dark synagogue bemoan a fellow *bokher* who claims to be driven "by some hidden force" to leave them. We do not see this mysterious figure for some time, until the camera finally pans to him in another dark corner of the *shul*, seemingly asleep but actually buried in thought. The two boys walk over and one of them asks, "Where are you going, Levy Yitzchok? To a brighter synagogue? Better Jews? God's grace is here." "The light of truth is everywhere," the other boy elaborates. "One need not search for it afar." "But one must search for it," Levy Yitzchok (Michael Goldstein) responds. He then slowly makes his way to the exit. "He'll lose his way," says the first boy. "He who seeks the truth will find it," says the second. As Levy Yitzchok (the first name clearly connoting his spiritual aspect) opens the door, a shaft of light streams in from outside, bathing him in an ethereal mist.

Our hero's quest takes him to verdant fields—presumably somewhere in the Russian Pale, though the exact location remains undisclosed. The perilous reality lurking just out of sight is brought to mind, however, as is the fabulous unreality of the setting. Relieved to meet a friendly Jewish farm boy, Avram-Yakov (Hershel Bernardi), indicating that "Jews are nearby," Levy is also amazed to find Jews who "farm the land" and "eat their own food!"

Avram-Jakov's family—with whom Levy spends the night, and by whom he is then cajoled into remaining to tutor the illiterate youngster—are as intrigued, and impressed, by the learned stranger as he is by them. Yet what begins as a transformative experience mainly for the "country bumpkins," for whom every word from the "divinely inspired" Levy "is a gem," becomes even more revelatory for Levy himself. Touched by his peasant hosts' generosity and basic goodness, for which he finds Talmudic legitimation in Rabbi Eliezer's adage "A man without land is not a man," Levy's true epiphany is triggered not by scripture but by sexual desire, for Avram-Jakov's spirited sister Tsine (Helen Beverly). Levy is initially threatened by his feelings for Tsine, who wears her own attraction to him on her sleeve. But his passion grows with the seasons in a process analogous to the planting cycle, and fittingly comes to fruition at harvest time, with the momentousness of the occasion underscored through a reprise of the emblematic image from the film's opening.

Levy's proposal of marriage to Tsine does not signify a rejection of mind in favor of body, however, but rather an amalgam of the two. For Tsine has undergone a profound change as well, learning not only to read and write from Levy, but also how to channel her initially charming but somewhat infantile emotionality into a more thoughtful concern for others. Ulmer brilliantly captures both the opposition and interconnection of spirituality and physicality, of heaven and earth, in several group shots in the family cottage, which frame the figures within a secondary frame created by a long wooden table below and a broad ceiling beam above.

Dialectical synthesis notwithstanding, the ending tilts toward the *musklyid* when a second betrothal is announced, between Tsine's sturdy older brother Hersh-Ber (Saul Levine) and the neighboring family's daughter Stera (Dena Drute). A bone of contention between the two families up to this point, their marriage is given the parents' blessing only after Hersh-Ber persuades Stera's skeptical father Elkone (Max Vodnov) of his worthiness by showcasing his "tough Jew" qualities, even threatening violence if Elkone deigns to harm his beloved.

The film's final pastoral image reinforces the privileging of *musklyid* over *yeshive bokher*, while also promoting the idealized view that the Jewish people's past glory and future hope lies in a healthy relation to Mother Earth. As Tsine and Levy walk hand in hand across the harvested fields past a plow prominently placed in the foreground, their trajectory diagonally away from camera connotes both the reclaiming of a bygone era and, especially in a late-1930s context, the realization of the Zionist dream. By going "back to the land," Levy has indeed found a "brighter synagogue" and "better Jews"—but only if "back" is taken to mean "return," not "retreat," and "the land" signifies not only the soil but also the former and future Land of Israel. In this way, Levy and Tsine's coming of age becomes a coming together of the ages, with the procreational symbolism of the personal and collective unions clearly marked in the camera's culminating tilt-down to a close-up of the plow, its blade embedded in the fertile soil.

The forging of a New Jew is literally represented in Ulmer's next Yiddish film, *Yankl der Shmid*. As the title further suggests, the narrative focus here is primarily on the *musklyid*, and it is his transformation that governs the story arc. Apprenticed from his youth to the village blacksmith, Yankl (Moishe Oysher) grows into a strong, virile young man with a taste for drink and an eye for the ladies. He also possesses an operatic-quality voice, which he displays both at work and at play, partly as a showcase for star Oysher's singing talent, but also as a sign that beneath Yankl's devil-may-care exterior beats a worthy Jewish heart. Unlike in *Grine Felder*, the catalyst for Yankl's spiritual makeover is not the land, or a fusion of *musklyid* and *yeshive bokher* elements. To the contrary, here the *yeshive bokher*, Raphoel (played again by Michael Goldstein), is portrayed as a *nebbish* (loser) of no use to anyone, least of all to his wife Rivke (Florence Weiss), who was forced into marrying him but continues to lust after Yankl. Nor does religious scripture play a role in bringing Yankl around, as it did for Levy via Rabbi Eliezer's Talmudic dictum.

Ultimately, however, Yankl's change in consciousness derives from the same basic source as Levy's—the love of a strong woman, in this case Rivke's cousin Tamara (Miriam Riselle). But if *musklyid* and *yeshive bokher* are to be taken allegorically, then so too must the women in *Grine Felder* and *Yankl der Shmid*. Only by embracing, not just a woman, but the female *principle*, both films seem to suggest, can *musklyid* and *yeshive bokher* achieve "true manhood." The difference between Tamara's and Rivke's metonymic function is that Tamara is more conscious of her transformative powers and more comfortable with them. This awareness and comfort level are emphasized in Tamara's confrontation with her uncle, Reb Aron (Yudel Dubinsky), who opposes her marriage to the roughneck, womanizing Yankl: "Do not speak badly of him. He is dearer to me than that dried-up *yeshive bokher* who courted me last year. I will make a man out of him."[4]

This takes some doing, for Tamara must deal not only with Yankl's primal urges but also with cousin Rivke, who transmogrifies into a femme fatale in a desperate attempt to win back her true love. In this latter regard, as well as visually, *Yankl der Shmid*, as Hoberman observes, "is closer than *Grine Felder* to the expressionistic noirs and thrillers Ulmer would make in Hollywood in the 1940s" (266). The noir aspect extends thematically to Yankl's near character backslide, and to Rivke's intimation of suicide in the nearby river when her seduction of Yankl fails; expressionist visual elements include the dark, shadowy interiors and Ulmer's "characteristic use of odd angles and bold perspective" (266).

Politically, the film retains a proletarian edge consonant with the Popular Front and socialist Zionism. The Russian connection, referenced in *Grine Felder*'s socialist-realist imagery, is even more explicitly marked in *Yankl der Shmid*'s onion-shaped spires and folk dances, and in its pervasive Marxist ideology. As Hoberman explains:

> Yankl, who sings an anthem to labor as he sweats in his smithy, is an explicitly working-class hero . . . Even [Anna] Appel's sympathetic *shadknte* [female matchmaker] is given a heroic proletarian dimension: "All week long we struggle for a living," she tells the smith in a bit of class-conscious coffee-klatching . . . A truly progressive girl, Tamara seems familiar with Freud as well as Marx. "A man knows so little of himself," she sighs when, after the designing Rivke leaves her husband, Yankl insists on taking his former mistress in as a boarder, just to prove she has no appeal for him. (269)

In replacing Rabbi Eliezer with Freud and Marx, *Yankl der Shmid* in no way renounces its Jewish lineage. To the contrary: in addition to the psychosexual and socialist links to Zionism, we have the fact that the founders of the psychoanalytic and communist movements, and a disproportionate number of the groups' leading members, were Jews. Moreover, Jews' inordinate attraction to the "talking cure" and a "classless society" are commonly explained in traditional Judaic terms—such as *tikkun olam* (healing the world), Talmudic exegesis, and the prophetic tradition (Gillman 56). Certainly, more opportunistic factors also play a role, such as the desire to create a more equitable political system that would finally allow Jews "to secure the most elusive prize of all . . . inclusion in the larger non-Jewish society" (Dollinger 4). What *Yankl der Shmid* and *Grine Felder* are proposing, however, through their transformations of *musklyid* and *yeshive bokher*, is that this new, more inclusive society must be predicated on a new, more expansive Jew.

DI KLYATSHE AND *AMERIKANER SHADKHN*: *SHRAYBERS* AND MATCHMAKERS

In *Di Klyatshe*, Ulmer expands and contracts the New Jew principle. The transformation, as in *Grine Felder*, entails a backward and a forward motion; however, the backward move here is not to the land but to folk wisdom, and forward not to Zion but to the New World. The film's romantic permutation also reveals a shift. The carriers of change are once again a young couple—Fishke (David Opatoshu), a lame-legged beggar, and Hodel (Helen Beverly), a poor blind girl—but the film's moral center, as well as its narrative mover and shaker, is the gray-bearded Rebe Mendele (Izidore Cashier), a *shrayber* (writer), bookseller, and spiritual factotum who takes up the troubled lovers' cause. And the trouble, this time, stems not from a particular social orientation or character flaw, but from eastern European Jewry's tribal insularity.

Intra-Jewish conflict, and ultimate reconciliation, are foregrounded in the film's opening scene, whose location is geographically specified. On the country road between the Jewish village of Glubsk ("Foolstown") and the more cosmopolitan city of Odessa, Rebe Mendele lies like a corpse in a horse-drawn cart. When a cart comes up from behind and its horse starts nibbling hay around the seemingly deceased Mendele's face, he awakens and angrily approaches the other cart's driver. The two men raise their fists for a fight, then suddenly recognize each other, and shake hands.

The film will return to this same setting and uplifting theme at the end, when Fishke and Hodel, at Mendele's urging and with his crucial assistance, take flight from the poverty, pestilence, superstition, and corruption of Glubsk toward the more modern and humane conditions of Odessa. The final image shows the couple in long shot from Mendele's point of view, silhouetted, as they ascend a low rise against the glow of a cloudless sky (apparently inspiring the film's American title, *A Light Ahead*). But the lighthearted opening and "enlightened" closing belie *Di Klyatshe*'s overall look and tone, which are relentlessly dark and bleak. Most of the film takes place at night, in the town's narrow alleyways, cramped living quarters, and cemeteries. In its canted lampposts, angular buildings, and expressionist shadows, Ulmer's Glubsk not only "suggests the confluence" of Chagall and *Caligari*, as Hoberman keenly observes (303), but, even more than *Yankl der Shmid*, it presages Ulmer's later immersion in the film noir cycle.

While Ulmer supplies the noir, Rebe Mendele, a stand-in for S. Y. Abramowitz, the author of the work on which the film is based, supplies the *Yiddishkeit*. Under his pen name Mendele Mokher Sforim (Mendele the Bookseller), Abramowitz was called the "Grandfather of Yiddish Literature" by Sholem Aleichem (Hoberman 300). Rebe Mendele's resemblance to his literary creator is reinforced not merely through the name and *shrayber*/bookseller occupation. In one scene in which he sells books and religious paraphernalia on the street, Rebe Mendele reflexively announces, in direct address to the camera, that in addition to prayer books, dime novels, and skullcaps, he "even" sells "books by Abramowitz." The irony of the "even" will become more bitter as the narrative unfolds, for as with the goods he peddles, the ideas Rebe Mendele propounds are both religiously and politically subversive.

The threat Mendele the *shrayber* poses to the Jewish establishment becomes an open secret when, at a meeting of the Glubsk city council, the councilmen express concern "because he may write about us in his books." Not that he doesn't have enough material already, given the council's refusal to fund a much-needed hospital in the town despite a growing cholera epidemic, which itself stems from a polluted river that the council has declined, and continues to decline, to clean. The spoken rather than written word gives vent to Rebe Mendele's religious rebelliousness. Raising his head to the heavens, he praises God's infinitude, then adds a Job-like plaint:

> Scattered over the globe are little Jewish cities. Thousands of years you gaze down upon them. You see their wretchedness, their misery, and keep silent . . . You listen to their sighs, you hear their groans in persecutions and massacres, and you keep silent. Oh, like a sick child to its mother will I lament to you! Oh, how it hurts! How can you look on and keep silent? How long will you torture us? When will there be an end?!

When his earthly and heavenly pleas fall on deaf ears, Rebe Mendele does what little he can to make a difference, starting with the hapless Fishke and Hodel. Following an ancient Glubsk custom, the cripple and the blind girl, as the poorest boy and girl in town, have been coerced into a "sacrificial" wedding in the cemetery to absolve the city of it sins, the real effect of which will be to stigmatize Fishke and Hodel as "the cholera groom and bride" and their offspring as "cholera children." Rebe Mendele coaxes the couple to go through with the humiliating ceremony, then secrets them out of town in his cart and onto the road he hopes will lead them "not to wretched need and bitterness but to a normal life full of joy." But whatever the future holds for them, the couple is justified in any case "to leave a city still in the Middle Ages that fights cholera with superstition."

Released in summer 1939, in the shadow of the German annexations of Austria and Czechoslovakia that brought nearly a million Jews under Nazi rule, *Di Klyatshe*'s biting tone and allegorical meaning were as clear as *Kristallnacht*. As the lowest of the low, the cripple and blind girl serve as metonyms for the perpetually marginalized and downtrodden Jewish people; and their flight from a "city still in the Middle Ages" represents eastern European Jewry's last best hope of escape from persecution, if not outright annihilation. The twist here is that the enemy is not merely without but within a Jewish collective backwardness which, however much effected by forces beyond their control, requires a complete reconstitution if the Jewish people are to survive. And this survival, in the New World or wherever Jews can find a safe haven, *Di Klyatshe* proclaims in no uncertain terms, calls for a New Jew as well.

Amerikaner Shadkhn, Ulmer's swan song to Yiddish film, examines to what extent the New World Jew fills the bill. The film ironically, in terms of genre, resembles Italy's fascist-era "white telephone" films: "romantic comedies in lavish settings, populated by men and women of leisure for whom love and marriage are life's greatest problems" (Hoberman 316). A superficial Jewishness informs the plot: a wealthy, second-generation American-Jewish Manhattanite, unlucky in love, turns to Old World inspired matchmaking as a last resort. But the film's subtext is only "too Jewish," dealing with an issue of increasing significance to American Jews: the threat to Jewish survival posed not by pogroms or concentration camps but by assimilation and acculturation.

That an irreparable rent in the fabric of European Yiddishkeit has already occurred is indicated right off the bat in the posh apartment, elegant clothes, and de-Judaized name of the film's protagonist, Nathan Silver (Leo Fuchs), but perhaps most tellingly in the pidgin Yiddish he and his friends speak in the opening scene's "bachelor party," as they call this most American, or at least non-Jewish, of customs. Other Americanisms such as "no sirree," "movie star," and "You said it!" pepper the dialogue, and the Americanization of the film itself is reflexively referenced in the party scene's climax, which parodies American gangster films. A shady-looking character in trench coat and fedora bursts in and pulls a gun on Nathan, then threatens to turn it on himself because Nathan has "stolen" his childhood sweetheart to be his bride.

When the tender-hearted Nathan calls off the wedding, making this his eighth aborted engagement, his mother turns to the family tree to break the losing streak.

Nathan's matrimonial problems, she explains, "run in the family." His Uncle Shya, back in the old country, was as healthy and prepossessing as Nat and yet as constitutionally unable to land a bride. So Uncle Shya decided to become a *shadkhn*, reasoning that by helping others he might also help himself. Nathan's response, and his mother's rejoinder, succinctly establish the film's survivalist/assimilationist dialectic:

> Nathan: But this is America, not Europe.
>
> Mrs. Silver: Family characteristics know no boundaries. They travel across oceans, over mountains.

And whatever obstacles familial bonds can't overcome, cinema can compensate for, as Nathan's fantasy immediately shows: Uncle Shya (Leo Fuchs with beard), basking in the glory of a wedding he has arranged, describes the *shadkhn*'s purpose in a manner that clearly spoke, at least to Jewish audiences at the time, to European-American relations as a whole: "He brings strangers together and knits bonds of friendship closer."

Nathan's American version of matchmaking, while played for broad comic effect, also satirizes the cultural transposition. The changing of his business name from Nathan Silver to Nat Gold raises the name's exchange value but also sends up the materialism of the enterprise; while his new business description, "Advisor in Human Relations," lampoons American euphemistic jargon. When Maurice (Yudel Dubinsky), Nathan's butler turned "executive assistant," misreads "relations" as "relishes, as in pickles," Yiddish humor's genius for unmasking pretentiousness through ingenuousness is once again revealed. Nathan's procedural innovations, however—having a lawyer, doctor, rabbi, and psychologist on staff to examine his clients before advising them—are no joke to New York's more traditional *shadkhonim*. Yet despite the old guard's bearded and black-hatted appearance, their American-style protest, replete with picket signs in Yiddish and English ("Better a *Shadkhn* Than a Shotgun," "It's Better to Do with A *Shadkhn* Than Never to Have Loved At All"), betrays their acculturation, and Nathan has little difficulty striking a deal with them that benefits all parties.[5]

The *shadkhn*'s traditional function, as Hoberman explains, was to mediate "between the material facts of an arranged marriage and the Jewish folk-belief that each marriage is divinely preordained. Perhaps the archetypal *shtetl* Jew, the *shadkhn* is at once the instrument of a divine plan and a *luftmentsh* [airman]" (318). Employing an American matchmaker to arbitrate tensions between Old and New World Jewishness was thus a master stroke, at least in a romantic comedy whose obligatory happy ending ensures—at least on the surface—a successful resolution.

When Nathan ends up marrying Judith Aarons (Judith Abardanel), a woman whose mother has hired him to find a husband for her daughter, but who falls in love with Nathan (and vice versa), the merging of the American Dream with its eastern European counterpart is posited as the best of both worlds, for the happily married couple and the Yiddish-language audience as well. It's left to the schlemiel Maurice to underscore, but also to problematize, the syncretism of American and Jewish ideals. After Nathan gives the matchmaking business to his assistant and one of the traditional *shadkhonim*, Maurice sums up, but also deconstructs, the arrangement: "Imagine! 'Maurice Zucker and Simon Schwalbenrok: Advisors in Human Relishes'—it's our dream, it's our dream!"

CONCLUSION

Ulmer's four Yiddish films propose, in varying degrees of urgency, the need for the forging of a New Jew in the wake of the demise of eastern European Jewry. That each film proffers a different alternative indicates the complexity of the problem and the difficulty in finding a viable solution under rapidly shifting historical conditions. Looked at from a postmodern perspective, however, Ulmer's New Jews need not be seen as separate and mutually exclusive models for Jewish identity, but can be seen rather as a fluid continuum of evolving, overlapping, recombinant identi*ties*. Nor is such a perspective necessarily anachronistic. The expression "two Jews, three opinions" may be of comparatively recent vintage, but a Jewish tradition of multivocality can be traced back to the Torah, whose ambiguities invited a host of heterogeneous interpretations in the Talmud and Midrash. Indeed, when taken together, Jews' diasporic existence(s), fragmented identity(ies), and indeterminate sacred text(s) have led David Biale, Michael Galchinsky, and Susannah Heschel, among others, to deem Jews a prototypically postmodern people. When we take into account the Jews' immigrant experience in the United States, a country that Jean Baudrillard regards as postmodern from its founding as a representationally based construction, Jewish imbrication with the postmodern condition expands exponentially.

Viewed through a postmodernist prism, then, Ulmer's "forging" of the New Jew must be taken in both its constructive and deconstructive senses—that is, as a reshaping and, alternately, as a *falsification* of identity. *Falsification*, here again, in the poststructuralist sense of Mary Ann Doane's notion of "masquerade" and Judith Butler's of "performativity," need not connote prevarication or deceit. Rather, as a concept it stresses the *fallacy* of inherent, immutable, unitary identity and thereby an opening of the "self" to its multiple facets and liberatory possibilities. Ulmer's Yiddish films point up the multiplicity of self in the way each character's New Jewishness reflects the contingencies of the specific historical moment in which the particular film was made. Their emancipatory potential emerges if the films are taken as a *body of work* in which a wardrobeful of identities are being tried on, sent back for alterations, and tried on again—in other words, when the idea of identity formation itself is being *tested*.

And what better proctor for such an examination than Edgar G. Ulmer? Born a Jew but raised oblivious to his Jewishness, he had Jewishness thrust upon him in adolescence; he not only rejected Judaism but converted to Christianity in adulthood; and he finally reclaimed his ethnic inheritance in early middle age—thankfully in a place, if not quite a time, when it was propitious to do so. Upon his early-1940s return to Hollywood, Ulmer, along with many of his fellow Jewish-émigré directors, would transmute his renewed Jewish consciousness into the emergent film-noir cycle.[6] In this way, his Yiddish-film period indeed can be seen as a stepping-stone for the more famous films to come, but not merely due to his growing aesthetic affinity for a darkly expressionist cinematic style. On a more fundamental level, his Yiddish-language work bears witness to Ulmer's growing existential awareness of what it meant "to be or not to be" a Jew.

NOTES

1. Ulmer's early career claims must be taken with a grain of salt. Among his wildest assertions were to have almost single-handedly invented German Expressionist cinema; to have served as a subject for one of Freud's psychoanalytic studies; and to have been related to Arthur Schnitzler (Grissemann 12). If you read what he alleged about himself, Bertrand Travernier observes, he would have had to have been "everywhere at the same time" (cited in Grissemann 12).

2. The fifth phase (1945–present), obviously beyond our purview here, consists of "modest and mostly unsuccessful attempts to revive Yiddish cinema in Poland, the United States, and, belatedly, in Israel" (Hoberman 8).

3. Barry Salt lists only seven "pure" Expressionist works, which, besides *Caligari* (and excluding *The Golem*), consist of *Genuine* and *From Morning to Midnight* (both 1920), *Torgus* (1921), *Raskolnikov* (1923), *Waxworks* (1924), and *Metropolis* (1926; 198).

4. The translated quotation here combines Hoberman's version (266) with the subtitles in the video I viewed. All the Yiddish film titles are according to Hoberman.

5. *Shadkhn* is spelled "shadchen" on the picket signs in the film. I use *shadkhn* to avoid confusion.

6. Other Jewish-émigré directors who contributed substantially to the film-noir cycle are Fritz Lang, Robert Siodmak, Billy and Willy Wilder, Otto Preminger, Curtis Bernhardt, Max Ophuls, John Brahm, and Anatole Litvak.

BIBLIOGRAPHY

Baudrillard, Jean. *Simulations* (New York: Semiotext[e], 1983).

Biale, David, Michael Galchinsky, and Susannah Heschel, eds. *Insider/Outsider: American Jews and Multiculturalism* (Berkeley: University of California Press, 1998).

Bogdanovich, Peter. "Edgar G. Ulmer," in *Who the Devil Made It: Conversations with Legendary Film Directors* (New York: Ballantine Books, 1997), 558–604.

Boyarin, Daniel. *Unheroic Conduct: The Rise of Heterosexuality and the Invention of the Jewish Man* (Berkeley: University of California Press, 1997).

Butler, Judith. *Gender Trouble: Feminism and the Subversion of Identity* (New York: Routledge, 1990).

Doane, Mary Ann. *The Desire to Desire: The Woman's Film of the 1940s* (Bloomington: Indiana University Press, 1987).

Dollinger, Marc. *Quest for Inclusion: Jews and Liberalism in Modern America* (Princeton: Princeton University Press, 2000).

Gillman, Neil. *Sacred Fragments: Recovering Theology for the Modern Jew* (Philadelphia: Jewish Publication Society, 1990).

Grissemann, Stefan. *Mann im Schatten: Der Filmmacher Edgar G. Ulmer* (Vienna: Paul Zsolnay Verlag, 2003).

Gunning, Tom. *The Films of Fritz Lang: Allegory and Visions of Modernity* (London: British Film Institute, 2000).

Hoberman, J. *Bridge of Light: Yiddish Film between Two Worlds* (Philadelphia: Temple University Press, 1991).

Krohn, Bill. "King of the Bs," *Film Comment* 19, no. 4 (July–August 1983): 60–64.

Salt, Barry. "From German Stage to German Screen," in *Before Caligari: German Cinema, 1895–1920*, ed. Paola Cherchi Usai and Lorenzo Codelli (Pordenone, Italy: Edizioni Biblioteca dell'Immagine, 1991).

Thissen, Judith. "Movies vs. Jewish Theater: The 'Grand Scandal,'" in *Entertaining America: Jews, Movies, and Broadcasting*, ed. J. Hoberman and Jeffrey Shandler (New York: Jewish Museum, 2003), 29.

Ulmer Cipes, Arianné. E-mail message to author, 3 November 2007.

———. Phone interview with author, 10 October 2007.

7

When You Get to the Fork, Take It

From Ulmer's Yiddish Cinema to Woody Allen

Miriam Strube

Since the beginning of moving images, Jews have been part of the film industry, both as actors and as producers. In America, Jews appeared in one-reelers as early as 1903, drawing on archetypes found in literature, vaudeville, and graphic humor. They also played an important role in the U.S. film industry. However, this role has not been an easy one. In *American Jewish Filmmakers,* David Desser and Lester D. Friedman point out that Jewish artists and businessmen have shaped the destiny of the film industry ever since Walter Selig moved his company to California in the early twentieth century (1).[1] Yet, for a long time, Jewish moguls were not keen on promoting either Jewish culture or Jewish actors.[2] As a story about Columbia's Harry Cohn illustrates, the prevalent attitude of the studio years was rather dismissive. When the director Richard Quine wanted to employ a specific actor, Cohn allegedly yelled: "He looks too Jewish! Around this studio the only Jews we put into pictures play Indians!" (1). Obviously, Jewishness was equated with unwelcome foreign traits. These studio moguls tried to achieve assimilation, both on and off screen, which led to a de-Semiticizing in film.[3] If the American movie showed Jews at all they were models of successful adaptation. Hollywood constructed "Americanism" as an effortless process of assimilation, an idealization of the road taken by the movie moguls themselves. Not survival but success, not making it *to* America but making it *in* America was emphasized. It was not until the end of the studio system in the late 1950s, and especially the growth of ethnic pride in the 1960s, that an evolution of American consciousness was marked. But even in early Jewish film, not all Jewish filmmakers depicted a smooth assimilation, especially not those of the Yiddish cinema.

In the following, I want to briefly describe Yiddish cinema before turning to Edgar G. Ulmer's four Yiddish films and, in particular, to his *Amerikaner Shadkhn* (*American Matchmaker*, 1940). With this film, I argue that Ulmer creates a Jewish American persona deeply steeped in neurotic ambivalence, a persona later employed, further developed, and popularized by Woody Allen, most notably in his Oscar-winning *Annie Hall* (1977).

YIDDISH CINEMA

Yiddish[4] culture in America, according to Patricia Erens (1976), has three defining aspects: first, a sense of humanity based on the notion of *mentshlekhkayt* (the ethos of the good man);[5] second, the acceptance of suffering as a fact of life; and third, the twin reaction to this condition, namely, humor and philosophical resignation—or, put differently, optimistic pessimism (8). This new American-Yiddish culture was at home neither in the Jewish past nor in the gentile present, and it therefore created a utopia shadowed by history—a utopia rendered desperate, complex, and poignant by a uniquely Jewish struggle for equilibrium between two worlds. Yet it is also important to point out that Yiddish was not used or celebrated by all Jewish immigrants. Often it was seen as neither entirely respectful nor completely respectable; for religious Jews, it was the language of the secular, whereas for the "enlightened" it signified nothing more than Jewish insularity.

In the nineteenth and early twentieth centuries, Yiddish culture was strongly expressed in live theater, whose prominence was gradually replaced by Yiddish cinema during the Depression in the 1930s. At that time, the Yiddish film companies were financially shaky independents catering to a clearly defined group of Jews (Erens, *Mentshlekhkayt* 48). While Yiddish artists and intellectuals embraced secular ideologies and opened themselves to their new surroundings, they simultaneously risked the loss of a significantly Jewish identity. In this respect, the Yiddish stage and screen were a means of identity formation. As J. Hoberman explains, it was not only entertainment but an antidote for homesickness and a source of collective identity, serving for its audience as half congregation, half extended family (17). Hoberman says:

> Novel for its audience, that broad, shifting spectrum of Jewish life between orthodoxy and assimilation, the Yiddish cinema is also novel in the history of cinema. Drawing upon an established dramatic and literary tradition, yet employing a language virtually unknown to the Gentile world and considered by many of its users to be only a "jargon," this was not just a national cinema without a nation-state, but a national cinema that, with every presentation, created its own

> ephemeral nation-state. A language charged with ideology, Yiddish was most important for those nationalists who rejected religion but resisted the Zionist insistence on a reconstructed homeland . . . Yiddish was not just a language and a folk culture but an entire Jewish world, a "*Yiddishland*." (5)

Initially, Yiddish cinema was as secular as Yiddish culture, often imbued with the perspective of the *proster Yid* (common Jew). For a long time it had a tendency toward sentimentality, yet it was a sentimentality leavened with comedy as well as with nostalgia and pathos. Looking at the development of Yiddish cinema, in his excellent book *The Bridge of Light*, Hoberman differentiates five different phases: The first, beginning in 1911 in the silent period and ending during World War I, coincided with the development of movies as a mass medium and marked the discovery of a Jewish film audience. The second phase began with the fall of the tsar in 1917 and extended a dozen years, through the end of the silent period. This phase was characterized by ambitious (albeit sporadic) attempts to make specifically Jewish movies. Less dependent than earlier films upon the Yiddish stage, these efforts drew upon the work of Yiddish and Jewish novelists. However, this period took place primarily in Europe. Conversely, the third phase, that of the early sound period, was an almost entirely American phenomenon. Less universal than the silent precursors, these were "exploitation" films attempting to attract the Jewish audience, ranging from canned vaudeville acts and cantorial virtuosity to Biblical pageants, political documentaries, and dubbed silent films. The fourth phase of Yiddish cinema is the best known. It began in 1935, mainly with the rejuvenation of the Polish movie industry. The first Polish-Yiddish film intrigued American producers and initiated a dialogue between Warsaw and New York. This so-called Golden Age coincided with the period of the Popular Front against fascism, and was characterized by international hits such as Joseph Green's *Yidl mitn Fidl* (*Yiddle [little Jew] with His Fiddle*; Poland, 1936), Edgar G. Ulmer's *Grine Felder* (*Green Fields*; U.S.A., 1937), and Michal Waszynski's *Der Dibek* (*The Dybbuk*; Poland, 1937). The final phase was concentrated in the immediate post–World War II period from 1945 to 1950 but, more generally, could be said to continue until the present. Returning Yiddish cinema to filmed theater, the fifth phase is characterized by a modest and rather unsuccessful attempt to revive Yiddish cinema in the United States and Poland, and also in Israel. But as "Yiddishland" dissolved into the American and Soviet mainstreams and was rendered obsolete by the creation of an actual Jewish homeland, the survivors of its Polish center dispersed throughout the world (343).

Throughout these five phases, the most persistent strain in American-Yiddish cinema was the family melodrama, with its images of domestic and psychic disintegration, of unhappy upward mobility, and of Americanized children rejecting or abandoning the parents who had made sacrifices for them. Such films dramatized the anxieties of immigrants over the disruptive effects that the New World might have on their traditional values. Probably in order to combat this anxiety, the wedding emerged as a ubiquitous symbol of the perpetuation of the Jewish people and their rituals in Yiddish cinema. Yet Hoberman points out the limitations of this symbol:

> Joyous or pathetic, comic or macabre, the wedding is the favored set piece of the Yiddish cinema. But this implicit emphasis on cultural continuity scarcely papers over the profound uneasiness that haunts many Yiddish movies. While pogroms, steerage, poverty, anti-Semitism, and other dismal facts of contemporary Jewish life are downplayed, Yiddish cinema is hardly escapist. (10)

Just as in all secular Yiddish culture, in Yiddish American cinema there is a tenuous connection between traditional Jewishness and American culture. As a consequence, these films are often self-contradictory, depicting a double consciousness and competing images of successful assimilation and the yearning for the simplicity of the *shtetl.* Often these competing notions are portrayed in antithetical perspectives. For example, the classic *Tsvey Shvester* (*Two Sisters*, 1938) neatly breaks down into antithetical worldviews: arranged marriage (which was the rule in the nineteenth-century *shtetl*) versus romantic love, "old-fashioned" versus modern, Yiddish versus American. However, implicit in these dichotomies is an urge for totality, the desire for a self-contained and complete Jewish world.

ULMER'S YIDDISH FILMS

Ulmer has been praised as one of the most versatile filmmakers (Schürmann 1), who "continually reinvented himself" (Isenberg, "Perennial Detour" 4). One of his many sides is his Yiddish cinema, although it is little known. (Erens, for example, does not even include him in her lengthy study *The Jew in American Cinema.*) During a four-year interlude and on a tiny budget, Ulmer made four films aimed at a Jewish audience, which were presented in the United States with English subtitles: *Grine Felder*, *Yankl der Shmid* (*The Singing Blacksmith*, 1938), *Di Klyatshe* (*The Light Ahead*, 1939), and *Amerikaner Shadkhn*. After *Amerikaner Shadkhn,* no further Yiddish films were made during World War II.

Ulmer was a self-identified secular Jew and, as George Lipsitz notes concerning Ulmer's ethnic films, he believed "that cinema as a medium had a responsibility to educate and communicate, that it belonged as much to people striving to define their ethnic identity as it did to investors seeking profits." (198). While Ulmer did not speak Yiddish, he was very familiar with the Yiddish theater scene on New York's Lower East Side.[6] In fact, during his first visit to New York, he was introduced to Yiddish stars from Second Avenue, "the second Broadway," such as the famous actor Maurice Schwartz.

Together with Green's 1936 classic *Yidl mitn Fidl*, *Grine Felder*, Ulmer's first Yiddish film (released the following year), was highly acclaimed both critically and commercially. Indeed, these two movies were the most successful Yiddish films ever made.[7] They created an upsurge in Yiddish culture and Jewish consciousness,[8] and they revitalized Yiddish cinema and gave it international status. Hoberman explains that these Yiddish hits were celebratory in a way that

> earlier Yiddish talkies had not been. Suffering was not glorified. Neither was political action—yet the image of Jewish fertility, cooperation, and folk resilience suggest a conscious countermythology in opposition to the virulent ideology of Nazi anti-Semitism. (235)

Green and Ulmer, Hoberman explains, combined a romantic nostalgia for shtetl culture with a far more sophisticated and ambitious filmmaking than that of American *shund* (235).[9]

Grine Felder (starring the distinguished actors Helen Beverly, Michael Goldstein, and Isidore Cashier) was so popular that it not only won the best foreign film entry at the Paris Film Festival in 1938,[10] but allegedly required a police presence to control the huge crowds during the first few days of its run in New York. Although this film of a Russian *shtetl* was shot in New Jersey, many praised its authenticity; for instance, *Der Tog*, a leading Yiddish daily newspaper, applauded it for its depiction of Jewish rural life and the authenticity of its language (cited in Schürmann 33). *Grine Felder* is based on a play by Peretz Hirschbein, which was adapted for the screen by Ulmer and the veteran Yiddish stage actor Jacob Ben-Ami, who also codirected the film. It is an unsentimental and lyrical rustic comedy displaying a sense of longing for roots. Furthermore, it celebrates an idyllic world of wholeness, in which work and religion, man and nature, and parents and children are happily reconciled (Hoberman 251). By offering a look at this world, the movie creates a number of positive Jewish images. Interestingly, Talmudic learning is presented as secondary: education of the heart is privileged over religious dogma. By focusing on the natural landscape as well as the *folksmentsh* (man of the people) and his connection to his idyllic surroundings, the film idealizes the common man and his spirituality; but it is a spirituality gained through embracing the material world rather than denying it. The film, as Stefan Grissemann puts it, dreams of the union of man and nature (115).

Ulmer's second Yiddish film (again, set in eastern Europe but shot in New Jersey) is also based on a literary text, namely David Pinski's 1906 Yiddish classic *Yankl der Shmid*. Adapting this drama as a vehicle for Moishe Oysher, a renowned actor, cantor, and star of Yiddish radio, with a supporting cast mostly drawn from the Yiddish Art Theater, the producer Roman Rebush and Ulmer engaged Jacob Weinbert to compose the musical score and the playwright Ossip Dymow to rework the drama for film. *Yankl der Shmid* turned out to be less successful than *Grine Felder* despite the almost unanimously good reviews, many of which complimented the film on its literary qualities.

This folkloric and montage-filled musical focuses on the blacksmith Yankl (Moishe Oysher), a working-class hero. Portrayed as a womanizing drunkard who is constantly philandering, he ends up marrying Tamara (Miriam Riselle), a poor orphan. Because of his relationship with Tamara, he finally becomes a *mentsh*—a conscientious worker, husband, and father (the baby, in fact, is Ulmer's infant daughter). This naturalistic drama was one of the first Yiddish productions to present a psychological study of physical passion, although sexual desire is presented as both a primal drive and a source of ambivalence (Hoberman 265). In contrast to *Grine Felder*, religion barely exists in *Yankl der Shmid*. Rather, the film celebrates *mentshlekhkayt* and the *proster Yid* in a very secular way.[11]

Ulmer's third film from this period, *Di Klyatshe* (or *Fishke der Krumer* [*Fishke the Cripple*]), is the most political, the most complex, and the least commercially successful of his Yiddish films.[12] The script was adapted from the 1869 satire titled *Masaot Benyamin Hashlishi* (*The Travels of Benjamin the Third*), by Mendele Mokher S'forim (also known as S. Y. Abramovitsh or as Mendele the Book Peddler), whom the famous Sholom Aleichem named the "Grandfather of Yiddish Literature." However, the prizewinning scriptwriter Chaver-Paver (né Gershon Einbinder), Ulmer, and Ulmer's wife Shirley jointly changed the script so as to soften Mendele's satire, which actually describes the *shtetl* Glubsk (literally "fool's town") as swarming with hucksters, beggars, and thieves, and as being surrounded by a moat of sewage (Hoberman 312).

Di Klyatshe is much stagier than *Grine Felder* (whose profits enabled Ulmer to produce this movie), and it is Ulmer's most expressionistic Yiddish film.[13] *Di Klyatshe* deals with poverty, exploitation, corruption, and hypocrisy. In contrast to his earlier Yiddish films, Ulmer now offers a negative view of the *shtetl*, which seems to be mired in the Dark Ages. Life in Glubsk is depicted as miserable and archaic, and its religion as self-serving, hypocritical, and little more than superstition; even the dietary laws are perverted by commerce (Hoberman 302). *Di Klyatshe* contrasts Glubsk's life with the love story between the blind orphan Hodl (Helen Beverly) and the crippled Fishke (David Opatoshu). Both of them are pariahs who are nevertheless characterized by purity. Contrary to the corrupt village people, these two outcasts are not mercenary. Poor and thus unable to get married, they dream of a humble home in the big city of Odessa, in which they can live together. Strikingly, while his earlier Yiddish movies are nostalgic in focusing on the vigorous and healthy rural life in eastern Europe, Ulmer's *Di Klyatshe* looks at the *shtetl*'s deformation and hypocrisy, envisioning the city as the place for salvation. As Fishke says, "In a big city, there's more opportunity." At the end of the movie they are enabled to leave for the big city through the assistance of another central character, Mendele (Isadore Cashier), again an ideal of the *folksmentsh.* Mendele helps them flee their midnight wedding, which the elders have organized as a ritual in order to fight the town's cholera epidemic (instead of allowing modern medicine or sanitation). "The sequences end with the lighting of a streetlamp, a striking allusion to the battle between enlightenment and religious dogma . . . the town pariahs break free from the dark ceremony and make their way to the bright road toward the big city" (Isenberg, "Perennial Detour" 14).

It is thus significant that Ulmer's next and final Yiddish film not only shows the rural-urban dialectic, but actually takes place in a city—and not just any city, but one far removed from the *shtetl* and the Old World. Moreover, in contrast to Ulmer's three previous Yiddish films, which are derived from Yiddish classics, *Amerikaner Shadkhn* is based on the story of Ulmer's Viennese cousin Gustav H. Heimo, and the script was written by Ulmer and Shirley. They set *Amerikaner Shadkhn* at the Jewish heart of the New World, New York City,[14] as the establishing shot of New York manifests; and they have given us "a comedy in which we see what became of Fishke and Hodl's descendents in the city" (Krohn 64) as well as the roles that Yiddish-speaking Jews occupy there (see Noah Isenberg's "Permanent Vacation," chapter 1 in this book). One of these roles is the *shadkhn*, or matchmaker.

The figure of the *shadkhn* is well-known in Yiddish cinema. For instance, in the classic *Yevreiskoye Schastye/Menakhem Mendl* (*Jewish Luck*, 1925, based on Sholem Aleichem's story), the protagonist Mendl stumbles upon a book that contains a list of prospective brides and grooms, and hence he decides to become a matchmaker: "*Shadkhn*—that's a real profession!" The *shadkhn*, however, is usually a comic, if not a ridiculous, figure. In *Jewish Luck* this is underscored when, at the film's climax, the new matchmaker's career goes awry when the self-proclaimed "king of *shadkhonim*" unintentionally arranges a match between two young women. Yet despite being a comic and poor figure, the *shadkhn* is not without power. For one thing, his qualification of individual *yikhes* (social pedigree) makes him a social arbiter. Moreover, being a psychologist of sorts, he mediates between the Jewish folk-belief that, on the one hand, each marriage is divinely preordained and, on the other hand, material circumstances are consequential in an arranged marriage (Hoberman 318).

In Ulmer's film on a *shadkhn*, Leo Fuchs plays the matchmaker. Fuchs was a dancer-comedian from Poland who was first introduced in Yiddish cinema in *Der Mazldiker Bokher* (*Lucky Boy,* 1935). In the mid-1930s, he was touted as both the "Yiddish Fred Astaire" and the "Yiddish Ray Bolger." Cinematically, *Amerikaner Shadkhn* is a very simple, low-budget film (even by Ulmer's standards), shot almost entirely in the studio. Thus, it often disappoints with its bland action and its mainly set-bound and overly static *mise-en-scène*, which for the most part seems more like canned theater than a well-made film. However, as Grissemann rightly points out, the film, with its lavish settings mostly populated by people of leisure, tries to simulate the luxurious makeup of Hollywood films (139). This fact, coupled with the choice of the romantic comedy as genre, makes this film the most American of Ulmer's Yiddish films. From its very beginning, the film seems to show that only in America, and, more specifically, only in an American city, can the Jew—that is, the Americanized Jew—aspire to and ultimately attain wealth.

Accordingly, the focus is on an assimilated, rich Jew, namely, Nat Silver (Fuchs), who is an elegant and cultivated Jewish American businessman, a self-made man, and a respected member of New York's Jewish elite. Nat obviously has made it in America in terms of money, but his attempts at love and marriage have been repeated failures. He has a troubled relationship with women, as all of his seven engagements have been called off at the last minute.[15] The opening sequence shows Nat at his bachelor party in his stylish art deco penthouse on Central Park West (an address where Ulmer actually once lived), yet the atmosphere is not portrayed as happy and cheerful. That night, Nat is awakened during a dream of his approaching marriage to Shirley (the woman's image in Nat's dream is of Ulmer's wife Shirley). A distressed young man holding a gun has invaded Nat's apartment, and he reveals that only his own poverty prevents Shirley from marrying him instead of Nat—a fact, as the young man says in despair, that will lead him to shoot himself. This incident ends Nat's eighth engagement. As a consequence, Nat wonders why he has "such bad luck in these affairs," and he puts this question to his mother. His mother replies that it runs in the family: "You are just like your uncle Shya, you have inherited his luck . . . He thought by helping others he might help himself." Uncle Shya thus became a *shadkhn*, and Nat's mother encourages him to do the same. "Unbelievable!" Nat exclaims, "This is America, not Europe." But his mother responds that "family characteristics know no boundaries. They travel across oceans, over mountains." And so Nat decides to change his life by turning himself into a matchmaker, that is, by becoming more like his uncle Shya, whom he resembles both in character and in looks, an observation confirmed by a flashback showing Shya (also played by Leo Fuchs) in traditional clothing, performing a marriage—and doing so without wanting a fee, as he just wants to make people happy. Uncle Shya's own loneliness, which parallels Nat's, is underscored in the scene following the ceremony. While everybody dances, uncle Shya is all by himself, without a single person sitting by his side. Indeed, we do not even see the other people; we only see their shadows on the wall while they are dancing and celebrating the wedding.

Having decided to pursue his uncle's trade, Nat pretends to go to Europe while in fact staying in the New World, where he reinvents himself. He changes his name from Silver to Gold and opens a human relations bureau on Grand Concourse and 158th Street, becoming a modern—that is, American—*shadkhn*.

Given this plotline, Judith Goldberg persuasively suggests that the language—Yiddish—is the only major element that identifies *Amerikaner Shadkhn* as a Jewish film. In contrast, I would argue that *Amerikaner Shadkhn* is profoundly steeped in Jewish culture, and that it anticipated *the* Jewish film persona, namely Allen's urban neurotic, who became almost instantly and internationally recognizable. While the film indeed celebrates success in America, it also emphasizes that the confluence of the city and wealth do not necessarily produce happiness. The film is deeply ambivalent. Consequently,

Figure 7.1. Flashback: Uncle Shya, the traditional *shadkhn*. Courtesy of Ariannė Ulmer Cipes.

Figure 7.2. Lonely Uncle Shya, surrounded by shadows of people dancing. Courtesy of Ariannė Ulmer Cipes.

a contemporary review in the *New York Post* opened with the remark that after watching the movie "we're still not sure whether [*Amerikaner Shadkhn* is] meant to be a serious drama with a solution (boy meets girl) or a rollicking comedy, spoofing the marriage broker institution even now in vogue amid Jewish family circles" (cited in Hoberman 319).

Not only is the film ambivalent, but it is also about ambivalence, about being torn, about inbetweenness. It presents the concept of the Jew as a cultural hybrid with a double consciousness; psyches trapped between the old and the new, having to negotiate partial acceptance and partial rejection; and a feeling of urban anxiety, although it is an anxiety shown as not only painful but also funny—and hence bearable. If Allen can be called the father of this neurotic city-Jew persona, Ulmer can be called its grandfather.

AMERIKANER SHADKHN AND *ANNIE HALL*

"A man complains to his psychiatrist that his brother-in-law thinks he's a chicken. When the doctor suggests putting him in a mental institution, the man claims: 'I would like to but we need the eggs.'" This joke, with which

Allen closes his reflection on human relationships in *Annie Hall*, is a paradox typical not only of what I call the persona of the urban neurotic Jew but also of the film itself,[16] and of *Amerikaner Shadkhn.*

One of the most memorable sequences from *Annie Hall* is the well-known dinner scene in which the protagonist Alvy Singer (Allen), a New York Jew, meets the gentile family of his girlfriend Annie Hall (Diane Keaton). This scene is built around both the contrasting conversations of Jews and gentiles at dinner and the spaces that they inhabit: the cramped, urban interiors of the former are contrasted with the brightly open, rural exteriors of the latter.

Here, Allen's use of the split screen directly and powerfully displays the contrast between the two families. This dichotomy is further strengthened by the *mise-en-scène* showing the worlds of the gentile Hall family and the Jewish Singer family, focusing on their differing table etiquette and noise levels, the divergent colors of their worlds, and, by implication, their different approaches to life. Both sound and colors are expressive of their emotional states. The Halls have their meal at midday, in the bright light that pours in through their windows, a reminder of the nature surrounding the Hall mansion. Unlike the Halls, the Singers have their meal enclosed in a cavelike interior. In and from this small apartment, nature is nowhere to be seen—except perhaps on the flower-print dresses of the women (Mast 131). The Halls, however, wear, and live within, patternless, colorless neutrals such as whites, off-whites, beiges, and grays—that is, earth tones that Allen always associates with goyism (and which become an important leitmotif in *Interiors,* the

Figure 7.3. Woody Allen's famous dinner scene in *Annie Hall.* Courtesy of MGM Home Entertainment.

film following *Annie Hall*). Visually, the harsh, clean lines of the Hall dining room sharply contrast with the chaos of the Singers' dining room, beyond whose walls lie not the fields and trees of nature but the noisy rollercoaster of New York's Coney Island. The Halls speak, if they speak at all, quietly and politely, one conversation at a time, about such banal topics as the weather, swap meets, and boating. The Singers all talk at once, creating a loud, semi-articulate noise, discussing rather depressing subjects such as failure, hospital visits, and deadly diseases.

From Alvy's perspective, Annie's family lives in a bright, sunny world, which supplies them with good health, wealth, and a sense of belonging. Alvy, both distraught and impressed by Annie's family during an Easter dinner, turns to the camera and tells the audience that Annie's family looks really healthy and American, and adds: "Nothing like my family. The two are like oil and water." Alvy's claim that the family looks "American" is particularly interesting, for his family is also American in that they were all born in the United States. But Alvy sees himself as an outsider, not an American, as a stranger from the hated New York City, a world of pessimism and darkness, a world, as he explains, where people fast to atone for sins they do not understand. His feeling of being an outsider is epitomized in one of the film's most memorable subjective images, namely when Allen depicts Alvy in the garb of a Hasidic Jew.[17]

At first sight, the vision of Hasidic Alvy has a clear meaning—the "freaky foreignness" of Jews, strangers in the American heartland of the clean, bright, open, tasteful, normal gentiles. While many rest with this reading, Gerald Mast rightly recognizes that Allen imbues this distinctive contrast with several twists below its simple surface (132). The shot of Hasidic Alvy does not really convey the Halls' view of him, not even that of the Jew-hater Grammy Hall (Helen Ludlum); rather, it mirrors the way Alvy perceives the Halls' gentile consciousness. Alvy's vision relates as much to the clear contrast between gentiles and Jews as to his paranoia and persecution complex, his own insecurities and discomfort. Earlier in the film, this belief of constantly being the object of scorn and ridicule is denoted in more detail. Alvy perceives anti-Semitism everywhere—not only in the looks of the Halls, but also in the mutterings under strangers' breaths. Simple questions such as "Did you eat?" are, in Alvy's mind, elided in the vernacular American pronunciation as "Djew eat?"

Moreover, while the dinner sequence constructs a visual and aural binary contrast between Jews and gentiles, Allen deconstructs this very binary opposition in the scene following the dinner. Whereas Alvy only notices the bright lights and healthful appearance of the Halls, the viewer is aware that Annie's brother Duane (Christopher Walken) suffers from feelings that exceed Alvy's own profound pessimism. Sitting on his bed in a dimly lit room, which is even darker than the Singers' dining room, Duane tells Alvy that

Figure 7.4. Hasidic Alvy, a stranger in the American heartland. Courtesy of MGM Home Entertainment.

he wants to confess something. He then describes his desire to kill himself by driving into the headlights of an oncoming car. Alvy is himself preoccupied with death, which is reflected in the two books he has bought Annie on their first date (*The Denial of Death* and *Death and Western Thought*), and similarly in Alvy's passion for Marcel Ophüls' classic documentary film *The Sorrow and the Pity*. Indeed, Alvy often whines about his obsession with death, although he does not view suicide as an appropriate action or solution. He therefore leaves Duane in his dark room, saying that he is "due on the planet earth."

In *Annie Hall*, Allen clearly disrupts Alvy's notion of Jewish difference. However, he shows the peculiar position of Jews in American society, one that is marginalized and alienated—despite forms of assimilation. This form of assimilation does not lead to the total disappearance of Jewish identity. This inbetweenness, Allen seems to say, has an impact not only on Jews as a group and their sense of belonging, but also on the individual, who is left feeling insecure and unhappy. One of the coping mechanisms is an intellectual approach to life. As Mast suggests, the image of the Jewish intellectual replaced the stereotype of the "money-counting Jew" (138). Part of this approach is an interest in psychoanalysis. In *Annie Hall,* as well as in many other Allen movies, the protagonist has been in therapy for many years. However, despite the interest in it, there is also an underlying suspicion of the techniques of Freudian psychoanalysis as a means to better understand human behavior. In Allen's movies, this suspicion is emphasized by the fact that therapists usually do not aid in making the protagonist happy or countering his *anhedonia,* that is, the inability to feel happiness. Along these lines, *Annie Hall*'s title was originally intended to be *Anhedonia*. Consequently, the film does not conclude with a happy ending, with the reunion of the two protagonists. Alvy's relationship to Annie—like his two previous marriages to Jewish women—fails. *Annie Hall* is, as Frank Krutnik labels it, a nervous romance, which is a response to the sexual revolution of the '60s challenging the ideology of heterosexual romance and the patriarchal conceptions of sex and sexuality (Krutnik). It thereby revises the genre of the romantic comedy, whose death Brian Henderson famously declared in the late '70s (22).

Amerikaner Shadkhn obviously predates the nervous romance and belongs to the genre of the romantic comedy ending with a happy marriage. Despite such obvious differences, I want to point to a number of striking similarities, to typical Allen themes (Lee 35) that are anticipated in *Amerikaner Shadkhn*: existential issues, such as questions of Jewish identity, responsibility, and feelings of difference from and ambivalence toward WASP society; intellectual approaches to life; urban settings; neurotic insecurities and, in connection with this, the interest in, yet suspicion of, the techniques of Freudian psychoanalysis as a method for a better understanding of human thinking and life; and, last but not least, problematic gender relations.

Already the paradoxical title, *Amerikaner Shadkhn*, combines the very traditional Yiddish figure of the *shadkhn* with *American* identity and thereby alludes to the clash of cultures and the consequent state of double consciousness or inbetweenness, the inescapable ambivalence, that I have described as the core of *Annie Hall*. When, after his eighth failed engagement, the protagonist of *Amerikaner Shadkhn* decides to become a *shadkhn,* he does not simply copy his uncle's business or looks. Instead, Nat modernizes the matchmaker's image and Americanizes the business: he does not wear a beard and hat like a traditional *shadkhn*, but rather he dresses as a diplomat; and the sign on his door does not say *shadkhn* but "advisor for human relations," which his friend and butler Maurice (Judel Dubinsky) misinterprets as edible "human relishes." In order to strengthen this modernized version and make it more scientific, intellectual, and thorough, he also brings in specialists: a doctor, a psychiatrist, a lawyer, and a rabbi.

He is particularly proud of the psychiatrist, "an expert on love problems"—however, we never really observe her in action or see her accomplishing much, and Nat's new approach once again lends itself to a comic remark, when Maurice calls the new business "schadchenology." Nat also proposes to update the business using modern methods embodied in the "Schadchen Trust," which gives the matchmakers working for him a salary (while he—out of *mentshlekhkayt,* or guilt, or emulation of his uncle—works for free).

Ambivalence is further emphasized on the linguistic level. The film is filled with comic stutters and other jokes on language, and has nearly as much English as Yiddish. The degree of innocent alienation from tradition is reflected by the comic acts (Hoberman 337). Most characters mix Yiddish with English, especially typical American expressions such as "You are so nice," which is a favorite expression of Judith's mother. (Judith [Judith Ababarnel] is the young woman who will eventually become Nat's wife, thus ending the film traditionally with a Jewish wedding.) Yet the people using English are by no means presented as ideals of assimilation. They are shown as comic or even ridiculous figures, such as a series of silly and overly assimilated women (who are contrasted by comic figures symbolizing tradition, such as old *shadkhn* figures wearing beards and derby hats while protesting against Nat's new business). These people have not quite found their place in the New World, as they are either hanging on to old traditions or striving for assimilation, which Ulmer portrays as overassimilation. Despite this pursuit of assimilation, despite the fact that Nat and many other characters are Americanized, being Jewish still plays a role in their lives. It is neither Judaism (a main theme in *Grine Felder*), nor orthodox

Figure 7.5. The American matchmaker and his modernized version of "schadchenology." Courtesy of Arianné Ulmer Cipes.

and conservative faith (portrayed so negatively in *Di Klyatshe*), but a form of cultural Jewish identity. For example, when Nat looks for a possible husband for Judith, it is still important that he be Jewish; intermarriage is not even considered by any of the involved parties.

It is not only this focus on ambivalence and inbetweenness, but also the film's humor that marks *Amerikaner Shadkhn* as coming from a Jewish tradition. It is a humor that, according to Sarah Blacher Cohen's definition in *The Jewish Wry*, could be described as a collision of the serious with the profane, the sad with the joyful (11).[18] In one impressive and funny sequence, seemingly without transition, Maurice and Nat start a lighthearted drinking song,[19] despite the fact that Maurice is obviously seriously depressed at the beginning of the scene and Nat constantly seems to be suffering from melancholy. As Nat's sister Elvy (Anna Guskin) says at one point, he is a schlemiel, someone who has bad luck, who is "the hidden architect of his misfortune" (Reik 41), and who represents the antithesis of the macho type (Ziv and Zajdman viii). Americanized Nat is such a schlemiel figure. The end of his eighth engagement certainly was unfortunate; but his behavior toward Judith, his unwillingness to see her as the perfect match that she is and that he feels her to be, comes rather from his *anhedonia* and his troubled and ambivalent relationship to women. Gender relationships are further complicated by the urban surroundings:

> The City offers a setting for the exploration of the historical ambiguities of the Jewish experience. In the process of emancipation, the city is also the bridge from tradition to modernity. It makes the move from communal status to ethnic and personal identity possible. (Desser and Friedman 6)

In *Amerikaner Shadkn* it is Judith, above all, who recognizes this fact, in a scene in which she describes New York as a slippery skating rink. On this skating rink she likes to socialize with "crackpots," as her mother complainingly points out, that is, with "artists, actors, dancers, and other peculiar people." Here the simplicity of the Old World's *shtetl* is not to be found. In the New World, a new sense of identity and consequently a new shape of gender relationships spring from this *urban* experience.

CONCLUSION

Focusing on the main characters of *Amerikaner Shadkhn* and *Annie Hall,* one could claim that both Nat and Alvy are neurotic urbanites. They are modern and assimilated intellectuals, yet they are not fully at home in their urban American home. Moreover, Nat and Alvy are similar not only in being characterized by their feelings of inbetweenness, the assimilation and Americanization of Jewish identity into a non-Jewish lifestyle, but also in that they are schlemiel figures who feel and reflect their *anhedonia* and existential turmoil. This turmoil has its origins in the absence of Judaism in their lives but the presence of a Jewish sensibility; the humor; the intellectual and self-reflective approach to life; and, last but not least, their troubled relationships to women. The main difference between Nat and Alvy is a matter of position and degree: Allen not only moves the "crackpot" from margin to center, but also exaggerates the characteristics of this Jewish neurotic hero.

Bill Krohn proposes that Nat's marriage to a woman "who represents everything new, after the comic detour of the Schadchen Trust, signals Ulmer's acceptance of his own new identity: during and after the war years, he became a working Hollywood director, an ardent patriot, and supporter of the free enterprise system" (64). Similarly, Hoberman entitles the chapter on *Amerikaner Shadkhn* "Married to America." One could furthermore argue that in *Amerikaner Shadkhn* Ulmer does not just tell a story of a matchmaker, but he himself becomes a matchmaker, namely between Yiddish cinema and American film.[20] For this European Jew, the United States turned out not to be a detour, yet it was no place like home. Just as marriage is not easy for Nat, just as *Amerikaner Shadkhn* is filled with moments of in-between-ness, gloominess, and discomfort (despite the wedding at the end), Ulmer does not believe in love at first sight or a simple, romantic love. Rather, in psychoanalytical terms, he stresses *Beziehungsarbeit* (relationship work), which is unstable and never-ending. Thus, in a vein similar to Allen's deconstruction of a stable notion of Jewishness and his celebration of a particular American-Jewish culture, which is alienated and marginalized and therefore lends itself to insecurities not to be overcome by intellect or psychoanalysis, Ulmer emphasizes ambivalence, not the total disappearance of Jewish identity, in his final and most American Yiddish film on an assimilated, wealthy, urban Jew. An American idiom might serve as a symbol for his route: "When you get to the fork, take it." For a Jewish American persona created by Ulmer or Allen, there is no way out but this one.

NOTES

1. The only exception was Darryl F. Zanuck's 20th Century-Fox, the "Goy Studio."
2. As Stephen J. Whitfield elaborates, there is no single definition of *Jewishness*. Whitfield also claims that the United States may be the site "that has most fully tested the category of Jew, where the definition is loose enough to embrace culture rather than religious belief or the identity of one's mother" (10).
3. See also Neal Gabler's thorough analysis in *An Empire of Their Own*.

4. Yiddish is a European Jewish language, which evolved during the Middle Ages. It is the vernacular of the Ashkenazim (from *Ashkenaz*, the medieval Hebrew name for Germany); and, like English, it is a fusion tongue, namely, an amalgam of High Middle German, Hebrew, various Slavic languages, and Aramaic.

5. In "From *The American Shadchan* to *Annie Hall*," Betty Yetta Forman describes *mentshlekhkayt* as "the standard of human decency and responsibility which formed the idea of shtetl life and the subsequent American immigration community" (6). Despite expectations raised by the title, Forman hardly devotes any attention to *Amerikaner Shadkhn*, and her article differs greatly from my approach and analysis.

6. New York's Lower East Side was the largest settlement of Jewish immigrants. In 1910, this city within a city reached its maximum density, cramming over half a million people into only a few square miles.

7. Theirs were the first sound films to "green" the Yiddish screen with extensive exteriors. The lyrical optimism of their movies stands in marked contrast to the sanctimonious guilt of the American generational melodramas, as well as to the morbid fatalism of later Polish films (Hoberman 235).

8. William Edlin praised the film in saying: "It is a joy and a great satisfaction to be able to state that *Grine Felder* is a film we can take pride in; a film which we can point to—the beginning of a new epoch in the experiment of producing American-made Yiddish movies" (cited in Hoberman 250). *Grine Felder* repeated *Yidl's* success. In *Literarische Bleter,* Nakhman Mayzel, who had recently left Warsaw for New York, lauded *Grine Felder* as an "outstanding artistic and financial success, unparalleled in the history of Yiddish film in America" (cited in Hoberman 251).

9. *Shund* is a term of contempt indicating literary or theatrical "trash" and denoting variously a vulgar display, an inept mishmash, a mass-produced trifle, or a piece of sentimental claptrap. *Shund* encompasses the full range of Yiddish kitsch, from the primitive Biblical operettas to grim domestic melodramas. It was the first art form expressing the distinctively American Yiddish community. True *shund* must be uplifting, pandering variously to nationalist, family, or religious sentiments (Hoberman 206, 207).

10. It should also be noted that in America, Yiddish films were considered to be "foreign," both by the general public and the New York State Board of Censors, even if they were made in New Jersey.

11. Hoberman compares these two Ulmer movies in filmic terms, stating that the "interiors are dramatically lit and exhibit his characteristic use of odd angles and bold perspective (for example, positioning outsized furniture in the foreground of the frame). The exterior set, with its onion-dome facades and plywood cottages, is far more elaborate than *Grine Felder's*. The pace, however, is less fluid" (266).

12. Yet it is worth pointing out that the fall of 1939 was the most successful period in the history of Yiddish cinema, as if Jews tried to express their solidarity at the movie hall. Therefore, as Hoberman argues, "the strong competition from other Yiddish releases was surely a factor. Indeed, given the film's disturbingly downbeat romance, continual emphasis on poverty and superstition, and blunt criticism of tradition, it could easily have performed even more poorly" (306).

13. "The performers tend toward stylized postures, and the frame is complicated by the use of foreground props. With its crazy angles and skewed lampposts, Glubsk

suggests the confluence of Marc Chagall and *The Cabinet of Dr. Caligari*" (Hoberman 303).

14. Noah Isenberg therefore rightly calls *Amerikaner Shadkhn* "almost a sequel." (See chapter 1, "Permanent Vacation," in this book.)

15. This is the main reason for the journalist Goldie Charles to assume that Ulmer's protagonist is homosexual, even though Ulmer never makes a clear reference on this account (Grissemann 140). However, I read his instability and "gender trouble" merely as traits of the Jewish neurotic urbanite on whom I focus in this chapter.

16. *Annie Hall* is *the* screen romance of the late 1970s. For Allen, as Neil Sinyard points out, "it marked a significant shift of direction, in subject (from cine-pastiche to self-revelation) and in persona (from stooge to sage). The film's huge popularity and Oscar-winning success (Woody winning Oscars for writing and direction, Diane Keaton for best actress, the movie being voted best film) testified to his remarkable dexterity in being able to transform private angst into public art" (46).

17. In contrast to Ulmer, at least as a child Allen spoke Yiddish (Baxter 11). He was brought up Orthodox, and until he was bar mitzvahed at thirteen he had to attend Hebrew school (Lax 33). However, he resented all organized faith. In his films all references to Judaism and Hasidic rabbis are derisive. This is the case from his first film, *Take the Money and Run* (1969), in which the protagonist agrees to be a "guinea pig" for a new drug. This drug turns him briefly into a rabbi discussing the Talmud.

18. Irvin Howe claims that at "the heart of Yiddish literature, often in its most earnest works, one finds Jewish humor—the homely anecdote or joke. It is a remarkable fact that this people of tragic destiny insisted on making laughter a major strand of their folk expression" (16).

19. The songs further convey two things: Ulmer's passion for music and, as Isenberg remarks in reference to Alexander Horwarth, music or musical figures as a means of highlighting the allegories of a typical emigrant situation (*Perennial Detour* 15).

20. Bret Wood sees this process of Americanization particularly on an aesthetic level. He points to the stylistic similarities between Nat's wedding party and the phantasmatic jazz orchestra in *Detour* (cited in Grissemann 144).

BIBLIOGRAPHY

Baxter, John. *Woody Allen: A Biography* (New York: Carroll and Graf, 1999).

Cohen, Sarah Blacher. "Introduction," in *The Jewish Wry: Essays on Jewish Humor*, ed. Sarah Blacher Cohen (Detroit: Wayne State University Press, 1990), 1–15.

Desser, David, and Lester D. Friedman. *American Jewish Filmmakers*, 2nd ed. (Champaign: University of Illinois Press, 2004).

Erens, Patricia. *The Jew in American Cinema* (Bloomington: Indiana University Press, 1984).

———. "Mentshlekhkayt Conquers All: The Yiddish Cinema in America," *Film Comment* 12, no.1 (January–February 1976): 48–64.

Forman, Betty Yetta. "From *The American Shadchan* to *Annie Hall*: The Life and Legacy of Yiddish Film in America," *National Jewish Monthly*, November 1977, 4–13.

Gabler, Neal. *An Empire of Their Own: How the Jews Invented Hollywood* (New York: Crown, 1988).

Goldberg, Judith. *Laughter through Tears: The Yiddish Cinema* (Fairleigh Dickinson University Press, 1982).

Grissemann, Stefan. *Mann im Schatten: Der Filmemacher Edgar G. Ulmer* (Vienna: Zsolnay, 2003).

Henderson, Brian. "Romantic Comedy Today: Semi-Tough or Impossible?" *Film Quarterly* 31, no. 4 (1978): 11–23.

Hoberman, J. *Bridge of Light: Yiddish Film between Two Worlds* (New York: Schocken Books, 1991).

Howe, Irvin. "The Nature of Jewish Laughter," in *The Jewish Wry: Essays on Jewish Humor*, ed. Sarah Blacher Cohen (Detroit: Wayne State University Press, 1990), 16–24.

Isenberg, Noah. "Perennial Detour: The Cinema of Edgar G. Ulmer and the Experience of Exile," *Cinema Journal* 43, no. 2 (Winter 2004): 3–25.

Krohn, Bill. "King of the Bs," *Film Comment* 19, no. 4 (July–August 1983): 60–64.

Krutnik, Frank. "The Faint Aroma of Performing Seals: The 'Nervous' Romance and the Comedy of the Sexes," *Velvet Light Trap* 26 (1990): 57–72.

Lax, Eric. *Woody Allen: A Biography*, 2nd ed. (Cambridge, Mass.: Da Capo Press, 2000).

Lee, Sander H. *Eighteen Woody Allen Films Analyzed: Anguish, God and Existentialism* (Jefferson, N.C.: McFarland, 2002).

Lipsitz, George. "The New York Intellectuals: Samuel Fuller and Edgar Ulmer," in *Time Passages: Collective Memory and American Popular Culture*, 7th ed. (Minneapolis: University of Minnesota Press, 2001), 179–210.

Mast, Gerald. "The Neurotic Jew as American Clown," in *The Jewish Wry: Essays on Jewish Humor*, ed. Sarah Blacher Cohen (Detroit: Wayne State University Press, 1990), 125–140.

Reik, Theodore. *Jewish Wit* (New York: Gamut Press, 1962).

Schürmann, Ernst. *The Primacy of the Visual: A Tribute to Edgar G. Ulmer* (San Francisco: Goethe Institute, n.d.).

Sinyard, Neil. *The Films of Woody Allen* (New York: Exeter Books, 1987).

Whitfield, Stephen J. *In Search of American Jewish Culture* (Hanover, N.H.: Brandeis University Press, 2001).

Ziv, Avener, and Anat Zajdman, eds. *Semites and Stereotypes: Characteristics of Jewish Humor* (Westport, Conn.: Greenwood Press, 1993).

FILMS CITED

Amerikaner Shadkhn (*American Matchmaker*, 1940)
Annie Hall (1977)

Der Dibek (*The Dybbuk*, 1937)
Der Mazldiker Bokher (*Lucky Boy,* 1935)
Detour (1945)
Di Klyatshe (*The Light Ahead*, 1939)
Grine Felder (*Green Fields*, 1937)
Take the Money and Run (1969)
Tsvey Shvester (Two Sisters, 1938)
Yankl der Shmid (*The Singing Blacksmith/Yankl the Blacksmith*, 1938)
Yevreiskoye Schastye/Menakhem Mendl (Jewish Luck, 1925)
Yidl mitn Fidl (Yiddle [little Jew] with His Fiddle, 1936)

8

A World Destroyed by Gold

Shared Allegories of Capital in Wagner's *Ring* and Ulmer's *Isle of Forgotten Sins*

Andrew Repasky McElhinney

Lord, smile on those who smile,
Hosannah!
Grant them the wealth to live in style.
Hosannah!
Pardon their crimes against the masses.
Hosannah! Hosannah! Hosannah! Hosannah! Hosannah! Hosannah!
May God bless Rockefeller,
May God bless Henry Ford
May God bless J. P. Morgan, too,
And his great treasure hoard.
God bless Big Oil and Coal and Steel,
Send them their just reward.
May God bless sex appeal,
When wealthy men get bored,
God keep their faith and profits high,
And though the poor may starve and die,
Make sure no Earthly court will try the rich
Who rule the Earth the way you rule the sky.
Almighty Lord!

—Bertolt Brecht, *Happy End: A Melodrama with Songs*, 1929, translated by Michael Feingold, 2006

THE BIRTH OF CINEMA OUT OF MUSIC

Before he acquiesced to the fact that only music can communicate what fails words and tableaux, Richard Wagner sought to mount *Gesamtkunstwerk*—

dramatic pageants where music, text, and special effects synthesize to create a total work of art, greater than the sum of its elements. With the advent of motion-picture photography just before the turn of the nineteenth century, the movement-image became the sibling to music, insomuch as both now possessed music's previously unique possibility of expressing the inexpressible.

Western cinema, and especially synchronized "sound" cinema, makes making "total works of art" almost accidental, as the medium inherently lends itself to cathartic, overpowering, all-encompassing spectacle whose root can be found in Wagner's operatic revolutions of the nineteenth century.

Radical new theater techniques had been in the Norse air since Georg Büchner left his observationist plays unfinished in the 1830s and they, perhaps because of their unfinished nature, elicited a startling, strange, new dramaturgy that moved narrative along at an unstable emotional pace. Though still underrecognized in its great significance, Frank Wedekind's most indelible contribution to post-Wagner world drama was fusing Büchner's disjointed (unfinished) hyperrealism with his own distinct form of burlesque, at a time when Scandinavian drama, especially Henrik Ibsen, ruled the stage with a revolutionary, "modern" approach to the representation of European psychology. For the first time on the Western stage, unsolvable ambiguity ignited both structure and content, melding the effect into one inseparable element of performance.

From Wedekind's experimental performance works, infused with Büchner, Bertolt Brecht synthesized much of his style, so much so that we can, on an elemental level, understand Brecht's theater as the flower of Wedekindian grotesque and Wagnerian *Gesamtkunstwerk*. Because of its privileged place at the intersection of German cinema between the wars, Brecht's theatrical influence was inseparable from feature-length cinema, especially once the sound era ostensibly relegated the movement-image to an imitation of theater. Brecht's theater speaks most pointedly today as the European exclamation of the first half of the twentieth century. As he himself tells us, "art is not a mirror held up to reality, but a hammer with which to shape it."

But indirectly, a sort of declawed Brecht permeates. His effects of alienation, seduction, and propaganda are used to trigger or merely to facilitate any old narrative today. Everything is Brechtian in our post-postmodern era. His use of the lurid, of the enticing-and-yet-forbidden, to fuel theater is the dramatic technique on which Western sound cinema (and its advertising) is based. Ultimately, when method is inseparable from narrative, the medium is the message.

With the premiere of *Happy End* in 1929, Brecht summarized this polyformatic genre that we see in his theater and in Western sound cinema's imitation of theater as "melodrama with song." Brechtian "melodramas with song" are the defining genre of the twentieth century because they provide a format in which entertainment and allegory can coexist in an easily digestible, and perhaps commercial, form.

To a large extent—and this is made all the more convincing an observation because of the existence of exceptions, like the work of Chaplin and Dreyer—Western sound cinema has consisted of individuals creating less ambiguous representations of the personality possibilities they understand to be relevant to the items they wish to juxtapose against them. Ergo, all cinema is allegory, just as all media is propaganda, and all theater is manipulation of illusion and disillusionment.

Germany from 1919 to 1933 was a creative golden age. In that era, German theater, silent cinema, and music fused European aesthetics into technique, and for over a decade produced the most indelible images and sounds of the twentieth century. Weimar Germany is now a time of legends—Reinhardt, Brecht, Wiene, Murnau, Lang, Pabst, Weill, Schoenberg . . . It was in this fertile milieu that Edgar George Ulmer came of age. Ulmer would go on to excel at cinematic "melodramas with song."

RECALLED TO LIFE

Western cinema has excelled at melodramas with songs—if, indeed, it is not almost totally comprised of them. Classics as diverse as *L'Atalante* (1934), *The Wizard of Oz* (1939), *Casablanca* (1942), *The Night of the Hunter* (1955), *The Searchers* (1956), *Dr. Strangelove* (1964), *Aguirre Wrath of God* (1972), *Jaws* (1975), *Stand By Me* (1986), *The Cook, The Thief, His Wife and Her Lover* (1989), and *The Rock* (1995) all fit into what we can consider the "melodrama with song" genre.

Ulmer made melodramas with songs in nearly every genre, often in diptychs—*Thunder Over Texas* (1934) / *The Naked Dawn* (1955), *Detour* (1945) / *Murder Is My Beat* (1955), *The Wife of Monte Christo* (1946) / *Pirates of Capri* (1949)—which afford Ulmer a first and last word on genre archetypes. Like Shakespeare or the Greeks before him, Ulmer frequently assembled preexisting narratives into a new, inherently more complex whole. Ulmer's reworking of *Hamlet* as *Strange Illusion* (1945), and his reworking of Wagner's four-part music drama *Der Ring Des Nibelungen* in *Isle of Forgotten Sins* (1943), are potent reimaginings of world classics, almost postmodern in the way their simplification for the screen illustrates core truths of the source that more straightforward productions often miss. Ulmer's deconstructions, usually heavily related to his budgets, are dramaturgical inventions unthinkable in any other circumstances than their own. It is this unique essentialism that propels intermittently moldy melodrama forward with a contrastingly sophisticated psychological expression of the profound uneasiness at the illusion of representation that any performance phenomenon offers.

Ulmer's cinema is remarkable because of its synthesis of Weimar-era theatrics at a time when the cinema afforded a massive world audience, and the European political upheavals of the 1930s created a direct migration from the film capitals of Europe, and especially Germany, to Hollywoodland, U.S.A. Ulmer's "golden hour" was his time at the Producers Releasing Corporation (PRC), where he directed some of his most evocative and distinct work, including *Bluebeard* (1944), *Detour,* and *Club Havana* (1945).

Ulmer's first major PRC movie was *Isle of Forgotten Sins,* first released in 1943 and later reissued as *Monsoon*. In it, Ulmer and composer-conductor Leo Erdody shape a dreamy South Seas adventure yarn into a meditation on philosophical themes developed in Wagner's *Ring* operas, expressing these dramatic concerns with liberal quotations of Wagnerian leitmotifs woven into the movie's almost constant underscoring. An understanding of Wagner, and the significance of each quoted *Ring* leitmotif, adds an immense layer of illumination and unexpected metaphorical depth to *Isle of Forgotten Sins*.

Figure 8.1. Film poster for *Isle of Forgotten Sins.* Courtesy of Arianné Ulmer Cipes.

CGI CAN NEVER TOP THIS!

Just as the first part of Wagner's *Ring, Das Rheingold,* begins with an unmodulated 136-bar prelude based on the chord of E-flat major (meant to represent the Rhine), *Isle of Forgotten Sins* begins with the sound of the sea. In Ulmer's work, the water sounds are followed by the swelling of an unseen orchestra and a camera pan over driftwood, on which the main titles appear. Erdody's overture fills the soundtrack, resembling an orchestra warming up before a concert. All sorts of musical phrases and percussive crescendos fly out of Erdody's pit, until this cacophony is overwhelmed by an unseen choir harmonizing, giving voice to powerful forces of nature that will eventually and apocalyptically deluge the human squabbling at the heart of *Isle of Forgotten Sins'* melodrama.

To illustrate the importance of the score's construction and its multiple authorship to the viewer, Erdody's credit reads "Music by ERDODY [. . .] ," the ellipses denoting that Erdody's contribution is the final redaction of music, and that his score will draw on other composers.

Isle of Forgotten Sins opens with a subjective, nearly point-of-view tracking shot that winds down a corridor of bedrooms in a vaguely Asian setting. It is clear that we are in a brothel and that a still-unseen madam is waking her "girls" to ready themselves for fresh sailors. The musical underscoring is a noodling oriental theme that Erdody and Ulmer use to connote the exoticness, and also the toil of the prostitutes.

Marge Williams (Gale Sondergaard) is revealed to be the madam of the brothel, called the Isle of Forgotten Sins, which officially operates as a legit nightclub with live music, food, and drink. Marge reminds the women that they are under heavy scrutiny by a magistrate who is seeking any provocation to close the place. Marge tells them to clean up the floor show ("All rough stuff is taboo"), and a gong announces the opening of the establishment for the night.

Marge has a special relationship with the new prostitute, Diane (Rita Quigley). In a private moment, Marge tells Diane that it's not easy when your "modesty has taken a beating" and reminds her that "giving patrons an eyeful is a stepping stone on [your] way home." Already, Ulmer has presented us with a world where love has been affected by capital, if not conjoined to it, and where capital and the pursuit of capital force individuals to do things that they would otherwise be uncomfortable with. In almost every one of his motion pictures, Ulmer treats money, as Al Roberts says so pointedly in *Detour*, as "paper crawling with germs." This is a direct correlation to *Der Ring*, where omnipotent power can only be achieved by theft, the violation of nature, and the forswearing of love.

In the tradition of other great Ulmer-film heroine portrayals like those of Janet Smith, Vera, and Jenny Hager, Sondergaard's approach to playing Marge is ambiguous. In her aside with Diane, we must ask the following: is Marge just trying to protect her investment in the woman? is she seducing her? or does Diane represent a daughter or a younger version of Marge herself? Ulmer often sets up these character dualities, as they serve to transform the under-written into the fertilely suggestive by the nearly total ambiguity of performance. In montage theory, this technique is named the Kuleshov effect.

The action of *Isle of Forgotten Sins* moves aboard a docked ship belonging to Jack Burke (Frank Fenton). Below deck, Burke has tied up shipmate Clancy (John Carradine). Stealing his money, Burke makes for the Isle of Forgotten Sins. Arriving there, he takes Marge to her office, tells her that her lover Clancy is dead, and proposes that they run off together. As Marge is weighing her options, Clancy bounds in, mad as hell, and he and Burke fight.

Burke and Clancy's sparring is gleeful and joyous; they attack each other with a verve and flirtation that physically illustrates the complex and often contradictory bonds they share. Almost immediately, the men break the table lamp and the room plunges into near darkness. Here, Ulmer undercranks the camera and the drama gains momentum by being captured in a jittery fast motion. Clancy and Burke's fisticuffs spill into the nightclub centrum, and in a matter of moments they have nearly destroyed the place. The patrons are greatly amused that the club is living up to its wild reputation. After Clancy has beaten Burke unconscious, a plantation owner named Carruthers (Sidney Toler) injects himself into the fray and leads the club in celebrating the new champ, buying all a round of drinks.

Money makes Burke and Clancy fast friends again. Clancy has recognized Carruthers, through his distinctive "banshee laugh," as a missing sea captain named Krogan. Six months earlier, Krogan had been captain of the *Tropic Star*, which sank under mysterious circumstances, taking its cargo of three million dollars in gold to a watery grave. Clancy surmises that Krogan sank the ship on purpose and reckons that Krogan must have the gold on his island, or that the treasure is still with the sunken ship. The appearance of Krogan's first mate, now using the name Johnny Pacific (Rick Vallin), confirms to Clancy that Carruthers is Krogan. Clancy tells Burke that there will be "so much money for both of us" that they will have "no reason to double cross each other." Clancy and Burke shake hands on joining forces and pledge to fight "back-to-back," not between themselves.

Chaos again erupts at the Isle of Forgotten Sins as a man falls from the balcony onto the main dance floor and dies, having been shot by Olga (Betty Amann), one of the dancers. The visiting magistrate places everyone in the club under "technical arrest," leading to riotous panic breaking out as patrons and club employees alike scramble to escape the law.

Burke, Clancy, Marge, and some of Marge's women flee in Burke's ship with the club's cash. They set their course for Moran Island, where Carruthers/Krogan has his plantation. Burke and Clancy plot to use the women as a distraction for Krogan and Pacific while they snoop around to figure out what has become of the *Tropic Star's* gold. For their part, Clancy promises Marge and the other women a share despite Burke's objections. Diane wants nothing to do with gold, and her forfeited share is claimed at gunpoint by Olga, who has also fled to the island.

The action switches to Krogan, Johnny, and their concubine Luana (Veda Ann Borg) on Moran Island. As they watch Burke, Clancy, and Marge arrive on Burke's boat, we hear the first Wagner leitmotiv quoted on the soundtrack, as shown in figure 8.2. It's Hunding's theme from Act I of *Die Walküre*, the second of Wagner's four *Ring* operas. In *Walküre*, Sieglinde has been separated from her twin brother Siegmund and forced into a marriage with Hunding, a warrior from an uncivilized tribe. Act I begins with Siegmund finding Sieglinde in Hunding's hut, where she lives as an abused sex slave. Wounded and fleeing pursuers, Siegmund asks who she is and where he is. Sieglinde replies, "Dies Haus und dies Weib sind Hundings Eigen," roughly, "This house and this woman are Hunding's possessions"; and, with that line, Hunding's leitmotiv sounds on a muted horn. In *Isle of Forgotten Sins*, the horn call represents the pending battle between Clancy-Burke and Krogan-Pacific, just as in *Walküre* it anticipates the Hunding-versus-Siegmund battle at the climax of the second act. In *Der Ring*, the horn's balefulness painfully evokes Sieglinde's imprisoning marriage to Hunding, and in *Isle of Forgotten Sins* it evokes the way the women are treated as objects by men.

In one of the most lyrical moments of *Isle of Forgotten Sins*, Marge and the other women go on a moonlit swim with Krogan and Pacific. The soundtrack merges music, the sound of water, and the chatting of the characters into an intriguing ambient soundscape; where the story is being told visually, the soundtrack is a muddled reflection of the emotions displayed and sug-

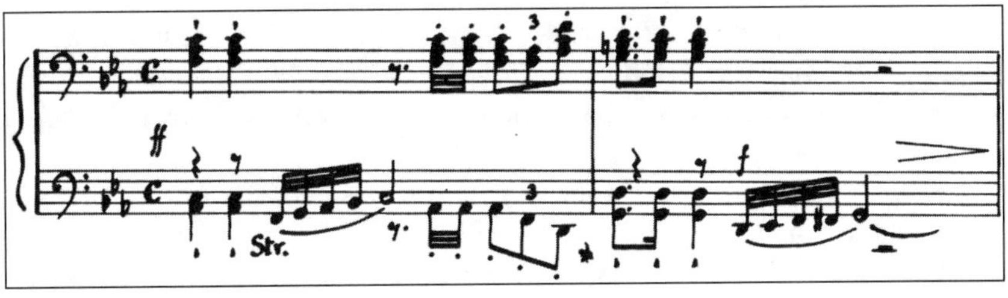

Figure 8.2.

gested on the screen. Ulmer's pioneering use of the limitations of his sound, where we get the gist rather than word-for-word audibility, anticipates Robert Altman's deservedly famous layered stereo soundscapes, and illustrates yet again Ulmer's miraculous skill at using the meagerness of his budget to his artistic advantage.

As Krogan forces himself on one of the women in the water, *Isle of Forgotten Sins* cuts to Clancy and Burke searching the plantation house. Clancy finds a map of where the *Tropic Star* went down, and he and Burke surmise that the gold is still at the bottom of the sea, ripe for looting.

Forty-two minutes into *Isle of Forgotten Sins*, the twenty-four-minute centerpiece deep-sea diving sequence commences. Clancy commands the ship and air bellows, while Burke goes down, an air line and microphone his umbilical cord to the surface. Burke is represented underwater by Ulmer photographing a puppet in a tank. The *Rheingold* E-flat-major Prelude chord emerges, as if from the depths of the brine, on the soundtrack.

In *Rheingold*, the head god, Wotan, in acquiescence to the nagging of his wife Fricka, has hired giants, Fafner and brother Fasolt, to build a home. With it, Fricka hopes for a hearth that will keep her adulterous husband from further infidelities. However, fearing the destruction of the gods, Wotan has turned Fricka's dream house into a fortress and agreed (earnestly or not—it is never clear) to trade Fricka's sister Freia, goddess of youth, to Fafner and Fasolt as payment for the castle (named Valhalla). Not only is Fricka outraged at this selling of her sister, but the race of gods clamors for Freia's return because they age rapidly when not revitalized by her magic apples. Wotan turns to crafty half-god, and sometimes adversary, Loge to help free Freia from his contract with the giants. Loge recounts how the Nibelung gnome Alberich has recently gained a gold hoard by stealing the magic Rheingold—which can only be taken from nature by the renunciation of love—and forging it into a magic ring granting omnipotence. Loge suggests that Alberich's booty, gained via the ring's magic, might prove a worthy substitute payment. Enticed, the giants agree to accept the treasure in lieu of Freia. Amorally but legally, Wotan and Loge then trick and trap Alberich, who under threat of death relinquishes the ring and the hoard to the gods, but not before he curses the ring, and all who come into contact with it, with envy, unslakable lust, and death. These events, in the concluding part of *Der Ring*, *Götterdämmerung,* result in the immolation of the gods and the rebirth of the natural world though a catastrophic flood.

In *Isle of Forgotten Sins*, we have a simplification of the *Rheingold* argument, where Ulmer reduces Wagner's panoptic *Ring* universe to a relatively elemental story of one pair of crime partners using a second to help them steal some gold—the equivalent of the *Rheingold* subplot wherein Wotan and Loge (re)steal the gold from Alberich, who first stole it from the Rhine. Just as Wotan is unwilling to renounce love but desires unlimited power and therefore needs Alberich to steal the gold, Krogan-Pacific need Clancy-Burke to obtain the treasure for them from the bottom of the ocean.

One of Wagner's greatest dramatic reforms was his attention to soundscape. His music, and music in general he would argue, is meant to invoke the drama as well as the movement within the created space—the descent and return to Nibelheim in *Rheingold* or "Siegfried's Rhine Journey" in *Götterdämmerung* are but the two of the most prominent examples of this "cinematic" technique in *Der Ring*. Wagner's dramatic innovations were not confined to the music and text of his shows; rather, with the construction of the Bayreuth Festival House, he moved performing art closer to installation and away from presentation by seeking a total effect. With that in mind, the Bayreuth orchestra pit is covered, so that the audience's vision is directed to the stage, and the sonorities of the instrumentation blend seamlessly with the actors' voices. Thus, the audience is immersed in the created world and therefore must navigate its own role in the drama and allegory at hand. The contemporary parallel to the effect of Wagner's covered orchestra pit and a movie's nondiegetic scoring, once we see the interchangeability of the disciplines of music drama, opera, and movies, is what we name the "cinematic."

At first, Burke's excursion under the sea in *Isle of Forgotten Sins* brings no sign of the treasure. He remarks to Clancy that there is "nothing but sand" at the bottom of the sea. On the soundtrack, the Rhinemaidens' lament for their stolen Rheingold punctuates Clancy's frustration. In *Rheingold*, the gold is stolen from its rightful place in nature, and through the power of the renunciation of love by Alberich directly, and Wotan indirectly, it takes on a supernatural importance that brings about the destruction of the world order. In *Isle of Forgotten Sins*, Ulmer/Erdody use this allusion to underscore how money taints love, and greed leads to destruction.

Clancy stirs the frustrated Burke on, telling him not to be discouraged because the gold's "got to be somewhere." Burke urges Clancy to "check the map." Dramatically parallel, the motif of Erda's warning of the gold's destructive force from *Rheingold* follows his line (figure 8.3). Clancy finds the wrecked *Tropic Star* and Ulmer/Erdody harness the exuberant music that accompanies the revelation of the treasure in scene 1 of *Rheingold* (figure 8.4).

For the next few minutes, quotations from *Rheingold*'s prelude, the Rhinemaidens' lament, and Erda's warning repeat on the soundtrack. Clancy ascends from the depths; his relief at being safely back on the surface is expressed by a repetition of the joyous "Rheingold Revelation" leitmotiv. All is not calm on the surface, however—as the *Rheingold* prelude sounds below, a tremendous monsoon (represented by naturalistic sound effects and the double exposure

Figure 8.3.

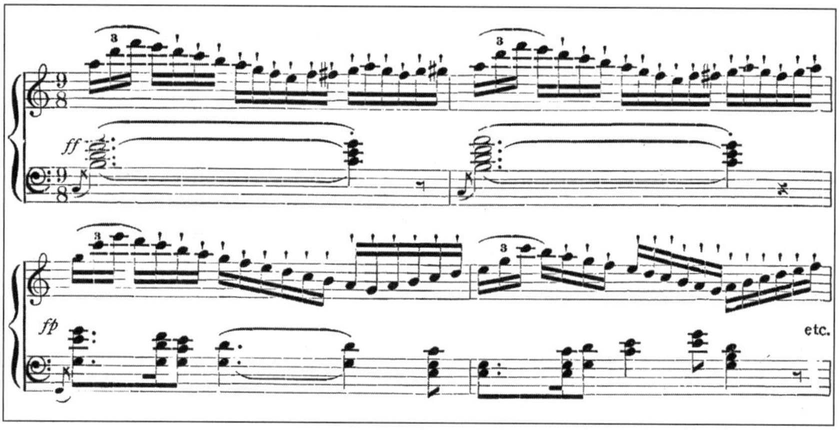

Figure 8.4.

of stock footage) builds in the sky above. Just as Wagner often incorporates diegetic sounds (e.g., anvils, steerhorns, fluepipes) into his total musical theater, Ulmer incorporates natural sounds to compound and contrast with Erdody's nearly overweening underscoring. The tension of this music–sound effects dichotomy mounts until it is expressed by the unseen chorus that sings a lively jig, recapitulating the narrative of the adventure for gold before us. In *Der Ring*, Wagner often has secondary characters reiterate major themes, using them to provide new details or explain situations differently from how we have previously understood them. Ulmer's/Erdody's vocal chorus provides this effect, but in a modern way—"modern" insofar as Erdody's choral song has an *alienation effect* from the drama at hand. Erdody's song asks the audience to consider the "why" of the adventure. Enamored of Greek drama, Wagner wanted the orchestra to replace the chorus. In *Isle of Forgotten Sins,* Ulmer uses Erdody's score as his Wagnerian Greek chorus. When lyrics are added to Erdody's music, the effect becomes Brechtian because, rather than drawing us further into the illusion, it questions the illusion, forcing the exploration of metaphor.

Clancy takes his turn diving, and Burke commands the ship in the face of worsening weather as Krogan-Pacific poise themselves to ambush the team. Unable to dive for the gold themselves, it is revealed that Krogan-Pacific have lured Clancy-Burke into doing the hard work for them. With its interwoven chords representing hard labor and mighty strength, the giants' leitmotiv from *Rheingold* is shown in figure 8.5, making explicit the affinity between Wotan-Loge using Fafner-Fasolt, and Krogan-Pacific using Clancy-Burke.

As Krogan orders his native minions to attack Clancy-Burke and take the gold, the Rhinemaidens' motif again fills the soundtrack; yet this time it is their reintroduction music from their final, more somber, appearance in *Der Ring*, at the top of Act III of *Götterdämmerung*. The familiar but transformed music of the Rhinemaidens' third *Ring* appearance underscores both the futility of humankind's quest for gold and the destruction that the gold wreaks, causing people to forswear love for tangible assists and therefore betray their souls. In *Isle of Forgotten Sins* the gold has distracted all of Ulmer's characters, save the sage native king of Moran Island, from the danger of the impending monsoon, just as in *Der Ring* the gold distracts nearly everyone from the impending Götterdämmerung.

The giants' leitmotiv appears again to accompanying Clancy-Burke's raising of the chest of gold from the sunken *Tropic Star*. Ulmer's/Erdody's Wagner quotes then shift to the music of the "Gods' Entrance to Valhalla" from the end of *Rheingold*. While outwardly celebratory, the music carries with it the knowledge that the creation of Valhalla has sealed the gods' fate, and that they have already begun to destroy themselves.

Clancy fakes having the bends so that Burke will bring him to the surface before the gold. As with Fafner and Fasolt, distrust and envy are core tenets of the men's relationship. Eventually in *Rheingold*, Fafner kills Fasolt for the treasure, and in *Isle of Forgotten Sins*, the suspicion of a double cross is never far from either Burke's or Clancy's mind. The fear that one man will desert the other to feed his self-interest permeates the diving sequence, and this is the same net of fear that most of *Der Ring*'s characters find themselves trapped in because of gold. Erdody works the giants' leitmotiv and the "Gods' Entrance to Valhalla" music into a feverish cycle, until the moment when the trunk of gold is tugged to the surface and the "Revelation of the Rheingold" quotation again sounds.

Figure 8.5.

As Burke helps Clancy on board, the giants' leitmotiv repeats yet another time. As Clancy "recovers" from faking the bends, the Valhalla music, that is, the music of false victory, further echoes in Erdody's underscoring.

Clancy and Burke take the chest of gold to a dark room. They open the chest, and the gold finally lies before them after their intense subterfuge and labors. Ulmer chooses to have the gold remain dark (and, without a close-up, loveless) in the chest. In a rare moment, Erdody's score is silent, the Greek "chorus" of *Isle of Forgotten Sins* muted while ghostly winds rage outside to accompany the scene. Burke pays his crew their share of the gold, and he and Clancy are left alone to haggle over the rest. Burke proposes a 2-to-1 split. Clancy objects, but Burke tells him that since he has furnished the diving equipment, boat, and crew, he deserves a larger share. Burke reminds Clancy that the knowledge of the gold was his. Clancy is unimpressed, as to him, the idea of something is not the same as the means to do it. In *Rheingold* this is directly analogous to Fafner telling Fasolt that he has more right to the gold because Fasolt wanted Freia more than he desires the Nibelung hoard and the Ring, which Wotan has substituted as payment. As they dispute the distribution of the gold, Clancy and Burke fight more violently than ever before, trashing the room and knocking over a lamp, which begins a fire as the monsoon approaches outside.

The finale of *Isle of Forgotten Sins* echoes the finale of *Der Ring*, in which Wotan's disowned daughter Brunnhilde ignites a fire that (supernaturally) rages out of control. After the immolation brings about the dusk of the gods, the Rhine waters rise, flooding everything in their embryonic fluids. In Wagner's world, the corrupt social order has fallen and is ready to be rebirthed out of nature. Whether this rebirth will be a perpetuation of the cycle or a new, better phase of humanity is the ambiguous question that Wagner's music meditates on in the final minutes of *Götterdämmerung*.

Krogan-Pacific board Burke's boat and interrupt Burke and Clancy's fight. They confine Burke-Clancy to a closet, which Pacific nails shut. Krogan-Pacific abscond with the gold and blow up Burke's ship, but Burke and Clancy escape at the very last minute as the monsoon hits Moran Island full blast.

Marge and the other women wait for the men to return to the plantation house. Olga reveals that she betrayed Burke and Clancy's looting plans to Johnny Pacific. As she and Marge are about to fight, Krogan and Pacific return with the gold and the news that Clancy and Burke are dead. Olga pulls a gun, demanding the gold; but when she goes to fire, her gat is empty. Krogan laughs at Olga, telling her that he neutered her gun, remembering her bad habit of shooting people, and knocks her to the ground with his hands.

Suddenly, Krogan turns a gun on everyone, including his partner Pacific, and claims the entire treasure hoard for himself. "As long as we're having a showdown," he says, "we might as well make it a good one." Pacific objects, saying that Krogan didn't know about the gold being on board the *Tropic Star* until he informed him. Krogan calls Pacific a "weak sister" who "didn't have innards enough to steal it" alone. With this final turn of events, Ulmer makes the parallels between the Krogan-Pacific and Clancy-Burke relationships explicitly clear. The couples are doubles for each other—there are no heroes where gold is concerned.

Pacific fires his pistol at Krogan. Krogan shoots back; and after exchanging six shots each, both men slump to the ground dead. At that very minute, Burke and Clancy waltz in, the former noting the "nice shooting" of his slain adversaries. Luana takes a gun off the floor and points it at Burke and Clancy. Burke removes the gun from her as if she were a child, and tells her that Clancy "can't give you the gold, but I can." Luana falls into Burke's embrace. As when Alberich lovelessly woos Grimhild with gold to mate and sire an heir, the women in *Isle of Forgotten Sins* all have their price for companionship.

At the very moment that Luana trades love for gold, the eye of the monsoon wrecks the plantation house and washes Burke, Clancy, and the women out to sea in an apocalyptic frenzy. In ragged, open waters, Clancy holds Marge and Diane to a piece of driftwood. Exhausted, Marge tells Clancy that she cannot hang on much longer. Clancy holds her, and himself, against the raft as Marge tries to sacrifice herself to the stormy sea. The monsoon rages harder, and we fade out on Clancy clutching Diane and Marge to the raft, as it appears that they may be, or are being, overcome by the waves.

For the coda of *Isle of Forgotten Sins*, we fade in on a peaceful skyline after the monsoon has passed. We find Marge minding the till at the Bird Cage Café. Erdody's oriental theme from the beginning of *Isle of Forgotten Sins* perfumes the soundtrack after a long absence. Marge stands by the cash register, a picture of an embracing Burke and Diane at its side. Clancy appears, looking disoriented. He pours himself a drink, and asks Marge for money for another scheme which he promises to fill her in on later. Marge gives Clancy the money, thrilled that her man needs her and always comes back to her, yet worried at what worse fate could result from Clancy's shenanigans. Clancy runs out, and Marge slams the register shut wearily. She is left looking after her man as we fade out on Sondergaard's wry smile.

THE MEDIUM IS THE MESSAGE

The most remarkable aspect of Ulmer's PRC films is their subjective use of the unconscious as a cinematic location, the tone of which places the entire context in a dream state. For Ulmer, it's the logical alchemy of the silent expressionist-philosopher awoken by the vulgar clamor of sync sound. The epilogue to *Isle of Forgotten Sins* in the Bird Cage Café easily plays as Marge's satirically bourgeois death dream, projected as she loses her struggle with the monsoon. Because everyone is alive and accounted for in the Café coda, it is a "happy ending" sure to please censors and studio brass alike. However, when examined, this happy end is anything but, as Marge finds herself trapped in the existential living hell of perpetually almost having what she most desires.

Detour possesses a similar dream ending. In the final shot, it is uncertain whether Al is narrating his capture by the authorities, or projecting a fantasy of capture that will absolve him of the constant fear of detention that torments him more truly than any physical incarceration ever could. In *Detour*, the law (represented by a squad car) finally catches up with Al by the side of a highway. The ridiculousness of the cops' putting him in the car; pulling away; and then having to stop to reclose the door, only to drive away again, is a detail—a final (?) detour—so preposterously mundane that it reiterates the complete stench of failure and almost-success that Ulmer assembles around Roberts with the skill of a slapstick comedian.

In these dreamy happy ends, Ulmer's synthesis of technique and material is at its most unquestionably successful. Moving the narrative into metaphor by harnessing the concept of "dream," Ulmer exposes his artifice, and this exposure better illustrates the narrative just presented than the actual first-person experience of spectatorship. Ever the psychoanalytic director, Ulmer moves praxis to this subconscious climax, which forces the immediate review of the action in the viewer's conscious, making the true experience of watching an Ulmer movie one of remembrance—most resplendently cathartic when experienced in personal retrospect. As a unique result, the memory of an Ulmer movie is often stronger than the experience of watching one, as Ulmer's cinema becomes dream.

In his famous February 1970 interview with Peter Bogdanovich, printed in *Who the Devil Made It—Conversations with Legendary Film Directors*, Ulmer remarks, "I really am looking for absolution for all the things I had to do for money's sake." It is easy to understand the frustration of a man more talented than his means, who was so crafty at making so much out of so little that his skill confined most of his cinematic expressions to B-programmers and genre exercises. In *Isle of Forgotten Sins*, both Krogan-Pacific and Burke-Clancy struggle with ideas versus means, and this film is but one example of Ulmer illustrating capital's destructive influence on creativity. From *The Black Cat* (1934) to *Ruthless* (1948) to *The Amazing Transparent Man* (1960) to *The Cavern* (1964), wealth is the constant antagonist to love and can only be achieved by love's renunciation. This Wagnerian struggle in

Ulmer festers until it tears an Ulmer movie apart in a "Liebestod"-like climax, always—sometimes insanely—celebrating the unconscious's true dominion over the soul.

As a result of Ulmer's unique dramaturgy, where catharsis is welded to memory, Erdody's musical underscoring abstracts his collaborations with Ulmer closer to ballet or opera than traditional sync cinema. As in opera, time in Ulmer becomes an emotional reality rather than a naturalistic one—the mise-en-scène lasts the duration of the created emotional phenomenon, rather than representing the actual time of interactions. Once created in the actor's deliberate performance, this emotional time is charted in the sculpting of spaces by Ulmer's camera, which induces an intentional vertigo in the spectator—which, in turn, places much of Ulmer's cinema in the dream state, demanding interpretation for full understanding. Tracking shots, such as the magistrate's entrance into the Isle of Forgotten Sins, reveal as much as they obscure, often doubling over the same studio space, oddly claiming it for multiple purposes within the same frame. Camera pullbacks remove spectators from the volatility of the characters' interpersonal interactions, presenting them as cosmic targets unaware of how at the mercy of their environment (often referred to as "fate") they are. Push-ins, as when Marge is waiting for the men to return with the gold, remove us from a larger panorama and focus the spectator on specific character obsessions, so empathetically illustrated as to threaten to overwhelm the thrust of genre/plot at any time. When Ulmer arrives at his climaxes, these obsessions overwhelm presentation and reveal themselves to be what the movie has really been about.

Finally, each Ulmer movie is a struggle between capital and love, bisected by vertical lines of light and divided into a primal binary between darkness and light. Because Ulmer rarely had the means to lavishly illustrate his scripts, the shadow plays he devises to represent that which he cannot conjure create a far richer presentation than all the gold in the world could buy. As Godard tells us, "Art attracts us only by what it reveals of our most secret self."

Note: Thanks to Madlon Laster, George McElhinney, and Frank Thornton.

BIBLIOGRAPHY

Bentley, Eric. *Frank Wedekind's "The First Lulu"* (New York: Applause Books, 1994).

Bogdanovich, Peter. *Who the Devil Made It: Conversations with Legendary Film Directors* (New York: Ballantine, 1998).

Cooke, Deryck. *An Introduction to Wagner's "Der Ring Des Nibelungen"* (London: Decca, 1968).

Deleuze, Gilles. *Cinema 1: The Movement-Image*, trans. Hugh Tomlinson and B. Habberjam (Minneapolis: University of Minnesota Press, 1986).
Fitzgerald, Gerald, et al., eds. *The Ring—Metropolitan Opera* (New York: Metropolitan Opera Guild, 1988).
Godard, Jean-Luc. "What Is Cinema?" *Les amis du cinéma* (1 October 1952, reprinted in *Godard, on Godard*, trans. and ed. Tom Milne, 1968).
Jarman, Douglas. "Berg: Wozzeck; An Introduction," in *Wozzeck Wiener 1987* (Hamburg: Polydor International, 1988).
Magee, Bryan. *The Tristan Chord: Wagner and Philosophy* (New York: Henry Holt, 2001).
Newman, Ernest. *The Wagner Operas* (Princeton: Princeton University Press, 1991).
Sarris, Andrew. *The American Cinema Directors and Directions, 1928–1968* (New York: Da Capo Press, 1996).
Styan, J. L. *Max Reinhardt*. (London: Cambridge University Press, 1982).
Wagner, Richard. *The Authentic Librettos of the Wagner Operas, Complete with English and German Parallel Texts and Music of the Principal Airs* (New York: Crown, 1938).
———. *Der Ring Des Nibelungen* (Decca, 1968).
———. *Der Ring Des Nibelungen, Recorded Live at Bayreuth Festival 1953* (Gala, 999791, 1994).
Weill, Kurt, and Bertolt Brecht. "Prologue," in *Happy End: A Melodrama with Songs* (Ghostlight, 7915584418-2, 2006).

9

Ulmer and the Noir Femme Fatale

Alena Smiešková

If during the silent era the audience had known him as a stage designer and a producer, and in horror films as a successful writer and an emerging new talent in the genre, it was the film noir where Edgar G. Ulmer used at best his experience with the German film expressionists such as Wegener, Murnau, Wiene, and Lang, and convincingly immortalized himself. Because what in many hands would be ridiculous and banal acquired, in Ulmer's hands, the subtle quality of the style, and what the mainstream would recognize as the drawbacks of seclusion and lack of opportunities that Ulmer exploited to the full brim. Therefore it is no surprise that he later became known as the "King of the Bs."

Film-noir poetics were ideally suited to low-budget "B" movies, as Schrader points out in his "Notes on Film Noir" (165). Ulmer's best films were therefore created in the period that Schrader describes "oddly both one of Hollywood's best periods and least known" (153). Such contrasting characteristics suggest that this era in American film can be seen (and I agree with this opinion) as "an immensely creative period—probably the most creative in Hollywood's history" (164). But at the same time, it is quite understandable that it was, for a long time, avoided and underestimated by the official criticism. Representations that were in harsh contrast with the dark poetics of film noir dominated American cinematography and culture at the time that the first film noirs appeared. The postwar period in the United States reflected a high degree of normative behavior in a number of areas of life, ranging from the family to institutions such as schools, hospitals, the army, and the government. It is precisely film noir, with its dark poetics accentuating corruption of character and institution, along with despair and alienation, that brings up the subversive view of an otherwise optimistically presented American reality. These values remained overlooked and undisclosed in the 1950s. For a long time film noir was perceived as "an aberration of the American character" (165). In contrast, the American Western was "more American" because its characters idealized fundamental qualities of American life, such as individualism, freedom, pragmatism, and the "American Dream."

More importantly, the subversive quality of film noir rests not only in the sociological interpretation of its elements; it is also deeply rooted in its style, choreography, and mannerist visual representation. It opens up the possibilities for unconventional solutions, unacceptable for Hollywood films of that time: unhappy endings, and the dislocation of female characters from familiar and acceptable positions. This is the quintessential difference, the quality that other mass-produced American films of the time did not and could not achieve. Last but not least, the noir films, together with auteur cinema, had an immense influence on the latest trends in contemporary cinema.

In her seminal essay "Lounge Time: Postwar Crises and the Chronotope of Film Noir," Vivian Sobchack acknowledges that the reference to external sources in no way resolves the internal logic of those films (129). Moreover, describing the social context of the noir-style films as "transitional," her understanding clearly comes closer than it seems to the understanding of the film-noir poetics of Schrader (131). In Schrader's view, the film noir is defined more precisely by the "more subtle qualities of tone and mood," in contrast to traditional conventions of the genre specified by the setting and conflict (154). And thus the social context that gives rise to a desire to restore the lost patriarchal order, as Sobchack asserts, generates the timeless world in the interspace between the past and present, populated by characters anxious of their futures, with fluctuating and unstable identities, disclosing the secrets of male and female sexuality, dominance, and submissiveness (131).

I would like to focus on three manifestations of film-noir style in Ulmer's oeuvre. The link uniting their interpretations is the character of the femme fatale. This chapter is grounded in the premise that Ulmer's heroines in *The Strange Woman* (1946), *Detour* (1945), and *Murder Is My Beat* (1955) represent disquieting versions of feminine beauty as a formal representation of unpresentable experience and concepts. I work with two approaches: the aesthetics of the film noir and the aesthetics of sublime sentiment.

In Jean-François Lyotard's reading, it is the model of the Kantian sublime, its function, and its operation that provide for both the logic and the impulses of contemporary art. For "the sublime . . . is an equivocal emotion" that arises in a "conflict between the faculties of a subject, the faculty to conceive of something and the faculty to 'present' something" (77). If we agree with Janey Place, in her text *Women in Film Noir*, that the world constructed in film noir is "paranoic, claustrophobic, hopeless, doomed, predetermined by the past, without clear moral or personal identity," then this world is "transitional" and must always be defined anew, as is also true of the identity of its characters (41). The irreconcilability of the realizations that something that resists figuration may still be conceived of in one's mind splinters the unified perception of reality and undermines the stability of its concept. Lyotard explains: "We have the Idea of the world (the totality of what is), but we do not have the capacity to show an example of it. We have the idea of the simple . . . but we cannot illustrate it with a sensible object which would be a 'case' of it" (78). Therefore the "Ideas of which no presentation is possible" as "the unpresentable" challenge representation in art (78). Thus, Kantian conflict can be understood as a philosophical equivalent of the aesthetic efforts that have marked the content and form of the construction of the world in film noir. When Schrader says that the "theme [in film noir] is hidden in the style" or that "it works out conflicts visually rather than thematically," his understanding accentuates the dominance of visual means of expression (166). It is therefore analogical to the possibilities of figuration to which the definition of the Kantian sublime extends.

It is interesting to note that Ulmer filmed *The Strange Woman* and *Detour* at approximately the same time. While *Detour* has become a cult film, after *The Black Cat* (1934) the most famous of his oeuvre, *The Strange Woman* belongs among the most neglected and least discussed in the overall context of his films. It may be because *The Strange Woman* is not a "conventional" film noir. As an adaptation of the novel of the same title by Ben Ames Williams, it is situated at the beginning of the nineteenth century in the busy world of a port town, which is populated by a variety of characters, ranging from the highest to the lowest and poorest. The class stratification creates a firm background with its stable social conventions and expectations. As the title suggests, the protagonist, Jenny Hager, is a strange woman, dislocated from the stereotyped roles assigned to women by nineteenth-century bourgeois society. The film is narrated from her perspective, and it is exactly her otherness that creates the dynamics and excellent visual stylistics of the film.

Hedy Lamarr, who stars in the film, was called an "angel and sinner" in a 1947 review of the film in the *New York Times*—the two words capturing the ineffable character of the protagonist. The film presents the transformation of Jenny Hager—a half orphan living with her drunkard father in the port town of Bangor—into the most influential and richest lady of the town (until her tragic end). Jenny understands from the very beginning that if she wants to change her predestined social status, she must count on her femininity: "I am going to be beautiful," she asserts in the opening scene. The scene is one of the examples of Ulmer's mastery. Ulmer did not need expensive stage design or an extensive budget: the dynamics of the story depend on the camera angle, the mise-en-scène, and the surprising editing. The minimalism at the end of the scene is the most impressive and foreshadows the development of Jenny's identity. At the beginning of the scene, Jenny, still a child, assures her father of their happy and prosperous future. The camera photographs her in a close-up, while at the same time the viewer can watch the eccentric detail in the corner of the frame, where her hand is playing with a strand of her hair. The detail here is equally seductive to that of Lamarr raising her eyebrow slightly in other scenes, in which she uses this mannerism to nonverbally complete the discourse of a seducer—for example, in scenes with the grown-up Ephraim. In the case of the former scene, her voice is accompanied by the vertical movement of the camera, and we suddenly see the same image in the river—a mirroring of the real Jenny. The image, like in a fairy tale, is suddenly blurred; and following the fade-out, the grown-up Jenny stands on the riverbank, as if born out of the narcissist reflection in the water. In contrast to Narcissus, however, Jenny at least temporarily escapes the self-destructive influence of her own sexuality.

The character of Jenny can be classified as the proto-noir femme fatale. She has, however, a lot in common with other types of strong femmes fatales in film noirs, such as the bar singers, hostesses, and models who act in roles where they deliberately construct their own images (Gledhill 17). In contrast to the typical femme fatale who appears in a film noir situated in the second half of the twentieth century, who has two possibilities—she can work or she can live off a man—for Jenny there is only one option: she can live off her husband only. Striving to achieve a new social status, she marries the most influential man in town—Isaiah Poster, the father of her childhood friend Ephraim. She becomes a respectable woman, and, in spite of the conventional solution, the character of Jenny defamiliarizes the role of a woman in marriage. She actively constructs her image of a charitable and merciful woman. After the church mass at which the priest has invited the congregation to donate money to build a new church, she sees that the rich of Bangor are silent, and she raises her voice: "If the men of Bangor won't give to the church the women will." Her rhetoric is decisive and self-conscious, and it subverts the hierarchy of dominance and submissiveness in the traditional representation of family. Thus, in spite of the fact that film noirs present an active and independent woman outside of the traditional family, Jenny, as the wife of a respected man, not only constructs her destiny but also builds her positive public image.

To illustrate the visual means that Ulmer uses to present the conflicting character of Jenny, I will mention one more scene. Ulmer's film is the most persuasive when he finds a formal expression for the undecidable rational and emotional situation that occurs when Jenny is passionate, manipulative, and beautiful at same time. At such moments, the spiral of seduction extends on; and due to the visual stylization, the viewer is as immersed in it as the characters in the film.

The scene I wish to discuss is a seduction scene that takes place after a family dinner, where Jenny, paradoxically, substitutes for Ephraim's dead mother. Ulmer's convincing iconography, based on the play of light and shadows, is a suitable counterpart to the menacing juxtaposition of domestic and gothic atmosphere at the beginning of the nineteenth century.

When Isaiah, Ephraim's father, leaves with the candle, Jenny extinguishes the lamp to light the candle on the mantelpiece. A few seconds after darkness has filled the space, Jenny raises the candle to her face; and her face, partly illuminated, creates one of the most beautiful moments in the film. Her white face stands out of the dark background, and it is beautiful and disquieting at the same time. One eye, illuminated by the candle, radiates her inner light and passion as she pretends to be committed to Ephraim; the other is buried in shadows. Her mysterious expression is underscored by an oblique shadow cast over her neck, dividing it to two triangles, white and black. When she leads Ephraim upstairs she lights the way with the candle. We leave the nineteenth-century gothic atmosphere, and, together with Jenny, we enter a ghastly, timeless world beyond any time specifications, sharply formatted by vertical and diagonal shafts of light that come from outside. Ulmer creates a visual counterpart to the ambiguity of values in this world, and the movement of the camera following the characters as they go upstairs redefines the dominant role in the family.

In this film, Ulmer constructs a genuinely complex femme fatale character. The film does not provide us with a Freudian resolution or social criticism of the patriarchal system; it provides a provocative version of reality and discloses the duality of the femme fatale—on the one hand a philanthropic saint, and on the other hand a woman driven by her unbound sexuality.

Detour is a classic film noir. Its visual qualities, as well as its story, are examples par excellence of the noir style. The plot is narrated in flashbacks, accompanied by the narrator-protagonist's voice-over. The pace of the film is seemingly slow; it moves "quietly" through a sequence of "almost" banal events, ultimately to its fatal ending. From the beginning, Ulmer works with the fragmented character of the protagonist and the space. Al Roberts, a pianist with a classical education, plays in a small nightclub in New York while living through his romance with his fiancée, Sue. Al's stability, his late-night shows with Sue, and his enamored looks while walking Sue home along fog-filled New York streets are undermined by the visual representation of the aforementioned scenes. Ulmer uses the low Dutch angle to produce the disequilibrium of the situation; dark and foggy New York streets are the visual counterpart to uncertainty and the upcoming dissonance in their life.

Sue leaves Hollywood to start her career, and Al decides to come to see her. He is almost penniless, and thus he hitchhikes. His journey across America on a highway is the entrance to a dark, surreal world, where the familiar becomes unfamiliar. Al moves within the space that Sobchack defines as "the common places from wartime and postwar time American culture" (130). These are the places intimately familiar to Al: "the cocktail lounge, the night club, the bar, the hotel room, the boarding house, the diner, the dance hall, the roadside café, the train and bus stations, the wayside motel," in his case also a gas station and a used-car lot and the highway (130). His life, however, in a sequence of events, disjoints from the common circumstances and leads to his tragic end.

The rhetoric of the protagonist is persuasive, and he insists that the tragedy of his life can be substantiated when he identifies the breaking point at which his prospects and his stable fortunes collapsed. In the opening scene, he introduces his retrospective recollection in this way: "I keep trying to forget what happened and wonder what my life might have been like if that car of Haskell's hadn't stopped." But as Jon Tuska claims in his work *Dark Cinema: American Film Noir in Cultural Perspective*, "the hamartia of the male protagonist is only rarely manifested as an error in judgment but rather is most often the consequence of a fatal obsession, usually with the femme fatale" (211). Roberts interprets tragic circumstances as an intrusion of fate into his life; he sees himself as entrapped in the circumstances without his free will, without the possibility of altering anything in his life. He says: "But one thing I don't have to wonder about, I know. Someday a car will stop to pick me up that I never thumbed. Yes, Fate or some mysterious force can put the finger on you or me, for no good reason at all." Everything in the film is presented exclusively through his perspective; the retrospective narrative is often interrupted, and the camera focuses on his face in a close-up. But similarly to other narrators in film noirs, his narration is also unreliable.

Roberts oscillates between two women—Sue, whom he follows to the West Coast, is his destiny, as is Vera, whom he meets on his way out west. Sue represents for him stability and, implicitly, the lost patriarchal order; Vera is a changeable and active element whose dominance Roberts does not want to admit: "The most dangerous animal in the world." She disquiets him with her ephemeral identity: at one moment it is that of a child, then suddenly it is that of a beast. When she introduces herself—"Call me Vera"—she shows that her present identity is only one of the possibilities.

In the instance of this film, I agree with Sobchack that the films circumscribed as "noir" are seen as playing out negative dramas of postwar masculine trauma and gender anxiety, brought on by wartime destabilization of the culture's domestic economy and a consequent "deregulation" of the institutionalized and patriarchally informed relationship between men and women (130).

Roberts's disequilibrium is presented in the film by two different representations of the femme fatale. Sue is a blond woman who, after a short episode at the beginning of the film, appears only in short sequences when Al tries to reach her by phone. In these scenes, Sue is photographed by a static camera; she is stiff like a puppet in a light-colored dress, sitting in an armchair and elegantly holding a dark telephone. Sue functions for Al as a part of the patriarchally institutionalized relationship: marriage. To the viewer, the scenes offer a chilling chimera that is miles away from the Sue that Roberts projects. The dissonance between them is tangible, documented by her clothes and the props in the environment occupied by Sue. The distance grows emotionally; Sue is self-controlled, and, in contrast to the excited and nervous Al who calls her, her responses are mechanical and emotionally disinterested.

Vera is Sue's other Self. She is dark-haired, passionate, energetic, and tangible. Al is more and more infatuated by her charm and manipulation. If Roberts speaks about some mysterious force, then Vera is the physical representation of this unpresentable concept. Although Ann Savage, who stars as Vera, appears only in the second half of the film, her appearance is unforgettable. The camera accentuates her physical beauty, and, with her mesmerizing looks and harsh, sharp words, she dominates each scene. Her accidental death corresponds with the feminist interpretation of the masculine desire to conquer fate.

There are only a few possible resolutions to the fatal relationship for the male protagonist in film noir. One of them, as Claire Johnston shows reinterpreting Lacan's psychoanalytic system in film noir, is that the woman must be found guilty and punished as a result of the "fault" in the Symbolic Order (111). In this case the male protagonist can be freed from his bondage to the femme fatale when she dies. One morning Roberts enters Vera's room to find out that he has accidentally strangled Vera with a telephone cable. In this scene, the camera angle is as if from Roberts's perspective; it moves from object to object, focusing and defocusing the lens. Now Roberts's earlier words sound like an ominous metafictional premonition: "If this would be fiction I would fall in love with her, marry her and made her a respectable woman, while she would make a sacrifice and die."

I have mentioned above that the ineffable quality of fate is materialized in the film in the character of the femme fatale. Both heroines can be classified as the "noir" femme fatale par excellence. While Vera is existentially present, Sue is only an illusion. The frame shot in which Sue reappears in Al's imagination in the reflection of the rear mirror shortly before he encounters "fate" is among the most fascinating in the film. The camera shows Al's face in the rear mirror of Haskell's car, which in the center of the frame is conspicuous in the darkness. Sue, singing in a close-fitting, glittering dress, appears in a fade-in/fade-out, with the shadows of musicians in the background. The shot's diagonal outlines and the low Dutch angle of the camera disrupt the compositional unity. The visual means of expression are the iconographic representation of Roberts's disturbed mind, and they foreshadow Al's submissiveness toward "fate."

A similar shot can be found in *Lost Highway* (1997), a cult film by David Lynch, when the protagonist's face makes a visible appearance in a car in the darkness of night. Lynch's film does not hide its affiliation with the film-noir style. The highway that becomes the fate of the male protagonist in *Detour* is the metaphoric loop in Lynch's metanarrative. Al Roberts makes "only" a detour on his way to beloved Sue, and there he meets Vera in a fatal encounter.

Another connotation that links together the worlds and characters of *Lost Highway* and *Detour* is their existential situation. After arriving in Hollywood, Vera and Al seek accommodation in a hotel under false names. When they enter the hotel room, Vera says with relief, "Home, sweet home." Her words are ironic—what could be more in contrast to home, and all its associations, than a hotel room? The hotel room represents everything that is fleeting, temporary, and unstable, and if this heterocosmos is the index of stability for Vera, then it signifies that for her—as well as for Lynch's characters and Al Roberts—there is no such thing as home.

Ulmer works with a very low budget and minimalist means. There are only three major characters. Ulmer uses only two sets, which he rearranges and alters depending on the setting. The shots filmed in the car are accomplished with a static camera and a movable background. In spite of this, the forced perspective, the expressionist motifs, and the nightmarish world grounded in fatalism produce the atmosphere of one of the blackest film noirs ever made in the classic period between 1935 and 1955.

The last film to be analyzed belongs to the end of the film noir period. *Murder Is My Beat* was produced in 1955. It is probably also because of this that the representation of the femme fatale differs in this film. Ulmer forms an alternative solution to the relationship between the male protagonist and the femme fatale Eden Lane (portrayed in the film by Barbara Payton).

In many respects, the film manifests its affinity with the noir style. It is the traditional model of the murder mystery and its investigation based on the premise of "Whodunit?"—in this case the investigation of the murder of mysterious Frank Dean. The epistemological search for the truth is, however, marked by the failure of the protagonist, a detective who must be called off the case after he has helped the main suspect, Eden Lane, escape.

The film has a nonlinear structure; its narrative is as if cut in half. The convoluted sequence of events formally corresponds with the complicated process of the search for the truth. The introductory part of the film shows the investigating detective Ray Patrick alone, in a motel. Eden, whom he has helped to escape, has disappeared again. Ray persuades his boss that he can finish the case because he believes Eden is the key to the resolution of the mystery. In the following retrospective narrative, we learn "how it all started." Then the plot returns to the present; and, after a series of many revelations, including the disclosure of infidelity, exchange of identity, blackmailing, and murder, the Dean case is resolved.

The resolution comes in a dramatic scene in which Dean's wife jumps from a moving train and dies. This scene formally reduplicates another key scene, which also takes place on a train at night. In that scene Ray, who has traced Eden to Dean's cottage in the mountains, is escorting her into the hands of justice. Eden spots Dean, a supposedly murdered man, at one of the stations. When she and Ray are alone in a compartment, she speaks excitedly about her innocence. Her blond hair, covered with a white bandana, and her white face, on a dark background, contrast with her deep, velvety voice. Ray starts to have doubts. He persuades himself: "When a man starts to doubt, what he presents as right must be right." In a scene almost identical to that of Dean's wife's suicide, they jump out of the train at a place where the train slows down. The camera shoots the empty darkness behind the opened door of the train, and in the following shot we can see Eden's body falling onto the pavement. The fall that seems to be fatal is, however, without consequences.

If Eden had died in this moment of the narrative, it would have been an accidental death very similar to the death of Vera in *Detour*. Ray would have acted in a manner dependent on his fatal attraction to the femme fatale. The motivation for such an obsession has been depicted in the previous scene in the mountain cottage. In accordance with the desire to restore the dominance of Logos and consequently the order in chaos that the murder investigation brings, the femme fatale would die accidentally and the successful cop would become a wreck and bump—similarly to the situation in *Detour*. This film, however, presents another solution. After the fall that seems to be tragic, Ray stands up and brushes off his coat, then helps Eden to stand up—and we already know the rest. After many obstacles and mysteries, the case is successfully closed. Ray has been suspended and no longer works for the police; however, he goes to work as a private eye, with Eden as a prospective Mrs. Patrick at his side.

At first sight, such a happy ending does not correspond with the dark poetics of film noir. However, if we agree with Johnston's interpretation, which offers the Lacanian solution of the conflict within the Symbolic Order, Ray has assigned the femme fatale a role in a newly restored patriarchal order, and in marrying her he has sublimated the fatal attraction within a socially acceptable framework (111).

Payton, however, in spite of this "predicament," remains the could-be-noir femme fatale in this film. Much of the construction of her character is rooted in the visual qualities of the film and her acting. Even though the film "may lack the classic dimensions of . . . *Detour* . . . it benefits from the presence of Barbara Payton as an ambiguous femme fatale" (Silver and Ward 191).

In this case, the scene at Dean's cottage in the mountains mentioned above is the most instructive. Ray approaches the cottage in a snowstorm. After enormous effort, which in the film looks more comic than persuasive, he opens the door of the cottage—which he can do only with a gun in his hand—and finds a gentle, unprotected woman with the face of an angel standing next to the mantelpiece, instead of a cunning, merciless murderess. Payton has something in her of Kim Novak from Hitchcock's *Vertigo* (1958) or Jean Seberg from Godard's *Breathless* (1959). Feminine tenderness blends with inner strength and endurance in her acting. "Ulmer extracts the maximum narrative tension from the viewer's uncertainty over Eden Lane's guilt, an uncertainty reinforced by Payton's portrayal of Eden in a 'neutral' manner" (Silver and Ward 191).

The mantelpiece scene reminds us in many aspects of the seduction scene described above in *The Strange Woman*. It seems for a moment that it is the hard-boiled cop who dominates the situation. When the interior light fades out because of a power failure, Eden comes closer to the mantelpiece to light the candles. There is a change in the field of dominance. Ray offers Eden a cigarette, and they smoke together, next to the mantelpiece. When Eden moves to the sofa and narrates her version of the story ("Maybe this is a new angle"), the camera focuses on her face in a close-up situated in the left part of the frame, while the rest of the scene remains in shadow; there is only a cigarette in Ray's hand, which is off center in the bottom right corner of the frame. It is the index of his presence when Eden starts to tell her version of the story. The frame composition shows that Ray's presence is no longer dominant. "Payton's performance permits the suggestion of instability beneath the surface calm of Eden's visage," and as a result of this Ray depends on Eden; she is the embodiment of truth for him in the case (Silver and Ward 191). Thus Ulmer repeatedly uses the beauty of the femme fatale to present the unpresentable.

During his analysis of the "unpresentable," Lyotard, interpreting Kant, asserts that modernist art, within which we can place Ulmer's stylistic approaches to film noir, is characterized by the nostalgic desire to present the unpresentable, the desire to find the form for that which is the unpresentable (81). As we have pointed out above, the world constructed in the film noir, more than that in any "A" Hollywood movie, produces a new, changeable, and subversive reality—it is intentionally "anti-realistic" (Gledhill 19). The conventional or simplified forms of representation are not suitable to present the disequilibrium. Moreover, as Sylvia Harvey asserts, "the dissonances, the sense of disorientation and unease, although frequently present at the level of plot and thematic development are . . . always a function of the visual style of this group of films" (Silver and Ward 171). Director Edgar G. Ulmer searches for the means of expression that could capture the semantic dissonances and the disequilibrium of the world presented, or of the fragmented identities of the characters. The curious camera angles; the composition of visual images and mise-en-scène; and the lighting, which ranges between light and shadow, help him to defamiliarize common and banal objects (172). In *The Strange Woman*, *Detour*, and *Murder Is My Beat*, the femme fatale character, in her various modifications from the proto-noir femme fatale to the could-be noir femme fatale, becomes the visual representation of unpresentable concepts such as altruism and seduction, fate and truth. Thus it is the character of the femme fatale that embodies the novel meanings and visual techniques that continue to make film noir attractive to audiences.

BIBLIOGRAPHY

Gledhill, Christine. "Klute, Part 1: A Contemporary Film Noir and Feminist Criticism," in *Women in Film Noir*, ed. E. A. Kaplan (London: British Film Institute, 1978), 6–21.

Harvey, Sylvia. "The Absent Family in Film Noir," in *Movies and Mass Culture*, ed. John Belton (New Brunswick: Rutgers University Press, 1996), 171–82.

Johnston, Claire. "Double Indemnity," in *Women in Film Noir*, ed. E. A. Kaplan (London: British Film Institute, 1978), 100–111.

Lyotard, Jean-François. *The Postmodern Condition: A Report on Knowledge*, trans. Geoff Bennington and Brian Massumi, Theory and History of Literature, vol. 10 (Minneapolis: University of Minnesota Press, 1988).

"Murder Is My Beat," in *Film Noir*, ed. Alain Silver and Elizabeth Ward, co-ed. Carl Macek and Robert Porfirio (London: Martin Secker and Warburg, 1979).

Place, Janey. "Women in Film Noir," in *Women in Film Noir*, ed. E. A. Kaplan (London: British Film Institute, 1978), 35–55.

Schrader, Paul. "Notes on Film Noir," in *Movies and Mass Culture*, ed. John Belton (New Brunswick: Rutgers University Press, 1996), 153–70.

Sobchack, Vivian. "Lounge Time: Postwar Crises and the Chronotope of Film Noir," in *Refiguring American Film Genres: Theory and History*, ed. Nick Browne (Berkeley: University of California Press, 1989), 129–70.

Tuska, Jon. *Dark Cinema: American Film Noir in Cultural Perspective*, Contributions to the Study of Popular Culture, no. 9 (Westport, Conn.: Greenwood Press, 1978), 199–215.

FILMS CITED

The Black Cat (1934, Edgar G. Ulmer)
Detour (1945, Edgar G. Ulmer)
The Strange Woman (1946, Edgar G. Ulmer)
Murder Is My Beat (1955, Edgar G. Ulmer)
Vertigo (1958, Alfred Hitchcock)
Breathless (1959, Jean-Luc Godard)

10

Detour's Detour

David Kalat

Once upon a time there was a motion picture called *Detour* (1945). It was a small, wiry thing, gristle and bone. It would have been the runt of any litter, except for the sad fact that it came from a litter of runts, movies made for pocket change and thrust out into the world without support, left to fend for themselves in a harsh and competitive environment.

What *Detour* lacked in polish and graces it made up for with a steely constitution. It was made of stern stuff, this angry little poem written in the language of failure and defeat. Its flickering frames contain a story of an aspiring artist whose talent would seem to merit one kind of fate, glorious and celebratory, but whose life is shuttled down a cruel detour to a very different destination. He begins his adventure dreaming of a new life in a sunnier world, and finishes up lost and lonely, an exile.

The grubby little picture flailed its way across movie screens in 1945 with no greater or lesser prominence than any of its impoverished brethren. It was a B movie, and such things have no shelf life. *Detour*, however, did. More than a half century later, film critics and fans were still falling over themselves to shower it with accolades. In movie parlance, *Detour* had "legs."

It was fashioned by a man named Edgar G. Ulmer, who, like some Jewish mystic of myth, had a habit of pulling clay from the ground and giving it his special imprint, such that it could come to eternal life, a golem. *Detour* was not Ulmer's only bid to cinema immortality, but it was his most distinctive and memorable. His own life had been touched by such detours: he was an artist of no small ability, whose destiny was redirected, stunted, misfired. For the pointy-heads who took up *Detour* as their cause célèbre, the film and its maker were a Möbius strip, art and artist endlessly reflected in one another.

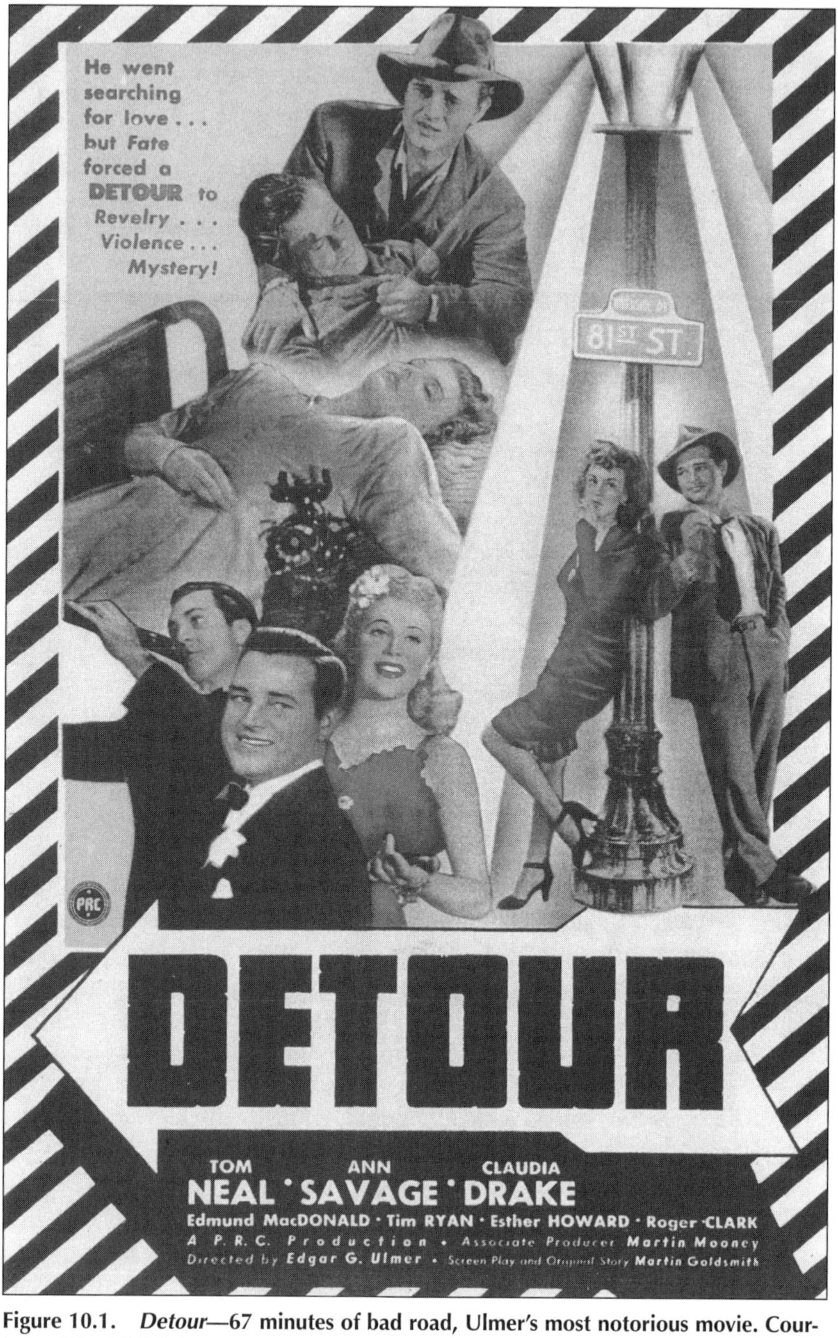

Figure 10.1. ***Detour*—67 minutes of bad road, Ulmer's most notorious movie. Courtesy of David Kalat.**

Ulmer has been called many things—"King of the Bs" is a common title. But the nickname says more about his circumstances than his role within them. Look past the fact that he made low-budget programmers, look only at the films themselves, and we can see he was heir to the grand traditions of German Expressionism, and a direct precursor and inspiration to the avatars of the French New Wave. That he worked in American genre pictures, mercenary as mercenary gets, makes his legacy that much more important: here was living proof that the world of European high-art cinema and American commercial moviemaking were not mutually exclusive.

Or so film historical conventional wisdom would have you believe. Real life is never so tidy.

PORTRAIT OF THE YOUNG MAN AS AN ARTIST

The story starts in those dusky years at the close of World War I, when a Mittel-Europäische artiste, his head full of demons, winds up on the set of various German Expressionist epics: *The Golem* (1920), *The Cabinet of Dr. Caligari* (1920), *Metropolis* (1927) . . . One could scarcely ask for a more auspicious time and place to be cutting one's eyeteeth, even if Edgar was only hunkered in the wings with a claw hammer, helping build the sets.

In 1924, Ulmer was jettisoned from the citadel of Universum Film AG (UFA) to start anew in America. Ulmer says this was done without consulting him, an overseas transfer he never wished for (Bogdanovich 565–66). Maybe so, but in hindsight we can see that this, the first of many detours to come, was fortuitous: the filmmakers with whom he was working at the time would soon be making the same leap to Hollywood, only more frantically, as the shadow of fascism descended across their safe European home. He was not the first of his kind to emigrate. Define "his kind" as you will—artist, intellectual, Jew, or just plain rational human being. It didn't take a rocket scientist to see that Europe was becoming a very ugly place to live (although, to history's great regret, too many rocket scientists chose to stay in Germany).

Ulmer touched down in the heart of Hollywood at Universal Pictures, where he apprenticed as an assistant director under the likes of William Wyler. Making quickie Westerns for Universal was the proverbial study in contrasts—from the sumptuous spectacles of German Expressionism to cranking out programmers like a string of sausages. It was also an education in the ways of the American studio system. Back home, the director was king. If Fritz Lang wanted to make a movie about a futuristic city riven by class divisions and threatened by a crazy humanoid robot, it was up to his producer to support that endeavor. Here, film ideas were cooked up by the front office and assigned to directors, who could be replaced should they wander too far off base.

Roughly a decade after first trodding American soil, Ulmer found himself called to the office of Carl Laemmle Jr., scion of Universal Pictures. Junior had watched the climbing profits of recent hits *Dracula* (1931) and *Frankenstein* (1931) reach unimagined heights. These films would still be making money for the studio in the twenty-first century, but Junior had no way of knowing that. More to the point, he had no way of knowing whether the trend had already peaked. Given the apparent popularity of Gothic horrors, it would seem a good bet to make another one and watch the cash roll in; given the huge expense of Gothic horrors, it would seem a terrible bet to risk so much money on an unknown. Faced with this dilemma, Junior had a brainwave. He decided to join the genre's top stars, Bela Lugosi and Boris Karloff, in the same film; slap on the title of an Edgar Allan Poe story; and market it as a successor to the *Frankenstein/Dracula* tradition, but made at a discount to hedge the bet (Bogdanovich 575).

It was a dog of an assignment. Ulmer was saddled with two of the most egocentric scenery-munchers in the business but given none of the special effects or spooky makeup that had made them stars in the first place. He was supposed to compete with Gothic thrillers that had cost three to four times as much as he was allotted (Palm 00:22:50). The Poe connection, such as it was, was of no use either, since by common agreement "The Black Cat" is an unfilmable story.

All Edgar had going for him was a cynic's worldview. He had grown up in the ashes of war with deprivation and want all around him, and it had imbued him with a sense of futility and dread that was to become quite fashionable. He didn't need supernatural monsters, since he was to pack *The Black Cat* (1935) with enough misanthropy to horrify even the most stalwart. If Ulmer's *Black Cat* were to be remade today, its story of moral ruin and grisly torture would be ginned up in the style of *Saw* (2004) or *Hostel* (2005). But in the discreet days of the mid-1930s, and in the subtle hands of Master Ulmer, the film was given an austere elegance that hovers queasily above its subject matter. The result is a gloriously "go-for-baroque" thriller that has justifiably lingered in memory over seventy years and counting. Ulmer had done something you'd expect from Superman—he had grabbed a lump of coal from the dirt and, in his hands, turned it into a diamond. *The Black Cat* put black ink in Universal's ledgers.

If you were to stop reading right now, it could seem as if this story has a happy ending. Edgar Ulmer arrived in Hollywood and made it big. But read on, and discover the next fork in the road.

In the wake of *The Black Cat*, Ulmer had earned the kind of creative autonomy he held most dear. He was allowed to pitch his own film idea to Junior, an adaptation of *Bluebeard* with Karloff as a serial killer. Go for it, said the boss. Budgets were drawn up, plans were afoot, posters were struck with Karloff's face and Ulmer's name. The movie itself, though, was not made. Ulmer left the studio, then he left Los Angeles, then California.

Fate had stuck out its foot.

SECRETS AND LIES

It is said that Ulmer tanked his career over a girl. Her name was Shirley. As a script supervisor at Universal she was paid to attend to details, to make sure things matched. And so it could not have escaped her notice that the man barking orders on the *Black Cat* set was a darkly handsome rogue with a syrupy Old World accent. The passion that bloomed between them came with a price: she was married. Or, to be more precise, she was married to Max Alexander—a Universal executive, Papa Laemmle's nephew, Junior's good buddy, and Edgar's boss. Their love was what one would call a bad career move (Knipfel 12).

Homewrecker Edgar and his slatternly bride were no longer welcome in Hollywood or anywhere the fury of the Laemmles could reach. These young lovers chose each other over career and comfort, accepting the uncertainties of the future so long as it could be faced together.

This is a fairy story.

Ulmer was a fabulist. He not only wove stories on film, he wove them from the fabric of his own life. His personal biography is a riot of exaggerations, half-truths, white lies, and unsubstantiated fantasy. He was by no means the first filmmaker to show a cavalier disregard for the facts of his life—indeed it is a fairly common enough human trait in all professions. Who among us does not prefer the shining fantasy of the person he or she wishes to be over the often disappointing and embarrassing facts of who he or she actually is? For most of us, this tendency is harmless; but when historians come calling to draw inferences and conclusions from the details of a person's life, it starts to matter whether those details were accurately recorded.

For example, Ulmer styled himself a Viennese native. Vienna was and is one of the seats of European culture, and made a perfect birthplace for an artist—but it was some hundred miles south of the truth. In fact, Ulmer came from the then-Czechoslovakia, from a town called Olomouc. This proved inconvenient to the man, so he filed it away in a drawer. It is a small point, but it lets a little doubt into the discussion about all the other points of Ulmer's life for which he is the primary research source (Grissemann 21–30).

"I had done pictures in Europe with Murnau and with Fritz Lang and designed sets for *The Cabinet of Dr. Caligari* and the golden pictures like that," Ulmer told Peter Bogdanovich in 1970 (562). Ulmer elaborated which pictures he had worked on with Lang: "*Metropolis*, *Die Nibelungen*, and then I worked with him later on a film called *The Spies—Spione*—a classic picture" (563). Bogdanovich was fascinated by these tales, and asked Ulmer to explain what his role precisely entailed:

> I was really Production Designer. At that time, up to the coming of sound, there were *two* directors on each picture: a director for the dramatic action and for the actors, and then for the *picture* itself, who established the camera angles, camera movements, et cetera; there had to be teamwork . . . With Murnau I invented a new role called "Production Design," which meant the designing of each and every angle. (563–64)

The classics of German Expressionism are celebrated today not so much for their stories but for their visual artistry. If Ulmer wants to take credit for those visual triumphs and relegate their named creators to having merely directed the actors, it would behoove him to offer up some proof. The credits on the film prints themselves and the archives of UFA are of no help to him, however. Ulmer may be telling the truth, but the documentary evidence does not back him up.

If you will forgive the personal digression, I wish to offer an anecdote by way of analogy. I was once employed as a color timer at a motion picture processing facility whose primary clients included several major stock-footage archives. Filmmaker Gus Van Sant was directing the feature-film adaptation of *Even Cowgirls Get the Blues* (1993). His picture used cranes as a symbol; but instead of filming new footage of the gangly birds for this purpose, he licensed some stock footage. Van Sant made many poor directorial choices on that misfired flick, so his ill-considered choice of some very grainy 16 mm shots of flying cranes was nowhere near the worst of his troubles; but it didn't help that this already crummy material ended up in the inexperienced hands of my youthful self to blow up to 35 mm. I performed my task ineptly, and assumed he would reject the resulting mess and go shoot something watchable to sub into its place. When I eventually saw the movie at a theater the following summer, I was shocked to see my miserable failings splattered across a forty-foot screen for paying customers.

I have since taken to telling people that I personally ruined *Even Cowgirls Get the Blues*. Although I have a point (my incompetence caused the film's central visual metaphor to come across as an amateur-hour reject), I am of course joking. The closing titles of that film list hundreds of names, and not only is mine not among them, neither is that of the company for which I worked. I contributed to the film, in a visible way, but it is absurd to pretend that my role was significant.

Ulmer may well have made sets on some of the golden oldies of Hoch-Deutsch Expressionismus, but in granting him that we can also safely assume that the absence of his name from the rosters was a signal of his importance to the finished product. He could do his job well, or he could do it poorly, but he was never other than a jobber on a massive endeavor staffed by lots of people—all of whom could affect the quality of the end product by doing their jobs well, or poorly.

Movies are not books. Auteur theory is a useful shorthand for historians trying to tease out what makes a movie what it is, but it is a simplification. Movies are made by teams, committees, armies. It takes a village to make a movie.

Edgar Ulmer wanted to think of himself as a *singular* artist, whose personal vision extruded through his works. He wanted to be an auteur. Hollywood is an industry, and has little room for the go-it-alone artist. Ulmer and Hollywood were destined to be an awkward fit.

In telling the story that Ulmer's promising career in Hollywood was derailed by a romantic indiscretion, Ulmer and his biographers safely answer the question with a grand romantic myth. Ulmer worked in the margins of the film industry the rest of his life because he had to, because he was kicked out of the mainstream, goes the story; he could have triumphed within the system if only, if only . . .

Edgar and Shirley went on the lam to flee Max Alexander's wounded pride. Their personal diaspora ultimately brought them to Producers Releasing Corporation (PRC), the most decrepit outfit on Poverty Row. Here Edgar would forge his legacy, shooting six-day wonders on budgets that would make Roger Corman seem profligate by comparison. Here he would eke out his professional existence, shut out of the big leagues, all but squandering his cinematic gifts.

Buried in this story is a secret, a hidden fact that casts doubt on the narrative surrounding it. At PRC, you see, Ulmer served as a de facto chief of production, choosing projects and overseeing other filmmakers in addition to those flicks he himself directed. Ulmer extended his creative influence throughout PRC during his tenure there in the 1940s. At this time, one of the producers working alongside him was a fellow Universal alum—Max Alexander. If Ulmer's trajectory away from Universal had been to flee Alexander, his arrival at PRC could not have put him any closer to the man.

STUNTED AMBITIONS

In the 1930s and '40s, it was bog-standard distribution practice to send out motion pictures in pairs. One, the A picture, was the glossy, star-studded primary feature intended to draw crowds; the flip side of the double bill was short and cheap, and it was intended to give those crowds a sense they had gotten a full day's worth of entertainment off their ticket fare. Eventually, the term "B movie" would morph into a reference to any cheaply made film, but time was it had a very specific meaning.

Big studios could make B movies as well as anyone. Better, even. But that was of little use, since the main concern for a B movie was not whether it was good but whether it was there. Since B movies were not marketed for themselves, it did not much matter what they were. For this reason, the realm of B-moviemaking was the best avenue by which independents could compete with Hollywood.

The publicity engines of the big studios profit from the illusion of Hollywood as a place where glamorous artists and creative visionaries express themselves for the entertainment of the world. Those publicists, however, toil in the service of a far less glamorous crowd of number crunchers, financial whiz kids, and corporate institutions. At its best, Hollywood is an almost magical balance between these competing worlds, in which the creative expression of talented celebrities does provide enjoyment to the masses and thereby profits to the men in suits.

Deep in the shadows of the Valley, there existed a twisted parody of Hollywood: a parallel world lacking nearly all of the characteristics one would normally associate with the movie colony. Its public face was neither especially creative nor in any way glamorous; its private sphere was too starved of cash to be called Big Business, except as a joke. But in this parallel world, they did make movies. It was a place affectionately called Poverty Row.

Ben Judell was a hardheaded survivor of Hollywood's low-budget trenches. In 1939, he decided to launch his own concern, initially named Producers Pictures. He lined up investors, some property on which to construct a studio, agreements with the distribution exchanges, scripts, and filmmakers, and set out on an ambitious program of aggressive picture making. In less time than it takes milk to go bad, he ran into dire financial problems. He poured too much money into the earliest productions, which faltered at the box office, leaving the second round of productions half-finished and out of funds. Pathe Labs was preparing to foreclose on Judell's unpaid lab bill of nearly a million dollars when his chief investor Sigmund Neufeld stepped in to take over. Judell shuffled off into the darkness, and Neufeld retooled the studio to more modest goals. He slashed the production schedule and lowered the bar, and the newly rechristened Producers Releasing Corporation started to make money instead of lose it.

This caught the attention of Seymour Nebenzahl, the savvy producer responsible for Fritz Lang's *M* (1931) and *Testament of Dr. Mabuse* (1933). As the Nazis took power, he and Lang had skipped out of Germany to stop over in France for a while, where Nebenzahl produced one of Buster Keaton's better talkie features, *The King of the Champs-Elysees* (1934). Not long after that, Nebenzahl came to America, like so many gifted European filmmakers of the age. The film world is divided into two camps: the dreamers and the pragmatists. The dreamers become directors, heads full of fancy, while the pragmatists become producers. Nebenzahl was a brilliant producer—which meant he was pragmatic. While Edgar Ulmer shuffled around looking for a studio to call home, Nebenzahl went and bought himself one. He invested in PRC, along with his partners at Pathe, who had noted the turnaround in the company's fortunes under Neufeld.

At this time, in the early 1940s, Ulmer was relegated to shooting newsreels for Pathe—a sad comedown for such a talent, but it paid the bills. He was in discussions with Paramount to join them as a staff director, to begin on a remake of *The Blue Angel*, starring Veronica Lake! As his talks went forward and his hopes soared, his bosses at Pathe suggested that PRC might be a good gig for a man of his skill. Nebenzahl was an old friend from the glory days of German silent cinema, and Seymour made it clear the job was his for the taking.

Posterity knows that Ulmer did not get the Paramount job, but not why. The contents of the discussions, the inner workings of the minds of the men who looked at Ulmer and said "no" . . . these things are lost to us. What we have is the result: Ulmer took the job at PRC, and laid down a personal myth that this was his desire. PRC was better suited to his personality. His talent at maximizing production value on minimized resources would prove a more valuable asset in an environment of want. He was never constituted to blandly sublimate himself to the wranglings of studio politics—"the Hollywood hash machine," as he famously called it in his conversations with Bogdanovich (592). In the fringes of Hollywood he would find a measure of creative control almost unthinkable in the big movie houses.

Three times it happened: three times he had an opportunity to prove himself within the system, and three times his fate was misdirected. The first was in 1935 with *The Black Cat*, when Ulmer saw his success opening doors—only to have them just as swiftly slammed shut. Then, in the summer of 1941, Ulmer negotiated with Paramount, only to wind up at an absurdist parody of a movie studio instead. The third and final grab at the ring came in 1946, when Ulmer's *The Strange Woman* returned him more or less to the

Hollywood mainstream; but his agent never took proper advantage of the situation, and nothing came of it. The notions that Ulmer was exiled because of the Max Alexander affair or because he opted for the freedom of independence do not bear scrutiny. These are excuses. Why, you ask, did Ulmer work on the fringes? The question is its own answer. Ulmer did not function within Hollywood. To ask why is to assume that he could have functioned within the system. Yet the evidence shows that given the chance, he did not. It does not matter what Edgar G. Ulmer thought about his choices; his destiny was set for him. At a place like PRC, he flourished. Might as well pretend he liked it.

DETOUR, MARK 1

Edgar G. Ulmer's *Detour* is the story of a frustrated artist, kicked around by fate. Al Roberts and his girl Sue are small-time musicians eking out an existence in a Greenwich Village nightspot. Sue harbors dreams of being discovered, and sets out west to seek fame and fortune. Al decides to follow her, and hitchhikes across country to catch up with his lost love. Along the way he is picked up by a driver, Charlie Haskell, with a wad of cash and some ugly scars on his wrist. Before Al finds out much about his mysterious benefactor, Haskell dies suddenly in a freak accident. Al realizes to his horror that he is trapped—no one will believe he did not kill the man, and so his only course of action is to act as if he did: hide the body, rob it blind, assume the dead man's identity, and run.

As the groaning noise of guilt and fear crowd his panicky brain, Al tries to seek comfort by finding someone even less fortunate. He picks up Vera, a grizzled wretch of a girl, at a gas stop, but is puzzled by her cold reaction to him. Too late, he discovers that Vera is the one who put the scars on Haskell's wrist. She recognizes the car but not its new owner, and concludes Al must have murdered Haskell for his money. Using this as blackmail leverage, Vera makes Al her slave.

His only escape from Vera's clutches is yet another freak death, as he unwittingly strangles her with a telephone cord during a drunken argument. Once again, Al has to go on the run, but this time there will be no end. Just running, endless running. He will never see Sue, never settle down in one place, never play music, never even hear his own name. His freedom is bought at a terrible price.

Throughout this grim tale, Al's voice narrates the cruel twists of his life with a tone of perpetual complaint. Film noir has a rich tradition of voice-over narration, but Ulmer's use of it here has a peculiar and interesting effect: there is a dissonance between what Al says and what we see, a disconnection between the events he describes and how he interprets them. It is a subtle thing, but the man who made *The Black Cat* without once showing a man denuded of his skin is a man who wields subtlety as a weapon.

The first note of discord is struck early in the narrative, when Al proposes marriage to Sue. Fans of Ulmer's frugal expressionism may be spending most of their attention on the fact that the director has rendered the streets of New York without even bothering to build a set, using just a couple of street signs and enough fog machines to blanket Texas. Within the swirling tendrils of fog, however, a tender romantic moment is going quietly awry. Every sweet nothing Al purrs gets thrown back in his face, and Sue's unsentimental response to his proposal is to announce coolly that she is pulling up stakes and heading to Hollywood. "Maybe you'll decide to come out, too, later on," is the best she can come up with to soothe his damaged ego, and it doesn't help much.

For the love of Al's life, the reason he will uproot his own life and go hunting for her across the nation, Sue is no great shakes. We see her in just three scenes of the film, and in none of them does she make much of an impression—aside from coming across a little callous in response to Al's profession of love. In the end, we do not really know much about her—and that is the point. Neither, really, does Al. He is not actually in love with her. He is fixated on his image of her, an idealized abstraction that has little to do with the real Sue and everything to do with Al's needs.

Every time Al opens his mouth, misanthropic poison spews out. Handed a tip by a customer, he eyes the ten-dollar bill in his hand and pronounces it "a piece of paper crawling with germs." Al, being a glass-all-empty kind of person, can see that the road to Hollywood is littered with the bones of the talented and the ambitious, and he decides to simply hunker down where he is and make a life out of grudging resentment. He doesn't believe in the future, and he is consumed by so much self-loathing that he honestly cannot imagine any better tomorrow. For all her flaws, Sue is the one solid anchor in his self-pitying world. Once she departs, he is likely to be sucked into his own personal black hole of despair. He either has to chase after her or surrender to nihilism.

The second glimpse into Al's fractured psychology comes when Haskell picks him up and offers to drive him all the way from Arizona to Los Angeles. It is a lucky break, the only one to come Al's way in the entire sad story, but he never reckons it as such. The first thing he does is set about examining the dental work on his gift horse. Through the narration we can see that there is no trace of humility or gratefulness in Al, just jealousy and contempt.

When Haskell dies, it as is if the story skips a groove. The audience scratches its collective head in mutual befuddlement: "Huh? What just happened?" It is never clear if Haskell perished from a heart attack, from cracking his skull on the rocky ground, or maybe as a result of some other detail denied us in the blankly abstracted sequence. In what should be—is—the key scene of the film, the threads binding cause to effect become tangled and torn.

It is here, when the film makes the least sense, that Ulmer's careful hand reveals itself most clearly. The entire story line hangs on the premise that Al believes no one would ever accept his innocence. If there were even the remotest possibility that Al could persuade someone that Haskell's demise was accidental, then Vera's blackmail attempts might not work. So Ulmer makes sure that not even we in the audience are convinced. Al, the narrator of his own story, cannot quite believe his own version of events either. For a crucial moment, the narration and the events on screen have slipped out of sync, and Al's fate has tumbled into the gap between.

For all his railings against how unfair all this is, Al never owns up to the possibility that he made this bed himself. He clicks his tongue in discontent about Vera's ungracious response to his offer of a lift, never appreciating the irony that he was just as diffident toward Haskell. He protests vigorously against Vera's labeling him a murderer, never pausing to reflect that his theft of Haskell's identity and belongings is every bit as illegal. Above all hangs the question of why he went after Sue in the first place, whether she was ever worth the trouble he visited upon himself in her name. She vanishes from the story even before she vanishes from Al's life, as if she was never more than a blond cipher.

There is a sleight of hand at work here, a sly juggling of what is shown to the audience, so adroit as to be all but undetectable. Ulmer's magic lies in the absences, the empty spaces. There's nothing up his sleeve, he says as he shows a minimalist tableau. *Detour* clocks in at scarcely more than an hour and has only four principal characters (two of whom are dispensed with before the halfway point), and the set designers took the week off, leaving the fog machines and back-projection screens to take up the slack. Ulmer once boasted, quite implausibly, of having been contracted by Murnau to build completely new sets for each and every change of camera angle (Bogdanovich 564). Ulmer treats *Detour* like a photonegative: if I can't have unique sets for every shot, how's about no sets at all!

In anything minimalist, what is present takes on added potency. With so much excised, the choices of what to leave in seem touched by some special significance. Consider Al's rejection by Sue. It is superfluous to the plot, insomuch as there are countless ways in which the story could have motivated Al to go trekking to L.A. As far as the plot is concerned, it matters little if Al is seeking a girl he will never find, or running from the mob, or on his way to start a new job. From a narrative point of view, Sue is a classic MacGuffin, a mere excuse to motivate the hero into action. Of all the myriad ways in which to accomplish this, Ulmer chose this one: a boy wants a girl, who does not much seem to want him back. It is a fragment of some untold tale, an unanswered question, a dangling participle.

What was removed that left a hole this shape?

DETOUR'S DETOUR

Martin M. Goldsmith was a drifter, thumbing his way across the Depression-ravaged remains of a once-great nation, secretly nursing the dream to write for the movies. In 1938, the vagabond author was skulking around studio lots in Hollywood taking menial jobs on soundstages in the hopes of rubbing shoulders with the icons of the screen. Every night, he bundled up his day's worth of vain hopes, frustrations, loneliness, and caustic bile and disgorged it into his typewriter (Doody, unpaginated foreword).

Come 1939 and he got this mess of venom and spite published by the Macaulay Company as *Detour: An Extraordinary Tale*. It was his second novel, written in a spartan language of clinical disgust.

Half of the book tells the story of Al, and his fateful misadventures with Haskell and Vera. Shuffled in between the chapters of Al's unhappy chronicles is a second story, Sue's. When she drops out of Al's life, her own story continues on its own tragic and wayward path. Sue goes west to seek her own fate, and is just as abused by the results.

Sue is an undistinguished dancer in an unremarkable nightclub in a flea-bitten town. She is neither more talented nor more lovely than any of the other dancers packed onto the stage alongside her, not to mention the countless others like her cluttering the numberless stages and clubs across the entire nation. To call them a dime a dozen would be a mathematical joke—a dime is worth more than that. Yet Sue, like all the others, dreams of being a star. One day she will be discovered, and take her rightful place in the gossip columns and fan rags. That her unlikely dream is shared by gaggles of starstruck girls never once impinges on her plans. Mistaking wishful thinking for manifest destiny, she quits her job and buys a ticket to Hollywood. The Dream Factory has that kind of allure, a power to overwhelm all logic with fairy-tale visions of glamour and fame. As any classicist will tell you, a siren song is no good thing. The call of Hollywood has lured numberless aspirants to their doom, washed up on the rocky shoals of L.A.

The girl named Sue finds herself in such an inglorious dead-end, slinging hash at a greasy spoon. She has by now forgotten Al completely, and set herself to hooking up with various men chosen for their potential to provide her with a comfortable future. By dribs and drabs she acclimates herself to the idea that she can benefit by leasing her body out to the highest bidder. Unlike Al, she never blames fate for her calumny; these are her choices, and she embraces them.

Although Al is never reunited with Sue, in a way he sort of is. Vera and Sue are kindred souls, separated only be a few degrees of ruination. Al, who never really knew the woman he professed to love, cannot recognize Sue in Vera, nor does he recognize in Vera the same coruscating cynicism that rules his own outlook. Vera—tubercular whore and professional blackmailer—is no more than a fun-house mirror reflection of Al and Sue's worst, most defining, qualities. As much as Al tries to position himself as an innocent victim of circumstance, this is the fate he has chosen. For him to loathe Vera and love Sue in the same breath is to draw absurd distinctions, to split infinitesimal hairs.

Goldsmith sold *Detour* to PRC in 1944 with the proviso that he pen the screenplay adaptation. It was his big break, his entree into the world of movies. In the years to come, Goldsmith would write a number of clever thrillers, earn his keep, and win an Academy Award nomination. Sometimes the right combination of talent and good fortune does produce happy endings after all (Doody). He worked with Ulmer and PRC producer Martin Mooney to summarize the story as a screenplay treatment in October of that year. The extent of Mooney's role in the process is opaque—neither Ulmer nor Goldsmith showed much inclination to share the limelight with a mere pencil-pusher—yet it was Mooney's name on the sixteen-page treatment submitted to the Production Code of America's office for approval (Biesen 164).

Joseph Breen, the chief censor for the motion-picture business, replied that PRC had to be out of its ever-lovin' mind if it thought the PCA would give its stamp to a dirty-minded story about prostitutes and murderers. Changes would need to be made: Sue could not be seen to sleep around, and the movie could not "reflect discredit on the motion picture industry" (Biesen, 164–65).

Ulmer and Goldsmith decided that the simplest solution to that dilemma was just to drop the Sue subplot altogether and leave the story focused on Al and Vera. Breen was anxious that Al not be seen to get away with anything illegal and insisted that the "criminal antihero is absolutely in the hands of the police with a guilty regretful narration" at the end (Biesen 164). Years down the road, critics enamored of *Detour* would praise its oblique, ambiguous ending. On screen, Breen's "crime never pays" finale gets a twist, as it is unclear whether Al is actually arrested or merely haunted by the fear of imminent arrest. The literal reading of the scene, the one favored by the cramped imaginations of censors, pales next to the horror of perpetual paranoia, a man hunted by his own shadow. Either way, Al is punished something fierce.

"Fate, or some mysterious force, can put the finger on you or me for no good reason at all," Al says as the film grinds to its grim conclusion. This is also, ahem, the last line of the novel—which grinds to the same grim, ambiguous conclusion. Every detail credited to Ulmer's genius—every quotable line of dialogue, every plot twist, every cynical jab in the ribs—comes intact from Goldsmith's book. Ulmer's "genius," such as it is, seemingly lies in faithfully translating the novel into flickering celluloid.

If this is true, then Edgar Ulmer was merely a conduit, not a creator.

DETOUR, VERSION 2.0

In 1992, the Earth shook: *Detour* was selected for the National Film Registry. If you did not just gasp in astonishment, then you must need some additional information. The National Film Registry selects twenty-five motion pictures each year based on their cultural, historical, or aesthetic significance. These films are then preserved by the Library of Congress as examples of enduring American culture. In other words, it is a measure by which the United States says, "This movie rocks!"

Although the only stipulated criterion for selection is that the motion picture must be at least ten years old, the fact is that the registry is not in the habit of honoring low-budget thrillers, B pictures, Poverty Row quickies, or any other category under which *Detour* might likely be filed. It was the film-historical equivalent of Michelin handing out a five-star rating to a lone McDonalds franchise off the turnpike. "We don't care for fast food, but hoo boy, them burgers are sweet!" To a viewer in 1992 interested in seeing what all the fuss was about, all this entailed was taking a five-dollar bill into a K-Mart or a corner drug store and rifling through the bargain-video bin, lousy with copies of *Detour*, each one sporting a different cover and different company's logo on the box.

This was the ignominious fate of this legendary film, abandoned and orphaned. PRC had long since gone out of business, and the B-movie market had vanished altogether. Preserving and maintaining motion pictures is no easy or inexpensive task—that is why the National Registry only bothers with a couple dozen a year. Major media companies with a stake in the continued exploitation of a film may keep its elements in some vault, but in the absence of such economic incentives there is no reason to expect that a film will have been kept around in any particularly good form. *Detour* had lapsed into the public domain, leaving no media company with an exclusive right to its distribution. And so, no one had a solid incentive to keep it around.

In the intervening years, *Detour*'s exhibition on television and in secondary theatrical markets had ensured a healthy supply of 16 mm prints. Murky, dupey, contrasty things, these amateur-gauge reels of film made the inexpen-

Figure 10.2. *Detour* 1992—A misbegotten remake that sheds light on why Ulmer's original has become a classic. Courtesy of David Kalat.

sive production look even crappier. Unimpressive though they were, these 16 mm reels were plentiful, and in the age of public-domain video, they would guarantee a proliferation of poor-quality video copies.

Meanwhile, an individual collector had been spending his time and money amassing a private archive of old movies. Wade Williams III is an oversize sort of personality, the kind of man who unironically prints up his letterhead with a threatening WWIII logo. He takes his hobby seriously, and woe betide the fool who does not take Williams equally seriously. Where possible, he had been buying up original negatives and copyrights. *Detour*'s copyright had escaped his grasp, but he had acquired an original 35 mm camera negative, and rights to the book underlying the film. One was more valuable than the other, but which one was which depended on your point of view.

In an environment of rampant video piracy, Williams was reluctant to use the *Detour* negative to strike a high-quality video edition. Once it was out in the world, he would have little protection from those who would try to burn off copies of his work and sell it as their own; and the lack of copyright status discouraged him from allowing the negative to be used. It was a white elephant, an object of value that could not be exploited or enjoyed, merely hoarded.

The book, however . . .

It occurred to Williams's devious, scheming mind that he had a back door to claiming ownership of *Detour*. He could undertake a remake, and copyright that. That the book contained an entire second storyline not used in the 1945 film helped justify the remake as artistically valid, while at the same time Williams would show an almost slavish desire to pay homage to Ulmer's version. He would shoot in black and white (at least partially), using the same minimalist techniques as Ulmer, and maintain the 1940s setting instead of updating the film to modern times. (Williams once told me that he used the same car that had been used in the original film. I didn't at the time clarify with him whether he meant the same model of car, or the exact same vehicle, although I got the impression he meant the latter. I have never found any evidence to support this claim.) Instead of shooting in widescreen, Williams reverted to the 1940s full-frame standard—partially to mimic the original cinematography, but also as an acknowledgment that his film was destined for a life on video and cable TV. To top it off, Williams tracked down the son of actor Tom Neal, who had played Al in the original, and cast him in his father's role. Tom Neal Jr. looks strikingly like his father, which gives the remake a queer déjà-vu vibe.

Filmed in Kansas City, Missouri, Williams's *Detour* is a clumsy, half-formed wreck. Shot on video and given a chintzy synthesizer score, it gives off the acrid air of an amateur production. The actors are awkward on camera, giving theatrical performances better suited to the stage. Tom Neal Jr.'s voice-over narration is badly spoken, as if a rehearsal read-through had been recorded and used as is.

The new and unimproved *Detour* had its premiere and one-week run at the Fine Arts Theater in Kansas City in February 1992, before moving on to home video through VCI and cablecasts on HBO. The 1945 film on whose blueprint it was modeled was winning accolades still, forty-some years after its birth—winning the highest honor Congress would bestow on a movie—while Williams's *Detour* followed its inevitable slide into obscurity.

Williams's mistake is not obvious. He did what seemed logical. He had a time-tested story and a cinematic approach that had proved itself. He stayed close enough to Ulmer's vision to take few artistic risks, yet he added new material and ideas into the mix to keep it from being a pointless exercise in hero worship. If he had limited financial resources or actors of questionable talent . . . well, these limitations had been Ulmer's, too. All Ulmer had to do was usher Goldsmith's prose onto the screen; certainly anyone could do the same.

Evidently, this is not the case.

Looking coldly at the transition from Goldsmith's *Detour* to Ulmer's *Detour* one could draw the conclusion that Ulmer played little role in making the film what it was. But a movie is so much more than just a filmed story, and while it is true that many of the more obvious merits of *Detour* can be credited to Goldsmith, this does not mean that Ulmer was not, in the shadows and margins and subtle details, contributing less obvious values.

THREE *DETOURS* MAKE A RIGHT

In examining the differences and discrepancies between the three versions of *Detour*, then, it is easy to see that there are successful choices and misfired mistakes, and that history has adjudged Ulmer's rendition to be the best balance between these extremes. There are substantial plot details, characters, and lines of dialogue common to all three versions, and therefore these variables can be canceled out of the equation. Of what remains, some of Ulmer's choices were prescribed for him: the seamier aspects of the novel were forbidden by the censors from inclusion in the 1945 film, for example. Even Ulmer's famously parsimonious use of back projection and abstracted sets were as much forced on him by circumstance as they were matters of choice: the film was shot in June 1945, when wartime restrictions on location shooting would have forbidden much else (Biesen 165).

The legend goes that Ulmer cranked the picture out in six days. I dare you to find a reference to *Detour* that does not repeat the six-day myth. Years later, his daughter Arianné Ulmer Cipes pulled out PRC documentation (for a film on Ulmer's career); the documentation clearly states a generous fourteen-day schedule—essentially the same production block that Universal had given him for *The Black Cat*! (Palm 00:42:00). Pretending he had made it faster and cheaper gave Ulmer a way to buff his image as a miracle worker, and provided a handy excuse for any of *Detour*'s rougher edges. In fact, he had little to apologize for—*Detour*'s rough edges, visible though they certainly are, simply correspond to the lean prose style of the novel, which is written as the literary equivalent of a low-budget quickie.

In his cast selection, Ulmer made inspired choices. Since the film eventually devolves into a two-hander, the casting of the two leads was critical. As Vera, Ann Savage gives the performance of her life. Neé Bernice Lyon, she was an army brat whose attempt to break into Hollywood initially resulted in a frustration not unlike that experienced by Vera herself—she was a failed actress who was left to sell her body when nothing else was available. The early 1940s found Savage working just unbilled walk-on parts. Her primary line of business at that time was as a pinup girl, quite popular with the troops—a gig that rewarded her most rudimentary physical assets but said nothing about her talent. *Detour* represented a major break for the struggling actress. "I had never had a good part like that," she would later say (Palm 00:39:00). In stark contrast to what had gone before, Ulmer sought to conceal her glamour, hiding her beauty behind dirty makeup and greasy hair. He encouraged her to scream and sneer, to disregard what was ladylike. "I often tell young actresses—if you can play Vera, you can play anything" (Palm 00:40:00). The Academy of Motion Pictures Arts and Sciences agreed, and in 2005 praised her as an "icon and legend." Following *Detour*, her career took off, with Savage often cast in femme-fatale roles, costarring five times with Tom Neal.

Like Savage, Neal was given a role that connected to his own personality and life. He was educated as a lawyer and a boxer—two professions in opposite spheres, perhaps, but also just different ways in which to fight. There was a simmering, seething anger in Neal, a latent violence that he held in check (at certain times more than at others). In *Detour* he played a man driven to self-destruction, and afterward he followed that maleficent detour to his own doom. Neal's first wife was an actress whose attention he did not fully command. They broke up, got back together, broke up again—and along the way Neal flew into a jealous rage at a rival, beating the other man to a bloody pulp. For this sin he was blacklisted in Hollywood. Having all but lost his career, he then lost her, too. Neal's second wife was claimed by cancer. By his third marriage, Neal's commitment to undying love was no longer seaworthy: he shot this woman in the head, and was sentenced to prison (Muller 179).

Detour skirts around the biographies of its makers. Forged in the fire of a writer's frustration, it started off as a way for Martin Goldsmith to vent. Goldsmith's most personal novel would come to be seen as Edgar Ulmer's most personal film, starring actors whose lives flitted through a similar orbit. The magic of *Detour* is in the curious circumstance by which Goldsmith's

Figure 10.3. Edgar G. Ulmer—a maverick filmmaker whose films outshone their humble origins. Courtesy of David Kalat.

angry screed turned out to be fully transferable—what was "personal" was also universal. Wade Williams III's mistake was in thinking that this unique alignment of artists and opportunities could be reduced to a simple formula, to be repeated decades later, to anything resembling the same result.

"I really am looking for absolution for all the things I had to do for money's sake," Ulmer told Bogdanovich (603). It is a statement that could just as easily have been uttered by anyone else involved in this classic film. In *Detour*, they found it.

BIBLIOGRAPHY

Biesen, Sheri Chinen. *Blackout: World War II and the Origins of Film Noir* (Baltimore: Johns Hopkins University Press, 2005), 162–66.

Bogdanovich, Peter. *Who the Devil Made It: Conversations with Legendary Film Directors* (New York: Ballantine Books, 1997).

Doody, Richard. "Foreword," in *Detour: An Extraordinary Tale*, by Martin M. Goldsmith (O'Bryan House, 2005).

Goldsmith, Martin M. *Detour: An Extraordinary Tale* (New York: Macaulay, 1939).

Grissemann, Stefan. *Mann im Schatten: Der Filmemacher Edgar G. Ulmer* (Regensburg: Paul Zsolnay Verlag, 2003), 21–30.

Knipfel, Jim. "Fate Stuck Out Its Foot," *NYPress*, 11–17 November 1998, 12–14.

Muller, Eddie. *Dark City: The Lost World of Film Noir* (New York: St. Martin's Griffin, 1998), 177–79.

FILM CITED

Edgar G. Ulmer: The Man Off-Screen (Michael Palm, director; New York: Kino International, 2004).

11

Fantasy and Failure in *Strange Illusion*

Hugh S. Manon

> Desire is propped up by a fantasy, at least one foot of which is in the Other, and precisely the one that counts, even and above all if it happens to limp.
>
> —Jacques Lacan, *Écrits*

Since its release in 1945, critics and fans alike have found it difficult to identify the genre of Edgar G. Ulmer's film *Strange Illusion*, and with good reason. Initially billed as both a "psychological drama" and a "romantic mystery," the plot of the film is not so much a generic hybrid as an unpredictable string of non sequiturs—abrupt shifts in narrative, soundtrack, and mise-en-scène that seem designed to call attention to generic difference per se. Beginning with its distinctive opening framing device—the cryptic, fog-enshrouded dream of the film's young protagonist, Paul Cartwright (Jimmy Lydon)—the film's first act plays like a noir amnesia film turned inside out. The problem is not that Paul fails to recognize what is right in front of him—that his mother's suitor, Brett Curtis (William Wellman), is an insidious and perhaps murderous villain. Rather, Paul's crisis is that his dream has revealed the true state of things all too clearly. Far from suffering a loss of memory, Paul knows things that he cannot possibly know, and must convince others that his outrageous, seemingly paranoid accusations about Curtis are nonetheless valid. Indeed, the film's major trope can be summed up in a single line, delivered by Paul to his confidant, Dr. Martin Vincent (Regis Toomey): "This may sound kind of crazy, Doc, but that dream is beginning to happen."

As in an amnesia film, Paul's conflict begins with the realization that he is at one remove from the reality that surrounds him—a reality in which his friends and family refuse to believe that the seemingly benevolent Brett Curtis is anything other than what he appears to be. Unlike in an amnesia plot, however, Paul is not hermetically sealed out of the truth of his circumstances, but instead sealed in. He does not investigate; he only confirms, with all of the expected answers dropping right into his hands. In terms of genre, then, if the film is supposed to be a mystery, then why is the enigma so elementary, so easily solved? If it is a romance, then why do both Paul and Curtis appear so casually unconcerned with—and even allergic to—their supposed love interests? If it is a suspense thriller, then what do we make of Paul's immunity to persecution, and the fact that his foreknowledge negates any real tension or surprise, while guaranteeing that in the end there can be no twist? Moreover, if (as many critics have argued) *Strange Illusion* is a film noir like Ulmer's other 1945 film, *Detour*, then why are the women Paul interacts with so virtuous and decent, and why is the film's ending so cloyingly optimistic?

Perhaps the most surprising of the film's many generic and tonal shifts occurs when Curtis, the film's purported villain, is revealed to be exactly what Paul suspects him of being: not only a serial perpetrator of so-called "perfect crimes," but also "the cruelest man in the world."[1] When Curtis arrives at Restview Manor, a local sanitarium, for a moment the film shifts into full-on noir mode, revealing both Curtis's true identity as a legendary criminal mastermind named Claude Barrington, and his collaboration with his former psychiatrist, an equally insidious character named Professor Muhlbach (Charles Arnt). In a clandestine exchange of dialogue, we learn that the two men are already engaged in a plot to exact revenge on the family of the deceased Judge Albert Cartwright—and especially his young wife Virginia (Sally Eilers), Paul's mother. Although the specific reason for Barrington's revenge is left ambiguous—having something to do with the deceased judge's "meddling interference"—their past history is clearly motive enough for Barrington to hatch an impossibly risky plot: ingratiating himself with the Cartwright family, marrying Virginia, killing her in some undetectable fashion, and then inheriting her considerable fortune.[2] Most implausible of all, Barrington's sudden reappearance confirms that, for him, to have murdered the judge and gotten away with the crime was somehow just not satisfying; he now must abuse the dead man's family. If all this reads a bit like a soap opera, the film is that, too, as well as a kind of Gothic romance, a 1940s teenpic, and a Shakespearean adaptation, with Curtis playing Claudius to Paul's Hamlet. The film begs not so much for an accounting of the specific quality of these generic components, as for an explanation of the impulse to "repeated genre-shifting" itself.

In the pages that follow, I argue that one way to rationalize the generic instability of *Strange Illusion* is to understand the entirety of the film's narrative as representing the interior of Paul's psyche—the daydreams of a young man who has himself perhaps watched too many movies. From the moment Paul awakens at the film's beginning, to the final sequence when he is knocked unconscious—only to resume the dream, this time more optimistically—the events we witness on the screen are not Paul's objective reality, but his elaborate *fantasy*. In Lacanian psychoanalysis, fantasy can be understood as a framework of incomplete scenes, a landscape of imagined lack into which one escapes in order to escape a confrontation with the Real of his or her desire. In the words of Slovenian philosopher Slavoj Žižek, whose elaborations of the Lacanian notion of fantasy are foundational to this project, fantasy "provides the co-ordinates of our desire"; it "constructs the frame enabling us to desire something" (*Sublime Object* 118). As I go on to explain, the psychoanalytic conception of fantasy is useful not only in explaining Paul's plight, but also in contextualizing the distinct and occasionally bizarre techniques through which director Ulmer, the infamous auteur of Poverty Row, puts his stamp on Paul's story. Indeed, the more tenuously artificial and cheap-looking Ulmer's techniques become, the more readily we may be convinced that the arrival of Curtis/Barrington does not represent an invasion of Paul's "real reality," but rather the central element in a fantasy frame through which protagonist Paul Cartwright gradually learns how to desire.

IN (BETWEEN) DREAMS

Albeit an anachronism, the single film that does the most to illuminate the formal and narrative strangeness of *Strange Illusion* is David Lynch's *Mulholland Drive* (2001), a feature-length experimental narrative whose often confusing plot can convincingly be explained as the elaborate dream of Diane Selwyn (Naomi Watts), who for most of the film appears only within the dream, as Betty Elms (also Watts). The problem, of course, is that the viewer is likewise "inside" Diane's dream from the moment the film begins, and remains there for over two-thirds of the film's running time, never questioning that Betty Elms is anything other than a "real" person.[3] A similar textual comparison is afforded by Robert Altman's *Images* (1971), in which the viewer, often without realizing it, is transported inside the psychotic point of view of protagonist Cathryn (Susannah York). When Cathryn's now-dead ex-lover reappears at a country cottage, initially nothing indicates to the viewer that he is an apparition, and this shifting between the two "levels" of reality that Cathryn experiences fuels a number of horrific shocks as the film unfolds. Recently, a number of more mainstream films, such as M. Night Shyamalan's *The Sixth Sense* (1999) and Alejandro Amenábar's *The Others* (2001), have similarly manipulated the viewer's perspective by locating the action wholly inside a false reality without any objective perspective to provide context.[4]

All of the aforementioned films, however, benefit from their appearance in an era in which audiences are more amenable to being unwittingly immersed in unreality. Audiences are thrilled when, at the end of *The Sixth Sense*, it is revealed that Dr. Malcolm Crowe (Bruce Willis) has been dead all along, and that for an hour and a half we, like Crowe, have been unaware of our own delusion. *Strange Illusion*, I argue, is equally manipulative (and equally unapologetic) in delivering the psychic interior of its protagonist packaged as objective reality. The difference is that our nostalgic view of the 1940s, coupled with the "aw shucks" wholesomeness and youthful naiveté of Paul—whose trusted perspective underwrites most of the narrative—effectively prohibits us from assuming the worst: that the film is deluding us from beginning to end. Particularly curious in this regard is the fact that the narrative never accounts for how Paul could have dreamed Curtis's actions and motives in the first place. Moreover, once Curtis is recognized as Barrington and shot by the authorities, the film simply ends, as if psychic detection were a common and accepted practice and no explanation were required. The viewer is left to surmise that it was all an uncannily accurate hunch on Paul's part, or a perhaps a hyperextended episode of déjà vu.

At the same time, owing to its repeated emphasis on Freudian theory (note the volume of Freud cheated out toward the camera on Paul's desk), we can easily arrive at a second, pop-psychoanalytic reading of Paul's prescience. It is well-known that Ulmer was interested in psychoanalysis, and part of the film's topical appeal at mid-century derived from its invocation of Freudian theory—the script's nominal attempt to exploit what the film's promotional materials clumsily label "the unexplainable subconsciousness [*sic*] and the interpretation of dreams."[5] In *Strange Illusion*, the source of the protagonist's crisis is ostensibly Oedipal. As the film begins, Paul is in the process of discovering that his mother, a widow of two years, has developed an interest in another man, and that this interest could lead to marriage, thus obviating Paul's status as his mother's primary partner. The result is Paul's dream of an ominous male who has come to take his mother away. Translated into waking life, Paul's dream appears to come true when Curtis appears on the scene to court Virginia, and before too long he begins to resemble the master criminal Barrington (a pun on "barrier," which is what he threatens to become for Paul). Consequently, Paul initiates an investigation to reveal Curtis's true identity, thus overcoming the (potential, new) father in order to regain access to the mother.

Paul's visions can be understood as symptomatic of a family-wide denial that has been going on since the judge's death. Stirred up by the arrival of Curtis, this repressed traumatic material slowly burbles out of the unconscious and back to the surface, albeit in a transformed way. This, of course, represents the orthodox Freudian reading of the film, and an interpretation that is not lost on the film's writers. Freud's theories are given voice later in the film by Muhlbach, albeit in a Hollywood-ized form: "In some cases, filial devotion to a mother goes beyond the borderline of normality. It can frequently produce hallucinations . . . I believe it is your emotional aversion to your mother's remarriage which produces these neurotic symptoms."

The problem here is that a hallucination, as we commonly understand the term, is by definition at odds with reality, and far from a predictor of events to come. Perhaps in *Strange Illusion*, as in the films by Altman, Lynch, Shyamalan, and Amenábar, the problem is not that dreams are self-evidently encroaching on reality, but that the dividing line(s) between "objective" reality and Paul's distorted interior psychology has been camouflaged too well. In this way, the viewer is left unaware that any such shift has taken place, or at least is unclear as to what "reality" we occupy at any given point.[6] In other words, the "hallucination" Muhlbach describes is not an aberration within Paul's psyche, but instead a pervasive "other" logic of which Paul himself is the symptom. If this hypothesis holds true (or at least cannot be easily dismissed), then given its appearance in 1945 *Strange Illusion* must be considered far more radical than the more contemporary films I have mentioned above.

Ulmer provides abundant indicators that the film's opening and closing frames are in fact Paul's dreams—that he is really asleep. The rest of the film is something else, but if this "something else" into which Paul awakens is not reality, then what is it? To reiterate, my contention is that in a profound flaunting of Hollywood narrative, generic convention, and common-sense oppositionality, when Paul wakes up at the beginning of the film we are not transported into his normal "objective" reality, but instead into Paul's own highly idiosyncratic subjectivity. But a crucial question immediately arises. If the body of the film is really Paul's fantasy, why then is it so dramatic, full of conflict, and psychologically painful? The answer is that this is fantasy in a specifically Lacanian sense—an imagined scene full of incompletion and inaccessibility which permits the protagonist to continually redefine and reorient his desire.

According to Lacan, dreams and fantasies are neither synonymous, nor are they unrelated; however, they are both bound up in the question of what, for the human subject, constitutes "awakening." Žižek notes that "the Lacanian thesis [is] that it is only in the dream that we come close to the real awakening—that is, to the Real of our desire." Žižek continues:

> When we awaken into reality after a dream, we usually say to ourselves "it was just a dream," thereby blinding ourselves to the fact that in our everyday, wakening reality we are *nothing but a consciousness of this dream*. It was only in the

> dream that we approached the fantasy-framework which determines our activity, our mode of acting in reality itself. (*Sublime Object* 47)

In such an arrangement, what we call "reality"—the symbolic landscape into which we "awaken"—is to a greater or lesser degree always a fantasy, a framework that exists to support our desire, furnishing us with a route toward satisfaction but not with satisfaction itself. The dream is not, then, itself a fantasy. Instead the dream is a kind of "near approach" to jouissance that we never approach in reality, but which nonetheless predisposes us to certain fantasies that keep our desire, and thus our "reality," up and running. In a strong sense, then, Paul's predicament anticipates a line delivered by Eden Lane (Barbara Payton) in Ulmer's 1955 film noir *Murder Is My Beat*: "The only way that I can wake up from this nightmare is to go to sleep." For Paul, the problem is not that he cannot wake up from a frightening dream, but that he cannot go to sleep and thus exit his nightmarish, conflict-driven fantasy. In the section that follows, I argue that such an interpretation is borne out not only by what Paul says and does (i.e., the dialogue and actions scripted for him), but also by the "strange" manipulations of film form brought to bear by director Ulmer and his filmmaking cohorts. In other words, Paul's engagement on the plane of fantasy is set in high relief at the precise moments that Ulmer's style flares up.

DIME-STORE AESTHETICS

According to Frank Krutnik, Ulmer's notorious film *Detour* is of particular interest not because of the director's ability to transcend budgetary limitations, or make them disappear on screen, but rather because of his willingness to embrace and even "play up" the clunky, at times cardboard, artifice that appears in low-budget films almost by default:

> The blatant coincidences around which the narrative turns, together with the enclosed world of the film (exaggerated by its very low budget: the minimal cast and settings, the use of stock footage), serve to de-emphasize realist denotation and to suggest that everything within the film is a projection of the hero's psychic disturbance. (126)

This same unusual synergy persists in *Strange Illusion*, but with the added benefit that the film's narrative centers directly on its protagonist's "psychic disturbance." In the previous section, I read against the grain of the film's framing device to establish Paul's narrative as bearing the structure of fantasy. In this section, I examine three distinct stylistic repetitions in Ulmer's film, each of which both complements and helps to produce such a reading. The formal manipulations I examine are as follows: 1) the use of cheap-looking scale models as evidentiary sites, 2) the appearance of highly artificial, unnaturally close rear projection as a signifier of Paul's skewed relation to reality, and 3) a combined use of camera movement and nondiegetic musical cues to frame the story's inciting incident. Such highly artificial manipulations of film form, I argue, not only make viewers temporarily aware that they are watching a movie, but also express the implausibility of what the film's protagonist supposedly experiences as real, creating a sense that Paul does not participate in the film's various encounters and discoveries so much as they are privately screened for his benefit alone.

In *Strange Illusion*, scale models appear in two separate instances, each of which relates to the death of Paul's father. Common in both high- and low-budget films of the period, Ulmer's use of scale models would be insignificant if not for the mutual associations they create. The first scale-model sequence appears in Paul's initial dream and depicts a delivery truck pushing his father's sedan in front of an oncoming train. It is a dimly lit and relatively desolate country setting, suggesting that no one was around to see the incident. If we are not convinced that the train is a model, everything becomes clear when the engine makes contact with the car. There is no explosion or crunching of steel. Instead, the sedan is nudged along the railroad tracks with all the violence of a salt shaker sliding across a kitchen counter. This lack of large-scale inertia is our best clue that, despite the detailed rendering of the models, nothing "really real" is happing here. Significantly, too, the perspective is never explicitly attributed to any character in the film; it belongs solely to the mise-en-scène of Paul's dream. Consequently, the sequence resounds more as a schoolboy fantasy of what violent death must look like, rather than anything approaching realism.[7]

The second scale-model shot appears near the end of the film, when Paul and Muhlbach go to the roof of the sanitarium to try out the professor's binoculars. Much of the scene's tension derives from Paul's recklessness: he walks around with the binoculars held up to his eyes, paying no attention to the edge of the roof and nearly stepping off. When Paul spots an abandoned farm building and inquires about it, the professor's facial expression reveals deep concern, even suggesting that he would like to shove Paul off the roof to his death. Whereas the train crash scene that Paul sees in his dream can only be imaginary—revealing a scene that no one was there to see, and from a high-angle vantage point that seems suspiciously impossible to occupy—the shot through the binoculars decodes in precisely the opposite manner, as a real, material discovery. Out there in the countryside is an abandoned building—a perfect location to dispose of crime-scene evidence—and in the next scene

Paul and Dr. Vincent set out to explore it. The important point, however, has to do with the palpable artifice of the tiny scale-model barn. Like the model railroad we have already seen, the barn seems like a child's toy, designed to declare its own status as a fake. Framed with a binocular-shaped matte, the shot of the barn likewise correlates with the high artifice of Paul's dream world, at the very least suggesting that, in this film, all bets are off as to what is real and what is imaginary. Is Paul imagining that two years ago Muhlbach was standing at that very same spot, watching through his binoculars as Judge Cartwright was killed by the train? Is it possible that everything we see in the film represents a retrospective fantasy launched from Paul's own (now permanent) room at the sanitarium? Perhaps the stoic, pipe-smoking Vincent is not Paul's family physician, but instead his personal psychiatrist?[8] Or does Paul demonize Muhlbach because *he* is Paul's full-time psychiatrist, working hard to extricate Paul from the ever-present fantasy frame he inhabits? It seems to me that all these interpretations remain viable, provided we understand this film not as striving for realism and failing, but as playfully enjoying the gaps in its own aesthetic.

Related to Ulmer's use of scale models is his highly artificial use of rear projection. As in *The Sixth Sense*, where a sudden temperature drop signals that a ghost is present, Ulmer's rear-projected scenery indicates that what we see is not "Paul's sight" in some quasi-objective sense, but rather "Paul's vision"—in other words, his fantasy. Film noir scholar James Naremore has remarked that Ulmer "may be the only Hollywood director of the period—aside from Orson Welles—to deliberately exploit the artificiality of back projection" (148). Such an assessment applies not only to *Strange Illusion* and, obviously, *Detour*, but also to a number of Ulmer's other films. A particularly instructive instance of rear projection appears in the second act of *The Strange Woman* (1946), after Jenny Hager (Hedy Lamarr) informs Ephraim Poster (Louis Hayward) that she wants him to kill her husband Isaiah (Gene Lockhart) on a river trip into Maine logging country. As the party proceeds through the rapids in a canoe, a highly artificial rear-projected backdrop sets in high relief the tense moment of truth—an intent to murder witnessed only by the film's audience. "High relief" is the proper term for it, too, since the images of the two key players, father and son, appear "raised" against the not-so-real backdrop. They are spotlighted, circumscribed in a snow globe of intrigue, not by the film's lighting, but by the rear projected unreality itself. Yet is this not precisely how Paul's fantasy appears at various points throughout *Strange Illusion*—as a snow globe viewed from the inside, in which we are always aware of some vague, circumscribing limit point, or edge, where the fantasy ceases?

In *Strange Illusion*, Ulmer's use of rear projection is most remarkable in a night scene in which Paul peers out a front window of the sanitarium. Paul sits on a windowsill and witnesses Curtis/Barrington, who has previously stated that he never learned to drive an automobile, behind the wheel of a black sedan, with Muhlbach in the passenger seat. As they pull away, Paul notes the license number, yet the movement of his head appears out of sync with the images in front of him, as if he is preoccupied or slightly dazed. This mismatch between foreground and background action is only exacerbated by the angle from which the rear-projected footage was shot; it makes Paul appear entirely too close to the sedan, as if he were hovering ghostlike in space, just behind the car. My point, of course, is neither to critique this shot as "bad filmmaking," nor to suggest that the artifice is purely intentional. Rather, we might more profitably explain this shot and others like it as *successful failures*—moments at which formal flaws (occurring for whatever reason) directly complement the film's scripted plot. In other words, although it would be impossible to describe "in general" how a fantasy looks, Paul's view out the window captures precisely this sense of the ineffable in fantasy. The space we see simply doesn't "add up," creating an uncanny sense that Paul's perspective is not divorced from reality, yet not entirely married to it either.

Having interpreted the narrative of *Strange Illusion* as Paul's extended daydream, while suggesting that Ulmer's embracing of artifice demarcates both the "strangeness" and the limit points of the fantasy, it seems reasonable to ask at what point, if any, Paul's fantasy begins. To answer this question, I contend that we need only identify the moment at which Ulmer's style becomes noticeable as such. Following the opening dream sequence, the film's first stylistic flourish occurs just after Paul awakens at Vincent's cabin. The two have decided to go fishing and are casually dropping lines into an idyllic pond—a nice opportunity for relaxation, and perhaps also for Paul to daydream. In the midst of this placid scene, a mysterious figure approaches. The tone of the nondiegetic music is ominous, and a left-to-right tracking shot follows the man as he draws closer. When the camera pushes in to a shot of the boat on the pond, we are delivered a strong sense of the mystery man's perspective, and the conventions of horror film lead us to believe something is horribly wrong. Perhaps he has come to eavesdrop on the men, or even kill them. Then, just as abruptly, all is well. "Hi there," the man calls out, waving. Vincent returns, "Hiya, Mac. What are you doing down here, spying on us? You old fox!" The tone of the music changes to gleeful conviviality, and the voyeuristic camera movement stops. Mac (Vic Potel), the game warden, has come to deliver a letter to Paul, and the contents of this letter can be understood as the first of a series of highly unlikely, yet equally concrete (in a word, surreal) details that constitute Paul's fantasy. Paul scoops a fish out of the water (trusty metaphor for the unconscious), and they proceed to shore.

The letter is from Paul's father, who died two years prior under mysterious circumstances. Paul explains the unusual situation to Mac as follows: "Dad left a series of letters with the office of his estate. I get one every few months." Such a scenario begs the question: why would an apparently healthy man leave letters of advice for his son when he had no reason to expect his demise was imminent? Is the unlikely letter real to begin with, or a figment of Paul's fantasy? The thrust of the letter involves an admonition to Paul, which he reads aloud to Vincent:

> It will be your responsibility as the man of the family to protect your mother and Dorothy by being constantly vigilant of their associates. I have always guarded your mother, who is so much younger than I, for in my experience I've had ample opportunity to observe the cunning of unscrupulous impostors.

The words directly recall the shadowy figure in Paul's opening dream, a tall man in a fedora whose face we cannot see, but who both Paul's mother and his sister Dorothy (Jayne Hazard) mistake for Paul's father. Vincent responds: "Fits right in with your dream, doesn't it? A curious coincidence." Curious indeed, as one would logically imagine Paul's dream to have *followed* a letter such as this, rather than anticipating it, and in such literal terms. Although one might endlessly speculate about which events in the film are fantasy (and to what degree) and which represent a more objective reality, there is no better place to begin than Paul's receipt of the letter. Is the judge's admonition what sparks Paul's fantasy, or is it the first major element in the fantasy itself? Either way, these are the terms in which Ulmer's film begs to be examined.

HAVE YOU MET LYDIA?

In the parlance of psychoanalysis, the term "fantasy" does not designate the imaginary realization of an unrealizable desire (e.g., having sex with a supermodel, winning the lottery), but rather the staging of a scene in which lack itself appears. In his book *Looking Awry*, Žižek explains the purpose of fantasy:

> Fantasy is usually conceived as a scenario that realizes the subject's desire. This elementary definition is quite adequate, on condition that we take it *literally*: what the fantasy stages is not a scene in which our desire is fulfilled, fully satisfied, but on the contrary, a scene that realizes, stages, the desire as such. The fundamental point of psychoanalysis is that desire is not something given in advance, but something that has to be constructed—and it is precisely the role of fantasy to give the coordinates of the subject's desire, to specify its object, to

> locate the position the subject assumes in it. It is only through fantasy that the subject is constituted as desiring: *through fantasy we learn how to desire.* (6)

If the film as we experience it is Paul's fantasy, a crucial question remains: in what specific way is he learning to desire? Or, more concretely, in the final analysis what does Paul take to be the object that will satisfy him? Although the film seems to suggest that his mother's safety and happiness is Paul's primary goal, this interpretation overlooks the deferral of romance between Paul and the relatively minor character Lydia (Mary McLeod), who professes an infatuation with Paul early in the film. Moreover, in the film's closing image it is Lydia and not Virginia who promenades into the future with Paul, and this telos suggests that Paul's fantasy has more than anything primed him to desire the normative, heterosexual union that appears in the closing seconds of so many classical Hollywood narratives.

Despite her paucity of screen time, the character of Lydia nonetheless serves three major functions in the film. First, Lydia appears early on expressing an obvious romantic interest in Paul, only to be ignored when Paul notices that his father's portrait has been removed from its prominent location above the downstairs fireplace and relegated to an upstairs study. In this instance, she is a marker of Paul's increasing obsession with his mother's newfound romance, and his possible mental disturbance. Second, Lydia appears in the Cartwright's swimming pool as an object of Curtis/Barrington's visible lust. The significance of this scene becomes clear only later, when Lydia reveals to Paul that during that same afternoon at the pool, Curtis, unseen by any of the other guests, "swam underwater, got a stranglehold on [her] and started kissing [her]." Finally, as I have described above, Lydia appears in the film-ending dream sequence, locking arms with Paul and walking off toward the horizon and a hopeful future together.

Given this trajectory, I want to suggest that in the final analysis it is Paul's union with Lydia, and not solely his relationship with his mother, that the film's lengthy fantasy works to resolve. In other words, the entire procedure of suspecting Curtis to be an evil mastermind, researching his background, voluntarily entering an insane asylum, and, finally, proving that Curtis is Barrington and that he killed Paul's father is a roundabout way for Paul to come to sexually desire Lydia (and women in general) as "she who needs to be protected." The film is abundantly patriarchal on this count, and the fact that Lydia functions as a kind of junior counterpart to Paul's mother is precisely the point. Lydia needs to be desired by the lecherous criminal other, and then protected from him, in order to finally be desired by Paul. In other words, Paul does not need Lydia to replace his (barred, inaccessible) mother, but rather needs for her to take up a position analogous with Virginia's—becoming a woman who, according to the posthumous letter Paul receives (or fantasizes receiving) from his father, needs to be guarded and protected with constant vigilance. When Curtis arrives on the scene, the logic of Paul's deduction is juvenile: a man has come to replace my dead father, therefore he must have killed my father. In a decidedly noir convolution, it is precisely the fact that everyone is so infatuated with the benevolent Curtis that confirms his guilt in Paul's eyes. Like every other failed noir plot, Curtis/Barrington's scheme is "perfect, too perfect," and Paul's theoretical question to Curtis about the possibility of committing a "perfect crime" only underscores the paradox.[9] Yet this sense of undetectable perfectionism is precisely what makes for a perfect fantasy frame.

To be clear, then, Barrington is the primary object of Paul's fantasy. Correspondingly, more than any other person, object, or event in the film, it seems reasonable to assert that Barrington does not, in any objective sense, exist. Cunning to a fault, Barrington is nothing but a conduit for Paul's desire for Lydia, a catalyst that permits him to pair up with her in a socially acceptable way. In *Enjoy Your Symptom*, Žižek agues that

> Psychoanalysis sustains . . . the exact opposite of the usual, commonsense opinion according to which fantasy figures are nothing but distorted, combined, or otherwise concocted figures or their "real" models, of people of flesh and blood that we've met in our experience. We can relate to these "people of flesh and blood" only insofar as we are able to identify them with a certain place in our symbolic fantasy space, or, to put it in a more pathetic way, only insofar as they fill out a place preestablished in our dream—we fall in love with a woman insofar as her features coincide with our fantasy figure of a Woman. (5–6)

By fantasizing, in appropriately juvenile, cartoonish terms, what he would do if he were an expert criminologist like his father, Paul comes into his own desire, fully assumes it, and can thus proceed into a heterosexual coupling with Lydia. In a strong sense, Barrington's behind-the-scenes admission early in the film is exactly what Paul needs to hear: "The boy's as persistent as his father was." Coming out of the mouth of the world's greatest criminal, such a compliment is as pure a schoolboy fantasy as we are likely to witness; yet the comparison of Paul to his father as a man of Law is exactly what permits Lydia to assume her position as protectable, and thus desirable. In many ways, Paul's is the quintessential mid-century heterosexual male fantasy.

CONCLUSION: DOING THE MATH

While Paul's patriarchal quest for justice is precisely what sets the stage for his coming to desire Lydia, her pursuit by Barrington serves a secondary function—one that allows Paul to reconcile another remarkable aspect of his father's desire, and assume it as his own. I am referring specifically to the striking youthfulness of Paul's mother Virginia, whom both of her children refer to simply as "the Princess." Although never mentioned in dialogue, the numerical age of the film's various characters is a matter of some concern, since in a worst-case scenario their respective ages test the very limits of biological possibility. Paul is an American law student, which makes him at least twenty-one or twenty-two (actor Lydon's real-life age in 1945), and his looks and mannerisms suggest he could not possibly be older than twenty-five. Also odd is the fact that Virginia is described as "so much younger" than the judge. Assuming she is thirty-seven (the same age as Eilers), and that Paul is neither adopted nor a child from a previous marriage (something the film scrupulously avoids mentioning), Virginia would have been pregnant with him at around age fifteen.[10] Our clues to Judge Cartwright's age are even more obscure, since he does not appear as a living character in the film, and the only image presented of him is his looming oversized portrait above the mantelpiece. Painted at least two years before the story begins, the portrait of the judge makes him look around sixty, which suggests he was forty or so when Paul was born. All of this is speculative, of course, and although we can hypothesize endlessly about the unspecified ages of fictional characters, such speculation does have its limits. There can be no question, for instance, that in the person of Virginia, the judge married a (very) young woman, almost certainly less than half his age. Yet is this not precisely the aspect of Curtis's character that Paul (and presumably the film's viewer) find both startling and loathsome: that he is an older man attracted to young girls? Perhaps it is this mathematical problem of Paul's own birth, including the possibility of his conception in a lecherous affair, that the protagonist cannot bear, and which his fantasy of Barrington seeks to reconcile.

An even more interesting arithmetical problem occurs, however, between the film's opening dream and its parallel at film's end. In the opening dream, the frame is divided by an ominous silhouette whom we later find out to be Curtis/Barrington. In the closing dream, this figure has been vanquished, and as the film fades to black we see *two* equally black silhouettes proceeding toward the camera. Visually recalling the earlier scene, the film again asks its viewer to "do the math": one has been subtracted, and two appear. In what sort of logic can we say this: *one minus one equals two*? The answer is the logic of psychoanalysis itself, provided we understand Curtis/Barrington in his role as barrier or blockage. Once the barrier is recognized, dealt with, and thus removed from the (fantasy) scene, a couple forms. Yet the couple cannot proceed as such without this blockage having been surmounted. In other words, in order to commence coupling, Paul needs to fully assume his desire, which is not at all to say his satisfaction. Only through Paul's encountering the blockage as a site of lack, and fantasizing a way to deal with it, can Lydia occupy her position as "beyond-the-problem"—in other words, as desirable. The act of subtraction becomes an addition, or at least a kind of connection.

Whereas critics have tended to view the film's optimistic, even saccharine ending in Paul's dream ("Look, Mother, we can see ahead!") as out of sync with the majority of the film's conflict, such a reading overlooks the film's absolute final image. In the final shot, Vincent comes on screen to lead Virginia away, and she is replaced at Paul's side by Lydia. United at last, they proceed forward; but instead of approaching a sunny horizon, their image gradually darkens and goes black—a strangely uninverted parallel with Barrington's image in the film's opening sequence (see figure 11.1). If Paul has indeed learned to desire as his father desired, the inky blackness of Paul's and Lydia's silhouettes must be read not as a final, conflict-ending resolution, but as a pure repetition of the barrier that brought them together, an ongoing fantasy which, as it unfolds through the years, will inevitably require more fantasies, and more barriers.

Figure 11.1. One minus one equals two—the concluding frames of *Strange Illusion* (1945).

NOTES

1. The description appears in the film's pressbook as part of a suggested tagline for theatrical exhibitors: "Women dreamed of his kisses! But a boy's dream revealed him as the cruelest man in the world!"

2. The plot hatched by Barrington and Muhlbach is equivalent in audacity to the outrageous scheme concocted by Vera (Ann Savage) in Ulmer's *Detour*. Not only does Vera insist that Al Roberts (Tom Neal) continue to maintain the identity of the dead Charles Haskell Jr. (a lost heir who stands to inherit a fortune), but she also wants Al to masquerade as Haskell *in front of his own family*. Like Vera, who is convinced that the family will fail to notice that the false "Charles" does not look the same, or recall any of the details of his own personal history, Barrington seems to think he can persist in a loveless marriage, without ever being pressed on his own past history, and ultimately murder his wealthy new spouse without so much as an eyebrow being raised.

3. Lynch's *Inland Empire* (2006) is much the same in this regard. Moreover, all the films I mention here owe a considerable debt to Maya Deren's famous experimental short *Meshes of the Afternoon* (1943), wherein the series of images we receive is framed with what seems to be a more objective perspective from "outside" the dreamscape—a perspective which only comes at the end.

4. Although the connection is most obvious in the case of *The Others*—which centers on a woman and two young children living in an isolated mansion—in terms of structure, the literary progenitor of all the films I mention must be Henry James's *The Turn of the Screw* (1898). In James's novella, we view the story's events through the eyes of a narrator whose truly pathological unreliability remains (arguably) unconfirmed until the very last sentence.

5. The phrase appears in the film's pressbook under the heading "Sparkling Array of Stars in PRC Drama."

6. Even a film so unabashedly surreal as the *Old Dark House* parody *Sh! The Octopus* (William C. McGann, 1937) in the end gives a nod to the viewer, revealing that its incomprehensible plot has all been a dream. To omit such an acknowledgement, as I believe *Strange Illusion* does, is to invite the very kind of cognitive confusion that classical Hollywood cinema seeks to avoid.

7. The scale-model sequence of the train crash also appears at the midpoint of the film, when Paul has a flashback to his earlier dream; however, no new footage has been added. For my purposes here, the content of Paul's abbreviated flashback does not require further interpretation.

8. It is unclear throughout the film how Dr. Vincent is related to the Cartwright family; we know only that his sister lives somewhere in town, near the Cartwright estate. The film's pressbook indicates that he is the "family physician" and "an old family friend," and although we can infer this from the film, the connection is never explicitly stated. In many scenes he seems like a ghost himself, magically popping into view whenever Paul needs to confide in a father figure. Vincent never suffers in the film, and despite his active involvement in the pursuit of Barrington, he is never in danger. Except for a couple of brief exchanges of dialogue with other characters, it is as if he exists for Paul alone.

9. Numerous film noirs employ this same wry plot device, in which two characters publicly discuss the topic of "the perfect crime," while the audience knows that one of them is in the process of committing just such a crime. For examples of this motif in films released around the same time as *Strange Illusion*, see *Conflict* (Curtis Bernhardt, 1945), *Fear* (Alfred Zeisler, 1946), and *The Stranger* (Orson Welles, 1946). For a psychoanalytic reading of film noir's revision of the myth of the perfect crime, see Manon, 34–39.

10. The borderline impossibility of the various characters' respective ages has its parallel in the film's dialogue. In a lavish dinner scene, Curtis/Barrington pokes fun at Virginia's skills at arithmetic, telling the gathered guests that "she subtracts by counting backward on her fingers." The result, he says, is her conclusion that "ten minus five equals six." Given her son's age, perhaps Virginia is accustomed to such "creative accounting."

BIBLIOGRAPHY

Krutnik, Frank. *In a Lonely Street: Film Noir, Genre, Masculinity* (New York: Routledge, 1991).

Lacan, Jacques. *Écrits: The First Complete Edition in English*, trans. Bruce Fink (New York: Norton, 2006).

Manon, Hugh S. "Some Like It Cold: Fetishism in Billy Wilder's *Double Indemnity*," *Cinema Journal* 44, no. 4 (Summer 2005): 18–43.

Naremore, James. *More Than Night: Film Noir in Its Contexts* (Berkeley: University of California Press, 1998).

Žižek, Slavoj. *Enjoy Your Symptom: Jacques Lacan in Hollywood and Out* (New York: Routledge, 1992).

———. *Looking Awry: An Introduction to Jacques Lacan through Popular Culture* (Cambridge, Mass.: MIT Press, 1992).

———. *The Sublime Object of Ideology* (New York: Verso, 1989).

12

The Naked Filmmaker

Bill Krohn

During the '30s and '40s, Edgar G. Ulmer was not merely invisible, but masked. The films he made during the fifteen years after he was blackballed as a director for the majors were as personal as his one film for Universal, *The Black Cat*; but like that film, which was made within the norms of Universal's horror productions, they expressed personal qualities within two distinctive—and distinctively different—support systems: the ethnic communities with which Ulmer identified himself during the last half of the '30s, and the B-movie studio where he spent most of the '40s, Producers Releasing Corporation (PRC). One task of critics in recent years, because of the rediscovery of the ethnic films, has been to try to reconcile these two faces of Ulmer.

But there are still two decades—the '50s and the '60s—which remain virtually unexplored. As usual, this has a lot to do with distribution; but the PRC films remain relatively unseen outside specialized circles, too. The real obstacle to appreciation of these films is that Ulmer's first two decades have become the property of people who are more interested in the mask than in the man. This is obvious in the case of the Yiddish films, which have benefited from restorations and screenings conducted by institutions passionate about Yiddish cinema *in general*; but something similar has happened for a larger audience to whom Ulmer means, above all, the PRC films. The centrality which cinephiles in America and Europe alike accord to those films has at least as much to do with the love of B films *in general* as it does with Ulmer.

But while there is no contradiction between the production constraints Ulmer assumed and a high—even excessive—degree of self-consciousness in the films that resulted, there are distinctions of quality to be drawn, and in this respect I would say that the '40s was a less creative period for him than either the '30s or the '50s. After an astonishing start with *Tomorrow We Live*, which was made independently and picked up by PRC, *My Son The Hero*, *Girls in Chains*, *Isle of Forgotten Sins*, and *Jive Junction* have little to recommend them beyond the fact that Ulmer made them. It was only after achieving a certain amount of power within PRC that he was able to make five masterpieces—*Bluebeard*, *Strange Illusion*, *Detour*, *Club Havana* and *Her Sister's Secret*—where the genres adopted are subverted as creatively as Yiddish, Ukrainian, African American, and Navajo cultures are in the films of the ethnic period.

By contrast, I count ten masterpieces in the '30s and seven in the '50s, where the only films that fall below that level are two shorts—*Genevieve de Brabant* and the pilot for *Swiss Family Robinson*—in which producer interference and inexperienced actors sabotaged projects that are, even then, considerably more interesting than, say, *The Wife of Monte Cristo*. If we add *Ruthless*, *Carnegie Hall*, and *Pirates of Capri*, films Ulmer made while he was breaking free of PRC (which had in any case ceased to exist as such), and two late masterpieces, *Beyond the Time Barrier* and *The Cavern*, we have a very high assay of gold to dross for the period when he was functioning as a true independent, without the disguises that earned him, in the '30s, the sobriquet of "Director of the Minorities" and, in the '40s, the title "King of the Bs"—which afterward stuck to him like the coat of Nessus.

The aim of this chapter is to sketch the field to be explored, limited somewhat arbitrarily to the films released (with the exception of the pilot) in the '50s. Much spadework still remains to be done, because Peter Bogdanovich's definitive Ulmer interview broke off for reasons of health, never to be resumed, on the threshold of that decade. My sources, identified by letters when cited in the text, are conversations with Shirley Ulmer (S) and Arianné Ulmer Cipes (A); family letters archived at the Herrick Library; an unpublished interview with Bertrand Tavernier by Michael Wilson (BT); critical studies by Bret Wood (B) and Tag Gallagher (G); contemporary reviews by François Truffaut (FT) and Jean Domarchi (D); and interviews by Tavernier and Luc Moullet (T/M). The "Past Service Record" Ulmer wrote after he stopped making films (U) supplies an unimpeachably accurate chronology for this period.

THE MIRACLE OF ST. BENNY

Too many critics have assumed that the themes of *Detour* are all Ulmer had up his sleeve—this survey will proceed from other assumptions. I still remember seeing outraged fans of Ulmer, the master of film noir, storming out of a screening of *St. Benny the Dip* (1951) at UCLA, despite the fact that the look of the film is not that far from the New York scenes at the beginning of *Detour*; while even its plot (three crooks trapped into running a skid-row mission by the clerical collars they have put on as disguises) seems to express the theme of entrapment by fate which that brilliant act of self-mythification imposed on critics as the theme of Ulmer's work, and life.

But if we look at how *St. Benny* was made, important differences begin to appear. Actually filmed in New York, unlike *Detour*, *St. Benny* achieves a miraculous fusion of sets and real locations. Ulmer had already filmed on New York locations for *Carnegie Hall*, made a year before Jules Dassin and Stanley Donen did the same thing, and New York at least was aware of him by now—a caricature of him directing *St. Benny* on a crowded New York Street was spread over two pages of the *New York Times* during production. He had initially come back from Hollywood (U) to finish shooting *So Young So Bad* (1949), a more ambitious version of *Girls in Chains* produced by Harry and Eddie Danziger, two wealthy producers (not to be confused with Oscar Dancigers, Bunuel's Mexican producer) who were then just starting their own career. It is unclear how Ulmer met the brothers, but after *So Young* they offered him *St. Benny*, which he took because of a love for the stories of Damon Runyan, which had been imperfectly consummated in *My Son, the Hero*.

The screenwriter of *St. Benny* was to become a lifelong friend to Ulmer. Described by one reviewer as "the Theodore Dreiser of the detective novel" and by Arianné Ulmer as "a typical Jewish socialist," John Roeburt was a denizen of Greenwich Village who wrote hard-boiled detective stories. His script for *St. Benny*, written under Ulmer's supervision, is a mixture of humor and drama as seamless as Ulmer's blending of New York streets with forced-perspective sets (a specialty from his days as a production designer) that open pockets of dream and reminiscence in a Runyonesque tale of scoundrels redeemed by charity. Lionel Stander, making his last film before the blacklist, was handed some of the best lines, but the most beautiful is spoken by an anonymous hobo who leaves a suitcase full of money at the mission before committing suicide: "I've been a shadow on the Earth."

Much of *St. Benny* takes place at night, which makes possible the alchemy by which Ulmer fuses reality, soundstage, and dream; but the result has nothing to do with film noir and everything to do with the magical realism of two F. W. Murnau films he worked on, *Sunrise* and *Tabu*. The film's night mood also grew out of John Roeburt's reported habit of wandering the city streets at night (A), like the bishop and his assistant Wilbur, who go wandering every night in hopes of finding the three fugitives—three men in a city of six million, Wilbur complains, only to be told that before he can find the three, he has to first find himself. "Four men to find in a city of six million," says the bishop, whose air of perpetual distraction makes him one of the most believable Christian mystics ever put on screen. "That improves the odds considerably, doesn't it, Wilbur?"

"Just my lousy luck. Of all the cars that came along, I had to get in that one," whines Roberts in *Detour*—*St. Benny the Dip* turns that point of view, which is not the filmmaker's (G), inside out. Ulmer had always been fascinated by Roman Catholicism, but was kept from expressing his interest by the prejudices of Shirley's Jewish parents (A). The story of a pickpocket's redemption, *St. Benny the Dip* stands midway between Robert Bresson's *Pickpocket* and the streetwise sentiment of *Pickup on South Street*. When I commented to Shirley that the scene where Stander comes home to the wife he had abandoned showed an extraordinary feeling for the lives of poor people, she commented that Ulmer could do that "because he had been so poor himself."

THE MAN FROM PLANET MURNAU

The film Ulmer spent the rest of 1950 making, *The Man from Planet X* (1951), introduces us to three Hollywood professionals who worked with him throughout the decade: Aubrey Wisberg and Jack Pollexfen, two independent producers, and Ilse Lahn. Lahn was Ulmer's former (Viennese) girlfriend, Arianné's godmother, and an agent at the Paul Kohner Agency, which represented émigré filmmakers (e.g., Wilder, Wyler) and blacklisted writers during the '50s. She was Ulmer's agent after he went freelance and the line producer of *Murder Is My Beat* (written by Wisberg) and *The Daughter of Dr. Jekyll* (written and produced by Wisberg and Pollexfen, who performed the same functions on *Planet X*). She introduced these two "Hollywood characters" (S) to Ulmer, who persuaded them to push back their start date to give him time to prepare the picture properly, doing substantial rewrites on the script before starting the six-day shoot; painting the glass painting of the rugged tower where much of the action was set; and supervising postproduction (U). The scenes inside the scientist's castle were filmed on sets left over from the Hal Roach Company's *Joan of Arc*, obtained with the help of Mrs. Samuel Goldwyn, a regular Ulmer supporter (A). Although it started production after Howard Hawks's *The Thing*, Ulmer's *Planet X* was the first of the wave of '50s science-fiction films to make it into theaters. Made for $41,000, according to the autobiography of its star Robert Clarke, it was picked up by United Artists and grossed $1.2 million.

Like *The Black Cat*, *The Man from Planet X* is haunted by memories of Ulmer's Expressionist past, in particular Murnau's *Nosferatu*, a film that he told *Cinefantastique* he only saw after it was finished. The most obvious allusion is the glass painting of the castle's tower, which according to Clarke was the first thing that greeted him and his costar Margaret Field (the mother of Sally Field) when they went to Ulmer's house before the start of production. When Clarke looks up at the tower in the film, we see a second tower sprouting asymmetrically from its top—the observatory of Dr. Elliot, the father of Field's character. The shot recalls the hero's first glimpse of Count Orlock's castle in *Nosferatu*, which also has an asymmetrical, hornlike appendage sprouting from its top.

To heighten the impact of their spaceman, the producers did not credit the actor playing him, creating a mystery that has only recently been solved: it was a small actor named Pat Goldin (A), who spent most of his time complaining, according to Clarke. Did Ulmer suggest this strategy? He certainly knew of the mystery surrounding Max Schreck, the actor who is designated in the credits of *Nosferatu* as having played Count Orlock—in fact, he deepened it when he told *Cinefantastique* that he had heard that the character was really played by Hans Ramo, a screenwriter even more obscure than Schreck. The resemblances and differences between the mask worn by Goldin, which Ulmer designed, and the makeup of the actor in Murnau's film are particularly interesting. It is as if Ulmer had squashed Orlock's face to produce a smooth, rounded surface like an African ceremonial mask, turning the huge eyes to slits while retaining the pointed protuberances of ears, nose, and chin, made less prominent by the enlargement of the head. A light inside the spaceman's helmet gives him his own portable Expressionist lighting effects, which contribute greatly to the mask's eeriness.

Field, the first to see the visitor, says, "It was as if the face had been distorted by pressure." Later, when Clarke sees the extraterrestrial ship with its lights flashing on and off through the fog, he notes that it looks like "a giant diving bell," to which Dr. Elliot replies that the difference between "space" and water is just a matter of density. To ensure that we get the point, his next line is a complaint about the "everlasting fog that passes for climate" on the remote Scottish island where he has set up shop to observe the imminent approach of Planet X near to Earth. The fog blankets every exterior scene, like the omnipresent night in *St. Benny*, masking the poverty of the sets and creating a dreamlike ambience which suggests that our planet, for the inhabitants of Planet X, is like the bottom of the sea. (Nu Gel, the substance used to produce the fog, made everyone on the film sick.)

When Ulmer told *Cinefantastique* that he had inverted "un lieu commun" in *Planet X*, he was talking not about the conventions of '50s science fiction, which this film predates, but about the conventions of the horror film going back to *Nosferatu*. His reversal of the meanings of *Nosferatu* affects single images (the ship plowing through the fog, which in this case brings salvation) as well as the plot, which appears at first to be completely conventional: like Karloff in *The Black Cat*, the alien in *Planet X* is one of Ulmer's variations on the basic Murnau plot, in which a sinister figure (Count Orlock, Tartuffe, the father in *City Girl*, the priest in *Tabu*) threatens a happy couple's union. This aspect of the plot is underlined by the film's opening, which takes place just before the climax, as Clarke's voice-over broods over the fact that "it's been 48 hours since they took her." When the flashback recounting events up to this point is over, he finds Field a hypnotized prisoner inside the spaceship—to what end we are never told. Even the alien's hypnotic powers are a technological version of Count Orlock's: a beam of light emitted from the top of the ship that enslaves the will.

But despite appearances, the alien is benign. Suspicious of humans at first, he changes when Clarke saves his life, putting away his weapon and spreading his hands to show that he is unarmed. After that he follows his benefactors home like a lost puppy, only to be tortured by Elliot's disreputable assistant, Mears, who plans to use whatever scientific knowledge he can extract from him to become rich and powerful. Only then does the alien kidnap the heroine and enslave men from the nearby village to build an earthen rampart around his ship as protection, while waiting for his dying planet to come close enough for his people to escape, following a directional beam from his ship, to a world where they can survive. Mistrustful police and soldiers destroy him and his ship, condemning to death by freezing the other inhabitants of Planet X, which is glimpsed in a stunning sequence as it approaches the Earth and recedes: "A being arrives from a faraway plant . . . looking for a new world where he can live," Ulmer told *Cinefantastique*. "Sent as a scout and coming as a friend, this being immediately finds himself confronted by the persecutions of a scientist from our planet."

"Scientist" refers to Mears, who is the equivalent of Renfield, the real-estate agent in Nosferatu ("The real estate agent Renfield was a strange man, and unpleasant rumors circulated about him."). Mears's past transgressions—"He should've gotten twenty years," says Clarke—are also only alluded to: all we know is that he "upsets" Field, who wants him out of the castle. In keeping with Ulmer's systematic inversions of *Nosferatu*, Mears is the alien's tormenter, not his slave—his misdeeds put the visitor on the defensive, provoking humanity to destroy him, and with him the possibility of knowledge that "might have been mankind's greatest blessing," as Clarke says at the end. "Or its greatest curse," he adds, exemplifying the confused vision of all the human characters. Immersed in fog that is as dense as the sea to the "scout" who visits them (the fog of the material world, for those who insist on a Gnostic reading), they can only see his features distorted by the weight of an oppressive atmosphere that "passes for a climate," which keeps them from recognizing the face of their savior.

KING OF THE As

The other pole of Ulmer's career in the '50s was Europe. As Arianné explains, when he returned there to make *Pirates of Capri* Ulmer suddenly found himself working with "A" talent again, so throughout the decade he kept going back, struggling to get projects off the ground in Germany, Italy, France, and Spain. The first after *Planet X* was supposed to be *The Queen's Mark*, a costume picture for the Danzigers. Lured to Spain with that promise, he found himself instead making *Babes in Bagdad* (1952), a comedy about a revolt in a harem starring stripper Gypsy Rose Lee and Paulette Goddard. He took the project on because he was again promised *The Queen's Mark* as his next; similar promises enticed him to produce the mysterious German film *The Perjurer* in 1956 and to take over directing *L'Atlantide* from Frank Borzage. Ulmer spent over a year making *Babes* at a studio in Barcelona, also directing a Spanish version, *Muchachas en Bagdad*, that was nineteen minutes longer. The only extant prints are a black-and-white 16 mm print of the English-language version struck for TV, and a restoration of the Spanish version in 35 mm, with some reels in color and some in black and white. I hope someone unearths the French version someday (*Les mille et une filles de Bagdad*), which may have been what Truffaut saw and described appreciatively as "Voltairean high comedy."

Ulmer wrote to Arianné while preparing *Babes* that he was calling in "Cousin Roeburt," who had worked such wonders with *St. Benny*, to rewrite the dialogue, citing as a model the gangsters who find themselves playing supporting roles in a Shakespeare play in *Kiss Meet Kate* (L). Only one character in *Babes*, the villain's henchman, actually speaks with a Brooklyn accent—he becomes almost touching when he is ordered to kill everyone after the robbery of a trading caravan, including his own men. Reassured when he learns that "everyone" doesn't include him, he says humbly, "Thanks chief—for a minute I thought I was done for, too." This kind of inspired nonsense buoys a tale which Truffaut called "Voltairean" because of its theme (harem wives liberating themselves from their tyrant husband by outwitting him using the arts of illusion, deployed by a magician named Omar—Ulmer?), and because of a climactic episode in which the tyrant is transformed into a beggar whom no one recognizes, until he begins to believe his new identity himself—an enchanting episode which particularly impressed Tavernier. Ulmer illustrates the theme of illusion with shadows and reflections in water while the various tricks are being played, and the ballet of the man-fish trapped in the great net sums up the feminist plot, with the net remaining in place throughout the last sequence so that the humbled tyrant's renunciation of his harem can be filmed through it.

For his first color film, Ulmer designed sets using a limited palette to make the most of the limitations of two-strip Cinefotocolor technology. (He is credited as the film's production designer.) Contrasted gradations of dark red and aquamarine, as well as black and white, paint a "Bagdad" where visual motifs from the entire Middle East cohabit deliriously. One has to conclude from his remarks in an interview done while filming *L'Atlantide* (T/M) that, like Orson Welles and Allan Dwan, Ulmer still preferred black and white, but adjusted by doing more long takes when obliged to work in color:

> In a black-and-white film on a normal screen, you have to tell the story with many short shots. The dialogue doesn't matter. What matters above all is the image. . . . That fragmentation is not only a practical advantage, but above all an artistic one. You can give a visual rhythm to the film, as you cannot do with the "ten-minute take." A long take remains theatre, even when the camera moves.

Studying the impressive formalism of *Muchachas* helps us put in perspective the broken rhythms of Ulmer's next color experiment, *Geneviève de Brabant*, which he shot but didn't edit. The episode is part of a three-episode film (intended for theaters, but also as a pilot for a TV series, according to Arianné) produced by Victor Pahlen and starring Hedy Lamarr as an actress in a traveling theater troupe who plays, on successive nights, Geneviève, the Empress Josephine, and Helen of Troy. *Loves of Three Queens* is the only film Ulmer ever walked off of, after endless problems with Lamarr, when her rich husband bought the production from Pahlen and the director found himself working for his impossible star (A). The film, on which Ulmer received an "associate director" credit, was finished by Marc Allegret. Ulmer's fragment about a peasant-turned-queen condemned to death by her husband after being falsely accused of adultery by a man who desires her himself has been rightly praised for its medieval simplicity (G). My regrets about it are twofold.

On the one hand, despite the fact that Ulmer, true to his theory of color filmmaking, had frequently substituted camera movement in and out of long masters for editing, the editor stuck with the job of putting the pieces together botched it. On the other hand, knowing that Ulmer had a large hand in all phases of preproduction on the remaining episodes, I deeply regret that he only filmed this one, which has a distracting campy subtext because of Lamarr's sexual notoriety on and off the screen. She is more interesting as Josephine and Helen, in episodes that redeem historical "bad girls" by invented backstories. Jospehine, it turns out, cuckolded Napoleon because he loved History more than he loved her. He divorces her to marry Marie Louise of Austria and produce an heir, leaving her devastated at the end of her episode, like Helen at the end of hers. In *Helen of Troy* Menelaus, wanting war with Troy for economic reasons, asks his wife Helen to seduce Paris while he rallies his allies, then uses her elopement with the man she has come to love as a pretext for the war. When the besotted Menelaus takes her back after the death of Paris, her last words—"I pray that no woman will ever be as desolate as I"—throw an ironic light on the happy ending of *Geneviève de Brabant*, when the husband who condemned Geneviève to death takes her back after realizing his error.

These martyred women, sisters of the enslaved women in *Babes*, pave the way for those in Ulmer's other '50s films. *Loves of Three Queens* (aka *Eternal Femina*) would also have added to this theme a more serious play with the idea of illusion than what we have in *Babes*: Because of lack of coverage, the editor was obliged to preserve Ulmer's editing plan, which shows us close-ups of the saintly heroine only as she is seen through the eyes of the people (the audience, whom we also see watching at the beginning of the theater performance) and the eyes of four men—her maligned and murdered male friend, her husband, her executioner, and the accuser Golo, who sees her face one last time in a vision when he looks into a pool before dying. Geneviève is an image—her curse, like Helen's, is her beauty, and how it is reflected in the eyes of her admirers. And all three women are played by a rather promiscuous actress who refuses at the end of the film to be bought by a wealthy man because she prefers the freedom of life on the stage—a feminist version of the ending of *The Golden Coach*, made the previous year.

ANNUS MIRABILIS

The time lost with Pahlen and Lamarr was soon to be redeemed. On 14 February 1954, Ulmer wrote to Arianné, now studying at the Royal Academy of Dramatic Art in London, that he was scouting locations in preparation for two films: *The Bandit*, which would start shooting on 15 March, and *The Long Chance*, which would start almost immediately after, on 22 April (L). The first film was brought to him by one of his European connections, producer Gaston Hakim, but was sold to an American producer and released as a pickup by Universal in 1955, retitled *The Naked Dawn*, because Hakim had run out of money (A). The second film, produced by Lahn and written by Wisberg, was called *Murder Is My Beat* when Allied Artists released it the same year.

Another way that Ulmer found access to "A" collaborators in the '50s was through the blacklist, because of his connection with the Kohner Agency. He told Bogdanovich that Alvah Bessie wrote *Ruthless*; and, thanks to the researches of Tavernier, we know that Julian Zimet wrote *The Naked Dawn* and Dalton Trumbo *The Cavern* (BT). From the scattered references to Zimet in *Hollywood Exile*—a blacklist memoir by his friend Bernard Gordon—we can infer that he lived in Mexico while writing his novel *The Young Lovers*, and *The Bandit* probably belongs to the same period. Ulmer never met Zimet and, according to two sources (BT, A), he filmed his script without changing a word—a claim which, if true, is understandable: it is a wonderful script.

Zimet's source, he told Tavernier, was "Chelkash" (1894), one of Maksim Gorky's early stories about tramps. Although contemporary detractors of Gorky saw the story as glorifying the romantic tramp and bandit Chelkash in contrast to Gavrilla, the greedy peasant he hires to help him pull off a robbery, English critic Andrew Barratt argues convincingly in *The Early Fiction of Maksim Gorky* that Chelkash is a destructive nihilist of the kind Gorky describes in a famous letter to P. Kh. Maksimov (December 1910):

> I love people who are active and vigorous, who value and adorn life, even if only a little, by a small something, if only by the dream of a better life. In general, the Russian tramp is a character more terrible than I succeeded in saying; this man is terrible first and foremost in his implacable despair and in the fact that he negates himself, expels himself from life.

Zimet's script, in which Chelkash becomes the bandit Santiago (Arthur Kennedy) and Gavrilla the Native American peasant Manuel (Eugene Iglesias), keeps some of the perverse master-slave relationship that the seemingly amiable Chelkash imposes on Gavrilla, as well as Gavrilla's blind struggles to assert his own dignity in response. Moments like Santiago's contemptuous gift of the stolen money, followed by Manuel's promise to "pray for him every day," are taken from Gorky's tale, as are the moments when Santiago's envy of Manuel shows through.

But Zimet introduces a third character not found in his source, Manuel's wife Maria (Betta St. John), who has been sold to Manuel by the *patron* to be treated like a farm animal, making her a poor cousin of the *Babes in Bagdad* and of Helen of Troy, who was sold as a slave to Menelaus. Maria attracts Santiago until he befriends Manuel, and after the robbery and Manuel's first attempt on Santiago's life, she begs the bandit to take her away with him. He resists until Manuel, ashamed after Santiago saves his life, confesses that he planned to kill him. As in the short story, this sudden expression of Manuel's buried goodness provokes Santiago's rage, and he decides to leave with Maria. "If Santiago rejects him, it is because he has the brusque revelation of a cowardly, greedy soul *at the very moment when it is another Manuel who is speaking to him*." (D). Jean Domarchi was closer than he knew to the truth when he compared *The Naked Dawn*'s "sudden changes of heart" to Dostoevsky—Gorky's story is more reminiscent of Dostoevsky than of Marx.

Zimet's Santiago has seen two revolutions fail, and when he sends a transformed Manuel and Maria off to pursue a third way that will be better than his own nihilism and Manuel's peasant greed, we can only imagine what that would be. Ulmer told the *Cahiers du cinéma* that he endorsed the ending imposed by Universal in part because he "fell in love" with Eugene Iglesias:

> Manuel is the real hero. Of course, Kennedy tries to revolt to preserve his moral integrity, but his revolt comes from an egocentric vision of the world, and he uses the money he steals only for his own pleasure, not to change a world living under oppression. Manuel, however, will discover true happiness, and do more good in the world than the bandit.

Only an examination of production records will show how this ending—more hopeful than Gorky's and probably Zimet's—actually came about; but even without knowing where Zimet's script came from, Ulmer understood it at least as well as Zimet understood Gorky, so that many of the best things in the film seem to come from the Russian source. Santiago's love for Maria, for example, is an equivalent for the one redeeming trait Gorky allows his bandit, his love of nature as embodied by the sea. When we first see her fetching water from the river (a necessity until Manuel finds water in the dusty hole he is digging), and later when we admire her bare legs as the water of her bath runs down them (standing next to a chicken), she embodies the possibility of a reconciliation between alienated Man and Nature—which first appears in Ulmer's work in *Green Fields* and only resurfaces in *Geneviève de Brabant*, achieving here its apotheosis through the linked symbols of Woman and Water. But Murnau's "nosferatus" also recognize that beauty and yearn to possess it, and Santiago finally turns out to be one of them.

Another subject for further research is the question of how, and in spite of what interference, the stunning formal qualities of *The Naked Dawn* were achieved. Ariannè remembers, for example, that Universal insisted on cutting close-ups into the first dance sequence in the cantina, which appears to have been shot as two linked long takes, and the appreciative close-ups of Santiago and Manuel do feel false; but the real tour de force in the cantina illustrates Ulmer's remarks about the "artistic advantages" of montage: at the moment Santiago extends an invitation to the dancer (the fabulous Charalita), the lighting changes (rose and yellow fill lights appear out of nowhere), and a sexual and musical rhythm is created out of brief shots built around images of female and male legs—a visual theme that begins with the legs of the bandits and their horses seen under the railroad car during the credit sequence, and climaxes with the Bunuelian eroticism of water streaming down Maria's naked legs standing next to the chicken.

The film's most moving scene also appears to be composed of two long takes, this time linked by a brief series of shot-reverse shots: Santiago seduces Maria with his tales of Vera Cruz (plan-sequence 1), then reacts with horror when she asks him to take her with him (shot-reverse shots), telling her that his life is anything but romantic and Vera Cruz, a plague sore (plan-sequence 2). Again, although Tavernier remembers the sudden reversal as happening in one uninterrupted shot, the shot-reverse shots, the rhythm imposed when the camera pans to exclude Santiago or Maria from the frame, and the cutaways to the one and the other reclining in the off-space show that Ulmer has not forgotten the lesson of Murnau: "To say the opposite of what one shot says, you need another shot that completes and reverses what the other one began." (Ranciere 45). Except that in this scene, thanks to spoken words, music, and colors that seem cosubstantial with Kennedy's and St. John's astonishing performances, the pupil has surpassed the master.

BEYOND *DETOUR*

The Naked Dawn is the apogee in Ulmer's work of a certain classicism; in *Murder Is My Beat*, made almost simultaneously, he has already become a modern filmmaker. Wisberg's script returned Ulmer to film noir, with much less money than he had to spend on *Detour*, but the two films couldn't be more different. *Detour* is a flashy, ironic, and rather heartless German avant-garde film of the '20s or '30s; but in *Murder Is My Beat*, Ulmer invests a whole array of illusion-busting devices with contemporary meaning, to create a stripped-down version of cinematic modernism with a beating heart at its center.

The film portrays the gradual disintegration of a cop (Paul Langton) assailed by doubts about a case he thought he had solved, then about his own ability ever to solve it. Even though hero and heroine are redeemed by the ending, *Murder Is My Beat* is as harrowing as *Vertigo* in its portrayal of *l'amour fou* (the cop has fallen for a woman, played by Barbara Payton, whom he helped convict of murder), and in its treatment of the theme of illusion that we first saw in *Babes in Bagdad*, whose humbled tyrant also goes from not knowing who the woman sitting in front of him is to not knowing who *he* is. When certainty about the woman named Eden, which was the anchor for Ray the cop's sense of identity, blows up in his face, all certainties dissolve. (The film was based on a story called "Dynamite Anchorage.")

Ulmer was excited about the technical possibilities of the new, sensitive black-and-white Pan X film stock and the small, portable lights he used for the first time on *Murder*, but he did not exploit them to achieve location realism. Rather, the new techniques freed him to build sets that could be filmed from all angles (A), enabling him, for instance, to include ceilings in the scenes where Ray is talking to his boss—symbolizing the Law whose servants they are. Certainly the new stock made possible the beautiful series of shots of Ray wading through a snowstorm to capture Eden. In this paroxystic sequence, Ray's face becomes a tiny black circle, and his trench coat transforms him into a duplicate of the white-skirted, black-faced figurine that was the murder weapon—the first of many duplicates that will proliferate as the mystery deepens. The effect is the opposite of realistic, as Ulmer emphasizes by adding animated snowflakes when Ray draws near his goal.

Rather than using his new flexibility to shoot on location, Ulmer filmed all the exterior scenes in the small town where Ray goes to solve the murder against glaringly obvious back projections, within which we can read the names of many nationally known consumer products: emblems of a society built on illusion, whose leading citizen is a philanderer and a murderer. Ulmer even undercuts the reality of the only genuine exterior in this part of the film, the motel where Ray's boss Bert finds him in the opening sequence. In a seedy long shot of a nondescript bungalow, Bert peeks in the window at his quarry; but this window has curtains on it, while the window Ulmer cuts to when he moves in for an over-the-shoulder shot is uncurtained. Through that second window, filmed on a soundstage, we see Ray lying pensively in bed, before Ulmer cuts again to take us inside for a close-up view of his worried expression.

This first series of ruptures in the fabric of reality sets up a formal and thematic opposition: an external world composed of back projections, stock shots, and depersonalizing long shots set against the intimacy of the interiors where all the scenes between Eden and Ray take place. When they spend their first night together, Ulmer cuts away twice to show the cabin snowbound in darkness, reinforcing the growing intimacy between the cop and the fugitive after the electricity goes out and Ray lights candles, noting that the clock on the mantelpiece has stopped, too. Their voices grow hushed and keep breaking off, letting us hear the wind outside before they resume the endless *coq à l'âne* (she doesn't know that the man she struck is dead) by which two strangers are coming to know each other, and falling in love without acknowledging it.

In the scene on the train when Ray is taking Eden to prison, after she has seen the man she is supposed to have killed on the train platform, Ulmer keeps cutting to the roaring train wheels to show the external world racing inexorably to a grim conclusion, while Eden pleads softly with Ray to believe her. "When a man begins to doubt that what he represents as right must be right," Ray's voice tells us, "he's beginning to come apart at the seams." After a few days as fugitives, they will both start to doubt that what she saw (another rear projection) was real, leaving them with nothing to trust but their feelings, which they finally give in to in a joyless motel room like the one in *Detour*: when they kiss for the first time, the score (superb as always in Ulmer's films) stops, as if any scrap of the illusory garment cinema spins for reality (majestically deployed in the "Vera Cruz" scene in *The Naked Dawn*) would distort the truth of a passion Ray has felt ever since he opened the door of the cabin and saw Eden inside.

BEYOND THE FIFTIES

Ulmer made two films in 1956. The first, which he produced, was his first German film since *People on Sunday*, *The Perjurer*, about which I have been able to discover nothing except that Ulmer had his first heart attack and Arianné was arrested as a spy during the location scout (A). Then Lahn called him back to Hollywood for the last of his collaborations with Wisberg and Pollexfen, *The Daughter of Dr. Jekyll*. The most influential words ever written about Ulmer, in Andrew Sarris's indelible 1968 manifesto *The American Cinema*, were about this film:

> Anyone who loves cinema must be moved by *Daughter of Dr. Jekyll*, a film with a scenario so atrocious that it takes forty minutes to establish that the daughter of Dr. Jekyll is indeed the daughter of Dr. Jekyll. Ulmer's camera never falters even when his characters disintegrate.

I think we can assume Ulmer was aware that the title was a giveaway. Clearly we know what the big surprise is going to be from the moment "Janet Smith" (Gloria Talbot) arrives with her fiancé George Hastings (John Agar) at the mansion of her guardian, Dr. Lomas (Arthur Shields)—so much so that Ulmer can skip the scene when Dr. Lomas gives Janet the bad news and cut directly to her announcing to a stunned George that she can't marry him. Everything is known in advance in *The Daughter of Dr. Jekyll*—as in ancient tragedies and some examples of present-day theater influenced by the theories of Brecht—including the fact that kindly Dr. Lomas, not Janet, is the werewolf that is killing off the locals.

First of all, we see Lomas's distinctive silhouette in a precredit shot of "Hyde," and when he turns to address the camera, the makeup is skimpy enough that Shields would be recognizable to a six-year-old as the monster when he appears later, spouting good-hearted Irish blather to cover his equally obvious intentions. In addition, the scenes of "Janet Hyde's" nighttime murders are superimposed over the face of Janet lying in bed and dreaming. Even as we share her vision of herself as a bloody-clawed, white-robed wraith stalking innocents in the forest, we see that she is watching the action—dreaming it—at the same time we are.

The sense that everything is known undergirds a visual style that again uses sensitive stock and portable lights for purposes alien to the canons of cinematic realism. With the exception of shots of a miniature mansion and Janet's nightmare visions, the film takes place in a real L.A. house, paving the way for the implausibilities that Bret Wood catalogs disapprovingly in a recent study:

> Staging the narrative in bright, spacious sets . . . Ulmer allows *Daughter* to flounder, with no effort made to conceal such anachronistic details as cheap casters at the base of Jekyll's sliding bookcase, lamps and fire-places with electric bulbs inside, and the sight of cars passing on a busy highway beyond the sets.

Ulmer's "baring of the device" in *Daughter* distracts Wood from a stylistic choice that he appreciates in *Strange Illusion*, where the bright daylight world of Paul's home and environs is the lie, and the dark nightmare world of his dreams is the truth (B). Ulmer used ultraviolet film to shoot Janet's eerie night visions—one of which reproduces a lakeside idyll from Murnau—with a night look that could never have been achieved with filters.

There are moments like this in the ethnic films, but in *The Daughter of Dr. Jekyll* the mythos of Murnau emerges intact and undisguised from the series of revisions which repressed it in the '50s. In *The Man from Planet X* the nosferatu appears evil, but turns out to be benign; in *The Naked Dawn* the nosferatu is charming and lovable, but turns out to be evil; and in *The Daughter of Dr. Jekyll* the nosferatu's feigned goodness is a mask for evil that fools no one but the characters. In all three films the happy couple survives his depredations, but only *The Daughter of Dr. Jekyll* allows the audience to see, with no concealment or deferral (every detail of those brightly lit rooms—including the lights—is sharply reproduced by deep-focus photography), the smiling face of lust and greed at work.

Ulmer would revisit the Murnau mythos once more in the '50s, with an original variation of his own—a maternal nosferatu, inspired no doubt by his own mother—in *The Naked Venus*, a nudie produced by Gustav Hakim and filmed in four days on sets and California locations. I have nothing to add to Tag Gallagher's appreciation of this powerful film except to point out that it contains the first example of a film-within-the-film in Ulmer's work since *Diagnostic Procedures*: a voyeuristic collection of scenes in a nudist camp, filmed by two unsavory private investigators for use as a lying document during a divorce trial. Gallagher is right to ignore the fact that the heroine is finally reunited with her feckless husband. Like Geneviève de Brabant's reunion with the husband who condemned her to death, this happy ending is one more film illusion by which Ulmer, and the alert spectator, can no longer be duped.

If there is a period in Ulmer's work that is truly bleak, it is the last one, in which his innate Gnosticism comes to the fore, producing as final statements versions of the two Gnostic myths transmitted to later ages by Plato: the "Myth of Atlantis" from the *Timaeus* and the "Myth of the Cave" from *The Republic*. But the groundwork for these terrible last works was laid in the '50s.

Before *The Naked Venus*, Ulmer made a thirty-minute pilot for a television series based on *The Swiss Family Robinson* (1958), which never sold. The wooden performances of the children in this short film sank it despite the efforts of their dialogue coach, Arianné (A); but Ulmer used his luxuriant Mexican locations to sketch the idea of Nature as a beautiful prison, an idea that would receive its definitive expression in *The Cavern* (1965). In fact, Ulmer first prepared *The Cavern* in 1957, and put more of that preparation than anyone probably realized at the time into this fascinating television oddity—just as he made *L'Atlantide* (1961) first as *Beyond the Time Barrier* (released in 1960, filmed in 1959), a science-fiction film about a postnuclear underground society where the idea of *The Daughter of Dr. Jekyll* is taken to its logical conclusion: since the tragedy has already happened, no catharsis, no feeling, is possible for the characters.

But no one who loves cinema can fail to be moved by *The Daughter of Dr. Jekyll*, which I love more every time I watch it. *Detour* will always be the darling of critics, as *The Naked Dawn* is of cinephiles, but it is *The Daughter of Dr. Jekyll* whose influence on Ulmer's filmmaking descendants, like Andrew Repasky MacElhinney (*A Chronicle of Corpses*), promises to endure into the new century.

BIBLIOGRAPHY

Domarchi, Jean. "Un nouveau romatisme," *Cahiers du cinéma* 58 (April 1956).

Edgar G. Ulmer Collection, Margaret Herrick Library, Academy of Motion Picture Arts and Sciences, Beverly Hills, Calif.

Eisenschitz, Bernard, and Jean-Claude Romer. "Entretien avec Edgar G. Ulmer," *Midi-Minuit Fantastique* 13 (November 1965): 1–14.

Gallagher, Tag. "All Lost in Wonder," *Senses of Cinema*, at www.latrobe.edu.au/screeningthepast/firstrelease/fr0301/tgafr12a.htm.

Krohn, Bill. "*The Naked Dawn*: Production, Sources, and Mise-en-Scène," in *Edgar G. Ulmer: Essays on the King of the Bs*, ed. Bernd Herzogenrath (Jefferson, N.C.: McFarland, 2009), 215–24.
Moullet, Luc, and Bertrand Tavernier. "Enteretien avec Edgar G. Ulmer," *Cahiers du cinéma* 122 (August 1961).
Ranciere, Jacques. *La fable cinématographique* (Paris: Seuil, 2001).
Sarris, Andrew. *The American Cinema: Directors and Directions, 1929–1968* (New York: E. P. Dutton, 1968).
Tavernier, Bertrand. Interview by Michael Henry Wilson.
Truffaut, Francois. "*The Naked Dawn*," *Arts* 559 (1956), reprinted in *Les films de ma vie* (Flammarion, 1975).
Wood, Bret. "Visions from the Second Kingdom," *Video Watchdog* 41: 22–32.
Conversations with Shirley Ulmer, Ariannė Ulmer Cipes, and Jay Cipes.

13

The Political and Ideological Subtexts of *The Naked Dawn*

Reynold Humphries

The action of *The Naked Dawn* concerns primarily three characters: the middle-aged Mexican bandit Santiago (Arthur Kennedy) and a young Mexican couple, Maria (Betta St. John) and Manuel (Eugene Iglesias). In the film's opening scene, Santiago and his companion Vicente steal merchandise from a train stationed in a border town. Vicente is shot by the railway guard and dies in Santiago's arms soon after. After hiding the loot from the robbery, Santiago encounters Maria and accompanies her back to the little farm owned by Manuel. Visibly attracted to the wife, who is not indifferent to him, Santiago nevertheless chooses to undertake the social and moral education of the husband. Having been paid for the merchandise, which he stole in order to line the pockets of the corrupt shipping agent for the railroad, Guntz, Santiago steals the rest of the man's money when the latter tries to cheat him, then spends much of it lavishly during a night that he and Manuel spend in a cantina. However, the young husband, tired of poverty, considers that money must be saved not spent, and plans to kill the bandit in order to live better. At the last minute he cannot do so. His wife turns against him when she discovers what he had planned, and she leaves with Santiago. However, they turn back when Guntz and two colleagues arrive and try to hang Manuel. Santiago shoots Guntz but the man succeeds in wounding him fatally before dying. Santiago insists that Maria and Manuel stay together, and they ride off. The last shot is of the dying Santiago.

Summed up thus, *The Naked Dawn* sounds rather banal, yet it is not. Two different plot summaries are included in the entry on the film on www.imdb.com; and, while one is close to the summary I have just offered, the other (much shorter) includes a highly problematic sentence: "Exposed to money, the fast life, and Santiago's anarchistic philosophy, Manuel (formerly simple and hard working) is in serious danger of being corrupted (and Maria is not immune either)." I interpret this as meaning that Santiago is a corrupting influence on Manuel, who is presented positively otherwise; and that Maria is also open to corruption because of Santiago. I consider that this perverts totally both the manifest level of the script and its various implications; and that, once we delve into the film's subtexts, we can deduce that this comment turns the "real" meaning of *The Naked Dawn* upside down, in a manner which is profoundly ideological. Much closer to the truth is an anonymous "user comment" on the same site that calls Manuel "ambitious" and a "naive, greedy young man." Let us start, then, by considering a certain number of elements provided by the script.

It soon becomes clear that *The Naked Dawn*'s key themes, discussed between the three main characters and, hence, explicitly elaborated on the level of the script, are love and money—in other words, the things that, according to the ideological clichés, make the world go round. When Santiago first comes across Maria, we see her from his point of view: she is squatting by the side of a river. Santiago is patently attracted to this pretty young woman, and, for reasons that soon become clear, she is hardly indifferent to him. What is striking, however, is the way Ulmer insists on the cross round her neck, exposed in such a way that it cannot but draw our attention not only to the cross itself, but also to Maria's bare shoulders. Similarly, a large cross hangs on the wall in the home of Maria and Manuel, or, to be more precise, on the wall just beside their bed. In the context of the film the symbolism is polyvalent. There is a possible clash between desire and the Catholic vision of married love, but there is also the notion of strictly gendered roles within the family: the husband provides food and lodging via his work, the wife her body as housewife and bearer of children. It is hardly surprising, then, that Santiago hopes the couple will be blessed in the near future with many children. Again, in the context, this can be seen as a cliché trotted out by Santiago to please the young woman, while simultaneously suggesting he finds her sexually attractive.

It is the way Ulmer chooses to shoot scenes in the farmhouse involving Santiago, Maria, and Manuel that starts to reveal the film's critical stance over questions of love, marriage, and money. Two crucial scenes involve Santiago and Maria on the one hand, and Santiago and Manuel on the other. Santiago shows a great interest in the tortillas Maria is making by hand and deplores the poor quality of those produced by machines. Maria informs him that she was sold to Manuel, who needed a woman to make tortillas, along with the land which the couple now farms. The former owners were a wealthy family who treated her like an animal. Since there were three sons, it is reasonable to suppose that the formula "like an animal" is meant to be interpreted along both class and sexual lines. She existed to satisfy their carnal lust and was therefore reduced to having the use-value of a donkey or a piece of merchandise. Indeed, even less value than that: she was "thrown in" along with the land in order to make the offer more attractive.[1]

This scene is shot with Maria on the left and Santiago on the right, Ulmer framing them together in the middle ground. When Manuel enters and offers Santiago some alcohol, both framing and composition change. Ulmer frames the two men in the foreground, which excludes most of the room, unlike in the scene between Maria and Santiago. Nor is there any crosscutting to show Maria going about the task of preparing a meal while the two men drink and talk. Maria has been simply excluded from the frame and is reduced to an offscreen existence. Ulmer's mise-en-scène here underlines the wife's secondary status, while at the same time hinting that Santiago, who has been perfectly at ease treating Maria as an equal, returns happily to a universe that is male dominated. If later events show that Santiago is far more conscious of Maria's rights as a human being than Manuel is, here Ulmer gives the impression that Maria, as a woman, has to fight for recognition, for the right to share on an equal footing a world where men take for granted their superiority. Arguably, her offscreen role here is the equivalent of her status when owned by the family.

One sequence in particular highlights Santiago's ambivalence toward women. As indicated in the summary, Santiago has hidden the booty from the railroad robbery that opened the film. Manuel now accompanies him to the border town where the robbery took place, where Santiago hands over the booty (wristwatches) to Guntz, the railroad shipping agent. When Guntz refuses to hand over all the money promised in exchange for the stolen watches, on the grounds that Vicente is dead, Santiago resorts to a simple expedient: he threatens to hang Guntz unless the latter gives him the combination of the safe. Santiago then proceeds to spend a considerable sum of money with Manuel at a cantina, where he pays a local dancer to perform for them. That she is not only a dancer is clear from the way she exhibits her body and throws herself at Manuel. The sequence is badly directed. Ulmer does nothing to curb the dreadful overacting of Iglesias, perhaps because he is also content to give a genuine pro like Arthur Kennedy minimal instructions, relying on his experience as one of Hollywood's finest character actors.[2] The scene does, however, serve a multitude of purposes. There is surely a parallel between the dancer and Maria, although the two women are very different. The implications of prostitution here take up Maria's bitter references to her adolescent past (both she and Manuel are barely twenty). Where one woman cooks and has sex as a dutiful wife, the other dances (and has sex) to please the male clients. The young wife was sold and had no choice; the dancer sells herself and has no choice either, despite her joie de vivre. She openly assumes her status as a body on show and her pleasure at this does not modify the criticism implicit in the parallels drawn between her and Maria. More important, perhaps, is the role played by money, which is to become the film's dominant theme.

The theme, of course, has hardly been absent up till now: Santiago and Vicente steal to live. Indeed, the theme of exchange would sum up best the role of both money and sex in the film. Santiago (in the presence of Manuel) exchanges the stolen watches for cash, then throws much of it around in order to celebrate his success and offer Manuel and himself, by proxy, the favors of the dancer (the film carefully avoids any suggestion of sexual "impropriety," a factor to which we shall return presently). Similarly, Manuel has exchanged cash for the farm (and Maria), a farm where Maria has no choice but to work as a wife and housekeeper.[3] However, following on from the cantina sequence, Manuel starts to show unease at Santiago's attitude toward money. Although he is quite happy to get blind drunk on tequila, be passionately kissed by the experienced dancer ("experienced," clearly, in more ways than one), and, finally, receive his share of the money (Santiago giving Manuel what he would in other circumstances have given to Vicente, a genuinely comradely act which I shall discuss below), Manuel does have problems with money; and the film uses this to introduce the question of conflicting social values and what is a crucial, but far from obvious, theme: that of betrayal.

In order to situate these aspects of the film, it is necessary to return briefly to the cantina sequence. A further element is the ambiguous behavior of Santiago: is he deliberately trying to get Manuel seduced by the dancer? If so, is that because he wants to seduce Maria and reckons this will be possible only by getting Manuel out of the way? However, this dimension disappears as from the moment the two men leave the cantina, for we never see the dancer again. Moreover, Santiago's generosity toward Manuel has not gone unnoticed: three Americans in the cantina attempt to rob the pair but underestimate Santiago, to their cost. It is therefore revealing that Maria should take Manuel to task for accepting Santiago's money. I would suggest this reaction is unconscious: she sees in the gift (there are no strings attached) a repetition of how she found herself to be a young wife, with Santiago standing in for the wealthy landowner. The fact that Santiago is neither wealthy nor a landowner (it is, precisely, Manuel who is the landowner, and who continues to treat Maria as if she were still some chattel) cannot overcome her bitterness. We can interpret Maria's reaction as an example of an ideological discourse of which the subject is an effect: for Maria, women cannot transcend their role as wives and bearers of children, but she is sufficiently liberated to speak her mind. She is promptly beaten by Manuel for daring to criticize him, which can only confirm her negative view of men and her own social function. All she can do is go about her chores.

It is in this context that we can best understand the way Ulmer insists on crosses; the question transcends completely that of religion and repression. Manuel condenses in his attitude toward money two ideologies: that of the church and that of capitalism. If there is no question of Manuel sleeping with the dancer, then it is because the script is not interested in using this form of "betrayal" in order to facilitate a relationship between Santiago and Maria. This latter relationship comes about for other, more explicitly social reasons, and it is these that the film's script has been at pains to introduce gradually and implicitly in order to avoid *The Naked Dawn* becoming a film with a "message." Manuel's status as husband and provider leads him to assume he has all the rights. Significantly, he introduces Maria to Santiago with the eloquent formula: "This is my woman." Fundamentally, nothing has changed for Maria: she has exchanged one master for another, which means that she is part of a system of exchange determined outside her control. In his attitude to money, however, Manuel falls under the sway of a specific aspect of capitalism: its "puritan" dimension. Thrift must take precedence over spending and pleasure; money must be saved or invested, or else it will be wasted. It is for these reasons that he turns against Santiago after the cantina sequence, which represents the return of the repressed and consequently provokes a profound sense of guilt on Manuel's part at having been, literally, so carefree. Manuel is a willing slave to the ideologies that underpin his actions and words, so much so that he tries to kill Santiago in order to get his hands on the rest of the money. Crucially, he asks Christ to help him, promising to make a contribution to the church. In other words, he is trying to buy a place in paradise and is thus behaving simultaneously like a good Christian and like a good capitalist, endowed with a pronounced sense of private property.

Manuel may be a Mexican peasant, but he bears a striking resemblance, ideologically speaking, to a lower-middle-class American husband determined to climb the social ladder! One aspect of the script speaks volumes when it comes to attempting to ascertain just what is going on in a film where, for all intents and purposes, very little happens; where there is little action or drama; and where words speak louder than actions. For *The Naked Dawn* is a very strange film indeed, a foreign body within the genre of the Western. That aspect is geography: where does the film take place? The answer is simple: a border town. But just how simple is that answer? Presumably Santiago and Vicente carried out their robbery on the American side of the border: both the shipping agent and the railroad guard are Americans, and the cantina is frequented by both Americans and Mexicans. We can also conclude that Manuel's farm is located some considerable distance from the border: a long drive in his broken-down truck is necessary to reach the town from the farm. However, nothing is made of crossing over from the Mexican side to the American side and back again: not only do Santiago and Manuel frequent the border town, but Guntz and his cronies drive down to Manuel's farm so that Guntz can get his revenge by hanging Manuel. As we shall see now, the border town is a signifier whose meanings open the film out into the terrain of politics and history.

The Naked Dawn makes no attempt to distinguish between the two sides of the border. This is hardly surprising, given that California used to belong to Mexico, until American patriots, early examples of the likes of John Wayne, decided otherwise ("Remember the Alamo"). Thus the region is represented in a way that homogenizes it, and I would argue that this has most interesting repercussions ideologically. There is a definite anti-imperialist thrust to the film's script here: a border town is as far as the Mexicans can go, but the Americans penetrate deeper into Mexican territory and expect to get away with a lynching. Clearly Guntz and his cronies have problems with geography: they behave as if they were in the deep South. We shall return presently to the question of American imperialism, but let us return first to the role of the family in the film. I have referred to Manuel's broken-down truck, which is a relic from the 1920s or 1930s. *The Naked Dawn*, however, is set at the time at which it was made, 1955, and Guntz's car obviously belongs to this period. Why should this be important?

One American academic, evoking such changes in postwar America as birth-control devices, has pointed out that

> many scholars and observers at the time feared that these changes seriously threatened the continuation of the American family. Yet, the evidence overwhelmingly indicates that postwar American society experienced a surge in family life and a reaffirmation of domesticity that rested on distinct roles for women and men. (May 9)

This information is relevant for *The Naked Dawn*. We can notice that, if religion is represented as a daily force in the lives of the young couple, the behavior of Manuel is perfectly in keeping with the values at work north of the border. In other words, the script is creating, via the couple, a state of affairs which, from an ideological standpoint, could be that of any young American couple. Thus Americans—and in particular young American women—could recognize themselves in the lives of Maria and Manuel, despite the ethnic difference. The fact that both Santiago and Maria are played by Americans further erases the notion of difference. As a result, it is gendered roles, class, and economics that predominate, rather than "Mexicanness."

This, of course, does not mean that Mexico has been wiped off the map. On the contrary, the script highlights the country's politics and history. In order to place this in the context of the making of the film—which is, after all, a Hollywood production—I wish to draw attention to a further passage in the volume quoted above:

> From the Senate to the FBI, from the anticommunists in Hollywood to Mickey Spillane, moral weakness was associated with sexual degeneracy, which allegedly led to communism. To avoid dire consequences, men as well as women had to contain their sexuality in marriage where masculine men would be in control with sexually submissive competent homemakers at their side. Strong families required two essential ingredients: sexual restraint outside marriage and traditional gender roles in marriage. The issue of sexuality was central to both. (May 99)

Apart from the first sentence, this could be a comment on the couple in *The Naked Dawn*, on the place of Santiago, and on the role of the dancer in the cantina sequence. Just as the bandit makes no attempt to help Manuel betray Maria's trust in her husband, beyond being kissed by the dancer, so he does not betray Manuel by attempting to seduce Maria. She, however, puts on a new dress in Santiago's presence in an obvious attempt to please him. Manuel is absent. Both Maria and Manuel are tired of poverty, but their reactions and behavior are diametrically opposed: he tries to kill Santiago in order to get his hands on the rest of his money, whereas she turns away in disgust from her husband and begs Santiago to take her with him. Manuel chooses the road to theft, even homicide, thus placing himself in the same category as men like Guntz, whereas Maria, who considers she has nothing to lose because she is still a sort of slave, chooses what she sees as freedom with Santiago.

He is tempted but refuses, and it is here that we can see at work what the summary quoted above calls his "anarchistic philosophy." The formula is clearly used negatively, and wrongly so. Santiago refuses any and every system of domination and knows full well that Maria will simply submit to him, a much older man, in the imaginary belief that he has given meaning to her life and she to his. Santiago is down-to-earth: "I would tire of you within a week." Hardly gallant, but at least honest, which is more ethical and not sexist. Although Santiago changes his mind after Manuel's attempt to kill him and rides off with Maria, leaving Manuel in a state of childlike collapse, he does not abandon him to be lynched by Guntz, and he dies saving Manuel so that the young couple can be reunited. As he dies, we hear the words he spoke to the dying Vicente.

In Vicente's death scene, Santiago tries to reassure his only friend: when he dies he will be welcomed into paradise by Saint Peter and will find there the plot of land he was denied in life. Vicente, a profoundly religious man, simply laughs. For he knows full well that the last years of his life have been led as the result of the betrayals of which he has been a victim. As Santiago says to him, "you have been wronged," rejecting explicitly the Christian notion of sin. The long death scene exists for the script to provide the spectators will all the information they need to interpret what follows.

In a few exchanges Santiago and Vicente go back over their lives together, and their discussion is an eminently political one. They both participated actively in the Mexican revolution but were denounced as "traitors to the revolution" because each wanted his own plot of land. Then came the counter-revolution: the generals promised land but betrayed everyone, as a result of which Santiago and Vicente became bandits. In Santiago's words, "we took a little of what they promised us." It very soon becomes clear that the script is evoking a precise historical event in order to make a political comment on revolution and betrayal. During the discussion Santiago refers to Pancho Villa as if they had known him. But if they had fought with Villa, both would now be old men: some forty years separate the struggles led by Villa and the time of the film's action.[4] The revolution being referred to implicitly is surely the Bolshevik Revolution and its disastrous aftermath under Stalin: enforced collectivization is the element chosen by the film to illustrate betrayal and disillusion. The script is asking: is it counterrevolutionary to want to own and farm land? Certainly private property was not in itself considered counterrevolutionary by Marx, for whom the public ownership by the proletariat of the means of production *in an industrial society* was the key issue in the march toward socialism. But *The Naked Dawn* is not concerned, at least superficially, with such a society, and the betrayal of the former revolutionaries by the generals who imposed a counterrevolution finds in the action of the film a precise parallel. Just as the generals obviously kept the land for the privileged bourgeois elite, so in the contemporary Mexico of *The Naked Dawn* a wealthy landowner sells a small plot of land to Manuel, who has worked in the United States in order to be able to buy it. *The Naked Dawn* is therefore concerned with the betrayal of a collective movement and its attendant hopes, but also with the ways in which modern society repeats those betrayals.

As I stated above, Vicente laughs scornfully when Santiago tries to reassure him about the afterlife by stating he will have a plot of land in paradise. Since Vicente is a religious man, he must believe in paradise, and so his laughter must mean something else. He is surely laughing because he understands that Santiago is falling again into the trap set by the counterrevolutionary generals: they promised land later, then betrayed their promise. Vicente may believe in life after death, but he knows full well that owning and farming a plot of land is not the same as having a place at God's right hand. Nor does the notion of a peasant owning and farming a plot of land exclude the collective, where peasants can exchange between themselves what each needs to feed, clothe, and generally provide for his family. The script seems to be implying that any genuinely communist movement (in the Marxist sense) risks being betrayed by those with either no understanding of the issues or no interest in applying after the event the values that went into making the revolution a success. In America in 1955 this can only mean a denunciation of Stalinism and, by extension, the American Communist Party. The question of betrayal, however, goes far beyond Stalin's betrayal of the Bolshevik Revolution.

The alert reader will have noticed that I have referred to Ulmer on a number of occasions when discussing the significance of an aspect of the mise-en-scène, whereas I have otherwise limited myself to evoking "the script." This has been deliberate on my part, since I have chosen to follow the film through to its conclusion in order to elucidate a certain number of themes and subtexts. Ulmer as director interested me inasmuch as he took certain decisions concerning the filming, whereas up till now the identity of the screenwriter was of no concern. What mattered was the question of themes: the family and gendered roles, money and betrayal. Of particular importance was the character of Santiago: he refuses to abandon Vicente, to leave the naive Manuel to his own (de)vices, to deceive him with Maria, and, finally, to lead her up the garden path in the same way as Manuel led her up to the altar. Although the credits list Nina and Herman Schneider as the screenwriters, we now know that they were fronting for screenwriter Julian Zimet, one of Hollywood's blacklist victims from 1951.[5]

Although Zimet chose to live in exile in Mexico, it would be unwise to interpret the function of Mexico in *The Naked Dawn* exclusively in those terms. One aspect of the film's action, however, does suggest that Zimet had in mind the relation between the two countries and the predicament of the exiles. The refugees from Hollywood joined other refugees who had been made welcome in Mexico: those from fascist Spain and Stalinist Russia.[6] They had to be careful not to get involved in local politics and had constantly to be on the lookout for attempts by the United States government to make life unpleasant for them. We would therefore be justified in interpreting the end of the film, where Guntz and his two cronies take a trip to Mexico to seek out Manuel and Santiago, as Zimet's way of indicating just how easily the American government, via the FBI, could operate south of the border.

Even more pertinent, I would suggest, is the theme of betrayal, where *The Naked Dawn* subtly raises the question of the hearings into communism in the movie industry that had started up again in February 1951. It was now no longer a question, as in October 1947, of giving the Right the chance to settle scores with the Left over union battles going back to the 1930s. When the House Committee on Un-American Activities (HUAC) returned to the attack in 1951, the rules of the game had changed radically. Now the person summoned to appear had a choice: either to refuse to answer questions about his or her Communist Party past and acquaintances, or to answer such questions. The former choice meant taking the Fifth Amendment to avoid self-incrimination: the CP was not an illegal party, but HUAC explicitly refused to grant it the status of a party, seeing it as a "conspiracy." This, in turn, meant immediate blacklisting by the studios. Once one agreed to say that he or she had been a member of the CP but no longer was, this was only the beginning. The witness then had to name those who had shared this tainted past life in order to be granted absolution and hence the right to continue to work in Hollywood.[7]

In his script Zimet carefully avoids suggesting that a fictional character is based on a real-life one. Rather, he sketches in the conditions under which sticking by a comrade, on the one hand, or knifing him in the back, on the other hand, became a matter, if not of life or death, but of working or becoming an exile. Manuel's readiness to kill Santiago and to ask Christ for help in exchange for money for the church thus finds a parallel in the decision taken by many members of the movie industry to destroy the careers of many friends and comrades (not necessarily members or former members of the CP, it might be added) in order to continue to "farm" their own particular "plots of land" within Hollywood. Thus Santiago's consistent rejection of any form of betrayal must be interpreted as standing in for the courage of those who stood up to HUAC and remained faithful to old friends and the political struggles that had brought them together in more ethical and committed times.

NOTES

1. In our sophisticated societies, it has always been common to sell, say, a sports car with a seductive young woman draped over the hood. We can also take Santiago's remark about industrial tortillas as a reference to burgeoning fast-food joints.

2. Kennedy was at home in Westerns, as his work with Anthony Mann (*Bend of the River, The Man from Laramie*) and Nicholas Ray (*The Lusty Men*) testifies.

3. Ulmer's mise-en-scène during the sequence in the cantina even suggests that the dancer is better off socially than Maria (and perhaps financially too). As we have seen, the framing in Manuel's home excludes Maria, whereas Ulmer crosscuts between the two men (sitting together at a table, exactly as in the farmhouse) and the dancer performing. She may be a spectacle, but she receives more attention and, especially, appreciation than Maria. As we shall see, it is thanks to Santiago that Maria can break free.

4. It was left to Sam Peckinpah to represent this period in *The Wild Bunch* (1969).

5. The House Committee on Un-American Activities (HUAC) first investigated communism in Hollywood in 1940, but the hearings that paved the way for black-

listing took place in October 1947. HUAC returned in early 1951. Zimet was never investigated; he saw what was coming and left for Mexico in 1951. Many blacklist victims were to live there: Dalton Trumbo of the Hollywood Ten (blacklisted after the hearings of 1947), John Bright, Hugo Butler and his family, and others. See the interview with Zimet in McGilligan and Buhle, 723–48. He discusses *The Naked Dawn* on pp. 733–35. He chose the Schneiders as they were family. For information on Mexico as the home to blacklistees, see the volumes by Anhalt and Rouverol (the widow of Hugo Butler). Ulmer had already worked with a future victim of the blacklist: Gordon Kahn, who wrote *Ruthless* (1948). He was also to become an exile in Mexico. On *Ruthless*, see Humphries, "Logic."

6. We must not forget that Trotsky found a haven in Mexico until a Stalinist agent murdered him there in 1940.

7. For an exhaustive discussion of the ritual of naming names, see Navasky. For an introduction to blacklisting, why and how it came into existence, and its effects, see Humphries, *Hollywood's Blacklists*.

BIBLIOGRAPHY

Anhalt, Diane. *A Gathering of Fugitives: American Political Expatriates in Mexico, 1948–1965* (Santa Maria, Calif.: Archer Books, 2001).

Humphries, Reynold. *Hollywood's Blacklists: A Political and Cultural History* (Edinburgh: Edinburgh University Press, 2008).

———. "The Logic of Contradiction and the Politics of Desire in *Ruthless*," in *Edgar G. Ulmer: Essays on the King of the Bs*, ed. Bernd Herzogenrath (Jefferson, N.C.: McFarland, 2009), 159–70.

May, Elaine Tyler. *Homeward Bound: American Families in the Cold War Era* (New York: Basic Books, 1988).

McGilligan, Patrick, and Paul Buhle. *Tender Comrades: A Backstory of the Hollywood Blacklist* (New York: St. Martin's, 1997).

Navasky, Victor S. *Naming Names* (London: Penguin Books, 1980).

Rouverol, Jean. *Refugees from Hollywood: A Journal of the Blacklist Years* (Albuquerque: University of New Mexico Press, 2000).

14

A Grave New World

Cast and Crew on the Making of *Beyond the Time Barrier*

Robert Skotak

It may be more mere coincidence than deliberate choice, or the result of some mysterious cosmic alignment, that found one of Hollywood's most notoriously "underground" filmmakers exploring realms beneath the earth in three of his last five films—*Beyond the Time Barrier*, *Journey Beneath the Desert*, and *The Cavern*. But there is something appealingly appropriate about Edgar Ulmer winding up in worlds hidden from the sun, rooting around in dark places where story and locale could be played off of each other with peculiar symmetry and resonance.

In particular, *Beyond the Time Barrier* was the grimmest, cheapest of the three, as well as one of Ulmer's most schematically accomplished films. The director dotes on the reciprocally repeated facets of this underworld, in plot structure, physical structure, and theme. The film is a bit like a fable, complete with its lesson, a kind of technological *Wizard of Oz* tale of journey; change; and, finally, return, as an older—quite literally—and wiser version of oneself. In this case, the trip originates in a here-and-now "Kansas," and it lands its hero in a temporal Oz populated by useless wizards.

As in *Fable*, some "big picture" realities about life must be learned or overturned. So it is here that the presumed safety of our world is an illusion. For Ulmer, the telling is affected by means of a brooding state of mind: *Time Barrier* clearly tries to create this in its overcast grays and blacks. To call it "a meditation" would be overstatement, skirting pretension. But, pretentious notion or not, Ulmer touches on at least three elements—Fate, Faith, and Duty—with some sincerity, amplified by his handling of tone, his physical scheme, and the earnestness of his effort.

In looking at the how and why of the film's making, one learns that a pervasive sense of fear provided Ulmer with the impetus to graft an Old World, vaguely Slavic weight onto what could have otherwise been, in the hands of a less dedicated filmmaker, a phoned-in job. His characters wander among a seemingly endless series of inverted monolithic pyramids that bring to mind, in their coldness, isolating places as diverse as the modern parking garages, storage vaults, and cemeteries. To accomplish the creation of even such a minimalist environment on the film's nearly nonexistent budget was to require a miracle of resourcefulness from this most inventive director and his crew.

In spite of its minor miracles—and though made with the participation of, among others, an Academy Award–winning art director, a legendary makeup artist, a world-class stunt coordinator, and some top character actors—*Beyond the Time Barrier* has been long ignored. Some vast flaws—an embarrassingly amateur performance; special effects created, it would seem, with paper cutouts; and some ludicrous makeup applied in the absence of the maestro Jack Pierce—seriously cloud any attempt at a fair viewing.

Beyond the Time Barrier could not, in all seriousness, be called a "classic," or even a "minor classic." It is neither remotely a landmark nor is it negligible. It doesn't fall easily into the "guilty pleasure" category. It is too grim and humorless. Nonetheless, it has some classic elements, some striking moments and tableaus, a unique experimentation with design, and a heartfelt, to a fault, sincerity in its message.

Ulmer brought to it his own individuality and a commitment to make the most of little, ending with an artful hand off of melodrama to meaning. Ultimately, it was his fight for a visual symmetry, one that could reasonably interplay with "content," that enabled him to place his hero at the emotional vertices of Fate, Faith, and Duty without pretense—no mean feat for a tiny B movie ostensibly about jet planes, monsters, and the atomic bomb!

In a process initiated by the writings of Myron Meisel in the early 1970s, Ulmer's film has been rehabilitated to some extent, primarily in recognition of its thematic relevance to the director's supposed, overarching "cinema of despair," which developed as his reputation grew. But no detailed look into the how of its making—how the wide variety of factors, both people and circumstances, came together to be imprinted with Ulmer's stamp—has ever been undertaken. What follows is an attempt at remedy.

THE TALE

For those unfamiliar, Major William Allison, an air force test pilot, played by Robert Clarke, throttles his experimental X-80 suborbital jet on a flight to the fringes of outer space. The flight is a success, and more than that: Allison not only breaks all speed and altitude records, he jumps out of the year 1960 and sixty-four years into the future, though he doesn't even realize it for an astounding amount of time. After discovering widespread desolation and an empty solar installation on the ground, he is taken prisoner by people of the year 2024.

Much of the tale revolves around Allison's confused wanderings among these subterranean survivors-of-terrible-disaster. With few exceptions, everyone in this underground citadel has been rendered deaf, mute, and/or sterile by a worldwide "cosmic plague" in which the ozone layer, destroyed by atomic testing, is allowing harmful cosmic radiation to bombard the earth. Various groups of survivors each have their own plans as to how best to use this intruder for their own purposes. Some view him as a "Scape"—one who has escaped contamination—who therefore offers the possibility of being bred with the leader's young and still-fertile granddaughter. Others—a group of scientists, fellow time travelers from the past—want to seize Allison's plane to escape this doomed world for selfish reasons.

Allison manages to regain his plane and return to his own time as chaos breaks out in the form a violent rebellion of homicidal mutants who have been released by the scientists. Allison's escape is at a price: the time shunting has subtracted years from his life, and he returns an ancient, withered old man shaken by prospects of humanity's fated future. Bedridden and dying, he pleads with the Pentagon officials to prevent it, leaving them stunned and frozen. But moments before a hopeless fade-out, salvation is glimpsed as one official sagely observes, "Gentlemen, we've got a lot to think about."

Ulmer's film had its humble beginnings years earlier, in the not-so-humble Wild West of the cold war era—the golden age of the atom, radiation, and fallout, when atomic bombs and guided missiles were being blasted into the once-upon-a-time pure desert air of the American Southwest with nonchalant regularity. It was then—the early 1950s—that a decorated former Naval photographer, Arthur C. Pierce, was taking the first steps away from image making and toward the written word. Hoping to jump-start a potential career in motion pictures, he took the plunge in 1954 and developed a lengthy—and, in retrospect, astute—screen treatment dramatizing his concern with the eventual consequences of this unchecked testing of atomic weapons. His passion for science led him to a science-fiction approach: his hero would be a test pilot who inadvertently breaks through time, "the last barrier"—also the title of his story—and stumbles upon a radiation-devastated future and the last dying remnants of humankind.

As a novice writer, not well connected in the business, he knew he'd have to steer his story toward a lower budget and keep things appropriately straightforward, for mass-audience appeal. Believing he'd done all the right things, Pierce was disappointed to find there were no takers. "The Last Barrier" wasn't to catch a glimpse of sunlight for another half-dozen years.

Happenstance would finally connect Pierce's dust-gathering concept with Ulmer in the fall of 1958. The link would be actor Robert Clarke, the B-picture leading man who had starred in Ulmer's *The Man from Planet X* in 1950. He and Pierce happened to share the same accountant secretary at the time the actor was looking for a script to follow up his own independent film, *The Hideous Sun Demon*. Hearing this when their paths finally crossed, Pierce immediately thought of his yellowing "Barrier" treatment. He met with Clarke, who outlines the story:

> It was a very fortuitous meeting that Art and I had. I recall that as soon as I began to read his story, I thought, "Gosh, this'd be an excellent follow-up to *Sun Demon*," because it was current; it had the element of the atomic bomb problems well written into it. It had a unique ending—which, frankly, was a bit of a steal from *The Lost Horizon*. And it had a lot of exploitable things about it, which I wanted. By that, I mean [a story] that wouldn't require the services of a highly paid star, but could go out on its own like *The Man From Planet X*, which hadn't required a well-known actor, but was successful strictly on subject matter.
>
> Art's story was quite up to date. It had these elements which could be highly advertised. It seemed to me to be well thought-out and well constructed. Art was a great one for detail and getting into the actual "science fact" of it.

Says Pierce:

> Science and science fiction had always appealed to me. When I decided I wanted to write in this area, I decided I had to develop a philosophy and approach. To me, there are two basic kinds of science fiction, one where the science is based on fiction and one where the fiction is based on science, and it was [the second category] that appealed to me. I had no science background [I had primarily a technical background], so I had to dig pretty deep. I read pure science a great deal. If your fiction is based on science, then you have some of the work done for you, and you can go on to say something about the real world with some credence.

Among Pierce's real-world concerns were the effects of radiation on the population, the biological time bomb that might be released—a theme that also interested producer Clarke—and the potential for weaving these elements of particular cold war era concern into a realistic fabric.

Pierce was engaged by Clarke to turn his story into a screenplay, the writer notes, "for peanuts! Six hundred dollars." In fact, Pierce was to struggle throughout the development of the screenplay: "Unfortunately, I was so poor

I had to write the script by candlelight! I had had my electricity shut off! At least I wasn't using an electric typewriter at the time. When it got dark, man, I had a stick on this side and one on the other . . . writing [about all this technology] by candlelight!"

A perfectly odd beginning for an Edgar Ulmer film. Time travel by candlelight.

ENTER ULMER

The fall of 1958 could have offered up a dozen reliable budget directors to helm Clarke's project, such for-hire stalwarts as Edward L. Cahn, Nathan Juran, Gene Fowler Jr., or Arnold Laven, any of whom would have turned in a workmanlike translation from page to screen. But fate, in the form of a small number of degrees of separation, helped Clarke's project toward a less mundane outcome: While working with Pierce to develop the screenplay, Clarke happened upon an old acquaintance, veteran production manager Lester Guthrie. The two had worked together a decade earlier on *The Man From Planet X*, a film that had—if nothing else—demonstrated the efficacy of atmosphere writ large when applied to science fiction, both from an artistic and practical viewpoint.

Guthrie urged Clarke to take "The Last Barrier" to John Miller, Guthrie's current employer, a man who had recently formed a motion-picture investment company. Miller was looking for properties to produce: He had already arranged for the funding of two as-yet-undetermined films via his association with a wealthy ex–military major named Robert Maden. Maden had raised $225,000 from investors in Texas, but he and Miller needed viable material to produce. Clarke got his script into Miller hands.

Miller quickly grasped the potential in the Pierce-Clarke screenplay. Rockets, monsters, and time travel. He submitted it—along with Jack Lewis's *The Amazing Transparent Man* and an unnamed third script—to the money group in Texas. "The Last Barrier" was immediately picked as the best of the lot, and a budget of $125,000 was allocated toward production, pending selection of a director. The smaller amount of $100,000 was assigned to the second script chosen, *The Amazing Transparent Man*. The two films were to be shot back-to-back, both to be produced in the Dallas–Fort Worth area.

After the very first skim of Pierce's script—with all of its ambitions and technical and visual challenges—Guthrie collared Clarke flat out: "If you want to get the most out of this picture, I would highly recommend Edgar Ulmer!" Ulmer had slowed his output somewhat in recent years and was available. Says Clarke: "Edgar's ability to get more out of a script, and put more on the screen for less money [than anyone else] was very well known. He'd already done that on *Planet X*." Indeed, the ambitious, highly successful earlier film had been shot in six days for under $40,000!

Clarke knew he'd be a fool to not jump at the chance.

Like the investors, Ulmer found the script full of potential visually, intriguing with a few novel twists, if not quite ready to shoot; and he signed on to direct not only Pierce's script, but also the smaller *Amazing Transparent Man*—knowing, going in, that the time-travel story needed a lot of "shaping up."

Ulmer's involvement clearly and quickly helped skew the project away from what could have been nothing more than standard Saturday-matinee fare. Under his guidance, it darkened gradually toward something overcast and forlorn, a tale in which it might or might not be Too Late. Therein, gloomy elegiac overtones lay, nascent, waiting to be unveiled by the hand—and eye—of the director.

A number of elements on the raw pages no doubt appealed to Ulmer's impulses to viscerally depict not only impending chaos, but certain defining images and "strangeness," per se: Allison's disorienting discovery of the air base in a sudden shambles moments after take off; the mad laughter of the caged subhumans crawling about their dungeon; the reasoned yet confusing plotting and counterplotting of the future people; the doom-laden air hanging over the citadel; its silence before the chaos of the mutant revolt and the stillness following it; the Supreme's grief as his last hope is destroyed; and the humorlessness and unrelenting downwardness of the story arc. Amidst the naïveté and the melodramatic development, here was a lone figure, Allison, a modern "everyman"—aided now by technology—feeling his way through blind alleys and wheel-spinning cul de sacs, a character who could be shown with some sympathy.

When asked about her husband's attraction to worlds like the one of *Time Barrier*, Shirley Ulmer—his script supervisor and "springboard" on this and many of his films—points to his, to her, emotional core: "Edgar was a bleak visionary. The moors. Bronte. Brooding. This was Edgar. He always, *always* had to go emotionally to the most serious places." Essentially abandoned by parents and family as a youth, he fell into the realm of thinkers and questioners. Great minds of avant-garde and expressionistic exploration in cinema and theater mentored his formative years: Reinhardt, Murnau, Lang. Add to that the numbing madness of World War I, that cruel, dehumanizing hell into which men had been pitched. Such intellectual and chaotic intensity could scarcely not have informed his youth, laying before him not just the possibilities of the theater of the absurd but the temptation to succumb to life as such a theater. Or at least to live at its brink.

"This is a harsh thing to say," confesses Shirley Ulmer, "but I believe the line between genius and sanity and insanity is very, very fine. Edgar certainly was a genius, and that fine line was [definitely] there." But she insists—and many might sense this upon viewing his vast filmic output—he was deeply religious, *philosophically*. She draws a correlation between her husband's personal credo and the conclusion of one of his films: "Remember the last line in *Ruthless*?—'Keep searching.' That was his message. He was always trying to keep the door open. Searching." And that message, she insists, crops up again in *Time Barrier*'s last line, "We've got a lot to think about"—and this drew Ulmer toward the story.

This particular script was premised on the real dangers to the planet of the rampant spread of atomic radiation. This, according to both his wife and his daughter, Arianné, he feared with great concern at the time. This fear had grown deeper roots in Ulmer by the late '50s, spurred, initially, by his work on *Damaged Lives* (1933). By Shirley Ulmer's account, the need to wear lead aprons while she and her husband were in the presence of the invisible particles instilled in him a lifelong apprehension of radiation and "the Bomb." It should come as no surprise then that Ulmer—frequently viewed in the critics' arena as a man gripped by the notion of how "unseen forces" might act upon and complicate the fate of his characters—would be drawn to the dramatic impetus of forces working at the unseen atomic level, which could impact the entirety of humankind.

Beyond the overt, direct carnage atomic weaponry had been shown to produce, Pierce's script opened up areas less apparent, even to a prophetic extent—raising, if in no great detail, the issue of the potential destruction of the earth's ozone layer and what that would mean for the human race. His character General Karl Kruse—a fellow time-traveler-by-accident in the story—posits an interesting variation on global warming issues currently in debate. Pierce had thought a great deal about the problems of radiation and pollution for many years: "I knew about the ozone layer and its [vital] purpose," he explained in the late 1970s. "In my script, I called the result of its destruction the 'cosmic plague.' I used that theme in three other films. It was a real concern of mine." Though Pierce confessed that no one knew at the time of his script—the 1950s—what effects aerial contamination and atomic testing would ultimately have on the ozone layer, his instincts held that it was extremely vulnerable and subject to destruction, with potentially dire consequences for life on earth..

Though polar opposites in most ways—the science-leaning Pierce a long way from Ulmer's "dark Romanticism"—Pierce's themes, at least, were close to Ulmer's heart.

In the era of M.A.D.—mutually assured destruction—in which the United States and the Soviet Union found themselves matching stockpiles bomb for bomb, missile for missile, in an effort to maintain an apocalypse freeze, Ulmer could view Pierce's tale as a little fable of Man struggling to move forward in a world where much action negates most other action, where Man is seeking a path to break free of a claustrophobic Grand Impasse.

For two months prior to production, in early 1959, Ulmer chopped away at the script at a series of meetings with Pierce, Clarke, and production manager Guthrie, trying to bring it "into his own," emphasizing certain beats, subtracting all traces of humor, and looking to give it shape and style. Working with Ulmer was no small ordeal, Pierce recalled. He was pushed and prodded through endless requests for changes in dialogue, tone, structure, and characterization. In later years, Clarke pointed frequently not only to Ulmer's talent, but to his belligerence and intensity in the creative areas. "At times, Edgar was very hard to work with. He could be a real son of a bitch . . . Along with his enormous talent, he had an enormous ego to match!" At one point, exasperated and fed up by Ulmer's unending requests for rewrites, Clarke recalled Pierce jumping up from his chair and angrily snapping his pencil in two under Ulmer's nose, barely containing a physical attack. Ulmer was irritated, but appeared, according to Clarke, relieved at having provoked such emotion in the normally even-keeled writer.

Years later, Pierce didn't recall the incident, but confided, "Edgar was a tyrant! And he was *ponderous* in an old-fashioned way. Everything with him was *ponderous*!" adding, in the next breath, enigmatically, "But I liked him. He was marvelous."

Ariannè Ulmer Cipes—Ulmer's daughter and Clarke's costar in the film, under the stage name Arianne Arden—provides some insight into such incidents: "Dad would deliberately enrage people if he thought that was the only way to get to somebody, to bring them out. First he would try to do it in a nice way, but if he was hitting a brick wall and just wasn't getting 'the juice,' he would say, 'O.K.' and go after them and [force it] out."

A comparison of the earliest drafts with the final reveal Ulmer's darker influences. The scene in the pit with the mutants takes on an almost abstract quality with Ulmer. The villainous captain is given sympathetic moments. There is a greater emphasis on the competing factions in the future and the growing disorientation of the unwilling time traveler, and an expansion of his final moments with the Supreme, underlining the hopelessness following the final riot.

Ulmer also saw fit to break away from Pierce's straight linear telling, reformatting *The Last Barrier* into a three-act "present—flashback—present" structure: Major Allison takes off, disappears off radar, and returns only moments later, after which he tells his story—his adventure in the future—via flashback. Only the closing shots reveal the "shock": the pilot's face, which was that of a young man in the morning, is now—a few hours later—ancient and wrinkled because of his passage through time. The new structure put the audience into a more passive, "helpless" position that emphasized the fracturing of time for the purposes of greater subjectivity.

Throughout the rewrite, Ulmer struggled to add "meat" wherever he could. His attention was drawn to the great potential for invention presented by a peculiar pattern a study of the script revealed: all of the action and conflict revolved around "threes." Test pilot Allison moves through three distinct time periods to confront a threesome that holds sway over the world of 2024—the Supreme, the Captain, and the Supreme's granddaughter—who, in turn, are opposed by three scientists—Professor Bourman, General Kruse, and Captain Markova. Allison is then caught in a baffling interaction between three mutually opposed factions—the ruling party, the scientists, and the mutants. His actions are set against three phases of time—past, present/future, and a potential altered past. Even his test flight is laid out in three stages, and there are three mathematical factors involved if Allison is to reverse his time-jump.

Each point is a facet, a fracture of a greater piece that Allison must put together to move forward. Here was something Ulmer could explore through storytelling, science and design, threes-within-threes, and a potential overarching stylistic device that could form a uniquely Ulmerian uniting principle. Out of this arose one of Ulmer's more visually bold moves, the attempt to translate the intellectual theme of threes into the physical environment of the production, to reflect story conflict in the film's very *physicality*. Means of such amplification immediately presented themselves, a few by good fortune and coincidence, and they were embraced by Ulmer. For example, the interceptor jet that Pierce and Clarke had selected to represent the experimental X-80 of the script was Convair's highly advanced F-102a, noted for its broad, three-point delta-wing aerodynamic. Its cockpit, composed of subsets of triangles and angles, made for a suitable "time capsule" for the hero. Even his helmet—the MA-3, the most advanced high-altitude, impact-resistant, fringe-of-space military headgear available—could be used to frame Allison's face in its notably triangular visor for long stretches of screen time.

Building on this to near obsession, Ulmer changed the young heroine's name from "Terrene" to "Trirene." He would later order up scene transitions in the form of a triangle, the cumulative effect of which was a kind of endlessly echoed motif of complementary subsets within subsets suggesting, long before the theory had been widely put forth, the fractal nature of all things. Certainly it was a principle that likely would have gone completely unexplored by the vast field of for-hire directors working in even less-dim budgetary recesses of film at the time, and one that indicated Ulmer's personal involvement.

Regarding the extent to which Ulmer considered *Time Barrier* close to him or "serious," Ulmer Cipes notes,

> This film fell midway between earning a living and [issues close to] his heart. He certainly didn't set out to do films like *Jive Junction* and *Girls in Chains* at PRC [from his heart]. These were not films he would've personally pursued: They were assigned. But he did set out to do *Time Barrier* . . . He found science fiction challenging. He found it philosophically interesting. He found that—like theology and religion—it could be used to examine [big] issues, that now you could do the same thing through science fiction, and it provided you a tremendous scope of possibilities.

Like the literature of fable and allegory, and like Dickens's *Christmas Carol*, the eye of modern science-laced fiction allowed one even to see, as needed, across time and space; to witness the future consequences of one's actions in the past; and, like Scrooge, to become informed about alternate possibilities, even "second chances." Through technology, destiny might be challenged. With time travel, Ulmer could take on Fate itself.

NOTES FROM THE UNDERGROUND

For reasons traceable to a misinformed guess on the part of one writer in the early 1970s, it has long been reported that Ulmer's stylized citadel was nothing more than a "found" location, that the film had been put into production in haste to take advantage of a standing "futuristic exhibit" at the Texas Centennial Fairgrounds. While it is true that shooting took place at the famous Fair Park, no such "exhibit," often referred to in print, ever existed: the fairgrounds merely provided a huge, empty building to house the construction and assembly of the large, ambitious sets, which were designed and wholly fabricated for *Beyond the Time Barrier* (and which, it should be noted, served in redressed form as the basis for Ulmer's attic set in his subsequent film, *The Amazing Transparent Man*).

It is in the visualization of *Time Barrier*'s sets that Ulmer's attempt at plot-image-theme symbiosis came alive: Pierce's initial script had described 2024 as a world of rounded tunnels and circular chambers. Aside from the practical considerations—curved shapes being notoriously expensive and time-consuming to construct—Ulmer reportedly wasn't excited by the idea. What he was particularly interested in finding, according to Pierce, was a design that could also be used to tell the story, that could do so inexpensively, and that was based on scientific principles..

Harkening back to the halcyon days of German expressionism, as well as the Russian avant-garde constructivist movement, the cold realities of the story's future suggested sharp edges and maze-like wanderings to Ulmer. Angularities. Rectilinear forms and angles offered great visual prospects for the "moderne," and had the potential for creating a dialogue between the physical and the three-point story motifs, the latter leading ultimately to an obvious geometric counterpart, the triangle. As such, the three-sided template, as a physicality, opened the door to innumerable applications, including doors!—and walls, mirrors, passageways, and entire rooms. And there was a science to it.

In one of the rare on-record accounts from Ulmer about the film—possibly the only one—a near-obsession with the shape, in the glaring logic of it, is apparent:

> The triangle is one of the most important figures in geometry and in higher mathematics. The triangle is essential in buildings, [in a] bridge or a tunnel, where it is a basic element. I think that in the future, everything will be built in the most economical form, the most scientifically practical. That is why I chose the triangle, the same as [between] scenes. The sets and settings were based on the triangle. I wanted to use that shape as much as possible . . . With respect to *Beyond the Time Barrier*, I [perhaps] overdid myself with the settings. (Eisenschitz and Romer 6–7, my translation)

His latter observation may have met with disagreement from champions of style and artifice; for this was, for once, a small science-fiction movie that actually *had* a style!

Ulmer Cipes recalls: "The minute Dad had the triangle idea, it went from there. I can remember him sitting and showing [me and Mom] a lens and how a lens opens and closes in a camera, and his saying, 'That's the way I want the triangles to open and close as a door, like an iris.' He saw it as that."

To transform Ulmer's ideas into physical reality, Clarke and the director, in a particularly wise move, sought out the services of accomplished Academy Award–winning art director Ernst Fegte. The German-born designer was a smart choice in many ways. As the art director of Hollywood's first major science-fiction film, *Destination Moon*, he had displayed remarkable ingenuity and resourcefulness in the face of that film's modest budget and huge challenges. Years under contract in the '30s and '40s at Paramount had gained him wide-ranging experience on subjects as varied as *Frenchman's Creek* (1944)—for which he won his Academy Award—and the ghostly classic *The Uninvited* (1944). The fact that he was well-versed in German expressionism made him a kindred spirit with Ulmer, and put them both on the same page aesthetically, as well as in practical matters. Fegte explains:

> I had known Ulmer from Joseph Urban days. He used to be a draftsman for Urban in New York. A fellow Viennese, Urban was, and Ulmer was with him for many years as his sort of right hand. He had a *lot* of talent. Urban as the

Viennese designer for the Metropolitan Opera, needed such a man, and Ulmer did a beautiful job for him . . .

I worked very closely with Ulmer. That was the same kind of association I had had with George Pal [on *Destination Moon*]. We were just like this [crossed fingers]. *Time Barrier* had all been pre-staged. I knew what had to take place from a production point of view and from the staging point of view, and Ulmer went along with these ideas. He thought it was great at the time. And if we didn't have much money, we had fun.

Destination Moon was made like you make a class "A" picture. In other words, what money had to be spent had to be spent to make a good production. But *Time Barrier*, that was a different production altogether. Here the money was *tight*.

You had these survivors living underground sometime in the future; the people who had survived had to live there because of radiation [on the surface] . . . So you had your cast in all these underground chambers and tunnels in the story. And the question became "what does this place look like?" and, from a production point of view, "how do we create it?" Remember, we didn't have any money!

Now, in the script, what was described were these sort of "caves" carved out so people could live in them. Stone caves. I don't recall exactly, but Ulmer wanted something different, more interesting than rocks, rock walls. He talked about this idea of "geometric sets" he had. Geometric sets. He wanted a look based on triangles that he could use for his lighting, to get all kinds of lighting effects and so on . . .

I thought not just about triangles, but pyramids somehow. And how you could use four-sided pyramids to create a lot of different opportunities for sets using—or repeating—just one basic shape. So we talked it over, and he liked it. I made a small study model. Then he had the idea to invert them, so I then took this four-sided pyramid idea and made twelve of these things in miniature with upside-down pyramids, resting on their points. And Ulmer went for it. He added some panels that would open up as you needed to get from place to place [and so on].

What we did to make these: He wanted to make them lightweight—which they had to be, really—so they were just wood frames covered in muslin. I made twelve of them, big pyramids, all out of thin framework covered in stretched muslin and painted . . . We put those together in the big warehouse building at the fairgrounds in Dallas, which was big as a soundstage. The local crews I used, well, they got through it, but they had a hard time. [Those pyramids] would interlock: We clamped them, as I recall, together at the top, and the whole bunch would stand on their own. Would, essentially, be self-supporting. That simple. And since [they were] light, we could carry one away, or two, with the grips, open up the space or maybe make a room. . . . And that's how we did that, our "future world."

So from the basic set of twelve inverted pyramids, everything was made, all the different chambers could be made. By rearranging these things and regrouping them.

> When I designed this [*Time Barrier* set], I really went back to what I could remember of *Cabinet of Dr. Caligari*—which was a fabulous movie—and things of that nature. The look of these films—the lighting and the sets. Expressionistic, yes. And *Beyond the Time Barrier* conveyed a feeling, the emotions exactly. That's what I tried to do here in a modest way, but I just didn't have the money, and when I think of all the sequences that took place in this key set that I had, it was amazing that I could change it into something else. Shifting around the props and curtains and all the kinds of different pieces I used to make it look different each time!

Here, in 1959, Ulmer was taking inspiration from the earliest traditions of motion pictures and early-twentieth-century theater, stylistic minimalism, or representation. This approach not only allowed Ulmer a means to depict his scientific and aesthetic scheme, but solved his budget challenges. A Zen-stroke of which Ulmer's mentor, Max Reinhardt, might, with justification, have been proud.

Figure 14.1. Bleak faces, grays, and shadows: Ulmer's "sad" future. Courtesy of the Robert Skotak collection.

Figure 14.2. Test pilot Allison (Robert Clarke) in space-bound "time cockpit." Courtesy of the Robert Skotak collection.

CASTING

Casting had to be handled in two parts: The larger speaking roles were cast out of Los Angeles. Secondary parts—military personnel, citadel extras, and the mutants—were handled in the Dallas–Fort Worth area. As to these smaller parts, individuals were invited for tryouts at small theaters there, the casting sessions overseen, according to Don Flournoy (who was part of the Dallas cast), by Baruch Lumet and his young, not-yet-famous son Sydney.

Ulmer Cipes recalls that her dad had made an arrangement with the Paul Kohner Agency, which represented him, for the casting of three key parts: Kruse and Bourman—the renegade scientists—and the Supreme. Respectively, the roles were filled by the Hungarian Stephen Bekassy, the Dutch John Van Dreelen, and Vladimir Sokoloff, a Russian. Their distinct accents must have projected, to Ulmer's mind, something of an Old World quality onto this new world, another means of creating disorientation and sudden *change* for the pilot; for clearly the speech patterns of the future are far removed from

Figure 14.3. Futuristic-cubistic "dungeon," imprisoning mutant rebels. Design by Ulmer and Ernst Fegte. Courtesy of the Robert Skotak collection.

the flat, colloquial dialogue of Allison's preflight associates. It is as if he has landed in a foreign land, which, indeed, any sudden jump out of time would appear to be to the "jumper"!

Ulmer cast his daughter in the role of the duplicitous female scientist, Captain Markova, again reaching for a "foreign" feel. She explains:

> My father said that I had a European quality, because I'd spent so much time growing up there. [This quality] may be in my patterns of speech or something. But there is a slight edge of something "foreign" about me. And he felt I was kind of a cross between Gale Sondergaard, whom he adored and had worked with, who could be marvelous and "evil," and Hedy Lamarr. So that was the persona he was creating, the character [he was] creating for this film.

She adds her belief that her father had come up with the character name, since "we'd lived for a time in the apartment of [dancer] Alicia Markova, right about the time of *St. Benny the Dip*." Aside from the name, the dancer was to suggest an approach to *Time Barrier*'s "Markova" to Ulmer in other ways.

They eventually found their female lead in the person of Darlene Tompkins. The eighteen-year-old multiple beauty contest winner possessed not only the

Figure 14.4. Ulmer characters dominated by geometries. Shapes parallel three-way plot points. Courtesy of the Robert Skotak collection.

appeal and mime skills necessary, but she was available and affordable. It turned out to be an ideal choice. In spite of little experience and virtually no on-set rehearsal time, Tompkins would later be singled out in reviews for her commendable job. The "full bloom of youth" she radiated stood her in good stead, as Clarke later observed, as a futuristic Eve to his Adam.

THE FAIR SETS

Following several months of production meetings and script revisions, the production packed up and headed for Dallas. A truckload of futuristic items from local prop-rental houses departed from Los Angeles in late March 1959, and made its way to the Texas Fair Park to greet a crew gearing up for the shoot.

Hollywood had arrived—or at least a contingent of science-fiction/film-noir renegades!

Working out of inexpensive motels to save money, the principals shuttled daily to the sprawling fairgrounds where the majority of the film was to be

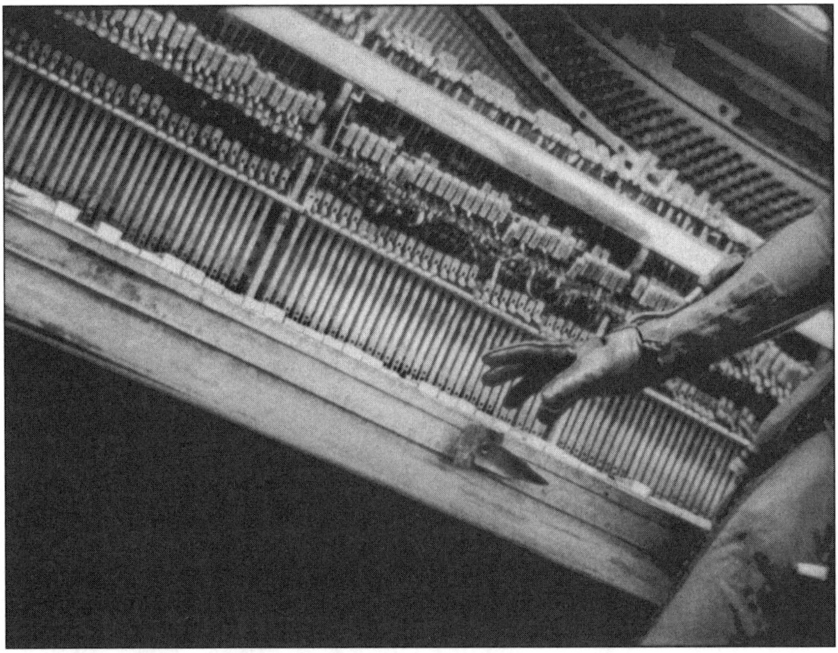

Figure 14.5. Pilot hand and piano keys: A striking visual-audio discord. Courtesy of the Robert Skotak collection.

shot. Guthrie had arranged for use of one of the fair's largest—and, with an inaugural date of 1904, oldest—pavilions, the Centennial Building, to house all the ambitious set construction and photography.

Fegte had arrived several weeks in advance of Ulmer and the Los Angeles group, and he had immediately hired a handful of local carpenters and put them to work constructing the sets. The Centennial Building's cavernous 94,000 square feet and 30-foot ceilings provided ample room for the giant erector set. On this echoing "soundstage," any question as to the film's thematic form would be glaringly clear: triangles and triangles and pyramids everywhere, taking shape, dotted by the occasional orb and plane, all eventually to be enshrouded in great, billowing curtains of military-surplus parachutes, hung about to dampen the sound. "The pyramids," explains Clarke,

> were actually put together in the building right there; Fegte, knowing that they had to be moved about during filming, kept that in mind during their construction. Ulmer went down about a week ahead of [the rest of us]. Being a multi-talented type of person, he wanted to know as much as he could about the layout of the sets so he could pre-plan his shooting. He was [after all] very much involved

Figure 14.6. Remains of the day, courtesy of a fortuitous abandoned airfield, Ulmer's "found set." Courtesy of the Robert Skotak collection.

Figure 14.7. Pilot Allison, promising change of Fate, proffers Faith. Courtesy of the Robert Skotak collection.

Figure 14.8. Trirene (Darlene Tompkins), Major Allison (Robert Clarke), and The Supreme (Vladimir Sokoloff). Courtesy of the Robert Skotak collection.

> with the production design. He was in complete agreement with the concept of the inverted pyramids. He knew that they were to be *mobile*, and that gave him peace of mind insofar as planning his shots.

Shirley Ulmer adds:

> The sets in *Time Barrier* were something else. Edgar used to get excited when he'd get a set built. He'd call me up and say "Get over here! You've got to see this"—and I'd seen it from its inception, so it was exciting for me too—but he'd almost had an orgasm on this one! He was like a kid with a toy!

"Dad loved Ernst Fegte," Ulmer Cipes recalls.

> The [triangles] had wheels on the bottom . . . The sets were being changed hour by hour. You could change them during lunchtime! All of it was orchestrated. The changes were all designed for each day's work . . . Fegte and Dad did work together on moving things, but most of the production decisions came from Dad and the cinematographer. It was not only pre-staged, but heavily rehearsed, like a ballet.

Figure 14.9. Decontamination chamber: Time traveler finds himself the focal point of opposed factions, angles, and options. Courtesy of the Robert Skotak collection.

A model of futurism, form, and efficiency, tongue and groove. Amplifying the notion of "three," the sets were a ubiquity that was to make *Time Barrier* one of the most shaped, visual transliterations of intellectual-conceit-turned-image ever applied to an erstwhile '50s "throwaway" picture. It was a far cry from Pierce's stone caves and round tunnels, but it still evoked a sense of the subterranean in its cubistic collection of vertices, which implied buttressing stalactites and weight overhead.

The *ideas* behind the sets were clear even to those brought in just for a few days of extras work. Malcolm Thomson was a drama student from Southern Methodist University. As a guard who was to wind up skewered on the business end of Markova's knife, the Ulmer-Fegte construction left him with a strong impression a half century later:

> I have no idea which building was used to build the sets, but what was built there was mind-boggling! Even then I was a design freak and a bit inclined to futuristic speculations. I knew at that age—19—about *Caligari*, about Murnau, Eisenstein and Pudovkin. And in *that* set—in Dallas of all places—I felt part of the scenographic world. *That* was inspiring.

THE SHOOT

To allow Fegte and his small crew time to finish set construction, exterior sequences were scheduled first. Filming began early on Wednesday, 8 April 1959, with veteran cinematographer Meredith Nicholson behind the camera. First up was Allison's landing at and exploration of the devastated Sands Air Force Base. Under appropriately heavy overcast skies, the crew set off for the ramshackle remains of what once was Eagle Mountain Marine Air Base, a 410-acre site located on the edge of Eagle Mountain Lake in Tarrant County, some eighteen miles outside Dallas.

The wet tarmac, leafless bare trees, and low, gray sky provided a suitably dreary backdrop for Ulmer's frame and the test pilot's confused wanderings. Allison finds the remains of his commander's office, a shattered section of highway, and overturned vehicles.

This first day's work would eventually provide one of Ulmer's more concentrated mood pieces. The director picked out interesting details. A dilapidated piano left in the wreckage provided a "found moment." Ulmer has his pilot stumble against it and strike a fittingly dead chord. In the silence and hollow wind, it evokes emptiness as successfully as might costly effects. Says Clarke:

> We moved around there pretty freely. The runway was pretty much grown over with weeds and grass, but the control tower, what was left of it, was still there. We shot in an area that was maybe a half-mile or so. Edgar picked out some of the best remaining aspects of the base as it was then. I thought he did an excellent job of covering it and getting the most out of it production value-wise.

It was in this type of grim environment that Ulmer's inclinations toward imminent collapse and thresholds of destruction could and did thrive. Other images included the following: a severe up angle holding the time traveler against the crumbling control tower; a wind-blown street as shot from a gliding dolly; and a caved-down officer's desk. In a chancy move, Ulmer had Nicholson shoot a "lock-off" of the Eagle Mountain control tower with Clarke moving through, framed to allow for the possibility that the sleek F-102a Delta Dagger jet (which could not be landed on the overgrown runway) could be split-screened into the shot later—a type of risky, time-consuming effort usually avoided by more budget-nervous directors.

Having been blessed with good, cold "bad weather" on a perfect "set," Ulmer had moved through his first day freely, creatively. That would not be the case as the crew moved onto the highly classified Carswell Air Force Base in Fort Worth for three days of work on the film's "bookends"—Allison's take off and emergency landings; his arrival and meeting with his superior,

Colonel Martin; the arrival of Pentagon officials; the briefing and hospital-room scenes; and the climactic, face-to-face meeting of the officials with the suddenly aged pilot.

Work at Carswell required special clearances for the entire crew, the assignment of special badges, and strict observation of restrictions. Some of the military's most advanced planes and the latest ground-to-air computer-management systems were installed at the base. Not surprisingly, the sequences shot there reflect the limitations and have a visually flat and "by the numbers" appearance.

Nicholson was able to photograph the parked F-102a from a matched angle to complete the second side of the split-screen shot begun at the abandoned airfield the previous day. Fortunately, the weather had remained consistent, or the composite could never have been assembled. For the film, the jet would now appear in the same shot with the wrecked control tower and Clarke, though existing in actuality some twenty miles apart.

At every step, Ulmer sought production value and realism whenever he could squeeze it in, even when barely possible. Says Clarke:

> We were very excited about [trying to get] a B-36 as it was taxiing along. We were so hopeful that the actors playing the officials from the Pentagon would get their dialogue correct and that their car would move just the way it should so the camera could get the plane taxiing in the background. And it worked. We got lucky.

A local historian, intimately familiar with Carswell's history and the making of the film, pointed out, as if common knowledge, that beefed-up security measures had been taken with the cast and crew because of the small bodies that had been brought to the base from Roswell, New Mexico, in the late 1940s! Ulmer, had he known, no doubt would have tried to get those into his frame too.

Guthrie had arranged to complete the casting begun in Los Angeles with tryouts to be held at the Knox Theater in Dallas. Readings were held to select the remaining speaking, bit, and extra parts.

The popular Top 40 DJ from Dallas's KILN radio station, Ken Knox, was chosen to handle the largest non-L.A.-based role, that of flight commander Colonel Martin. His dry Texas accent was a fairly accurate foreshadowing of later Houston Space Center mission-control patter.

Cast members were also drawn from area drama clubs and local TV stations. Ulmer tapped Don Flournoy and Thomas Ravick, two young "little theater"/TV actors, to play the two mutants with speaking parts.

On Monday, 13 April, the crew moved into the Fair Park Centennial Building for the remainder of the production. First up were scenes in the Supreme's chamber, the largest of the citadel sets, which was dominated by a huge, triangular "all-seeing eye" view screen, and which included several large plinths serving as the Supreme's "power desk"; several of Eero Saarinen's famous tulip chairs; a big moon-ball light hovering overhead; and not much else. Minimalism is Ulmer's order, both an aesthetic and budgetary choice. Nothing adorns. It is a study in Feng Shui Moderne, where angles and spheres are balanced and reduplicate. There is no warmth, and there are no decorations. The lack of secondary dressing is deliberate: there are no papers or books, wall outlets, or reminders of "outside" of any kind. The only recollections of the past—several portraits—are filed away. Other than the chairs, there is no other concession to human sentiment or amenities.

Aside from the big overhead "moon," Ulmer's secondary geometric theme—the circle—occurs in the form of three orbs that are conspicuous on the leader's desk, which seem to be placed there either for their magisterial implication or to suggest some mystical import. They are opaque and black, like crystal balls that have been shut off or have no future to tell.

Allison is interrogated by the ruling triumvirate—the Captain (Red Morgan), the Supreme, and Trirene. It is a long and fruitlessly circular confrontation. By the end of it, neither Allison nor the rulers have a clear idea of why he is here, how he got here, or what should be done with him. Can he be trusted?

Progress was slow the first day. The building was unheated, and a frigid cold quickly took its toll. Park officials had to be called in to thaw the bathroom pipes. Some crew members became ill. And the chamber sequence—thirteen and a half pages of long takes—tested the producer side of actor Clarke. Even decades later, he remembered vividly the discomfort and tension he felt during the scene, the impact of each and every delay weighing on him and the tiny budget—blown lines, camera miscues, lighting problems, unwanted background sounds. And then there were the major concerns over the performance—or nonperformance—of the actor playing the Captain: Boyd "Red" Morgan had been hired to help choreograph the fight scenes and handle stunt work. Both he and his brother Stacey—hired for the same reason—were considered among the best stuntmen working in the field at the time. Red Morgan, however, was no actor, at least not for the kind of interaction and dialogue required for the interrogation scene. His visible discomfort, flat delivery, and inappropriate "western" accent grated on and seriously undercut the actors playing opposite him. Says Clarke:

> Red Morgan was hired mainly because he was a stuntman and Les Guthrie gave him the part, but insisted Red be paid on a kind of [one price] basis, as both a stuntman and as an actor in order to save money. We couldn't afford what Red

> usually got even as a stuntman alone! He was a good stuntman, [but] I don't think he professed to be a very good actor. And, of course, he had the accent that really didn't fit . . . He just didn't have the ability to give that part what it needed. And it's too bad.

Clarke on film indeed appears as uncomfortable at times in the scene as he actually was—perhaps, ironically, as is appropriate from a dramatic standpoint, considering the scene's content. Ulmer Cipes comments: "Red was impossible. Dad tried to loosen him up, but with a limit on retakes, it just could not work." And there were neither time nor funds to dub his part. The fortunes of low-budget film production!

Both Clarke and Ulmer were also conscious that this was Tompkins's first time in front of a feature motion-picture camera. By her own account, Clarke helped lead her through some of these scenes. Clarke observes,

> Darlene was a sweet young gal and was trying very, very hard to do a good job, which, without dialogue, was a difficult assignment . . . And we thought she did a good job of portraying this "mutant" with a sweetness. She was demure, she was pretty, and she didn't overdo it. Edgar was very kind to Darlene. She was new to the business, and he was very patient with her.

Unlike in the case of Morgan, little performance was demanded of Tompkins on the first day, and she appeared relaxed. As a winner of twenty-one of the twenty-five beauty contests she had entered, Tompkins had training in poise on cue, though, she recalled, the "no more than three takes" general rule did create pressure. Added to that, she'd had a minor personal, behind-the-scenes disaster that day: As, perhaps, a concession to the "bobby-soxers" in the audience—but certainly a questionable one, given the setting sixty-four years in the future—the crew had decided to alter her hair into a ponytail. "The hairdresser," Tompkins recalls, "without asking, had grabbed a handful of my own natural hair and cut it off in the back and replaced it with that ponytail 'fall.' It was terrible. I couldn't believe she did that."

Clarke found it helpful, as an actor playing a major dialogue scene with two "novices," to anchor himself with veteran character actor Sokoloff. The Stanislavsky-trained Russian proved a wise choice by Ulmer. Sokoloff's half-century experience as an actor ensured a high degree of professionalism and the gravitas Ulmer wanted for the part. This was not cookie-cutter casting of what could have become, as was typical of the time, a well-worn science fiction character type—the cold, steel-fisted ruler. With age, along with what one observer called a "beatific" sweetness, etched in his every pore, he not only anchored Clarke, but radiated the ennui and the sadness that Ulmer had brought, appropriately, to the story: The Supreme and his granddaughter were to become the heart of the future; any joy that might have otherwise existed was drained away by the dread realization that, for humankind, there was no going back. The Bomb had reigned over all.

Sokoloff had much to draw upon in conveying Ulmer's sense of loss. His wife had died some ten years earlier, leaving him alone. He had no other family or relatives, and he carried a heavy air of melancholy about him. His physical appearance was aided by the artistry of another Hollywood legend who'd been brought in by Ulmer, Jack P. Pierce. The makeup genius Ulmer had worked with on his first major film in the United States, *The Black Cat*, Pierce had been the sole creator of some of the most famous motion-picture "creature" icons of the twentieth century, among them the original Frankenstein's monster, the Wolfman, Dracula, and the Mummy. Unceremoniously dumped by Universal after decades of sterling service when they "modernized" in the late '40s, Pierce had eventually turned to independent productions, such as *Time Barrier*.

Pierce handled all the character makeups on the film. Morgan's "Captain" became something of a "Dr. Morbius," the noteworthy character portrayed by Walter Pidgeon in *Forbidden Planet*. He fitted Sokoloff with a silvery hairpiece, not only to further age him, but to suggest long exposure to radiation; this was matched by a pallid complexion, evocative of weariness, a waning of life. Loss.

Day 2 in the citadel began in the "pit." Arthur Pierce's script called for Allison to be thrown into a slimy dungeon full of grotesque human mutations, providing Ulmer with room for stylish horror. A fight breaks out. Allison is able to overcome the creatures and, threatening to break the arm of one of them, gleans fragments of information. Little of it makes sense: They consider Allison a "'Scape," someone who "ran from the plague." What plague? The responses raise more questions than answers. These creatures—or their type—left to starve aboveground, psychotic and twisted, repeat over and over, "We'll kill all of you."

The Captain's guards reappear and free Allison. Trirene has convinced the Supreme that he can be trusted, and he is allowed to be free.

In staging the sequence, Ulmer and Fegle abandoned the standard notion of an Alexandre Dumas style creaking dungeon, creating instead a trap-like confluence of lines, angles, and shadows, the film's most overtly expressionistic set. Metal bars crisscross like a Picasso-spun spider web. The mutants' clawed hands shadow onto the triangled walls. The actors in the pit chortle, Renfield-like, and scurry up the stairs, bald human rats.

The scene is played at a certain madhouse pitch, a study in exaggeration and tableau, with an overemphasis in delivery and posture unusual in the late-1950s SF-horror cycle. "To Edgar, everything was larger than life," Shirley Ulmer commented when asked about the scene. "He embroidered everything, his staging, everything. He really and truly saw everything bigger than it was, including this. He projected that [idea], and his actors felt it, his cameraman felt it."

Playing the dungeon scene as something "bigger" than it was, staging it as a mental snake pit, Ulmer could correlate atomic testing with insanity.

But what should have been a successful culmination was seriously marred by production problems. The "pit" turned out seriously underpopulated. Nine mutants "able to fight" were originally to be hired to fill the scene; but for lack of money or time, only four actors—Flournoy, Ravick, and two nonspeaking extras—were brought in for the sequence. Hardly the threat to the entire citadel the script intended. Worse, the required "monstrous" bald-head makeups are completely unconvincing. Again, for reasons unknown, Jack Pierce was not available to apply and blend the makeups he'd tested with great success prior to production. In place of Pierce's seamless bald application and the distorted ears of the script, the production's hairdresser was pressed to apply cheap, costume-store rubber bald caps, which were wrinkled, ill fitting, and poorly blended.

Flournoy, who was to speak the lion's share of "subhuman" dialogue in the pit, gave it his best, bad makeup and all, delivering lines with intensity—half-mad with rage, half in delirium. Now a respected dean at a major university, he comments on this odd film experience with mixed feelings: "At the time . . . I was on the production staff at WFAA-TV, Channel 8 in Dallas–Fort Worth, mostly directing [commercials]. I had graduated from SMU with a baccalaureate degree in Fine Arts as a theater major. I had been in many plays."

But he was a bit unprepared for the more extreme realities of this particular low-budget film production:

> Given [this] theater background, what surprised me about *Time Barrier* [was that] there was no rehearsal and very little run-through prior to shooting. I recall being shocked that they were going to take the mutant scene in the pit without much more than a brief, on-the-spot explanation of what the scene was going to look like. It was even harder because none of us ever saw a full script, just the pages we were working on.
>
> I do recall trying to quickly work up a character based on what they were telling us . . . [but] I [also] remember little about my makeup, except that I was working at the TV station at the time, trying to balance schedules, getting quickly into and out of mutant character. The makeup was a mess, a greenish-brown color, as I recall, something like axle grease. Jack Pierce was not involved in anything having to do with the mutants.

Says Clarke:

> The mutants were "little theater" actors and certainly were capable of being in these scenes, playing the mutants like half-crazed human beings. Yes, I was very

> concerned about the bad appearance of their makeup, but there was nothing we could do about it by that time . . . I just hoped that the lighting was subdued enough to cover the obvious. [Those bald heads] looked like bathing caps covered with makeup. Unfortunately, they showed. It was probably the poorest part of the movie.

It was fortunate that screenwriter Pierce had flown in to his native Dallas and dropped in to watch filming that day, as he volunteered to help fill in the nonexistent mutant "crowd." Covered in green-goo makeup, he added his body to the scene in progress, in what he called his "Hitchcock cameo." There was another plus: Pierce was bald and didn't need the help of a fake rubber cap. The man who had written the scene would become its only believable "mutant"!

For years he wondered what had happened to the other "Pierce" on the film, the makeup expert capable of making the mutants truly memorable, and *realistic*.

He never found out. Nor did anyone else.

That day was also the first day Arianné ("Arden") Ulmer worked, in the role of the femme fatale, Captain Markova. Her director father and script supervisor mother gave particular attention to the performance of their "Markova"—she tiptoes stealthily off after spying on the Captain; moves among the dark, triangular rows; stabs a guard; and, like some fanatic revolutionary, frees the mutants: "Hear me, fellow prisoners. You're free. The citadel is yours. Hear me, mutants. Come out of your pit of death. Our time of vengeance has come. Follow me, soldiers of revenge. I'll lead you to the Captain. To food. To freedom!" Says Ulmer Cipes:

> Part of the reason Dad wanted me to do this film was to help me out with some footage that would assist my agent with my screen career. I had been trained in ballet and had also been trained at the Royal Academy of Dramatic Arts in London, and with Stella Adler in New York. All of my movements were to be choreographed, mostly by me, with the approval of Dad and Meredith Nicholson, the cameraman. This was also true of the ending [the mutant riot], to maintain the same tone throughout the film.

This concern for tone was true, certainly, not only for her movements, but in her line delivery as well, carefully matched to a "plan." In calling out to the mutants, she explains that her speech "was meant to be rather an inspirational tone, which I tried to achieve using the rhythm of the St. Crispin's Day speech from *Henry V* . . . [from one] of our favorite personal recordings that were available after the release of [Laurence Olivier's] *Henry V* as a film."

This proactive stance toward specific line delivery was somewhat out of character for Ulmer, according to Clarke:

> Edgar was not the kind of director like, say, Ida Lupino, who I'd worked for a couple of times, who'd get into it as an actress or actor. Edgar was more concerned with the camera movement, or whether the scene sounded right, or if there was too much dialogue or whether this should be cut, etc. He was great on story, great on keeping the picture moving—the pace—on keeping the camera moving to create perspective, to give the impression of a much bigger picture than just doing little head and shoulder shots and staying in one camera position.

True, line delivery was less a concern than the physical travel of the camera to create space and shape within the frame, as well as the transitory dynamics of objects and people across and through the frame. A case in point was that cat-like, tiptoed prowl of Markova's, dagger in hand, en route to liberating the mutants. Ulmer Cipes notes,

> Dad mostly choreographed the rhythms of my movement . . . not that much with my lines, really. The movements, however, were very carefully choreographed. [Since] I had a background in ballet, Dad knew he could utilize me that way. He knew what foot I was going to land on and where the camera could be, where the light could be, in particular in the "knifing" routine.

She describes another key to Markova's character:

> My hairdress in the film is a ballet dancer's hairdress. At that time, ballet dancers didn't leave their hair loose. They always wore it in a chignon or braided and, of course, the braid [which I had] was very Russian-looking. This again was the anti-Russian feeling, which is a joke, because my parents, when I was a child, were very pro-Russian at the time that the Russians were partners with the U.S. during the war, before things turned around. We were always sending bundles to Russia to be helpful. So Dad had an affinity for Russia. He had been there and knew the Slavic world . . . so he was very much at home with Russian culture and music.
>
> But the bugaboo at that moment—the making of *Time Barrier*—was definitely anticommunist.

Both Ulmer's daughter and wife emphasize the preeminent place music and sound held in his work, the audial aspect dominating his visuals at times but, by and large, always subservient to the total "form." Markova's approach to the mutants' lair and their subsequent liberation derives much of its effectiveness from the barely repressed "bedlam" beyond the dungeon bars. The maniacal laughter and shrieks of his extras, thickened and layered through an "echo chamber" in post, not only explains the need for the pit, but dramatically foreshadows the mad vengeance to come. Says Shirley Ulmer:

> The laughter was Edgar's idea. It was put into the script. He needed that "bedlam" effect for when [Markova] was talking down the steps to the mutants. He

> made them talk hysterically. I remember him talking to Arianné [about this] at the time. He said, "Just a minute, darling. We're going to put a sound track in there. It'll be like the sound of *insects*." Edgar "heard" things like that as well as visualized them.

Which is why scenes like this in the film play larger than they are, tilting toward the representational through an accumulation of self-reinforcing visual and audio brushstrokes.

The five-and-a-half-page pit scene—Allison's interrogation, the fight, the stabbing of the guard, and the liberation—was, remarkably, set up and shot entirely within four hours! Next, the "dungeon hallway" became, with a quick re-dress, a tunnel leading off the decontamination chamber, for earlier scenes of Allison's arrival. Then into the chamber itself, as neat a re-creation of science-fiction pulp illustration as one could imagine. Ulmer moves through the action quickly, encapsulating in tableau Allison's sudden Kafkaesque role, centering him in a convergence of angles, and strapping him inside an oversize bell jar, the focal point of an unspeaking judgmental circle that is armed with a mystery ray. He is a radioactive pariah, a futuristic boy in a bubble. As with the pit, the combined efforts of art director Fegte and cinematographer Nicholson, under Ulmer's hand, have created a stage of shadows and shapes that, if cheap, establish the territory with visual shorthand. One gets, in an instant, that this is the future; that it is hard, oppressive, and technological; and that fate seems to orbit between the new captive and the young woman who intervenes to free him.

The intersecting lines defined by lit and unlit planes help place, group, or separate characters like chess pieces, the very superstructure that shapes their world focusing their importance as well as insignificance.

Achieving the lighting effects was a major challenge for *Time Barrier*'s cameraman, Nicholson. Before this, he'd worked with the second unit on the epic chariot race in *Ben Hur*, where he had his pick of crew, equipment, and monetary resources. Here, every one of those things was nearly nonexistent, and every penny was in question. Ingenuity, instead, was the call of the day. Nicholson comments on his interplay with Ulmer:

> We didn't have drawings. There wasn't time for that! What we did was, we stayed late and talked it over in the evening. We'd go over all the angles and carefully work it out with Ulmer the night before. I liked him because he always knew what he was going after.
>
> Those sets were simple, but you could move them around and make one set look like a lot of different places, with lighting too. And I really tried to re-light them in different ways to create greater changes yet. We'd use soft light [as in the woman's bedroom] and hard light for other scenes. For that [mutant] pit,

> Edgar wanted me to light that to create a "spooky" effect. For a lot of this, I had to take the fresnels off my lights to get those hard shadows, but then we'd need a lot more light.

This was to cast, for instance, the shadows of the mutants' clawing hands up onto the walls.

Shirley Ulmer notes that the film's stark "cubistic lighting" came from earlier days in her husband's career. "Edgar was executing Schüfftan's ideas on this picture. This expressionistic look could never have been done in color; *Time Barrier* could *never* have been shot in color, artistically."

The production went into extended hours on day 8 with nine pages of long-winded expository dialogue, falling mainly to Bekassy and Van Dreelen. Here, in the engineering lab, they lay out the complex back-history of the world since 1960, as well as the "how" of Allison's sixty-four-year time jump. It was a very stressful day, and the stress is visible in Clarke's uncomfortable performance, as in his earlier scenes with Morgan. The problem this day was as follows: Bekassy had difficulty remembering his dialogue, due in part to the lack of rehearsal time. "We did maybe ten or twelve takes," Clarke recalls. "That was a lot since we usually did no more than three! [Stephen] was worried sick he'd blow a line and delay the schedule," especially during one of Ulmer's extended dolly setups. Considering the film's budget, pushing the schedule was never an option. Falling behind would mean script pages would be torn out to make up for lost time, and Ulmer, by all counts, would never have stood for that.

Bekassy began to perspire heavily, so much so that he had to play parts of the scene with his arms folded across his chest!

On the second-to-last day, the insert walls were removed from the standing pyramid group to create the "major junction area in the citadel," as described in the script: "A huge chamber, a junction area of a complex tunnel network. It is built on several levels, connected by ramps. The walls and ceiling are angular, carved of natural stone combined with concrete reinforcements, creating a modern, abstract impression."

Much of this was greatly simplified. The notion of levels, ramps, and natural stone could not be practically realized. But it was possible to create a reasonable amount of scope by opening out all the pyramids for scenes of Allison's first views of the underworld; various establishing angles of the silent population moving about; and, ultimately and especially, the mutant riot at the end of the film. Lighting, dolly tracking, and composition would imply greater variety.

Flournoy, who, as one of the mutants, was to romp through this main junction in the riot scenes, observes:

> When I reported for work out at Fair Park, the sets were already built and shooting was underway. I had studied set design and helped build sets. The upside-down pyramids, the repeated pattern of triangles, the spare angular lines, were striking to see, very otherworldly, but quite dysfunctional. The cast and crew were always ducking to keep from hitting their heads and had to pick up their feet to move through the openings which served as doors. It was an economical approach, however, for [Ulmer] was able to use the same basic set over and over from different angles with minimal changes.
>
> This underground world which Ulmer created was a graphic representation of the extremes of order and chaos, at least as I read it. The rigid, mechanistic world of the Citadel power elite—citizens and guards in tailored outfits marching at 45-degree angles to each other, in contrast to the slimy dark forces kept locked away in the pit.

At the same time, he maintains that certain aspects didn't gel:

> As it turns out, the ordered world was managed much better than the world of chaos. The way the story was told offered little to help the viewer understand the smoldering underside of that society, or even fear it . . . Better to have left what was beyond the gate [in the pit] to viewer imagination, using sound effects, letting the horrors of the underworld register on the faces of the talent [rather than] using too few mutants and borrowed footage . . . Why the mutant sequences on the stairs were done with so few actors, I can only guess.

In theory, the *impression* of more was all that mattered within the kind of representational approach Ulmer took to the production. His daughter, privy to her father's overview, comments:

> Dad chose in *this* film—not in all of them, but in this film—a real *theatrical* quality, because it was a minimalistic study, almost a German Expression film, unlike a *Detour*, where he'd go for a very natural quality. This [*Time Barrier*] is much more stylistic, and it was looked at from that vantage point [by Dad].

In the big junction Ulmer stages his climactic revolt, not only with a widened frame but also—in order to allow better coverage—by taking advantage of this production's first use of a second camera. The interplay of humans on the run, fleeing and fighting, and the tumbles, flying fists, gunfire, and shrieking laughter is caught from both floor-mounted and dolly-track cameras, and it results in a kind of ballet-mania that makes something energetic and fluid out of the small number of extras (production paperwork indicates twenty-eight) and pitifully smaller number of mutants (five). Critic Myron Meisel long promoted *Time Barrier* as among Ulmer's best, singling out not only its geometric configurations but its deliberate rhythms, similar to *Kagemusha*. And here, in this riot, those rhythms come most to the fore. In fact they are staged with a degree of dark glee, as the militant mutants deliver on their earlier promises to "kill, kill, kill all of you!"

This was Red Morgan's chance to redeem, in part, his nonperformance, translating Ulmer's battle plan into a series of stunt gags and exchanges. According to Ulmer Cipes,

> None of this happened extemporaneously. Dad had designed this so that [groups of people] should be moving a certain way and other groups should come through [another way]. He wanted to have some interesting fights. Again, we had a really small cast, and it had to be choreographed to give you impact and action because you're dealing with so few people. It was all deliberate, especially all the scenes with extras running through the corridors and so on. It was all highly designed.

Allison, Trirene, Kruse, and Bourman slip through the battle scene, tracked by Ulmer's gliding camera. Vignettes play out: women, seized by hysterical mutants, spin to the ground and are ravaged; mutants and "mutes" tumble head over heels; guards mow down mutants; mutants spring into the air. Flournoy, a highly active participant in that action, observes,

> The mutant attack was well-orchestrated. Lots of flowing movement, plausible encounters with guards and citizens. I don't remember much of the specifics except that we were very physical, which led to an unfortunate incident: In overpowering a guard, I took away his gun and hit him in the mouth with the butt, knocking his front teeth out. I felt terrible about it, but in the melee it happened.

Clarke recalls another type of mishap:

> In this fight sequence, one of the extras would bump into the pyramids and the canvas material would "waver" like it was in the wind, and the shot would have to be redone . . . The falls these guys took in the action shots were tough, because the floors were concrete and falling on that was tough.
>
> Their action was directed by Red Morgan. He did a fine job of the stunts and of making us a good climactic fight sequence, with as much action as he possibly could . . . I don't think Edgar gave too much [stunt] direction other than want[ing] the mutants to be as crazy in their appearance, as demented in their actions as they could be. His direction was more involved in creating the shots, moving the camera, in his pacing of the scenes.
>
> He used the dolly quite a bit . . . which would sometimes include panning movements to give the picture a bigger feeling [because these were] techniques used on bigger pictures.

On Saturday, 18 April, day 10, the last scenes in the Centennial Building were captured. Bourman betrays Kruse, then threatens Allison. The two fight. Trirene is accidentally shot . . .

Clarke could barely move in his pressure-laced high-altitude suit, but "I had to do my own fight stuff since we didn't have enough money to hire a stunt double for me." Besides, no one else would fit in the suit!

Clarke and Van Dreelen took away painful memories of skinned knees, sore elbows, and tumbles on hard concrete. There was no other way to shoot the scene in the time available.

Clarke and Tompkins played her dying scene in a set with the look and feel of a '40s melodrama, noir shadows against deco geometrics, with Nicholson shooting through gauzy "romantic" diffusion. Tompkins, lying with chocolate "blood" running on her side, struggled to play at "dying," and she later recalled fighting to control her breathing and trying to keep her eyelids from fluttering. Again there was no time for multiple retakes.

The overall tone is a reflection of Ulmer's lifelong admitted schism, the wedding of the theatrical, the melodramatic, with the meaningful: the melding of real-life concerns with the artifice of Germanic romanticism.

Ulmer's days, early in his career, on four-day, Yiddish-language shoots, and with nonexistent crews on "black" locations and in faux Ukranian countrysides in New Jersey, represented true independent filmmaking: filmmaking by the skin of the teeth, budgetless but undaunted, armed solely with a camera and creative chutzpah. And so Ulmer found himself returning to—or reduced to—these roots at the very end of *Beyond the Time Barrier*: The production had wrapped out of Fair Park without having filmed the key scene, the justification of all that had come before, the shock reveal of the inexplicably aged test pilot and his fade-out warning, ostensibly about the "cosmic plague"—in reality the Bomb. "[My dad] was fascinated with fear of the bomb," his daughter emphasizes. "This is what this story was about."

With a skeleton crew and no set, Ulmer was forced to film the end scene in true "independent film channel" style—home-movie, handmade-movie style, using a single cameraman, a couple of lights, and a bed borrowed from a previous location. The scene was arranged to resemble a section of a hospital room, but it was shot in the cheap motel they were staying at.

Elevating this beyond a homemade movie were the talents of legendary makeup master Jack Pierce, tasked, on the last day, with "aging up" thirty-nine-year-old Clarke to an eighty-plus-year-old man. Says Clarke:

> My old-age makeup was applied like Pierce did with Karloff on *Frankenstein*, by beginning about four in the morning. He started with what he called 'rice paper,' to give me a crinkly look. He applied it in small pieces over my entire face to give it a real wrinkled look. The rice paper was applied with spirit gum to stick it to my skin. It made my skin contract. The paper was thinner than tissue paper. You could literally see through it. He put that all over my face and then did a makeup job of skin color over it and used a whitener on my hair.

The major's pitiful end condition is not entirely a cruel act of fate; it is also a credible key toward opening up an alternate course of history. Through no fault of his own, Major Allison has been robbed of his "best years." By depicting this with a degree of physical verisimilitude, and urging Clarke's performance, Ulmer's last images help step the film up from the intermittent serial shenanigans and quasi-villainous "melodrama of the future" episodes.

Ulmer needed the scene to work if his film was to have any real purpose. Clarke remembers the director prodding, almost taunting him, pushing for performance with a capital P:

> I'll say this about Edgar, insofar as his artistic appreciation of others. It was hard to get a compliment. [But] at the end of that scene, he got a little gooseflesh on his arms, and he kind of rubbed them with a shudder and said, "That's the first time you've made me feel this picture." He was trying to compliment me in his way, saying that I'd touched him in an emotional way with my acting. And I was flattered really, even if it was kind of a left-handed compliment, because I respected him very much.

Filming was finally completed. Remarkably, they'd worked the entire production on a certain amount of faith that the footage was acceptable, since all of the exposed negative had been shipped to Consolidated Film Labs in Los Angeles for development, sight unseen. There had been no dailies.

POST-DRAMATIC STRESS

Although *Time Barrier* and *Transparent Man* weren't filmed concurrently—contrary to oft-repeated rumor—they were most definitely cut that way. Editor Jack Ruggerio huddled with the director and the two films at General Service Studios for several weeks following the director's return to Los Angeles after completion of the second film.

There was a certain amount of urgency hanging over the editing rooms. Ulmer had made a deal with an Italian producer to take on the epic tale of *Hannibal*, to be photographed in Europe. Ruggerio had to work fast. Ulmer's input had to be grabbed quickly before the director disappeared into the Alps.

Ulmer brought his notions of conceptual and physical geometrics, which had informed the entire shoot, to the editorial process, striving to string the individual pieces together in a manner somehow consistent with the film's overall scheme. To accomplish this, he turned to a simple, old idea that had been more or less out of fashion since the 1940s: optical "wipes" in the shape of triangles, he felt, could be used to segue between various episodes in the future world sequence. It was a very "so-old-it's-new-again" gambit, though some critics were quick to jump on it as more "old" than "bold."

Ulmer worked with versatile composer Darrell Calker to produce the wide-ranging score, military to modern to melancholy. Ulmer's passion for music encouraged Calker and the sound-effects editor to experiment with electronic tones, alternating with classical cellos and violins. If a bit thin and creaky on occasion, the score underlines Ulmer's changing time frames and mood—at times salutatory, at others forlorn, warm, resigned, and, finally, sad—the emotion by which the director characterized the entire film.

With *Time Barrier* almost completed, Ulmer moved off to handle *Hannibal*'s march, likely confident that his cinematic "house" was in order.

But . . .

PLAN B: AIP

Shortly after Ulmer left the project, his film was to take an unplanned left turn down a path as unpredictable as that of his lead character: Seeking to promote his two features, executive producer John Miller, according to producer Clarke, "became enamored of an old time movie pitchman named Kroeger Babb, and bought into his scheme." Miller was persuaded to invest tens of thousands of dollars in a "sure-fire" promotional campaign involving giveaway prizes. Babb's plan required massive region-to-region saturation advertising, and an investment of over $100,000, and it was implemented with multiple bookings in Oregon.

In the dead of winter.

Nobody came.

Complete wash.

Within weeks, Miller's company, having bet the house against this "sure win," folded, deeply in debt. He was forced to turn over ownership of both of his films to Consolidated Film Labs, for nonpayment of bills.

The lab, in turn, immediately put the film on the auction block, hoping to offset their own losses with a quick sale. For the amount owed against the two films, $75,000 each, that ne plus ultra purveyor of exploitation movies, American International Pictures, quickly acquired distribution rights.

Ulmer was away and unaware that his film was now to undergo an AIP makeover. Retaining editor Ruggerio, AIP executives ordered immediate cuts. Establishing scenes with officials shot at Carswell were first to go. Noting several places to "open the film up," primarily to provide fodder for print ads, posters, and trailers, AIP approached Howard Anderson's effects studio to create several new establishing shots. Consequently, what had originally been a scripted shot of a giant, isolated solar-power dish became a vast complex resembling—though not intended to be—a city. Elsewhere, in place of a crudely made, live-action prop representing the elevator to the engineering lab, AIP commissioned a matte painting. To disguise the lack of "mutants," the AIP execs inserted stock shots of a dungeon full of shaggy "lepers" taken from another of the company's recent acquisitions, Fritz Lang's *Journey to the Lost City*—not *Island of Lost Souls*, as has been printed elsewhere. Remarkably, the eye-popping mismatch between Ulmer's clean geometrics and the decayed stone of Lang's film, between the hirsute "barbarians" of the latter and the sterile, clean-shorn mutant inmates of the former, wasn't seen as a problem by AIP.

The most significant alteration came, however, in AIP's extensive overhaul of the film's structure. Pierce's first draft had told the story in a straightforward, A-B-C fashion, which Ulmer had made Pierce alter into a flashback structure during preproduction, presumably with the idea that a mystery at the top of the story would add tension. That was how he shot the film. But now AIP saw fit to restructure it back to Pierce's first-draft, linear telling—shearing it, in the process, from nearly 80 minutes to its current 75-minute running time.

BELIEVE IN ME

Only a handful of people in the world—those few who happened to live in Oregon in 1959 and attended a screening—chanced to see Ulmer's intended version of *Beyond the Time Barrier*. What has circulated since is AIP's "retake." If somewhat off-visioned, no one doubts it still remains an Edgar Ulmer film—all things, and contributors, considered.

Despite the warmth of some of its on-screen participants, namely, Clarke, Tompkins, and Sokoloff, a coldness hangs like morgue air throughout. Critics—those who bothered or noticed at all, and, at that, only in later years—tended to focus on its despairing zeitgeist, earning it few supporters. Yet another nightmarish Ulmerian world, constructed from his presumed dark impulse to trap his zombied characters in one more blind alley of fate, in one more pointless maze, where they can be drained of volition and left in some state of ignominy. Indeed, there is some reasonable support to that intent contained in the last slowed frames of *Time Barrier*, which hold poor Allison as if in helpless seizure, staring into the viewer's eyes with black terror, a possible director's vision of "how things are."

Then there are the major's parting words to the grieving Supreme: "No, it is not the end. If we believe, there is always hope . . . You will not live in a world of darkness." These are Ulmer's words in Pierce's script, the transcendence of his dark German romanticism, the assertion of will amidst accidents in time, perplexing manipulations, and other victimizations.

FINAL TALLY

For producer Robert Clarke, *Time Barrier* left mixed emotions. There were the moments of inspiration working with Edgar Ulmer, the cast, and the crew. There was the satisfaction of having *created*. And yet there was not insignificant pain and regret:

> We were constantly concerned about money. I can't overemphasize the budget problems that were rampant throughout the [making of the film] . . . For instance, the machinery in the background of the Engineering Lab was just a huge photograph! We couldn't afford the set! If we'd had another $50,000, it would have made a tremendous difference in the scope of the coverage and allowed us to get some exteriors so obviously needed to give the feeling that we were actually underground. We could've set up something outside to shoot my approach to the city, but we didn't have the money for that type of construction.

And worse were the financial and career losses that followed, for which there was never to be any compensation: "It was a terrible disappointment. I broke my neck to make the picture and then was cheated completely. It was a terrible lesson." And it was one from which he was never to fully recover, but one he never regretted.

Arthur Pierce continued to write scripts in a similar vein in the decades that followed, struggling often to survive in his favored genre, until his death in 1987. But *Time Barrier* always held a special place for him. His most gratifying recollection? Seeing gigantic displays promoting the film years later in Hong Kong, and crowds lined up around the block to see it. Regarding Ulmer, he says: "[In spite of our battles,] he did everything I would've done. He followed the script to the letter . . . We had some good elements in it. With a little more money and color, we could've made a real classic."

Shirley Ulmer couldn't have disagreed more regarding the notion of color. In her opinion, the film required black and white, not only for its graphic qualities to work, but to enhance the serious tone which, she stresses, her husband had sought—had sought in the service of a strong message:

> Edgar was very concerned about [the effects of] radiation at the time because of all the [atomic] testing that was going on . . . That was fearful to him. . . . He *was* concerned about this, and that is part of what interested him about this film. It was his *theme*. He was always so unhappy when audiences didn't get

> his message. He was trying to say something here and was grateful that some people got it.
>
> Edgar went to sleep with these pictures. That's why they still live after all these years. After all, these were all cheap little nothing deals. There was no real money in them.
>
> His pictures were his children.

Through actor Vladimir Sokoloff, whom her dad loved, according to Ulmer Cipes, Ulmer was able to convey much of the feeling of descending darkness. Through Sokoloff, he shifted the tone from melodrama to something resembling real drama, equating personal loss with world loss. Ultimately, his daughter notes, "Dad felt that sadness was important in telling the story."

From his few comments on record, it is clear that Ulmer was attracted to both theme and image in the story, and to the potential for the ineffable interplay between the physical and the emotional—an indulgence extended well beyond the limits of most of its B-movie kin. The film attempts to triangulate a relationship, if tenuous, between shape, theme, and emotion, to make that which is otherwise composed of "pieces" speak as one.

Significantly, he spoke of it specifically as a "terror" film, referring notably to the terror springing from mutation, depicted by the loss of hearing, speech, and the ability to reproduce, and, in the case of the mutants, the descent into madness. It is the terror of humankind forced to live in a virtual tomb: "We have returned to the cave," the Supreme asserts with profound sadness, "where Man first lived on Earth. We have returned to our birthplace to die."

But through Allison's pledge to "belief," underlined by Ulmer through the Supreme's reborn faith, amplified by the sincere melancholy of Sokoloff's persona, the director yields his fatalism to the deeper sentiment of survival. The pilot flies off to engage history. Reintegrating with the ghost of his former self—shown as the merging of the dual X-80s in space, the future and the past, the twin avatars of "the Possible and the Impossible"—Allison overtakes Fate. Having fulfilled his duty, he leaves the rest up to us.

"I believe" are the last words from the future.

BIBLIOGRAPHY

Eisenschitz, Bernard, and Jean-Claude Romer. "Entretien avec Edgar G. Ulmer," *Midi-Minuit Fantastique* 13 (November 1965): 1–14.

This chapter also draws excerpts from interviews I conducted between 1976 and 2008 with Edgar Ulmer's collaborators, as listed below, on the film *Beyond the*

Time Barrier: Robert Clarke, producer/actor; Arthur Pierce, screenwriter/assistant editor/extra; Shirley Ulmer, script supervisor; Ariannè Ulmer Cipes, actor; Ernst Fegte, art director; Meredith Nicholson, cinematographer; Darlene Tompkins, actor; Don Flournoy, actor; Russell Marker, actor; Malcolm Thomson, extra; Roger George, special effects; Robert Maden Jr., son of executive producer.

15

Invisibility and Insight

The Unerasable Trace of *The Amazing Transparent Man*

Alec Charles

The year is 1960 and the setting is a remote and threatening homestead—haunted house meets American Gothic. The narrative's crucial backstory involves the murder of a mother. The film is shot in black and white, and centers around acts of theft, absurd disguise, and extraordinary murder. The story starts with a thief on the run: a thief who ends up dying in the isolated house. During the course of the narrative, the forces of law and order lurk in the background, at once threatening and obtuse. One might, of course, be forgiven for mistaking this film for Alfred Hitchcock's *Psycho*—rather than Edgar G. Ulmer's *The Amazing Transparent Man*. Ulmer's film charts the unlikely adventures of one Joey Faust (Douglas Kennedy—an actor who had, incidentally, appeared in three episodes of *Alfred Hitchcock Presents* between 1956 and 1959), a professional safecracker who is sprung from jail by prospective master criminal Major Paul Krenner (James Griffith), his moll Laura Matson (Marguerite Chapman), and his sidekick Julian (Red Morgan). Krenner has kidnapped the daughter of physicist Peter Ulof (Ivan Triesault), in order to force Dr. Ulof to conduct experiments in invisibility. Ulof and Krenner turn Faust invisible, and, on their behalf, Faust conducts a number of audacious robberies. Krenner's ambition is to create an invincible army of invisible men, but his plans are thwarted when Faust—urged by Ulof—eventually turns against his paymaster in order to save the world from his transparent tyranny. Faust and Krenner die together in the ensuing conflagration; Ulof and his daughter Maria escape.

The Amazing Transparent Man opens with a shot of a wailing siren, a shot reminiscent not of *Psycho* but of Hitchcock's very first talking picture, *Blackmail* (1929). This is not the only influence of Hitchcock's oeuvre apparent in Ulmer's picture. Echoing a technique exploited by many of Hitchcock's films—and most obviously by *Psycho*—*The Amazing Transparent Man* repeatedly explores and subverts uses of subjective camera work in order to challenge the moral and psychical stance of the audience. It is a film of unusual ambiguity: although it may be viewed as an ostensibly proselytizing tale of the eventual redemption of a man called Faust, it is at the same time a film in which the most morally acceptable character, indeed the drama's moral heart—Dr. Peter Ulof—to some extent represents a reincarnation of Dr. Josef Mengele.

Ulof is a former Nazi scientist, a character responsible for the death of his own wife, a man who seeks atonement in the salvation first of his daughter and then of the entire human race: "My wife had died of experiments I was forced to perform on her in a concentration camp . . . all my patients wore hoods. I couldn't see their faces. I didn't know my wife was one of them." Ulof's wife became his victim because her identity was hidden from him—because she became invisible to him; and his punishment is to reenact this cycle of invisibility and moral blindness. Ulof has lost his own soul in what Holocaust survivor Primo Levi (42) calls the "indecipherable inferno" of the Final Solution—a process which sought to destroy the souls of its perpetrators and its victims alike: "their souls are dead" (57). It is only through the course of Ulmer's narrative, and specifically through Ulof's relationship with Ulmer's protagonist—not Josef but Joey Faust—that the scientist may regain his own humanity, his own soul.

If high modernity took place in, as T. S. Eliot put it in his *Four Quartets*, "the years *l'entre deux guerres*" (26), then the postmodern period may be seen as falling between two holocausts: the holocausts of the Second World War (Auschwitz, Belsen, Hiroshima, Nagasaki, Dresden) and the apocalyptic nuclear (or, in today's terms, terroristic) holocaust to come. This much is evidenced in the preoccupations of some of the most significant American and British authors and filmmakers of the period: Kurt Vonnegut and Martin Amis, for example, have written of both past and future holocausts; indeed one might suggest that postmodernity seems to lie somewhere in between *Schindler's List* and *Dr. Strangelove*.

It should come as no surprise therefore that Edgar G. Ulmer—an Eastern European Jewish American filmmaker—might be alerted by his heritage to posit these themes within his work; and *The Amazing Transparent Man* in fact quite overtly presents a discussion as to whether the proliferation of weapons of mass destruction is worth the risk of that final holocaust. The film takes place in an atmosphere of heightened cold war nuclear tensions: it was released three years after the death of Joseph McCarthy and the launch of Sputnik, two years after the United States accidentally lost a hydrogen bomb off the coast of Georgia, the year after Fidel Castro came to power, and two years before the Cuban Missile Crisis.

Perhaps most significantly, however, it was released just three years after Jack Arnold's similarly titled *The Incredible Shrinking Man* (1957), another tale of nuclear angst—a fable of a man who is mutated, alienated, and made "tyrannical" and "monstrous," and who is eventually destroyed by radiation. Specifically, that film's protagonist is destroyed by a radioactive cloud that mushrooms toward him across the ocean—a cloud, perhaps, from one of the United States' atmospheric nuclear tests (such as 1954's notorious detonation on Bikini Atoll), tests that were to be outlawed by the Partial Test Ban Treaty of 1963. *The Incredible Shrinking Man*'s Scott Carey (Grant Williams) imagines a world in which humanity is to be reduced (as he has been) to virtual nothingness by "other bursts of radiation, other clouds drifting across seas and continents"—and yet this bleak vision of atomic atomization finally holds for Carey some possibility of redemption: "Smaller than the smallest, I meant something too. To God there is no zero. I still exist." The apocalyptic tenor of *The Incredible Shrinking Man*—as of *The Amazing Transparent Man*—is met and countered by an almost Messianic fervor. America's nuclear paranoia is balanced (and perhaps at the same time enhanced) by its sense that it is a nation blessed—and therefore due to be redeemed—by God.

Although the title of Ulmer's film perhaps reflects the success of *The Incredible Shrinking Man*, it may actually have been forced upon Ulmer by Universal's ownership of *The Invisible Man* (1933). Yet just as F. W. Murnau's *Nosferatu* seems to benefit from the fact that, for copyright reasons, it could not call itself *Dracula*, so this film's recourse to *transparency* rather than *invisibility* (even though the character is patently—transparently—invisible rather than transparent) opens a set of oppositions and ambivalences (between transparency and opacity), which the film repeatedly embraces in its quest for individual and societal self-knowledge. Its protagonist is, in the words of Ulof, "a man who has unlocked every door except the one to his own soul. Now he has the key."

The Amazing Transparent Man may be considered by many to be flawed to the point of absurdity—and yet that very absurdity, as a defining characteristic of the postmodern alienation in which the film is grounded, may not be artistically inappropriate. Christopher Marlowe, Johann Wolfgang von Goethe, and H. G. Wells meet Luis Buñuel, James Whale, and Hitchcock: the result is as disturbing and as interesting as one might expect it to be.

PERSPECTIVE AND PERSPICACITY

The film's subversion of subjective camera work and editing techniques (sometimes intentional, sometimes apparently inadvertent) adds to these disturbing ambiguities in ways that contradict the classical structures of cinema

Figure 15.1. Melodramatic irony: Ulmer's film encompasses classical tragedy and postmodern absurdity. Courtesy of Arianné Ulmer Cipes (private collection).

narrative (as depicted by Christian Metz, 63), and, more specifically, recall Slavoj Žižek's readings of Hitchcock's use of his camera to disrupt conventions and expectations and to posit his audience within sites of alienation and monstrosity (249).

Ulmer's protagonist's invisibility is inconstant, even capricious. Faust becomes partially—then fully—visible in the middle of robbing a bank (an act by which he follows in the footsteps of Claude Rains's original invisible man) and flees to his getaway car, in which Laura—Ulmer's film-noir femme fatale—is waiting for him. "What's the matter?" she asks—as if she has not noticed he is no longer invisible—as if his invisibility itself is somehow invisible.

Shortly thereafter, Faust announces that he has had enough of the situation. "You just can't go off and leave me," Laura says—at which point he again turns invisible. It is almost as if his invisibility were psychosomatic, or at least triggered by his psychological state and by the exigencies of the plot. "Why do I keep appearing and disappearing?" Faust asks. The cause of his visual inconstancy is surely his moral and emotional ambiguity.

The film's visual ambivalence is embraced by its subjective camera work. Ulmer draws attention to the ambiguity of the camera's subjectivity when, near the start of the film, Faust throws a sheet over the camera. (Ulmer performs a similar effect in *The Black Cat*, when the hero—David Manners—throws his jacket over the camera, and then pulls a blanket from the lens as he tucks himself up in bed.) The blatant subjectivity—indeed the self-conscious fallibility—of Ulmer's camera work is at its most obvious and incongruous when, toward the end of the tale, security agent Drake (Edward Erwin) points his binoculars at the scene of the film's climactic explosion. We can tell we are seeing through Drake's binoculars because of the binocular-shaped aperture through which we are shown the scene; yet, unlike most binoculars (at least, unlike most binoculars in the early 1960s), Drake's pair have a marvelous capacity to cut from angle to angle and from shot to shot—even from long shot to close-up—as if they were showing a preedited piece of film.

The apparent clumsiness of this piece of direction is not necessarily as accidental as it may at first seem. On a number of occasions throughout the film, Ulmer is repeatedly playful—even deceptive—with his camera work, as if to emphasize the visual ambiguities of the scenario. It is notable that Ulmer's emphasis on subjective camera work begins immediately before Faust becomes invisible: as the invisibility machine prepares to do its work, we see the world for the first time through Faust's eyes. It is as if Ulmer is stressing the relationship between vision and visibility, and therefore between invisibility and an uncertainty of actual and moral vision.

Indeed, on several occasions, Ulmer stresses that Faust's invisibility is not even visible to the camera itself. Shortly after Faust has first been turned invisible, he speaks to Major Krenner; we see Krenner from the invisible man's point of view. The camera—which, we assume, still represents Faust's perspective—pans to a door some distance away. The door opens; and Faust (apparently—that is, nonapparently) goes through. The film's self-consciously subjective camera has been shown to be fallible: it no longer shows the invisible man's point of view (as both the camera and the audience had assumed it still did); Faust has moved invisibly away, and this is something which the camera has failed to see.

Shortly afterward, Ulmer repeats this trick: he presents a shot of Krenner, as Faust speaks to him, from Faust's point of view—except that this time it's a window (rather than a door) behind Krenner which then opens in the middle of this pseudosubjective shot. It is not just that Faust is invisible: Ulmer seems to be telling us that even his perspective is invisible.

Of course, one reason for this piece of camera work might simply be that the camera itself was static: it was able to pan around, but not to track forward. There is a similar sequence, however, when Faust enters the vault of a bank, in which the camera appears to show the scene from the protagonist's point of view—panning around and also tracking forward until it reaches a doorway, where it stops. Again (perhaps because the camera was unable to fit through the doorway—it was only twelve years earlier that Hitchcock had been obliged to lift the walls of his studio set for the camera to glide through, in order to maintain the single-shot flow of *Rope*), it seems that the protagonist has moved on ahead of the camera, as we see through the doorway a bag of cash rising from the table in the next room.

Tracking shots are remarkably scarce in *The Amazing Transparent Man*—and when they do happen (as when the camera follows the invisible Faust away from the nuclear vault), they only last a second or two. Shot/reverse-shot sequences are similarly rare: most dialogue scenes are shot in long tableaux. The film's limited budget and fortnight filming schedule no doubt prompted this technique; and yet it works surprisingly well, complementing the narrative's atmosphere of alienation.

One notable use of the shot/reverse-shot formula comes during the emotionally defining dialogue between Faust and Laura right at the heart of the film. Yet the camera does not—as is usually the case—assume each character's approximate position. Here, the "reverse" shot is not in fact the precise reverse of the first shot—it appears to come at 60 (rather than 180) degrees from the original shot. It appears that the camera has been positioned at a single point—the third point of an equilateral triangle which it forms with Faust and Laura, as it cuts and turns from the one to the other—and, rather than meeting *each other's eyes*, it is at *this* point that the two characters' sight lines approximately converge. Of course, this would have helped to reduce filming time; yet again it provokes a somewhat disquieting effect, as if the two characters are not quite looking at each other. This failure of their gazes to meet suggests a deeper disconnection; it also continues to bare the film's devices—in a quasi-Brechtian effort of alienation—by indicating the presence of the camera itself.

Cinema constantly emphasizes, and at the same time erases, the subjectivity of the filmmaking process. By installing the camera in the place of a character, the spectator comes to assume that the camera is underpinning that character's subjectivity, rather than usurping it. The shot/reverse-shot technique is central to this process. As Kaja Silverman writes,

> the viewing subject, unable to sustain for long its belief in the autonomy of the cinematic image, demands to know whose gaze controls what it sees. The shot/reverse shot formation is calculated to answer that question in such a manner that the cinematic illusion remains intact . . . The gaze which directs our look seems to belong to a fictional character rather than to the camera. (202)

Yet here, the exact opposite process takes place: the cinematic convention is laid bare, and the effect is both disruptive and disturbing. François Truffaut once praised Alfred Hitchcock's camera work for being "almost invisible" (47)—here, conversely, we discover that the invisibility of the subject has rendered the camera visible. The invisibility of Hitchcock's camera work renders his subjects directly visible and apparently real—while the great director remains at once aesthetically invisible and morally opaque—but it is the very visibility of Ulmer's direction that makes his technique so extraordinarily transparent and his subjects so unnatural and unfathomable.

ALLUSIONS AND ARCHETYPES

Ulmer's film is swathed in a convoluted web of cultural allusions. Could Joseph Faust, for example, be named after the Austrian Canadian actor Joseph Furst—a performer who went on to epitomize the eccentric scientist in a series of television and film roles during the sixties and seventies? Probably not. More convincing, however, are the film's references to its director's own oeuvre, and to the classic narratives of fictive and filmic horror.

The Amazing Transparent Man echoes elements from some of Ulmer's better-known earlier works. Like *The Black Cat* (1934), the film features a central European scientist scarred by his experiences of war; and, also like *The Black Cat*, its narrative climaxes with its two rivals battling to the death in a desolate house which then explodes. Like *Detour* (1945), it tells the tale of a man on the run from the law and from his own conscience, a man whose flight from justice only exacerbates his criminality. But perhaps most significantly, like *Bluebeard* (1944), *The Amazing Transparent Man* offers a self-conscious tribute to the myth of Faust.

We may witness in Ulmer's film a series—an interrelated sequence—of literary and cinematic archetypes, or indeed a set of allusions to various manifestations of a single archetype: that of the diabolically insane scientist, Faustus or Faust (in Marlowe's, Goethe's and F. W. Murnau's versions); Frankenstein (in Mary Shelley's and Whale's versions); Dr. Jekyll (in Robert Louis Stevenson's and Rouben Mamoulian's versions); and the invisible man (in Wells's and—again—Whale's versions). These figures are encapsulated at first within Ulmer's Dr. Ulof and then within Joey Faust: indeed, insofar as their possibilities of redemption are irrevocably intertwined, the relationship between Ulof and Faust represents an amalgam of these different incarnations of that one archetype. In naming his own invisible man Faust, Ulmer seems directly to be pointing out the parallels between these related figures. "I'm in hell . . . I have no soul," laments Fredric March in Mamoulian's film of *Dr. Jekyll and Mr. Hyde* (1931); and Ulmer's Faust and Ulof share this immanently Faustian condition.

Margareta, the heroine of Murnau's *Faust* (1926), gives birth to Faust's son in the snows of winter—at which point Murnau stresses his Christian allegory by showing carol singers in front of a nativity scene, singing of the baby Jesus born "in the depth of winter." In comparing the birth of Faust's son with the birth of Jesus, Murnau posits Faust somewhere in between Joseph and God. (Is not this, after all, Faust's transgression: is not he, like Frankenstein, the ordinary mortal, the Joseph, who would be God?) Ulmer's Joey Faust is both a Joseph and a Faust, an ordinary Joe who (in Ulof's words) "may some day be declared a martyr . . . a man who sacrificed himself"—a man who surrenders his God-like powers in an act of Christ-like self-sacrifice.

In making these Faustian allusions explicit in his own tale of invisibility, Ulmer also specifically exposes the Faust myth's influence upon Whale's adaptation of Wells's *The Invisible Man* (1933). Whale's protagonist Griffin (Claude Rains) speaks of having the "power to walk into the gold vaults of the nations, into the secrets of kings, into the holy of holies"—and, while Ulmer's Faust strolls into bank vaults, Goethe's Faust and Marlowe's Faustus fraternize with monarchy. In fact, Marlowe's Faustus actually penetrates the "holy of holies"—the inner circle of the Pope. Moreover, Faustus enters the papal chambers while remaining "invisible to all" (49)—beneath Mephistophilis' magic girdle of invisibility.

Whale's Griffin is a scientist who "meddled in things that man must leave alone." In that respect, he resembles Faustus or Faust—or, for that matter, Shelley's (or in fact Whale's) Frankenstein. Like Faustus and Faust, Griffin is restless and capricious in the employment and enjoyment of his powers: he doesn't choose to rule the world, but for no apparent reason he causes a train crash that kills a hundred people; and, when he robs a bank, he scatters his loot in the street. These superhuman figures remain tormented by the "helpless absurdity" (Wells 121) of their existence: they embody not only the angst but also the ennui of modern being. Wells's Griffin speaks of "the things a man reckons desirable . . . no doubt invisibility made it possible to get them, but it made it impossible to enjoy them when they are got" (121). Or, as Mephisto tells Faust in Murnau's film: "Nothing satisfies you."

These invisible men assume the very status of gods, insofar as God's power is to see all while remaining invisible—insofar as God is that which, in Derrida's words, "holds me in his gaze . . . while remaining inaccessible to me" (33); yet the impossibility of their desire necessitates that it must remain eternally unsatisfied. The extraordinary mutations—the virtual apotheoses—which these characters undergo foster a sense of alienation, which provokes a defensive megalomania. Even the overwhelmingly sympathetic protagonist of Arnold's *Incredible Shrinking Man* aspires to mastery over his microcosm: "I resolved that . . . I would dominate my world." While Wells's Griffin rants insanely of establishing a "Reign of Terror" (125)—perhaps echoing Frankenstein's monster's threatened "reign" (Shelley 204)—Claude Rains's incarnation goes further: "I shall offer my secret to the world, with all its terrible power! The nations of the world will bid for it—thousands, millions. The nation that wins my secret can sweep the world with invisible armies!" The villainous Krenner in Ulmer's *The Amazing Transparent Man* appears directly inspired by Rains's vision: "My aim is to make an entire invisible army." Yet Krenner not only echoes Griffin; he also recalls his Faustian original. In the second part of Goethe's tragedy, Faust offers the Emperor his service in battle: he calls forth an army of spirits who have assumed "transparent shapes of crystal purity" (324).

Ulmer's earlier films also, of course, display an interest in the story of Faust. *The Black Cat*—the tale of a Satanist who refuses to surrender his dead wife to death—perhaps owes more to Faustian obsessions with Helen of Troy than to the Edgar Allan Poe tale (288–300) from which it takes its name (but nothing of its plot: its credits announce that it was merely "suggested" by Poe's story). But it is, as suggested above, Ulmer's *Bluebeard* which most obviously draws upon this archetype. The film's protagonist, Gaston Morrell (John Carradine), is an artist and puppeteer who—at the opening of the film—performs a puppet version of Goethe's *Faust* (a scenario perhaps reminiscent of the shadow theater near the start of Murnau's *Faust*). Morrell is influenced by a Mephistopholean agent; and—just as Faust kills his betrothed's brother—he ends up murdering his beloved's sister. Morrell has previously murdered Jeanette, his favorite model, because he has discovered that she is a "low, coarse . . . creature" rather than the epitome of moral and aesthetic beauty that his paintings of her had tried to synthesize. This first murder traps him within a cycle of killing: "Every girl I painted turned out to be Jeanette . . . Every time I painted her I had to kill her again." His insanity results from the impossibility of the satisfaction of his remorseless desire; his psychosis reflects the madness of Norman Bates as of all these insatiable Faustian figures and invisible men.

During Margareta's brother's funeral—in both Goethe's and Murnau's versions of *Faust*—the medieval hymn *Dies Irae* is sung: "quidquid latet adparebit" (Goethe 124), "all hidden things must plain appear." These tales of invisibility announce that the concealed must eventually become visible again, and this revelation of the hidden produces that effect which Freud called "uncanny." That which is revealed is that which must be concealed, by invisibility, as by Norman Bates's disguise: the unsatisfiability of impossible desire.

Hitchcock's Bates murders his mother's lover and his mother; Wells's Griffin is indirectly responsible for the death of his father—as Frankenstein is for the deaths of his brother, of his adopted sister and wife, and of his father; Faust murders his fiancée's brother, and is responsible for his fiancée's death and the death of his own soul; Morrell kills his ideal woman and his lover's sister; Vitus Werdegast (Bela Lugosi) in *The Black Cat* has lost his wife but tries (and fails) to save his daughter; Hjalmar Poelzig (Boris Karloff) in the same film has lost his wife (Werdegast's wife) but preserves her body and marries his own stepdaughter (Werdegast's daughter); and Ulof has killed his own wife—but eventually redeems his lost daughter—just as Joey Faust has become alienated from his wife but eventually redeems himself for the sake of his absent daughter.

These transgressions of the familial imperatives of civilization (the superego) and of nature alike foster binds that are humanly impossible to break or to escape. It is only through recourse to divine manifestations of self-sacrificing love (*agape*) that some of these characters—including Ulof and both Fausts—are able to redeem themselves. These narratives—like acts of psychoanalysis—unveil for their protagonists the horror of the impossibility of their situations and, by implication, the nature of their ultimate moral choice. It is specifically this act of uncanny revelation that cinema so often appropriates from literature and myth, and, in doing so, finds so appropriate to its own modes of storytelling.

In the original folktale of Bluebeard, Bluebeard's wife discovers a secret room in her husband's castle, a room which, like Poelzig's cellar, contains the bodies of his dead wives—just as the cellar in Poe's "The Black Cat" conceals the walled-up corpse of the narrator's wife (288–300). This unveiling of hidden monstrosity represents a function for which film finds itself extraordinarily apt.

The myth of *Duke Bluebeard's Castle* was adapted into opera by Béla Bartók. Its libretto was written by another Hungarian "Béla"—not Lugosi, but Balázs, a writer better known for his work as a theorist of cinema. In his study of the *Theory of the Film*, Balázs describes cinema as "the flickering of . . . bloodless shadows" (280); yet he understands that these spectral and translucent forms have "revealed new worlds . . . concealed from us . . . the souls of objects" (47). Cinema's own soullessness reveals the secret soul or innate soullessness of its subjects; it makes opacity and even invisibility transparent; it manifests the impossible within a realm of possibility.

In Ulmer's *The Black Cat,* Poelzig remarks to Werdegast: "You say your soul was killed and that you have been dead all these years . . . Did we both not die here . . . ? Are we any less victims of the war than those whose bodies were torn asunder? Are we not both the living dead?" Karloff and Lugosi—better known as Frankenstein's monster and Count Dracula—may both represent the living dead; yet, during the course of the film, Lugosi's character experiences a moral and spiritual resurrection. Like Ulof, Werdegast is traumatized by the horrors of world war; like Joey Faust, he is a former prisoner; but, like both men, he is not incapable of redemption. Unlike Griffin, Morrell, and Poelzig, but like Goethe's Faust—though unlike Marlowe's Faustus—his soul can be whole again. Faust, Joey Faust, and Werdegast discover redemption—but only in death.

A latter-day version of Alexandre Dumas' Edmond Dantès, Werdegast returns home after years languishing in prison in search of vengeance—but eventually finds redemption rather than revenge. In *The Amazing Transparent Man*, both Joey Faust and Ulof have escaped from physical prisons—Ulof from the concentration camp in which he had once experimented upon his own wife, Faust from a more ordinary jail cell—but both remain trapped within their own psychical, spiritual, and moral incarcerations. In saving his own daughter, Ulof also saves himself; but Joey Faust can only redeem his soul by sacrificing his own life. He refers to his prison as a "concrete tomb"—yet it is a tomb from which, like Christ (but unlike the death-obsessed Poelzig), and like Lugosi's Werdegast (but unlike Lugosi's Dracula), he returns to save all humanity, and therefore to redeem his own humanity.

Werdegast's redemption is made evident from his first appearance: Ulmer shows his reflection in the window of a railway carriage, a moment that signifies that for once Lugosi's character is not without a soul. Joey Faust's redemption is also related to his appearance (or lack of it): if simulacra or superficial appearances mask a profound absence, then his invisibility disguises and therefore marks an innate presence; this transparency not only cannot erase, but in fact emphasizes by its attempts to erase, the traces of his psychical, moral, and spiritual being—his physical translucence fosters a mode of lucidity. Wells's Griffin comments that a man is "more transparent" than glass (91); and external invisibility can therefore eventually make the soul itself appear.

As Al Roberts (Tom Neal) comments in Ulmer's *Detour*: "Did you ever want to cut away a piece of your memory and blot it out? You can't, you know—no matter how hard you try." Roberts, on the run from the law, has assumed the identity of the man he fears he might be suspected of killing; however, in that guise, he (inadvertently) kills a woman. At the end of the film, he casts off his false identity (as under that identity he is suspected of murder), but he cannot reassume his own identity. (He has been listed as dead: the dead man whose identity he assumed has, in fact, assumed Roberts's identity.) Like Morrell, Poelzig, Bates, and the original invisible man himself, he is caught in an inescapable double bind; these characters are imprisoned in paradoxes of their own making. Joey Faust and his literary namesake (like Werdegast) only manage to escape—and to reassert their identities, their selves, and their souls—through acts of self-immolating love. Both Fausts willingly exchange their godlike physical invisibility for human spiritual transparency—which is the ultimate manifestation of visibility.

Wells's invisible man in death returns to visibility, as he becomes "faint and transparent as though . . . made of glass" (148). Claude Rains's incarnation becomes similarly visible; yet he is redeemed (as he dies) by the presence of his beloved Flora Cranley (Gloria Stuart). Whale's inclusion of this love interest turns Griffin from Marlowe's irredeemable Faustus into Goethe's redeemed Faust: rather than merely pursuing his impossible desire (embodied for Faustus and Faust in the figure of Helen of Troy), he may be redeemed by human love (embodied for Faust, but not for Faustus, in the figure of Margareta). Morrell, by contrast, pursues *Bluebeard*'s heroine not because of who she is, but because, like Faust's Helen, she represents an impossible ideal—in that she replaces Jeanette (whom he murdered because her reality did not live up to his ideal). She also represents Faustus's own Margareta (the figure who might have redeemed him, but who cannot, because—unlike Faust—he does not love her as herself, but only as his route to an impossibly narcissistic form of redemption). Morrell has that much in common with Hitchcock's Bates—who murders Marion Crane because she cannot replace the mother he has murdered, and cannot therefore absolve him of his original sin.

At the end of Whale's *The Invisible Man*, Griffin's face is gradually superimposed over its absence: nothingness becomes skull and sinew and finally facial features, the opposite of the original invisibility process that Ulmer presents in *The Amazing Transparent Man*. *Psycho* concludes with a somewhat similar shot: the skull of Mrs Bates is superimposed over Norman Bates's own face. Bates, of course, cannot be redeemed: he is a Faust who has murdered his Margareta and vanquished his Helen of Troy, an Oedipus who has destroyed the very object of his Oedipal desire. As Griffin is responsible for the death of his father (and from that point on in Wells's novel—well before his assumption of invisibility—finds himself alienated, an outcast), so Bates has killed his mother's lover (the father figure); and he has also killed his mother. The impossible desire (the desire for the perfect redeeming Other)—in Bates's case his desire for his mother—is at once negated and exacerbated by the fact of her murder; and Bates therefore continues to seek—and to annihilate—these figures of redemption in the vicious cycle of this paradox. *Bluebeard*'s Morrell and *The Black Cat*'s Poelzig languish in remarkably similar situations; and, just as Faust and Faustus damn themselves through their faith in their false idol, Helen of Troy, Morrell and Poelzig destroy themselves by trying to recapture their own lost figures of false salvation.

In *The Amazing Transparent Man*, however, redemption takes place through acts not of impossible desire but of impossible love, love which takes place both on an individual and a historical scale: Ulof's love for his daughter, and Joey Faust's (eventual) love for the world—and for his own unseen daughter. Faust is not redeemed by his attraction to Laura, an attraction which is superficial, ephemeral, and inconstant: unlike her Petrarchan namesake, she fails to inspire him to spiritual immortality, nor—despite the name of the actor who played her (Marguerite Chapman)—does she prove to be Joey Faust's Margareta; indeed, she represents a false and empty vision of romantic love. She is Faust's Helen of Troy, or the bride of Frankenstein.

As we discover near the start of Ulmer's film, Joey Faust was betrayed by his wife (she informed on him), and he has a daughter whom he has "never been allowed to see." In these ways, his situation parallels that of Ulof, who has betrayed his own wife, and whose daughter is kept locked away from him—in order to ensure his cooperation in Krenner's experiments. Faust frees Ulof's daughter and Ulof; but it is only when Ulof invokes Faust's own daughter that he chooses to sacrifice his life for the sake of humanity: "I'm thinking of my child," Ulof tells Faust. "You should think of yours. Is this the kind of world you want for your child?"

Faust's daughter is his Margareta, the key to his salvation, just as Dr. Peter Ulof's daughter Maria is his Margareta—and, for that matter, his Madonna. If Joey Faust becomes Christ-like at the end of the film—a Joseph who through the divinity conferred upon Maria (as Madonna) becomes a figure of Jesus—then he is a Messiah who redeems both Maria (as Magdalene—who, for that matter, is also represented in the figure of Laura) and Peter (Simon Peter) when he rejects the plans for world domination advanced by (St.)

Paul—Paul Krenner. He simultaneously becomes another Joseph—not the stepfather of Christ, but Joseph of Arimathea, the convert said to have borne Christ's legacy, the Holy Grail.

This allegorical reading is perhaps reinforced by the incongruous name given to Krenner's henchman—Julian. Just as Krenner has secured Ulof's co-operation by kidnapping his daughter, so he has secured Julian's by promising to arrange for his son to be released from prison (a son who, Julian eventually discovers, is in fact dead). Julian is the film's third self-sacrificing father (another father who assumes the traditionally redeeming role of an absent mother). Could Julian therefore be named after that medieval anchorite Julian of Norwich—whose theology preached, for the first time, a vision of Christ as the loving, all-forgiving mother of humanity?

Joey Faust—redeemed by the memory of his own daughter, his daughter's reflection in Ulof's—has never in fact seen that daughter, and will never see her: his own invisibility reflects her own eternal invisibility to him. When Krenner refers to Faust's daughter, Faust threatens to kill Krenner if he "ever mentions [his] daughter's name again"—yet Krenner has not in fact referred to Faust's daughter by name. Is it therefore to be inferred that Faust does not even know his own daughter's name—that, unseen and invisible, she is also nameless and unnamable? If Joey Faust represents a Faustian everyman, then his daughter represents an anonymously universal figure of redeeming and redeemable humanity.

MONSTROSITY AND MORALITY

The setup of Ulof's laboratory is somewhat reminiscent of Frankenstein's in Whale's film of 1931—and, like Whale's version of *Frankenstein* and Wells's *Invisible Man* (but, curiously, unlike Whale's *Invisible Man*), it exploits radiation to work its scientific miracles. Wells's Griffin employs "two radiating centers of a sort of ethereal vibration"—not X-rays, he stresses, but another form of radiation as yet undescribed (95); Whale's Frankenstein, meanwhile, harnesses a radiation beyond the ultraviolet: "the great ray that first brought life into the world." Ulmer's Ulof uses a fissile material called X13: "its properties are different from other nuclear materials." These indescribable, invisible, and transcendental forms of radiation are, ironically, captured within an eminently visual medium. These films' fixations upon invisibility to some extent reveal cinema's anxiety that it can only describe the superficial, can only represent what can be seen; however, its futile yet noble (noble because futile) attempts to envision the unenvisionable suggest an awareness, even a tangential understanding, of the unenvisionable—and therefore allow for the possibility that its world of shadows may indeed hint at the reality beyond Plato's cave—that cinema may thus perhaps come to represent what T. S. Eliot, in his *Choruses from "The Rock,"* called "the visible reminder of Invisible Light" (*Poems*, 178).

Yet this is of course for cinema to overreach itself into the provinces of divinity: to become its own Griffin, Jekyll, Frankenstein, or Faust. In playing upon these literary and cinematic figures, *The Amazing Transparent Man* posits its narrative within a complex (and perhaps contradictory) web of allusions to their stories and characters. Joey Faust is at once Wells's and Whale's invisible man, Stevenson's and Mamoulian's schizoid protagonist, Shelley's and Whale's monster, and Marlowe's, Goethe's, and Murnau's lost soul; Ulof is Frankenstein but also another Faust himself (Ulof is old Faust to Joey's youthful Faust); their invisible daughters (concealed and absent) are Whale's Flora Cranley and Elizabeth Frankenstein . . . and Shelley's pair of angelic sisters, Elizabeth and Margaret (her narrator Walton's sister) . . . and Goethe's and Murnau's Margareta (Valentin's sister); Laura is Whale's bride of Frankenstein and Goethe's Helen of Troy; and Krenner is at once Mephistopheles and, as we shall see, *The Bride of Frankenstein*'s Dr. Pretorius.

Shelley's Frankenstein is something of a Faustian figure himself: "Like the archangel who aspired to omnipotence, I am chained in an eternal hell" (221). The first part of Goethe's *Faust* was published eight years before Shelley started writing *Frankenstein*; indeed, Shelley's novel alludes to one of Goethe's earlier works, *Leiden des jungen Werthers*, as one of the three books that the monster reads, the text from which he learns "despondency and gloom" (127–28). Frankenstein repeatedly calls his creation a "devil" or "daemon" (99, 101, 165, 169, 170, 198, 202, 203, 205): it is his crucial error to mistake his monster first for his savior and then for his Mephistopheles—just as it is Faust's crucial error to mistake Helen of Troy for his savior, his Margareta.

Yet Oluf, in *The Amazing Transparent Man*, finds in Joey Faust—his creation, his invisible self-reflection—neither a devil nor a false savior, but the route to his own redemption. His monster, his revenant—but also his younger self, one which (unlike Faust's) can redeem the fatal error of his own youth—becomes his Margareta and his Christ. Ulof is redeemed because his invisible man—whom he has created and at the same time destroyed (for the act of creation is fatal: the radiation which empowers Joey Faust also poisons him)—forgives him for his own creation and destruction and, in doing so, becomes a "martyr" who absolves his creator of that original sin. Mr. Faust in effect becomes the Dr. Jekyll to Dr. Ulof's Mr. Hyde—and vice versa. Something similar happens to Frankenstein—not in Shelley's novel, nor in Whale's original adaptation, but in Whale's sequel.

Whale's second Frankenstein film, *The Bride of Frankenstein* (1935), makes the connection between Faust and Frankenstein explicit through the introduction of the Mephistophelean Dr. Pretorius (Ernest Thesiger), a darkly enigmatic manipulator who practices "black magic" and who forces the reformed baron into a "supreme collaboration." While *Bluebeard*'s Morrell plays with his Faustian puppets (Carradine, coincidentally, also has a small role in Whale's film), Pretorius—like Goethe's Mephistopheles—has his own homunculus in a jar. In fact, he has six homunculi, one of which resembles "the very devil"—"There's a certain resemblance to me," comments Pretorius.

Joey Faust, like Werdegast, dies battling evil in an exploding house—as does Karloff's monster in Whale's *Bride of Frankenstein*. (It is perhaps ironic that Karloff pulls the lever that blows up the building and kills the villain in Whale's film of 1935: the previous year, in *The Black Cat*, Lugosi had done exactly the same thing to kill Karloff.) While Shelley's monster and creator end up destroying each other—and thus creating an Oedipal bind worthy of Norman Bates—Whale's monster ultimately redeems himself by saving his creator (and his creator's wife) and destroying himself, his own bride, and his creator's nemesis (the evil Pretorius, who has forced Frankenstein to continue his experiments by kidnapping his wife). Ulmer's Joey Faust similarly saves his creator, Dr. Ulof, and Ulof's daughter, by consigning himself and Krenner (who has similarly forced Ulof to continue his experiments by kidnapping his daughter) to oblivion. And, just as Frankenstein's monster's deathly bride dies in the ensuing conflagration, so Joey's own femme fatale is in the house when it is obliterated by an atomic blast—when it is literally blown (to quote from *The Bride of Frankenstein*—rather than from *The Amazing Transparent Man*) "to atoms."

The Amazing Transparent Man ends with an explosion and a choice: a choice addressed directly to the audience. The security agent Drake proposes that "this idea of an invisible army is quite interesting—imagine what our counter-intelligence could accomplish if they were able to become invisible whenever necessary." Ulof—an Einsteinian amalgam of nuclear physicist and Germanic moral philosopher—admits that "the Central Intelligence Agency has already discussed the possibilities with me. But . . . think of the danger if the secret [like that of the A-bomb] were stolen from us . . . Perhaps it would be better if we let the secret die."

Ulof's reluctance to share his dangerous knowledge recalls Frankenstein's—"You expect to be informed of the secret with which I am acquainted; that cannot be" (Shelley 53)—or, for that matter, Dr. Lanyon's reticence towards the end of *Dr. Jekyll and Mr. Hyde*: "What he told me . . . I cannot bring my mind to set on paper" (Stevenson 80). Yet Ulmer's ending remains ambivalent; as at the close of Wells's *The Invisible Man*, there is a suggestion that this knowledge cannot forever remain buried: "No human being save the landlord knows those books are there, with the subtle secret of invisibility and a dozen other strange secrets written therein. And none other will know of them until he dies" (Wells 150).

In the very last moments of Ulmer's film—and in the shadow of its climactic mushroom cloud—Ulof turns to the camera and directly challenges the audience to solve the film's central moral dilemma: "It's a serious problem. What would *you* do?"

Of course, this is no end-of-*Psycho* moment: Triesault's gaze into our eyes is nowhere near as penetrating as Norman Bates's final stare. Its moral and aesthetic naïveté puts it somewhere in between Chaplin's pleading polemic to the audience at the close of *The Great Dictator* (1940) and the thirty-second interval for audience debate near the end of Paul Annet's British schlock-horror classic *The Beast Must Die* (1974): "One of these eight people will turn into a werewolf. Can you guess who it is when we stop the film for the Werewolf Break?"

We may also recall in this context the words of another eccentric European scientist, namely, Van Helsing's address to the audience at the end of Balderston and Deane's stage adaptation of *Dracula* (74)—in which the renowned vampire hunter reminds us, on a note of ironic "reassurance," that such demons do in fact exist. (Perhaps fortunately, Tod Browning chose not to include this speech in his 1931 celluloid version of Balderston and Deane's play.)

One might even be reminded of Hitchcock's own laboriously worthy introduction to *The Wrong Man* (1956)—in which the master of suspense, in informing his audience that his film is for once based upon a true story, displays a straight-faced (even po-faced) and uncharacteristically maladroit lack of flourish (and of subtlety, ambivalence, and moral and aesthetic invisibility) that he was wise enough not to imitate in his addresses to the camera as he introduced his television series *Alfred Hitchcock Presents*.

However, despite these generally unflattering parallels, the clumsiness of Ulmer's ending (and indeed of his entire film) is perhaps balanced by a complexity and an ambiguity which are arguably imposed upon the text by its conditions and standards of production (most notoriously, the fact that it was shot in a fortnight, back-to-back with another Ulmer picture). Despite its proselytizing, *The Amazing Transparent Man* maintains this ambivalence—albeit in the clunking obviousness of Ulof's final question to the audience. The film may not offer much in the way of subtlety, but it does offer moral choice, and therefore the beginnings of responsibility.

LAST WORDS

Ulmer's Joey Faust is on the run. He has that in common with Roberts in *Detour*, and Morrell (eventually) in *Bluebeard*, and Poelzig (metaphorically) in *The Black Cat*. Cinema—as a fantasist and escapist medium—has often been interested in great escapes and fugitives. Yet, in its progressive and spectacular specularity, cinema is also a medium that prefers its protagonists not to turn their backs on the camera (at least until the final moments—when Chaplin or Bogart may be permitted to walk away); it therefore allows us to view their flights from their own perspectives—as well as from the perspectives of those they flee.

As Hitchcock once said, "The audience can run with the hare and hunt with the hounds" (Gottlieb 130). Indeed, in so many of Hitchcock's movies (*The Thirty-Nine Steps*, *Saboteur*, *Stage Fright*, *Strangers on a Train*, *I Confess*, *To Catch a Thief*, *The Man Who Knew Too Much*, *North by Northwest*, *Psycho*, *Frenzy* . . .), the protagonist is both the pursuer and the pursued. "Cat and mouse, cat and mouse," says Farley Granger in *Rope* (1948). "But which is the cat, which is the mouse?"

Morrell, Poelzig, and Roberts are similarly hunted hunters (either predators or scavengers)—while Joey Faust and Werdegast, conversely, shift from their roles as escapees to those of avenging (or redeeming) angels. Yet, irrespective of whether their paths lead to damnation or redemption, there remains something fatalistic and deathly in the inevitability of these role reversals. These constant to-and-fros come to resemble Freud's grandson's fort-da game: the game that consoles us against the immediacy of loss, and yet whose deterministic repetitiveness speaks of our drive toward death.

At the same time, there remains something immanently cinematic about this process. For are not these reversals, these switchings between the hunter and the hunted, no more than models for the structure of the shot/reverse-shot on which classical cinema is conventionally based? And, indeed, is not this conventional structure itself merely a model for these characters'—and our own—drives toward individual and global destruction?

BIBLIOGRAPHY

Amis, Martin. *Einstein's Monsters* (London: Jonathan Cape, 1987).
———. *House of Meetings* (London: Jonathan Cape, 2006).
———. *Koba the Dread* (London: Jonathan Cape, 2002).
———. *Time's Arrow* (London: Jonathan Cape, 1991).
Balázs, Béla. *Theory of the Film* (New York: Dover, 1970).
Balderston, John, and Hamilton Deane. *Dracula* (London: Samuel French, 1933).

Derrida, Jacques. *The Gift of Death* (Chicago: University of Chicago Press, 1995).
Dumas, Alexandre. *The Count of Monte Christo* (London: Penguin, 2003).
Eliot, T. S. *Collected Poems* (London: Faber and Faber, 1936).
———. *Four Quartets* (London: Faber and Faber, 1979).
Freud, Sigmund. *Art and Literature* (London: Penguin, 1985).
———. *On Metapsychology* (London: Penguin, 1984).
Goethe, Johann Wolfgang von. *Faust* (Wordsworth Editions, 2007).
Gottlieb, Sidney, ed. *Hitchcock on Hitchcock* (London: Faber and Faber, 1997).
Levi, Primo. *If This Is a Man* (London: Abacus, 1987).
Marlowe, Christopher. *Doctor Faustus* (London: A&C Black, 1985).
Metz, Christian. *The Imaginary Signifier* (Bloomington: Indiana University Press, 1982).
Poe, Edgar Allan. *Tales of Mystery and Imagination* (Wordsworth Editions, 1993).
Shelley, Mary. *Frankenstein* (Oxford: Oxford University Press, 1980).
Silverman, Kaja. *The Subject of Semiotics* (Oxford: Oxford University Press, 1984).
Stevenson, Robert Louis. *Dr. Jekyll and Mr. Hyde* (London: Penguin, 1979).
Truffaut, François. *Hitchcock* (New York: Simon and Schuster, 1985).
Vonnegut, Kurt. *Galapagos* (London: Jonathan Cape, 1985).
———. *Mother Night* (London: Jonathan Cape, 1968).
———. *Slaughterhouse 5* (London: Jonathan Cape, 1970).
Wells, H. G. *The Invisible Man* (London: Penguin, 2005).
Žižek, Slavoj, ed. *Everything You Always Wanted to Know about Lacan (But Were Afraid to Ask Hitchcock)* (London: Verso, 1992).

16

An Interview with Shirley Ulmer

Tom Weaver

Behind every great man, the old saying goes, there's a woman. In the case of legendary director Edgar G. Ulmer, "the Miracle Man of Poverty Row," the woman was his devoted wife Shirley, who script-supervised all his movies from the mid-1930s on—and who married Ulmer even though it meant years of major-studio blacklisting for both of them. In this interview, Shirley Ulmer talks candidly about her "tremendous journey" (her thirty-five-year marriage to Ulmer), the experience of working with him in the margins of Hollywood, and some of the many cult films they made on small budgets, in sixteen-hour days, and against all odds.

Born 12 June 1914 in New York City, teenager Shirley came out to the movie capital for the first time in the early 1930s, after her banker father had been wiped out in the Crash. While her dad tried to make a new start in California, Shirley met picture people and began working as a script supervisor. She was married to independent producer Max Alexander when she met and instantly fell in love with Edgar Ulmer, eventually divorcing Alexander—nephew of Universal president Carl Laemmle. Hollywood outcasts, Ulmer and Shirley were subsequently forced to work in the East, on Poverty Row, and at other small indie studios, where the indomitable Ulmer forged a remarkable career as a master of minimalism, with memorable movies like *Bluebeard*, *Detour*, *Strange Illusion*, *The Man from Planet X*, and others. Shirley was also a writer of screenplays, teleplays, and the book *The Role of Script Supervision in Film and Television*; in later years, she (along with her daughter Arianné) maintained a high profile keeping alive the memory of Ulmer and his highly personal films. They were collaborating on the documentary *The Edgar G. Ulmer Story* when Shirley's health began to fail. She died in July 2000. The following interview was conducted in January 1998.

Your father came out to Hollywood to make a new start as a banker or in the picture business?

In *anything* [*laughs*]! He didn't have any idea about the picture business, and banking was a no-no at that time. My grandmother (that's on my mother's side) knew a lady who was Willie Wyler's mother. I remember that Wyler's mother was very annoyed that the Hillcrest Country Club was anti-Semitic then. She was the one who introduced me to [MGM production executive Irving G.] Thalberg and so forth, and that's how I got to be a script supervisor, thanks to her and my grandmother and a lady by the name of Moree Herring, a script supervisor at Metro. Thalberg was very kind to me, he said, "If you want to be a writer and you want to be on sets and learn something about the business, being a script clerk is a good way for a woman." That was what really got me started in the business.

Were you already Mrs. Max Alexander at that point?

No, not yet. I wrote a little play that Pasadena Playhouse put on and I played a small, autobiographical kind of part in it. After the show, Junior Laemmle and Max Alexander came backstage. So we went out, Junior and Max and another girl, I think her name was Betty.

On a double-date.

Yes. I picked Max, who was Uncle Carl Laemmle's nephew, and then I sort of saw him exclusively during that entire summer. When the big [Long Beach] earthquake happened [in 1933], my mother said, "I've had it out here, let's go back to New York." We did, my mother and father and I landed up in Brooklyn, Kings Highway. I was very unhappy that they brought me back to New York. Max began telephoning me long distance, because he wanted to marry me. Finally I said yes, because I was very unhappy about living at home with my mother, who didn't like the idea of me going around meeting producers and trying to sell my scripts [*laughs*]! He sent me a train ticket and a thousand dollars to come out to California. I cashed the train ticket in and I bought myself a boat trip, a two-week trip on the Grace line, a boat that went through the Panama Canal and stopped off in all these different ports along the northern part of South America. It was very exciting 'cause I had a little flirtation on the trip [*laughs*]—I was quite a gal, I didn't realize it! I wasn't scared, I was going to marry Max Alexander, but I met [actor] Dane Clark on the boat. We had a little romantic thing going, but nothing serious. We didn't go to bed, but we did spend a lot of time together. Then I got out to California and I married Max.

Did you marry him because you loved him or to get away from home?

I married him to get away from home. I *was* very fond of him; he was a nice guy, but a very simple man. When we were first married, we went to Hawaii on our honeymoon, then we came back and lived in Uncle Carl's big house. Then we took a little apartment on Stanley in Hollywood. Uncle Carl helped us with furniture and all kinds of lovely gifts, and he was very happy with the marriage.

How did you meet Edgar Ulmer?

Max was hiring Edgar to work [as a second unit director] on *I Can't Escape* [1934] and he invited him to dinner at our apartment on Stanley. I was in the kitchen making a pot roast when I heard this man's voice that was so exciting to me—not just the accent, the timbre of his voice. I thought, "Oh what a crazy, exciting man, what a beautiful voice!" I went in the living room and Max introduced me, and that's how I met Edgar.

Then after we had dinner, Max made the mistake of saying he was very tired and he had a headache, and that *I* would entertain Edgar, go out to the movies or something with him. Well, I entertained Edgar . . . and that was the beginning of the end of Max [*laughs*]!

Where did you and Ulmer go that night?

We went driving out to the beach. I had never met anyone like him, his knowledge was . . . incredible! He made me feel *stupid,* really. I talked about the book that I was writing [*Sinners in Sight*] and he talked about his experiences as an orphan after the war, when he had been sent to Sweden, and all the people he knew were famous—amazing brains. And *he* had an amazing brain. It was a very exciting evening. He started me out on a tremendous journey which was forty-odd years of marriage with him before he died. It wasn't always *easy*—he was not faithful, I had to watch out for that! He even had a daughter out of wedlock while we were married.

Subsequent "dates" with Ulmer took place behind Max Alexander's back, correct?

Yes.

What was it like, being part of the Laemmle clan?

It was *horrible.* That marriage only lasted a *year*, dear. Sundays were a disaster; on Sundays you sat around the table with the whole family at Uncle Carl's house, and everybody who was a top person at the studio was invited. That was a big deal, to be invited. Uncle Carl (unfortunately!) liked me very much [*laughs*] and he had me seated there and he had me giving my opinions.

I remember one opinion I gave, I told him how I had seen Margaret Sullavan in a play in New York, I've forgotten which one, and I thought she was a great actress. He turned to Junior and he said, "You hear what Shirley said? Find out more about Margaret Sullavan!" And he later hired her! So *that was* my contribution to the industry! Uncle Carl had a tremendous estate—it got broken up into five or six estates. It was a huge hunk of land with *many* houses on it. He sold it when he sold the studio.

When you say that Uncle Carl "unfortunately" liked you, does that mean that you didn't particularly like him?

Oh, I didn't *dis*like him; he was a *funny* old man. But he was deaf, and you had to scream for him to hear you. He wouldn't use his hearing aid. He had very old-fashioned ideas, and he *never* forgave Edgar for taking me away from his nephew Max.

What was Junior like?

Junior was . . . weird. He was such a hypochondriac—he was always fighting some illness, some of them real and some of them, I think, imaginary. He wore Kotex to keep from catching cold on his penis—*that* I remember! By the way, there was once an article which said I was having an affair with the old man [*laughs*]. That was not true—that made me *mad*!

Did Junior live at home with his father?

Yes, he did.

If Max Alexander was part of the Laemmle family, why wasn't he making Universal pictures? Why was he making independents?

He had his own company, Beacon Productions, because he wanted to show that he could do something on his own. He owned a little studio on Santa Monica Boulevard. But he was on good terms with his Uncle Carl and he took care of Uncle Carl's business things. Uncle Carl owned that whole block on the corner—Melody Lane was a restaurant where *everybody* went, there on the corner of Hollywood and Vine. Uncle Carl owned that and the rest of that whole square block. Max used to collect rents and things like that . . .

In addition to running his own motion picture company.

Right. Max's other two uncles (on his mother's side) were the Stern brothers. They made the *Our Gang* comedies, and they were very famous and very wealthy.

The first movie you worked on was Max Alexander's I Can't Escape*?*

Yes, with Lila Lee. In those days, when you got divorced, you had to wait a year to get it finalized, and when I met Edgar, he was just finished with that year of waiting and he was celebrating. He had been married to a girl by the name of Joan Warner, whose name he used sometimes as a director. [Ulmer did some early directing under the name John Warner.] She was a society girl and she had a relative, I think an uncle, who was a vice-president of the United States. Edgar and Joan Warner had a little girl.

What are some of your memories of the making of The Black Cat*?*

The Black Cat would never have been made if "Uncle Carl" had not gone to Europe, that I *know*. Junior was a very psycho, mixed-up young man, and Edgar was playing psychiatrist for him or something [*laughs*]! And so Junior had a real *crush* on Edgar, they were very close. It was Junior who got Edgar to do *The Black Cat.* When the old man came back from Europe, he didn't even want to *release The Black Cat*, because it had classical music in it. He didn't like that, he said, "The public can't take classical music, *I* can't take it! It's no good!" [*Laughs*] So it was a very strange thing that *Black Cat* became successful.

What impressions did you get of Karloff and Lugosi?

Boris was an intellectual, a very nice, easy guy to work with. Bela was a *clown*. Bela told jokes, he told crazy stories that he was a *hangman*. On the set he did all kinds of funny things to get attention. He was showing off.

That's funny, because from everything I've heard and read, Lugosi usually kept to himself on the sets of his pictures.

Why he acted that way, I don't know. He invited Edgar and me to his home, which I understood at that time was a big deal. He treated his wife [Lillian] like she was a servant maid—that was *my* impression. I didn't like him for that, but I never said anything. He seemed to be very fond of Edgar and took direction nicely.

Was your visit to Lugosi's house during the making of The Black Cat*?*

No, *much* later, after the movie was made, after I started living with Edgar. (We weren't married legally yet, but I was living with him.) Lugosi invited us to his home, and I recall that in the foyer of the house, right where we came in, was a huge painting of him in *Dracula*. And, again, I remember him forcing his little wife around very harshly. I felt sorry for her.

Several film historians have written that Ulmer's "dark side" manifested itself on The Black Cat. *Is that true, or is that just modern writers trying to be dramatic?*

I've heard that, too. Maybe it did; I can't say whether it did or not. That early on, I didn't know he *had* a dark side—I just knew that he got *difficult* at times [*laughs*]!

Were you romantically involved with him when he was making The Black Cat*?*

Not until afterwards.

So it was just a coincidence that you were assigned to The Black Cat *as script supervisor.*

I wasn't *assigned* to be the script supervisor, I just wangled my way in there because I wanted to *watch* Moree Herring the script supervisor, I wanted to learn more from her. So I wound up doing all her notes. I didn't get any credit, but in those days, you *never* got any credit. It was mostly an occupation for men, believe it or not. At Metro, there was only one girl [script supervisor]—everybody else was male. They changed that when they found that these males, like Mervyn LeRoy and a lot of others who started there as script supervisors, would leave and become directors, and the girls would *stay*.

What was Peter Ruric, the writer of The Black Cat, *like?*

He was brilliant, really, but *cuckoo* [*laughs*]. He wasn't like any *ordinary* person I'd ever met. But very, very brilliant—Edgar adored him, and they were very close. He was one who used to show up for the Sunday luncheons at Uncle Carl's.

The Black Cat *was made very cheaply and very fast. Obviously you worked long hours.*

Oh, and *how*! Not only on *The Black Cat* but on *all* Ulmer films, it was usually a sixteen-hour day. You'd get to work at six in the morning and you were lucky if you got home before midnight. The cameraman on *The Black Cat* [John Mescall] was very, very good. He was already recognized as a top cameraman.

And Ulmer got along well with him?

Very good. He always got along with the heads of the departments. He didn't get along with anybody that was a four-flusher or anything, but he got along with all of his crews. His crews always loved him, and he tried very hard all the way through his life to get the same people again and again.

And you didn't *get the impression that Karloff and Lugosi were close friends.*

They weren't close friends if they were friends *at all*, they just were sort of polite to each other. But you could feel a certain amount of jealousy or *tension*, I should say, going on between them.

Even emanating from Karloff?

Oh, yes. He had a certain contempt, because Lugosi did act like a clown, he acted silly. I don't think Karloff, any more than Edgar or I, believed these stupid stories Lugosi told us!

Did Lugosi tell people his stories one-on-one, or did he hold court?

He would hold court. He was reserved on his other pictures—at least that's what everybody tells me. But not with *us*! But I thought he was excellent in the picture.

Who was better in the picture, Karloff or Lugosi?

They were both good, they were both right for their parts. Karloff didn't want to make the picture, he didn't want to be known as a horror actor. He didn't want to do this film, but when Edgar showed him his sketches and the sketch of the costume he [Karloff] would wear, he weakened and said okay. Jacqueline Wells [Julie Bishop] was a pretty girl and she did a fine job, and David Manners was good, too. Edgar was a very interesting director—he directed with a baton. He *timed* their speeches. He drove Hedy Lamarr [star of Ulmer's *The Strange Woman*, 1946] crazy because he timed the way she spoke with the baton, and would slap her on the ankles with the baton if she goofed [*laughs*]!

Was he using the baton as early as The Black Cat*?*

Yes. Once Edgar told Peter Bogdanovich that he was a frustrated conductor—Edgar was *very* knowledgeable. He read music and he always had scores around the house, and one year he taught a course at the Curtis Institute in Philadelphia [on music theory and history]. So maybe he felt he was conducting! For Father's Day every year, our daughter Arianné always gave him a new baton, because he broke them all the time. He would go crazy on a good Beethoven's Ninth or things like that, "conducting" in the living room while he was listening to the music.

Right in the middle of The Black Cat, *and then later, in the middle of* Bluebeard, *Ulmer includes a scene of comic relief.*

He usually did that on purpose, because he was worried about being considered too serious. He felt people needed comic relief and he tried to do comedy whenever he could. But he was not known for being a good comedy director.

Supposedly Karloff's Satanist character was based on several real-life people—one of them Fritz Lang.

Well, Fritz Lang was one of the few people that Edgar did not get along with, so I don't know. They spoke badly about each other [*laughs*]!

In the Bogdanovich interview, Ulmer said that Fritz Lang was sadistic and he couldn't get along with him. Then, a few pages later, he said Erich von Stroheim was sadistic and that he loved *him! What was the difference between those two sadists?*

There was quite a difference. Von Stroheim was very intelligent and a much more knowledgeable man [than Lang]. Edgar liked someone he could *admire.*

What were some of his cost-cutting methods on a movie like Black Cat*?*

He always got to a point where he would suddenly say, "Well, it's getting towards the end of the day. I'm gonna *cheat—and* you're gonna cheat along *with* me. We're gonna go *fast,* we're gonna do one take." They would call him "One-Take" Ulmer—the actors would get scared *[laughs]*!

That's one way to hurry things up! Peter Bogdanovich asked Ulmer, "How in the world do you do 80 setups a day?" and Ulmer said, "Ask my wife." Well, thirty years later, I'm asking.

How did we do eighty setups a day? Well, because he would do these one-take things. He used the dolly like nobody had ever used it before; he would make five-minute, ten-minute shots. He was always unhappy that they didn't make film reels longer [*laughs*]!

Are you in any of his movies?

I was in *Natalka Poltavka* [1937]; it was a case where a girl didn't show up at work one day and Edgar said, *"Go* get in her costume." But I was Edgar's script supervisor on everything after *The Black Cat,* from 1934 on.

Is he *in any of his movies?*

No. He didn't have the acting bug.

Even though he started out as an actor?

Well, he was a different kind of actor, he was a stage actor.

One of the most striking scenes in Black Cat *is the one where Karloff prowls through the basement where he has all his dead wives in the upright glass coffins.*

I *loved* that scene. *All* of his sets were to me incredible, *always*. On his preparation for every film, he spent a lot of time and energy on creating sets that were unusual. In those days, his use of plexiglas and glass and all the other crazy things he did was completely modernistic. He made wonderful sets.

An actress named Lucille Lund, who played Karloff's wife in The Black Cat, *says that Ulmer treated her nicely until he started to flirt with her and she turned him down. After that, she said, "he wasn't very nice at all."*

Oh, that's very likely [*laughs*]—I believe her! Edgar did not have much carrying-on with actresses, his playing around was not with people in the business. Hedy Lamarr, who he knew from school days, was probably the only one he *may* have had an affair with, but I'm even inclined to doubt that it was for very long. 'Cause he really didn't like her. But he got a performance out of her in *The Strange Woman* that nobody else ever got. Also in *Loves of Three Queens* [1953], which we made in Italy. [Editor's note: The three-part film (aka *L'Amante di Paride* and *The Face That Launched a Thousand Ships*) is comprised of the stories of Geneviève of Brabant, Empress Josephine and Helen of Troy. After Ulmer directed the Geneviève of Brabant story, he and Hedy Lamarr had a fight (Lamarr had "bought out" the producers and started giving Ulmer instructions). For the first and only time, Ulmer walked off a picture. Lamarr engaged director Marc Allegret to direct the other two segments.]

Did the Laemmles ever come onto the sets of any of these movies?

Just Junior. Like I said, we were lucky that *Black Cat* even got released because the old man was furious. When he came back, he was so angry at his son, who had allowed Ulmer to go so crazy and use classical music and crazy sets and all of this. He didn't like the film at *all*.

Next Ulmer directed Thunder Over Texas [1934], *which I've never seen. Was there anything about it that set it apart from other Westerns?*

Yeah, it was accused of being another *Little Miss Marker*, it was the same kind of story. I wrote that film [using the pseudonym Shirle Castle].

Did Ulmer seem out of place directing a Western?

No, he *liked* the idea. He wasn't too good at it, but he did it and he liked it [*laughs*]! He was fascinated because that was part of America that he knew nothing about. He used the name "John Warner" on that film—later, when I got annoyed, he stopped using it. I got annoyed because I thought maybe Edgar still cared for her [Joan Warner]. She had left him, and in their divorce she said he had slapped her. He never hit me, he was not violent in that way. He screamed like crazy, but he never touched me [*laughs*]!

Do you think he slapped her?

Maybe . . . if she made him *mad* enough.

Were you still married to Max Alexander when you did Thunder Over Texas*?*

Yes. Then I started living with Edgar without being able to marry him because I had to wait that whole year, and we didn't get married until '35. I legally married Edgar a few months before my twenty-first birthday. Before that, I lived with him for almost a year, which was unheard-of in those days, too! We were living in the Christie Hotel on Hollywood Boulevard.

When you did fall in love with Ulmer and decided to marry him, do you remember breaking the news to Max Alexander?

Well, he thought I was nuts [*laughs*]—*everybody* did! My own parents didn't talk to me for a couple of *years*.

And Laemmle-wise, what were the repercussions?

Oh, we were told that we'd never work in Hollywood again. He couldn't get a job—that's why we went back to New York.

He was told by who *that he would never work again?*

By everyone he called.

So there was no face-to-face confrontation with any of the Laemmles.

No, no, no. But [Hollywood] just didn't want him around.

Were things touch-and-go financially throughout all your years with Edgar?

Well, until we made *Carnegie Hall*, yes. I think [*Carnegie Hall* producer] Boris Morros saw to it that we had dough.

After living and working in the East far several years, you and Ulmer came back to Hollywood and started working at PRC.

Edgar met [PRC producer] Leon Fromkess, who was an accountant of sorts—a businessman—and a real movie buff. Edgar and he struck up quite a friendship. He was very nice, he *and* his wife Rita. She was a bit of a pain in the neck, because she was always around on the set and Edgar was always shooing her away! But a nice lady. Both of them were devout Christian Scientists. At PRC I was very busy looking up scripts for them and writing little cards with synopses of what the basic stories were about.

What memories of Bluebeard*?*

The script was written by Pierre Gendron—he was a sick man in that he was, I guess, a semialcoholic. That made it a little difficult to work with him. But he could write like a dream and he got along with Edgar beautifully. He had a wife whose first name was Mary and she assisted him, especially when he couldn't show up or was too far gone in the cups [*laughs*]!

Back in Ulmer's Universal days, right after The Black Cat, *he was going to make a movie about Bluebeard, so it must have been something that was in his mind even—*

It *was* very much in his mind right along, yeah. He had a lot to do with the writing, and Pierre and his wife put it down on paper properly. He was an educated guy, this Pierre, very well versed in literature. I might tell you that Edgar was terribly self-conscious because English was a second language to him. He could write wonderfully, hut he didn't trust himself, he always wanted [help from] somebody who was knowledgeable in the English language. Pierre was a fine writer, but a difficult man.

How was working at PRC different from working at one of the bigger studios?

Edgar had complete charge. *Nobody else* had a word to say. Fromkess was a very quiet man . . . his wife gave Edgar a little problem now and then, but Fromkess and Edgar got along very, very well. Or they *did* until *The Strange Woman* came about. Hedy Lamarr wanted Edgar to direct her, and so Fromkess made a deal and loaned Edgar out to [*Strange Woman* producer] Hunt Stromberg. I've forgotten what Stromberg paid but it was a very large sum. Edgar had been earning $200 a week on his contract with Fromkess, and Fromkess never gave him a penny of the extra money that he made by lending Edgar out to do *The Strange Woman.* That's when Edgar decided *enough is enough*, and *very* shortly thereafter, when his contract came due, he refused to work there any more.

In what way was Mrs. Fromkess a pain in the neck? What was she trying to do by hanging out on the sets?

Well, she was a frustrated moviemaker, I guess [*laughs*]. She was a good woman, and they had a daughter who died of cancer. Mrs. Fromkess also died at an early age.

Did Edgar Ulmer have input in the music of these PRC movies?

He had *all* the input! Everybody, Fromkess included, thought that he was crazy to want to do an operatic thing, the *Faust* [marionette show], in *Blue-*

beard, hut he insisted on doing it. And it *was* noted; in fact, *The Hollywood Reporter* gave us a very fine critique on it.

What do you remember about composer Leo Erdody and cinematographer Eugene Schüfftan, who collaborated with Ulmer at PRC?

Erdody and Edgar were bosom pals. Erdody was a fine musician. Erdody died very suddenly and it was a tragedy for Edgar—he didn't really get over it *ever.* He loved Leo Erdody. Erdody's father was a conductor in Hungary, and Liszt left Erdody's father his baton. The father gave the baton to Erdody, Erdody gave the baton to Edgar and Edgar used that baton when he was directing. That baton still exists.

Schüfftan was a big help. Schüfftan couldn't join the union [the American Society of Cinematographers], they wouldn't let him in, but he was *very* much around and in charge of the camera. He was a darling man. He was Edgar's favorite cameraman, and he and Edgar were very close friends. But Schüfftan couldn't learn English properly. Every sentence had words from five different languages [*laughs*], he had all these languages mixed up. And he made us laugh very much and he would get very hurt, but we couldn't *help* laughing. It was very strange and very funny. He was a man of many languages—all at once!

Talking to Bogdanovich, Ulmer called Bluebeard *"a very lovely picture." What were some of the parts of it that he particularly enjoyed?*

He enjoyed very much being able to do the *Faust* aria. Sonia Sorel, John Carradine's girlfriend, was good in that, too. Edgar *didn't* want her in it because he didn't like hiring someone just because she was John's girlfriend, but she surprised him and gave a very fine performance. As did all of them. Edgar felt that Carradine did one of his finest jobs in *Bluebeard.* And Carradine kind of agreed with him [*laughs*]!

Your daughter Arianné tells funny stories about Ulmer losing his patience and getting tough with actors who weren't giving him what he wanted. In all your years of working with Ulmer, what actor got it the worst? Who got it with both barrels?

Offhand, I think it might have been John Saxon [on *The Cavern,* 1966]—Edgar treated him pretty bad! But he got along with his women fine. He was known for pinching their ankles sometimes during a close-up, to get an expression [*laughs*], but none of them seemed to mind. They all got along with him.

How about behind-the-camera people? Did he ever get tough with any of them?

No. He got along beautifully with *every* crew. They were handpicked and they were all wonderful.

I like the flashback scenes in Bluebeard, *with the distorted sets and imaginative camera work.*

Beautiful camera work, yes. Those were the kind of touches that Edgar relied on Schüfftan for.

What more can you tell me about Carradine?

He was the Man Who Came to Dinner [*laughs*]! He and his son, who calls himself David Carradine, a funny little youngster. They had been living at the Garden of Allah, which was a very well-known place, an outdoor hotel with bungalows all around the pool area. It was very popular with the stars at that time. John brought his boy to dinner and he told us a sad story about this wife whom he was divorcing, the mother of David. She was trying to get back alimony, and he had to hide out from her. So he asked if he could stay with *us* awhile. So we always laugh—he was the Man Who Came to Dinner, but he stayed with us for *months* [*laughs*]!

So you got to know him quite well.

Of course, and also David, who was a wild boy who took our daughter Arianné to play with him. He called himself Captain Midnight and they would run all over the roofs of the buildings! It was so dangerous, it scared the hell out of me—I was always chasing him and scolding him [*laughs*]!

Did you ever regret letting Carradine move in?

Oh, no, he was *fun*. He could have been a professor of literature, really, and Edgar admired anyone who was that knowledgeable. When Carradine and David were staying with us, they stayed in Edgar's bedroom and Edgar moved back in with me. We had separate bedrooms but we usually slept in my bedroom. Edgar's room was always a mess—he had his drawing board there and all of his stuff, and he wouldn't allow anybody to come in and clean up [*laughs*]. That was Edgar's "bedroom." He'd go back and forth—he would spend part of the night in my bedroom and then go into the second bedroom. He was an insomniac and he would get up in the middle of the night and work. This second bedroom attached to Arianné's bedroom, with a bathroom between them. If Arianné was up late at night or if she went into the bathroom and the light was showing beneath the door, she could go in there and talk to him. Most of the time Arianné talked to him was in the middle of the night.

If Ulmer and Carradine were such great friends, why wasn't Carradine in more of Ulmer's movies?

Because Carradine got more money—he went on to become a *name*. When we used him, he was *not*.

What was Sonia like?

[*Pause*] I didn't like her too much, but she *was* a good little actress. We went to their wedding; my daughter was the flower girl and David Carradine was the ring bearer. It was in the Episcopalian church on Wilshire Boulevard and they dressed in Shakespearean costumes. It caused a little publicity, and people talked about it. Arianné and David scattered the rosebuds.

John Carradine in more than one interview mentioned directing one scene in Bluebeard. *Do you know what he's talking about?*

No. And I don't think he'd say that if Edgar were alive!

What do you think of Bluebeard*? Do you think it's one of Ulmer's better pictures?*

I certainly do. It's hard to name my favorites, I can't pick *one,* but I can say offhand quickly *Ruthless* [1948], *The Cavern* and *Detour* [1945]. And *The Naked Dawn* [1955] definitely. Those would be the ones that I would name off the top of my head.

I want to hear some of the great stories you have about The Pirates of Capri [*1949*].

During the bad period in the U.S. [the HUAC period], Edgar and I were off to Europe. We were never really bothered at all, although the FBI did come see us before we went off—two gentlemen came to the house on King's Road and asked questions about certain friends of ours. I remember in particular they were interested at that moment in Gale Sondergaard. We didn't know anything about where she joined [the Communist Party] or what she did, so I don't think we helped them! Then they gave Edgar an envelope with a special address on it, and said when we were in Europe, and we were meeting all these people who were suspect, Edgar could [write it all down and] mail it back to them. And he said he'd be delighted.

So now we were off to Europe [to make *The Pirates of Capri*] with a producer by the name of Victor Pahlen, who was quite a character. I think they did that movie *The Bad and the Beautiful* [1952] about him. He had a lot of charm, he charmed everybody to death, but he was a bit on the crooked side [*laughs*]! He had gotten a deal together with a lady from Egypt to do this *Pirates of Capri* in Italy. Edgar had gone on first, to get everything arranged, and then he sent me a lot of telegrams and lists of things he was going to need.

I arrived in Italy with Arianné, who was a little girl—oh, she couldn't have been more than eleven or twelve years old. We arrived at Campino Airport near Ostia. (Everything was bombed out pretty bad, from the war.) We got out of the plane and I had all these toys and books and things for Arianné. And some little Italian children started running after us. With all these bundles and everything, and trying to keep hold of the child, I was having a little problem! And these children were running after me, making me very nervous, yelling, "Jew! Jew!" And I thought, "Oh, my God, you mean they're anti-Semitic over here too?" So I was frightened. I later found out they were yelling at me "Giu! Giu!" meaning "Down! Down!" because I was schlepping all of these huge suitcases and wouldn't let go of them. They wanted to help me [*laughs*]! I didn't know a word of Italian beyond *arrivederci!*

I got into a little building there on the airfield and they opened up my suitcases and they immediately took away my cigarettes—I had a couple of cartons in there. They took *them* away. And there was no one there to meet us—I was looking for Edgar. Finally a lady came and she said she was sorry she was late, she was delayed. She had promised Edgar she would meet us. We could come to the hotel and rest a little and have a little something to eat, but then we had to catch a midnight train down to the location, which was in Taranto. I thought of *Canada,* that's the only Toronto *I* knew! "What are we doing in Toronto [*laughs*]?"

This was probably October–November and we had been told that sunny Italy was *warm*, so I didn't have heavy clothes with me. Not for the child and not for me. We rushed to that train and we made it all right, and, my golly, it was *freezing*. One of my memories is that I couldn't put my head down on the pillow. We had a private train compartment and it was lovely, but it was so cold that the pillow felt like a block of ice [*laughs*]. There was no stop in Taranto, we got off the train at a little village close by, and there we were met by a car and chauffeur and driven down to Taranto. Now, Taranto had been bombed to the ground by the English. There wasn't a building with [an unbroken] window in it anymore. We were taken to the best-looking building of them all, which had some boarded-up windows. We got in there, into a great big sort of lobby, round, with a very unattractive lady sitting in the center at a raised dais or desk. We called her "the Animale" later—"the Animal." She was a very unattractive and *ugly-acting* person. And there were a lot of *very* pretty young women running around, most of them with just towels wrapped around them. Nothing ever dawned on me [*laughs*]—I led a very sheltered life! We were shown to our room, which was stone-walled and no windows, but at least it sheltered us a little from the cold. It had a great big double bed and there was a little single bed for Ariannè over in the corner. It wasn't until maybe the second night that I realized where I was, because finally I asked questions. Edgar told me, "Look, I couldn't find any better accommodations. This is a whorehouse!" A legal, government-licensed Italian naval whorehouse. Later on, Edgar would tell this story—he said, "I'll bet you I'm the only man who took his wife and daughter to a whorehouse!"

And what happened to the envelope that the FBI asked you to bring along on the trip?

Oh, we destroyed it right away [*laughs*]!

What can you remember about the making of The Man from Planet X*?*

Last night I put on my goggles and I watched my *Man from Planet X* tape all over again, and I thought it was a *very* respectable, *nice* picture. It was made in 1950 at the Hal Roach Studios, produced by Jack Pollexfen, who was a rather shy man. We all almost died because of the use of Nu Gel to make the fog you see in the picture. It was a ghastly experience and we all got sick. When we made *Man from Planet X*, we were in a *terrible* rush, because we had a job coming up that would take us to Spain.

Planet X *was one of the few Hollywood-made movies that you did around that time. Which did you enjoy more, making movies in Hollywood or abroad?*

I don't know whether the right word is "enjoy"—they were hard work!

Both at home and *abroad.*

Yes. The experiences in Europe, of course, were much more exciting in those years, because they didn't know Americans like we didn't know them. We were strangers to each other. In *Man from Planet X* we had Robert Clarke [as the star], an easygoing guy, very nice person. I can't say enough nice things about him. [Leading lady] Margaret Field was the mother of Sally, and Margaret gave up her career and put all her efforts behind that little girl of hers. (It paid off!) Margaret was a very simple, pleasant, nice personality.

And the guy who played X [Pat Goldin]?

I think he was okay—*very* okay, actually. But he was a bit of a complainer! He'd complain about the gear. He didn't complain *bitterly*, but he wasn't too happy. Edgar called that [mask] a "douche bag"!

Robert Clarke talks about making $210 *for starring in that movie.*

Well, Edgar got about three hundred, so Robert Clarke didn't do so bad! *Man from Planet X* was made in a very fast and tense schedule. As I said,

Nu Gel was the product that caused the fog, and it caused us all to get sick. It was *horrible* to breathe. We didn't know any other way, Edgar couldn't get the effect if he didn't use the Nu Gel. So somehow or other, sick or not, we got through. We *couldn't* have a delay because Harry and Eddie Danziger [producers of Ulmer's earlier *St. Benny the Dip*, 1951] had promised us that we were going to make a picture in Spain. We had to get going.

Did you get the sense that Edgar liked the way Man from Planet X *came out?*

He wasn't that impressed, but he liked having done it, 'cause he *wanted* to do a science-fiction of that sort. But we were in such a rush to get it done because that crazy couple was cabling us all the time, the Danzigers. We went to Europe on a ship called the *Liberté*, and it was absolutely magnificent—I had a wonderful trip. We arrived in France and from there we took a car or a train into Paris and met the Danzigers, who proceeded to give Edgar all kinds of scripts and ideas. The Danzigers were a couple of Americans who became very successful . . . became English citizens . . . owned the Mayfair and other hotels in London . . . and now they were producing movies. They were nice, they were pleasant, but they just drove us *crazy* because they'd give Edgar ideas of pictures that they were going to make, and Edgar would prepare them. He spent six months, after rushing to get there, before finally they got the deal set to make *Babes in Bagdad* [1952] in Spain.

When we got into Spain, there was a problem: I used to be like the go-fer, and [before leaving the U.S.] I had packed all the film and everything we'd need and sent it to Paris, where the Danzigers were waiting for us. Then, when I heard we were gonna be actually shooting in Spain, I transferred it all to Spain. When we were in Spain and ready to go, we couldn't get all this stuff out of customs. You see, Ariranné was a junior high school student, and Edgar and I arranged for her studies to be sent from her junior high so she wouldn't fall behind. Unfortunately, amongst the many books that were sent in that shipment was a book called *For Whom the Bell Tolls*.

[Laughs] Oh, Franco's "favorite"!

Here's the way we got our stuff: We had in that film Paulette Goddard, who was married at that time to Erich Maria Remarque, the author of *All Quiet on the Western Front.* Remarque had a beautiful home in Switzerland, and Paulette had come over and stolen him away from Marlene Dietrich! Now Goddard was working for us in *Babes in Bagdad.* She had a lot of clout in Europe, and she went down to Franco. Edgar didn't dare let Franco even know his *name*, because Edgar had once been interviewed and called Franco "the butcher of Europe." It got a lot of publicity in Europe, and Edgar was worried that Franco would find out that it was him! Fortunately he didn't. Goddard went down there and fooled around with all these big shots of Franco's, and she got a special permit to get the stuff off the ship! I remember that, because we were going crazy waiting!

The other problem that Edgar had was, the girls they had gotten together for him were supposed to be harem girls, beautiful girls—and they *were*. But most of them had hair on their chests! And long hair under their arms and all over their legs. And they were infuriated when Edgar made them shave [*laughs*]! They thought they'd lost all their sex appeal. Back then, men *liked* the hairy girls over there!

Why did Ulmer become involved on Beyond the Time Barrier *and* The Amazing Transparent Man, *the two science-fiction movies he made in Texas?*

They were done for dough. We shot *Beyond the Time Barrier* at an air force base, and that's interesting in my memory banks because we had to wear special badges and we were body-searched going and coming from work at the base. Remember the old saying, "If you don't like the weather in Texas, wait a half hour, it'll change"? It was always on and off and weather-permitting calls—you never knew what the weather would be. We had a lot of terrible storms. Both of them [*Time Barrier* and *The Amazing Transparent Man*] were made quickly.

There was a rumor that Ulmer did not direct all of Amazing Transparent Man.

He directed the whole thing. In fact, he stayed on in Texas longer than I did—he sent *me* and Arianné home and he stayed on there, because he did his first cut down there. Douglas Kennedy, who played the invisible man in that, was a gentleman and Marguerite Chapman was a very nice, simple lady.

What do you remember about shooting L'Atlantide *[1961] in Italy?*

When we started, Frank Borzage was supposed to direct it, Edgar was a producer and Nat Wachsberger was the money man; he was a big producer in Europe, a Frenchman. (Actually, he was a Belgian, but he liked to be called a Frenchman!) Wachsberger and his wife Yvette [Lebon], a well-known actress, were quite interesting people. We started the picture and we were either one or two days in when we realized Borzage was so sick, he could hardly hold his head up. I was helping him the best I could, but I didn't know what to do about it—he was really in terrible shape. When Wachsberger came to visit us on the set, he saw what we were up against and he had a conversation with Mrs. Borzage and she agreed, and Frank Borzage retired. He never did another thing, he died shortly after. It was very sad—it was *awful*.

How much of the picture had he directed?

There was nothing in the camera, really—a couple of long shots done on the beach. We were just marking time until Wachsberger came and did something about it. Anyhow, we did it, and it was interesting. It was a tough picture to make, but it was interesting.

Why tough?

Under the circumstances, we were all pretty shook up about Borzage. But I think Edgar did a very good job, a *splendid* job on that picture. I remember Arianné [the movie's dialogue coach] teaching Jean-Louis Trintignant the dialogue phonetically—he didn't speak English. But he was awfully good-looking [*laughs*]!

What happened to Borzage got hushed up. The trade papers said he couldn't direct L'Atlantide *because of the "language barrier."*

Well, his wife didn't want that publicity, because he wouldn't get any more work. Which he *didn't* and *shouldn't* have gotten—he was a sick man.

Ulmer's last feature was The Cavern, *which he made in Europe.*

We had a good cast in *The Cavern*. Brian Aherne was in it and he was really excellent, and if you ever read his autobiography, he talks a little bit about *The Cavern*. He gives his sympathy to Edgar—and me, too!—because we were really having a very rough time. In our cast we had Aherne and Larry Hagman, who was a very amusing young man who kept me going—who kept *all* of us going. It was so cold on the location there, and Larry was a drinker at the time, and he had his little flask going. He brought along same instant soup tablets—bouillon—and he made cups of bouillon for all of us, and then he would put something in from his flask [*laughs*]! It was a Yugoslavian liquor called Slivovitz, plum brandy, and it was probably 100 proof, because we *felt* it. And it did warm us up [*laughs*]! So we were grateful to him! He was always carrying on with funny jokes. We also had Peter Marshall, God *bless* him—he was the steadying influence, a *wonderful,* wonderful, decent human being. And John Saxon, who was a nuisance, and who doesn't like Edgar very much because Edgar didn't pay much attention to him [*laughs*]!

When we all got over there, we met in Rome and we were told, "Everything is set, the dough is in the bank in Yugoslavia. We're off to Belgrade!" We took off from Rome and got onto the train. But we didn't see our luggage—we had taken two or three taxis [to the train station] and one taxi had all our luggage and none of us had seen that luggage arrive. I was seated with Edgar and Larry and Peter, and I remember Peter was upset because Edgar had rushed us so and he didn't have a toothbrush [*laughs*]! We had *nothing* with us but the clothes on our back. And we were all pretty hysterical and angry at Edgar about this! We arrived in Belgrade and, my God, there was no luggage. So here we were in a strange country *without* luggage, with just what we had on our backs.

The Hotel Metropole in Belgrade was a very beautiful hotel, but not quite finished off good. In the bathrooms there were no toilets, there was just a hole in the beautiful marble floor [*laughs*]! The first activity I recall there was going shopping with Larry Hagman, looking for big tubs that we could put down on the floor and make ourselves some kind of a quasi-wash place. All the store windows had things *in* them, but when you'd go inside the store, there *wasn't* anything. We were pretty upset. We only found one tub, which became a community tub, going from room to room. And it was winter, the snow was *way* up, up almost to my waist in spots, and very, very cold, and Hagman's booze was very welcome! In the hotel we had a woman who sat in uniform in the lobby, and if we wanted to receive or make phone calls, we had to do them down there on her phone. And when we went even onto location, there were two Yugoslavian officers assigned to us. It was *very* Communistic. We had a maid who had paper in her one pair of shoes because they had holes in them, and she wouldn't take another pair because she would be arrested. Horrible. The people were *lovely* . . . but frightened. There was great fear in the air.

Like I told you, the Hotel Metropole had marble floors, and Larry Hagman made a bonfire on the floor in his room [*laughs*]! He had his family with him—he had two little girls and his wife. A charming, lovely family. (He *is* a family man, as you can see—they've stayed together all these years.) Anyhow, he was gonna feed his family, and somehow or other he'd gotten hold of some sausages and he wasn't gonna take them outside, so he just made a bonfire in the hotel!

We shot for I would say three, four days, maybe a week on the location, which wasn't far from the main city of Belgrade. And all of a sudden, when Edgar went to the bank, he discovered that the money had been confiscated. And we got the news from others around us, from the [Yugoslavian] crew, that the country had a new minister, the old guy had been booted out, and there had been a lot of changes. And we better get the hell out of there!

Which you did.

They got us onto a workman's train that left in the middle of the night. We left like thieves in the night. And on that train, Edgar had the first signs of what he got later—a small stroke. He kind of half-passed out, he was not feeling good, and Peter Marshall was his "doctor" who was helping him and was so kind. I'm always grateful, Peter *really* helped him—he kept everybody from bothering Edgar while on the train.

The original plan was to shoot it all *in Yugoslavia?*

Yeah. And we were *stuck* now. Everybody was so good about it except John Saxon—of course. He was suspicious 'cause he didn't believe us that we *would* get financed again. We didn't have money there for a week or so, and everybody just said, "Don't worry, we're not gonna stop filming." Only John Saxon gave trouble.

You resumed shooting in Italy.

Yes. Edgar was in terrible shape, and now he had to try and find a cave, which he did, in the city of Trieste. As I can tell you, it was a very nerve-wracking experience. I thought that Larry Hagman gave the finest performance, not only of his life, but of anybody playing a drunken person who's out of control. He was really awfully good, and I thought Brian Aherne was lovely. The girl was Rosanna Schiaffino, and she was very pretty and very nice. Nothing spectacular—she never got anywhere, not like Loren and Gina Lollobrigida. But we thought she might, so we used her. It was all quite an experience!

In the mid-'60s, Ulmer finally tried to branch out into television.

That's right, that's why we came home from Europe. And also because I thought Edgar needed doctoring—I didn't know what was wrong with him. He was getting *terrible* migraines.

Edgar wrote thirteen scripts for *The Doris Day Show,* for which they didn't *pay* him. Doris Day's husband Marty Melcher took over, and then Melcher got a stroke and Doris Day's son said he didn't know anything about [the money Ulmer was owed] and he didn't pay him. We had to sue Doris Day and the suit went on for four, five years. Edgar was dead by the time I settled the suit with her for $3,000. I couldn't afford the lawyers.

The scripts he wrote were produced?

Yes. But no credit. The son said Edgar never wrote them, but he never met Edgar, he didn't know him.

What was Doris Day like to work for?

Edgar got along with her fine. She was friendly, but with a little ice, *always*. She had a *cold* nature. But she was pleasant always and on time and very professional.

At that same time I was still working as a script supervisor, for Jacques Demy and a lot of different directors here. I was working at Columbia on a film directed by Demy [*The Model Shop,* 1969] and I didn't finish that film, because I came home late one night and found Edgar on the floor. He'd had his big stroke. Unfortunately, Edgar had a *very* rough ending: For four years, one stroke after the other. He was unable to move, unable to talk. We communicated by my giving him an ink pad and holding his hand, and he would scrawl with the little movement he had in the hand—very little. He couldn't even raise his head, he had to be fed intravenously. It was four years of this agony. And he didn't like being in the hospital—he was at Cedars, and when the insurance people cut us off, I didn't know what to do. I went to the Motion Picture Home, and they said they would take him in for $400 a month if I would sign off all my belongings—car, jewelry, clothing, *everything* you have to sign off. I had to do it. We got him set up in a nice private room and they were very good to him and took care of him. I took him home every weekend—they arranged for the ambulance and . . . [*chokes up*]. Excuse me—this is horrible stuff, it was a horrible time. It was the toughest four years of my life.

You said you had to sign away everything. How did you still have a house to bring him home to on weekends?

The house was *gone*, I had taken an apartment. I had *nothing*, dear—really nothing! But I was lucky to be a good script supervisor, so I got work. Not steady—I worked sporadically. I made commercials, I made a lot of money doing commercials. There was a man by the name of John Hazard who took pity on me—he knew Edgar, and he kept me very busy, at least two, three commercials a month, and in those days they were paying two hundred, three hundred dollars a day. That got me on my feet again.

Are you surprised that, twenty-five years after your husband's passing, there's still so much interest in him and his movies?

I am shocked [*laughs*]—of course! I am *not* surprised at a *few*, because even before he died he had quite a little fan club going. Young people flocked around Edgar, and he loved it, and he told wonderful stories, and I wish I could tell them like he did.

Ulmer enjoyed the freedom to make his movies the way he *wanted to make them—that's part of the reason he worked at all these small studios. But would it have really broken your heart if he had been taken in by a big studio and went to work every day and made "bigger" movies, just maybe not exactly his way? Would that steady employment really have been a bad thing?*

I think it *would* have been, yeah. He wouldn't have made those particular movies that *he* picked. Let's face it, no studio would have okayed the kind of films he made.

So even with all the financial ups and downs—

I have no regrets. *None*. He was a man who gave me a wonderful journey—an exciting journey, an instructive journey. He broadened my horizons like no university could.

17

Karloff, Lugosi, Browning, and Whale

Edgar G. Ulmer, translated from the French by Bernd Herzogenrath

Karloff was able to play roles which were his speciality, since he could place himself into some kind of self-hypnosis when he was playing these figures . . . but not Lugosi. Lugosi was a great technician who knew the reactions of the audience very well.

* * *

With his very theatrical style, Lugosi knew how to captivate his audiences. Karloff was different . . . with him, you had to repeat, again, and again . . . Karloff rehearsed his roles and said: "I will show you what I am going to do." He detested his roles as monster, for the simple reason that he was absorbed by them. He thought of himself as a good actor—and justifiably so—but he knew that the audience was obsessed by the horror that was emanating from his different incarnations. For me, Karloff was continuing a direct lineage from Lon Chaney Sr. Chaney played the kind of roles in the Silent Era, which—as you can imagine—was very difficult: *The Phantom of the Opera*, *The Hunchback of Notre Dame*, etc. True, Lugosi thought he was Dracula—that was part of his life. But he reacted very theatrically in this respect. With Lugosi, for example, I always have to give directions such as "Please, don't overdo it! Cut another fifty percent! . . . You can do such things on the stage, but not here!"

* * *

This interview originally appeared as part of Bernard Eisenschitz and Jean-Claude Romer's "Entretien avec Edgar G. Ulmer" in *Midi-Minuit Fantastique* 13 (November 1965).

Tod Browning was maybe the first to watch what was being called "Fantasy" films at this time, made in Germany and Sweden; Murnau himself made some of those. After World War I, and in particular in Germany, the influence of E. T. A. Hoffmann was considerably bigger than the influence of Edgar Allan Poe. The fact that editors were using the talents of painters and illustrators made Grune, Murnau, and lots of others interested in this new style of expression. Browning knew all this, and it was he who put pressure on Carl Laemmle (before he changed to Metro), and before he became a specialist in this field. Browning knew every trick you could pull from a camera, and he knew the art of montage. It was he who had Jack Pierce, a makeup artist who had just arrived in New York, create masks and makeup—long before *Frankenstein* (1931). When Irving Thalberg left Universal and joined L. B. Mayer to found Metro Goldwyn Mayer, he was so captivated by Browning's imagination that he took Browning with him. In the beginning—I am talking about 1925—Metro had an excellent art department. They had made the famous Cedric Gibbons come from New York, where he had worked as a stage designer for the theater. And Browning, who knew the work of Wiene in *Caligari*, began to turn away from the expressionism of this period in order to embrace a concept one might call "baroque." Browning was an immensely cultured person, much more than the majority of the people. He was an expert in literature, and a specialist, not only on Edgar Poe, but on the whole English Gothic, where you find lots of these stories.

* * *

But we know extremely little about his private life, since he was a very reclusive person, a very introverted man. In the evenings, after work, Browning took his car and disappeared. He never joined you for a drink, nobody knew where he lived, and it was very difficult to approach him personally. He was a very strange man! I only knew one of his habits: when he was working on a film, in the break between takes, he used to gather the actors and technicians and tell the most extraordinary stories . . . I don't know any other director who was so passionate about his subjects . . . Browning was very successful with his movies. The tradition that he had implanted at Universal was taken up again immediately, so there was no year without a horror movie. Then James Whale was hired . . . You have to understand that in the Silent Era, visual effects were considerably more important with regard to realism than sound. Until the end of his career, Browning tried to keep a distance from the use of dialogues; he wanted to keep the visual effects. I always had this impression; although I'm not sure if the final version of the script was Browning's own or the scriptwriter's . . . I have this impression because each of his films, despite the various different scriptwriters, is always typical of his own personal style.

Note: For more information on Tod Browning, the "classic" of course is David J. Skal and Elias Savada's *Dark Carnival: The Secret World of Tod Browning, Hollywood's Master of the Macabre* (New York: Anchor Books, 1995); but see also Bernd Herzogenrath, ed., *The Films of Tod Browning* (London: Black Dog, 2006), and Bernd Herzogenrath, ed., *Tod Browning: Essays of the Macabre and the Grotesque* (Jefferson, N.C.: McFarland, 2008).

Filmography

The Border Sheriff **(Universal Pictures) U.S., 1926**

Director: Robert North Bradbury
Assistant Director: Edgar G. Ulmer [not credited]
Screenplay: Robert North Bradbury
Cinematography: Harry Mason, William Nobles
Cast: Jack Hoxie, Olive Hasbrouck, S. E. Jennings, Gilbert Holmes, Buck Moulton, Tom Lingham, Bert de Marc, Frank Rice
5 reels / B&W

People on Sunday / Menschen am Sonntag **(UFA, Paramount, MGM) Germany, 1930**

Directors: Edgar G. Ulmer, Robert Siodmak, Rochus Gliese [not credited]
Screenplay: Billy Wilder, Curt Siodmak, Edgar G. Ulmer
Producer: Seymour Nebenzahl
Cinematography: Eugen Schüfftan
Cinematography Assistance: Fred Zinnemann
Music: Otto Stenzeel
Art Direction: Moritz Seder
Cast: Erwin Splettstößer, Brigitte Borchert, Wolfgang von Waltershausen, Christl Ehlers, Annie Schreyer, Kurt Gerron, Valeska Gert, Heinrich Gretler, Ernö Verebes
73 minutes / B&W
DVD: BFI

Love's Interlude or *The Warning Shadow* (Peerless Production Inc.) U.S., 1932 [Unreleased]

Director: Edgar G. Ulmer
Assistant Director: Walter Sheridan
Screenplay: Edgar G. Ulmer, Florence Pollack
Producer: Adolph Pollack
Cinematography: Frank Zucker, Lester Lang
Cast: Dita Parlo, William Desmond, Tom Moore, Arthur Housman, Ruth Burns

Mr. Broadway (Broadway Hollywood Productions Ltd.) U.S., 1933

Directors: Johnnie Walker, Edgar G. Ulmer [not credited]
Screenplay: Ed Sullivan, Abel Green
Cinematography: Frank Zucker
Cast: Ed Sullivan, Jack Dempsey, Ruth Etting, Bert Lahr, Jack Benny, Mary Livingstone, Jack Haley, Eddy Duchin, Ernst Lubitsch
63 minutes / B&W

Damaged Lives (Columbia Pictures Corporation) Canada / U.S., 1933

Director: Edgar G. Ulmer
Screenplay: Donald Davis, Edgar G. Ulmer
Producer: Maxwell Cohn
Cinematography: Allen G. Siegler
Editor: Otto Meyer
Clinical Supervision: Dr. Gordon Bates
Cast: Diane Sinclair, Lyman Williams, Cecilia Parker, George Irving, Almeda Fowler, Jason Robards Sr., Marceline Day, Charlotte Merriam
69 minutes / B&W
DVD: Alpha Video (61-minute American version)

The Black Cat (Universal Pictures Inc.) U.S., 1934

Director: Edgar G. Ulmer
Screenplay: Peter Ruric, Tom Kilpatrick [not credited]
Producer: Carl Laemmle Jr.
Cinematography: John J. Mescall
Editor: Ray Curtiss
Music: Franz Liszt, Piotr Tchaikovski
Art Direction: Charles D. Hall
Costumes: Edgar G. Ulmer, Vera West, Ed Ware

Cast: Boris Karloff, Bela Lugosi, David Manners, Julie Bishop, Lucille Lund, Harry Cording, Egon Brecher
65 minutes / B&W
DVD: Universal

Thunder over Texas (Beacon Productions Inc.) U.S., 1934

Director: Edgar G. Ulmer [credited as John Warner]
Screenplay: Eddy Granemann
Producer: Max Alexander
Cinematography: Harry Forbes
Editor: George M. Merrick
Script Supervisor: Shirley Ulmer
Cast: Guinn "Big Boy" Williams, Marion Shilling, Helen Westcott, Claude Payton, Philo McCullough, Robert McKenzie, Ben Corbett
61 minutes / B&W

From Nine to Nine (Coronet Pictures Ltd.) Canada / U.S., 1936

Director: Edgar G. Ulmer
Screenplay: Kenneth Duncan
Associate Producer: William Steiner
Cinematography: Alfred Jacquemin
Editor: Ross Pitt-Taylor
Music: Maurice Metzger
Art Direction: Fred Govan
Script Supervisor: Shirley Ulmer
Cast: Ruth Roland, Roland Drew, Doris Covert, Kenneth Duncan, Eugene Sigaloff, Miriam Battista, Arthur Stenning
62/75 minutes / B&W

Natalka Poltavka (Avramenko Film Productions Inc.) U.S., 1936

Directors: Edgar G. Ulmer, Michael J. Gann
Screenplay: Vasile Avramenko, Michael J. Gann
Producer: Vasile Avramenko
Music: C. N. Shvedoff
Script Supervisor: Shirley Ulmer
Cast: Thalia Sabanieeva, Olena Dibrova, Fedir Braznick, Dimitri Creona, Lydia Berezovska, Peter Kushabsby
93 minutes / B&W

Green Fields / Grine Felder **(Collective Film Producers Inc.) U.S., 1936**

Directors: Edgar G. Ulmer, Jacob Ben-Ami
Screenplay: George Moscov, Peretz Hirschbein
Producers: Ludwig Landy, Roman Rebush
Cinematography: William Miller, J. Burgi Contner
Editor: Jack Kemp
Music: Vladimir Heifetz
Art Direction: Steve Goulding
Script Supervisor: Shirley Ulmer
Cast: Michael Goldstein, Helen Beverly, Izidor Cashier, Aron Ben-Ami, Anna Appel, Lea Noemi, Dena Drute
97 minutes / B&W
DVD: The National Center For Jewish Film

La Vida Bohemia **(Columbia Pictures Corporation) U.S., 1937**

Directors: John Alton, Joseph Berne, Edgar G. Ulmer [not credited]
Screenplay: José Lopez Rubio
Producer: Jaime del Amo
Cinematography: Jockey Arthur Feindel, J. Henry Kruse
Editor: Irving Applebaum
Music: Alexander Borisoff
Art Direction: Frank Paul Sylos
Script Supervisor: Shirley Ulmer
Cast: Rosita Díaz Gimeno, Gilbert Roland Miguel Ligero, José Crespo, Romualdo Tirado, Juan Toren
77 minutes / B&W

The Singing Blacksmith / Yankl der Schmid **(Collective Film Producers Inc.) U.S., 1938**

Director: Edgar G. Ulmer
Screenplay: Ben-Zvi Baratoff, Ossip Dymow, David Pinski
Producers: Ludwig Randy, Roman Rebush
Cinematography: William Miller
Editor: Jack Kemp
Music: Edward Fenton, Edwin Schabbehar
Script Supervisor: Shirley Ulmer
Cast: Moishe Oysher, Miriam Riselle, Florence Weiss, Anna Appel, Ben-Zvi Baratoff, Michael Goldstein, Lea Noemi

105 minutes / B&W
DVD: The National Center For Jewish Film

Cossacks in Exile / Zaporozhets za Dunayem (Avramenko Film Company Ltd.) U.S., 1938

Director: Edgar G. Ulmer
Screenplay: Vasile Avramenko
Producers: Vasile Avramenko, Michael J. Gann
Cinematography: William Miller, Leo Lipp
Editor: Jack Kemp
Music: Anthony Rudnicki
Costumes: Fedir Braznick
Script Supervisor: Shirley Ulmer
Cast: Maria Sokil, Michael Shvets, Helen Orlenko, Alexis Tcherkassi, Nicholas Karlash, Vladimir Sikevitch
110 minutes / B&W

Moon over Harlem (Meteor Productions Inc.) U.S., 1939

Director: Edgar G. Ulmer
Screenplay: Sherle Castle [Shirley Ulmer]
Producers: Edgar G. Ulmer, Peter E. Kassler
Cinematography: J. Burgi Contner, Edward Hyland
Editor: Jack Kemp
Music: Donald Heywood
Art Direction: Eugene Wolk
Script Supervisor: Shirley Ulmer
Cast: Percy "Bud" Harris, Cora Green, Izinetta Wilcox, Alec Lovejoy, Earl Gough, Zerita Steptean, Petrina Moore
68 minutes / B&W
DVD: Image Entertainment

The Light Ahead / Fischke der Krumer / Di Klayatshe (Carmel Productions Inc.) U.S., 1939

Director: Edgar G. Ulmer
Screenplay: Chavet Pahver, Mendele Mocher Sforim, Edgar G. Ulmer, Shirley Ulmer
Producers: Edgar G. Ulmer, Peter E. Kassler
Cinematography: J. Burgi Contner, Edward Hyland
Editor: Jack Kemp

Music: Dean Cole
Art Direction: Robert Benny, Edgar G. Ulmer
Script Supervisor: Shirley Ulmer
Cast: Izidor Cashier, Helen Beverly, David Opatoshu, Rosetta Bialis, Tillie Rabinowitz, Anna Guskin, Celia Budkin
94 minutes / B&W
DVD: The National Center For Jewish Film

American Matchmaker / Amerikaner Shadkhn **(Fame Films Inc.) U.S., 1940**

Director: Edgar G. Ulmer
Screenplay: Sherle Castle [Shirley Ulmer]
Producer: Edgar G. Ulmer
Cinematography: J. Burgi Contner, Edward Hyland
Editor: Hans E. Mandl
Music: Sam Morgenstern
Art Direction: William Saulter
Script Supervisor: Shirley Ulmer
Cast: Leo Fuchs, Judith Abarbanel, Yudel Dubinsky, Anna Guskin, Celia Brodkin, Abraham Lax, William Mercur
100 minutes / B&W
DVD: The National Center For Jewish Film

Shorts for National Tuberculosis Association & U.S. Health 1937–1940

Cloud in the Sky
Another to Conquer
Goodbye Mr. Germ
Methods of Diagnosis
Let My People Live
They Do Come Back
Mantoux Text
Life Is Good

Director: Edgar G. Ulmer
Springer Pictures Inc., 1940/1941
Industrial Pictures (42)
Commercials (8)

Military Films (Such as Series on *Celestial Navigation*)

Hostages (Angelus Pictures Inc.) U.S., 1941

Released by Paramount
2nd Unit Director: Edgar G. Ulmer

Hitler's Madman (Atlantis Pictures Inc. / P.R.C. Pictures Inc.) U.S., 1942
2nd Unit Director: Edgar G. Ulmer

Tomorrow We Live (Atlantis Pictures Inc. / P.R.C. Pictures Inc.) U.S., 1942

Director: Edgar G. Ulmer
Screenplay: Bart Lytton
Producers: Leon Fromkess, Seymour Nebenzal
Cinematography: Jack Greenhalgh
Editor: Dan Milner
Music: Leo Erdody
Set Decoration: Fred Preble
Script Supervisor: Shirley Ulmer
Cast: Ricardo Cortez, Jean Parker, Emmett Lynn, William Marshall, Roseanne Stevens, Ray Miller, Frank S. Hagney
63 minutes / B&W
DVD: Alpha Video

My Son, the Hero (P.R.C. Pictures Inc.) U.S., 1943

Director: Edgar G. Ulmer
Screenplay: Edgar G. Ulmer, Doris Malloy, Sam Newfield
Producer: Peter R. van Duinen
Cinematography: Jack Greenhalgh, Robert Cline
Editor: Charles Henkel Jr.
Music: Leo Erdody
Set Decoration: Fred Preble
Script Supervisor: Shirley Ulmer
Cast: Patsy Kelly, Roscoe Karns, Joan Blair, Carol Hughes, Maxie Rosenbloom, Luis Alberni, Joseph Allen Jr.
66 minutes / B&W
DVD: Alpha Video

Prisoner of Japan (Atlantis Pictures Inc. / P.R.C. Pictures Inc.) U.S., 1943

Directors: Arthur Ripley, Edgar G. Ulmer [not credited]
Screenplay: Robert Chapin, Arthur Ripley
Producers: Seymour Nebenzal, Edgar G. Ulmer
Cinematography: Jack Greenhalgh
Editor: Holbrook N. Todd

Music: Lee Zahler
Script Supervisor: Shirley Ulmer
Cast: Alan Baxter, Gertrude Michael, Ernst Deutsch, Corinna Mura, Tom Seidel, Billy Boya, Ray Bennett
64 minutes / B&W

Minstrel Man **(P.R.C. Pictures Inc.) U.S., 1943**

Director: Joseph H. Lewis
Screenplay: Irwin Franklyn, Pierre Gendron
Producer: Leon Fromkess
Cinematography: Marcel Le Picard
Editor: Carl Pierson
Music: Ferd Grofé
Art Direction: Paul Palmentola
Production Design: Edgar G. Ulmer
Script Supervisor: Shirley Ulmer
Cast: Benny Fields, Gladys George, Roscoe Karns, Jerome Cowan, John Raitt
Ulmer directed the first 5 days, and was 2nd Unit Director for the entire production.

Girls in Chains **(Atlantis Pictures Corporation / P.R.C. Pictures Inc.) U.S., 1943**

Director: Edgar G. Ulmer
Screenplay: Albert Beich
Producers: Peter R. van Duinen, Leon Fromkess
Cinematography: Ira Morgan
Editor: Charles Henkel Jr.
Music: Leo Erdody
Art Direction: Fred Preble
Set Decoration: Harry Reif
Script Supervisor: Shirley Ulmer
Cast: Arline Judge, Roger Clark, Robin Raymond, Barbara Pepper, Dorothy Burgess, Clancy Cooper, Allen Byron
70 minutes / B&W

Isle of Forgotten Sins **[reissue title *Monsoon*] (Atlantis Pictures Corporation / P.R.C. Pictures Inc.) U.S., 1943**

Director: Edgar G. Ulmer
Screenplay: Raymond L. Schrock

Producer: Peter R. van Duinen
Cinematography: Ira Morgan
Editor: Charles Henkel Jr.
Music: Leo Erdody
Art Direction: Fred Preble
Script Supervisor: Shirley Ulmer
Cast: John Carradine, Gale Sondergaard, Sidney Toler, Frank Fenton, Veda Ann Borg, Rita Quigley, Rick Vallin
81 minutes / B&W
DVD: Alpha Video

Jive Junction [UK title *Swing High*] (P.R.C. Pictures Inc.) U.S., 1943

Director: Edgar G. Ulmer
Screenplay: Irving Wallace, Walter Doniger, Malvin Wald
Producer: Leon Fromkess
Cinematography: Ira Morgan
Editor: Robert Crandall
Music: Leo Erdody
Art Direction: Frank Sylos
Script Supervisor: Shirley Ulmer
Cast: Dickie Moore, Tina Thayer, Gerra Young, Johnny Michaels, Jack Wagner, Jan Wiley, Bill Halligan
64 minutes / B&W

Raphael Wolff Productions with U.S. Army Forces, 1943

Coca Cola morale films for service men (4)
Army training films (12)
Army Hymns from Home (2)
Director: Edgar G. Ulmer

Bluebeard (P.R.C. Pictures Inc.) U.S., 1944

Director: Edgar G. Ulmer
Screenplay: Pierre Gendron
Producer: Leon Fromkess
Production Designer: Eugen Schüfftan
Cinematography: Jockey Arthur Feindel
Editor: Carl Pierson
Music: Leo Erdody
Art Direction: Paul Palmentola, Angelo Scibetta

Set Decoration: Glenn P. Thompson
Script Supervisor: Shirley Ulmer
Cast: John Carradine, Jean Parker, Nils Asther, Ludwig Stössel, George Pembroke, Teala Loring, Sonia Sorel
70 minutes / B&W
DVD: Image Entertainment

Strange Illusion **[*Out of the Night*] (P.R.C. Pictures Inc.) U.S., 1944**

Director: Edgar G. Ulmer
Screenplay: Adele Comandini
Producer: Leon Fromkess
Cinematography: Philip Tannura, Benjamin H. Kline [not credited], Eugen Schüfftan [not credited]
Editor: Carl Pierson
Music: Leo Erdody
Art Direction: Paul Palmentola
Set Decoration: Harry Reif
Script Supervisor: Shirley Ulmer
Cast: James Lydon, Sally Eilers, Warren William, Regis Toomey, Charles Arnt, George Reed, Jayne Hazard, Jimmy Clark
85 minutes / B&W
DVD: Alpha Video

Club Havana **(P.R.C. Pictures Inc.) U.S., 1945**

Director: Edgar G. Ulmer
Screenplay: Raymond L. Schrock
Producer: Leon Fromkess
Cinematography: Benjamin H. Kline, Eugen Schüfftan [not credited]
Editor: Carl Pierson
Music: Howard Jackson
Art Direction: Edward C. Jewell
Set Decoration: Glenn P. Thompson
Script Supervisor: Shirley Ulmer
Cast: Tom Neal, Margaret Lindsay, Don Douglas, Lita Baron, Dorothy Morris, Ernest Truex, Marc Lawrence
62 minutes / B&W

Detour **(P.R.C. Pictures Inc.) U.S., 1945**

Director: Edgar G. Ulmer
Screenplay: Martin Goldsmith

Producer: Leon Fromkess
Cinematography: Benjamin H. Kline
Editor: George McGuire
Music: Leo Erdody
Art Direction: Edward C. Jewell
Set Decoration: Glenn P. Thompson
Script Supervisor: Shirley Ulmer
Cast: Tom Neal, Ann Savage, Claudia Drake, Edmund MacDonald, Tim Ryan, Esther Howard, Pat Gleason
67 minutes / B&W
DVD: Alpha Video

The Wife of Monte Cristo (P.R.C. Pictures Inc.) U.S., 1946

Director: Edgar G. Ulmer
Screenplay: Dorcas Cochran
Producer: Leon Fromkess
Cinematography: Edward A. Kull, Benjamin H. Kline [not credited], Eugen Schüfftan [not credited]
Editor: Douglas Bagier
Music: Paul Dessau
Art Direction: Edward C. Jewell
Set Decoration: Glenn P. Thompson
Script Supervisor: Shirley Ulmer
Cast: John Loder, Leonore Aubert, Martin Kosleck, Charles Dingle, Eduardo Ciannelli, Fritz Feld, Eva Gabor
85 minutes / B&W

Her Sister's Secret (P.R.C. Pictures Inc.) U.S., 1946

Director: Edgar G. Ulmer
Screenplay: Anne Green
Producer: Henry Brash
Cinematography: Franz Planer
Editors: Jack W. Ogilvie, Carl Pierson
Music: Hans Sommer
Art Direction: Edward C. Jewell
Set Decoration: Glenn P. Thompson
Script Supervisor: Shirley Ulmer
Cast: Nancy Coleman, Margaret Lindsay, Phillip Reed, Regis Toomey, Henry Stephenson, Felix Bressart
85 minutes / B&W

The Strange Woman (Mars Film Corporation) U.S., 1946

Director: Edgar G. Ulmer
Screenplay: Herbert Meadow, Hunt Stromberg, Edgar G. Ulmer
Producers: Hedy Lamarr, Hunt Stromberg, Jack Chertok, Eugen Shüfftan
Cinematography: Lucien Andriot
Editors: John M. Folay, Richard G. Wray
Music: Carmen Dragon
Art Direction: Nicolai Remisoff
Script Supervisor: Shirley Ulmer
Cast: Hedy Lamarr, George Sanders, Louis Hayward, Gene Lockhart, Hillary Brooke, Rhys Williams, Alan Napier
99 minutes / B&W
DVD: Image Entertainment

Carnegie Hall (Federal Films Inc.) U.S., 1947

Director: Edgar G. Ulmer
Screenplay: Karl Kamb
Producers: Boris Morros, William Le Baron, Samuel Rheiner
Cinematography: William Miller
Editor: Fred Feitshans Jr.
Art Direction, Costumes: Max Rée
Script Supervisor: Shirley Ulmer
Cast: Marsha Hunt, William Prince, Frank McHugh, Martha O'Driscoll, Hans Jaray; As themselves: Walter Damrosch, Jascha Heifetz, Harry James, Vaughn Monroe, Jan Peerce, Ezio Pinza, Lily Pons, Arthur Rubenstein, Risë Stevens, Leopold Stokowski
143 minutes / B&W
DVD and VHS: Bel Canta Society

Ruthless (Producing Artists Inc.) U.S., 1947

Director: Edgar G. Ulmer
Screenplay: S. K. Lauren, Gordon Kahn, Alvah Bessie [not credited]
Producer: Arthur S. Lyons
Cinematography: Bert Glennon
Editor: Francis D. Lyon
Music: Werner Janssen
Art Direction: Frank Sylos
Set Decoration: Ray Robinson
Script Supervisor: Shirley Ulmer

Cast: Zachary Scott, Louis Hayward, Diana Lynn, Sydney Greenstreet, Lucille Bremer, Martha Vickers, Edith Barrett, Raymond Burr

104 minutes / B&W

VHS: Terra

Captain Sirocco / I Pirati di Capri (Film Classics) Italy / U.S., 1949

Directors: Edgar G. Ulmer, Guiseppe Maria Scotese

Screenplay: Sidney Alexander

Producers: Rudolph Monter, Victor Pahlen

Cinematography: Anchise Brizzi

Editor: Renzo Lucidi

Music: Nino Rota

Art Direction: Guido Fiorini

Script Supervisor: Shirley Ulmer

Cast: Louis Hayward, Binnie Barnes, Alan Curtis, Rudolph Serato, Massimo Serato, Mariella Lotti, Mikhail Rasumny, Virginia Belmont

95 minutes / B&W

DVD: Image Entertainment

So Young So Bad (Danziger Productions Ltd.) U.S., 1950

Directors: Bernard Vorhaus, Edgar G. Ulmer [not credited]

Screenplay: Jean Rouverol, Bernard Vorhaus, Joseph Than [not credited]

Producers: Edward J. Danziger, Harry Lee Danziger

Cinematography: Don Malkames

Editor: Carl Lerner

Music: Robert W. Stringer

91 minutes / B&W

St. Benny the Dip (Danziger Productions Ltd.) U.S., 1951

Director: Edgar G. Ulmer

Screenplay: John Roeburt

Producers: Edward J. Danziger, Harry Lee Danziger

Cinematography: Don Malkames

Music: Robert W. Stringer

Script Supervisor: Shirley Ulmer

Cast: Dick Haymes, Nina Foch, Roland Young, Lionel Stander, Freddie Bartholomew, Oscar Karlweis

82 minutes / B&W

DVD: Alpha Video

The Man from Planet X (Mid Century Films Inc.) U.S., 1951

Director: Edgar G. Ulmer
Screenplay: Aubrey Wisberg, Jack Pollexfen
Producers: Aubrey Wisberg, Jack Pollexfen
Cinematography: John L. Russell
Editor: Fred Feitshans Jr.
Music: Charles Koff
Art Direction: Angelo Scibetta, Byron Vreeland
Script Supervisor: Shirley Ulmer
Cast: Robert Clarke, Margaret Field, Raymond Bond, William Schallert, Roy Engel, Gilbert Fallman, David Ormont
71 minutes / B&W
DVD and VHS: MGM

Babes in Bagdad / Muchachas en Bagdad (Danziger Productions Ltd.) Spain / U.K. / U.S., 1952

Directors: Edgar G. Ulmer, Jerónimo Mihura
Screenplay: Felix Feist, Joe Ansen
Producers: Edward J. Danziger, Harry Lee Danziger
Cinematography: Jack E. Cox, Georges Périnal, José Luis Pérez de Rozas
Editors: Edith Lenny, Teresa Alococer, Angeles Pruna
Music: Jesus Garcia Leoz
Art Direction: Juan Frexe, Enrique Bronchalo
Script Supervisor: Shirley Ulmer
Cast: Paulette Goddard, Gypsy Rose Lee, John Boles, Richard Ney, Thomas Gallagher, Sebastian Cabot, MacDonald Parke, Christopher Lee
79 minutes / Color

Loves of Three Queens / L'Eterna Femmina / L' Amante di Paride (Cine del Duca, P.C.E.) Italy / France, 1954

Directors: Edgar G. Ulmer (directed the Geneviève of Brabant episode) [not credited], Marc Allégret
Screenplay: Marc Allégret, Vittorio Nino Novarese, Vadim Plemiannikov, Salka Viertel
Producers: Victor Pahlen, Hedy Lamarr
Cinematography: John Allen, Desmond Dickinson
Editor: Manuel del Campo
Music: Nino Rota
Art Direction: Virgilio Marchi, Mario Chiari

Script Supervisor: Shirley Ulmer
Cast: Hedy Lamarr, Milly Vitale, Massimo Serato, Cathy O'Donnell, Anna Amendola, Cesare Danova, Robert Beatty
90 minutes / Color

The Naked Dawn (Joseph Shaftel Productions) U.S., 1954

Director: Edgar G. Ulmer
Screenplay: Nina Schneider, Herman Schneider (Julian Zimet)
Producer: Joseph Shaftel Productions
Cinematography: Frederick Gately
Editor: Dan Milner
Music: Herschel Burke Gilbert
Art Direction: Martin Lencer
Set Decoration. Harry Reif
Script Supervisor: Shirley Ulmer
Cast: Arthur Kennedy, Betta St. John, Eugene Iglesias, Roy Engel, Charlita, Tony Martinez, Francis McDonald
82 minutes / Color

Murder Is My Beat [UK title *Dynamite Anchorage*] (Masthead Productions Inc.) U.S., 1955

Director: Edgar G. Ulmer
Screenplay: Aubrey Wisberg
Producer: Aubrey Wisberg
Cinematography: Harold E. Wellman
Editor: Fred Feitshans Jr.
Music: Albert Glasser
Art Direction: James Sullivan, Harry Reif
Script Supervisor: Shirley Ulmer
Cast: Paul Langton, Barbara Payton, Robert Shayne, Selena Royle, Roy Gordon, Tracey Roberts, Kate MacKenna
77 minutes / B&W

The Perjurer / Der Meineidbauer / Die Sünderin vom Fernerhof (Eichberg Film GmbH) Germany, 1956

Director: Rudolf Jugert
Screenplay: Erna Fentsch
Producer: Edgar G. Ulmer
Cinematography: Roger Hubert

Editor: Lilian Seng
Music: Friedrich Meyer
Art Direction: Max Mellin, Wolf Englert
Cast: Heidemarie Hatheyer, Carl Wery, Hans von Borsody, Christiane Hörbiger-Wessely, Attila Hörbiger, Joseph Offenbach
100 minutes / B&W

Daughter of Dr. Jekyll (Film Ventures Inc.) U.S., 1957

Director: Edgar G. Ulmer
Screenplay: Jack Pollexfen
Producer: Jack Pollexfen
Cinematography: John F. Warren
Editor: Holbrook N. Todd
Music: Melvyn Leonard
Art Direction: Theobald Holsopple
Set Decoration: Mowbray Berkeley
Script Supervisor: Shirley Ulmer
Cast: John Agar, Gloria Talbott, Arthur Shields, John Dierkes, Mollie McCart, Martha Wentworth, Marjorie Stapp
70 minutes / B&W
DVD: Image Entertainment

The Naked Venus (Beaux Arts Films, Inc.) U.S., 1958

Director: Edgar G. Ulmer
Screenplay: Gabriel Gort, Gaston Hakim
Producer: Gaston Hakim
Cinematography: Jacques Sheldon
Editor: Ronny Ashcroft
Music: Arne Hasse
Cast: Patricia Connelle, Don Roberts, Arianne Arden (Arianné Ulmer), Wynn Gregory, Douglas McCairn
77 minutes / B&W
DVD: Image Entertainment

Swiss Family Robinson (Transworld Artists) U.S., 1958 (one episode)

Director: Edgar G. Ulmer
Screenplay: Harold Jacob Smith
Producer: Edgar G. Ulmer, Henry F. Ehrlich
Cinematography: J. Charles Carbajal

Editor: Carlos Savage
Music: Lan Adomian
Art Direction: Edward Fitzgerald
Script Supervisor: Shirley Ulmer
Cast: Will Rogers Jr., Kasey Williams, Reba Waters, John Schmidt, Michael Schmidt, Donald Allain
30 minutes / Color
DVD: Allday Entertainment

Beyond the Time Barrier (Pacific International, aka Miller Consolidated Productions) U.S., 1960

Director: Edgar G. Ulmer
Screenplay: Arthur C. Pierce
Producer: Robert Clarke
Cinematography: Meredith M. Nicholson
Editor: Jack Ruggiero
Music: Darrell Calker
Art Direction: Ernest Fegté
Script Supervisor: Shirley Ulmer
Cast: Robert Clarke, Darlene Tompkins, Arianne Arden (Arianné Ulmer), Vladimir Sokoloff, Stephen Bekassy
75 minutes / B&W
DVD: Sinister Cinema

The Amazing Transparent Man (Pacific International, aka Miller Consolidated Productions) U.S., 1960

Director: Edgar G. Ulmer
Screenplay: Jack Lewis
Producer: Lester D. Guthrie
Cinematography: Meredith M. Nicholson
Editor: Jack Ruggiero
Music: Darrell Calker
Art Direction: Ernest Fegté
Set Decoration: Louise Caldwell
Script Supervisor: Shirley Ulmer
Cast: Marguerite Chapman, Douglas Kennedy, James Griffith, Ivan Triesault, Boyd 'Red' Morgan, Carmel Daniel
58 minutes / B&W
DVD: Alpha Video; Roan

Hannibal / Annibale (Liber Films, Chefordi) Italy / U.S., 1960

Directors: Edgar G. Ulmer, Carlo Ludovico Bragaglia
Screenplay: Mortimer Braus, Sandro Continenza
Producer: Ottavio Poggi
Cinematography: Raffaele Maschiocchi
Editor: Renato Cinquini
Music: Carlo Rustichelli
Art Direction: Amedeo Mellone, Ernest Kromberg
Script Supervisor: Shirley Ulmer
Cast: Victor Mature, Rita Gam, Milly Vitale, Gabriele Ferzetti, Rik Battaglia, Franco Silva, Mario Girotti (Terence Hill)
100 minutes / Color
DVD: VCI Entertainment

Journey Beneath the Desert / Antinea, l'amante della citta sepolta / L'Atlantide (C.C.M. / Fidès) France / Italy, 1961

Directors: Edgar G. Ulmer, Giuseppe Masini, Frank Borzage (uncredited)
Screenplay: André Tabet, Ugo Liberatore, Remigio Del Grosso
Producer: Luigi Nannerini
Cinematography: Enzo Serafin
Editor: Renato Cinquini
Music: Carlo Rustichelli
Art Direction: Piero Filippone, Edgar G. Ulmer
Script Supervisor: Shirley Ulmer
Cast: Haya Harareet, Jean-Louis Trintignant, Rad Fulton (James Westmoreland), Amedeo Nazzari, Georges Rivière, Giulia Rubini
104 minutes / Color
DVD: Sinister Cinema

The Cavern / Sette contro la morte / Helden—Himmel und Holle / Neunzig Nachte und ein Tag (Cinedoris S.p.A., Arwin Productions / 20th Century-Fox Corporation) Italy / Germany / U.S., 1964

Director: Edgar G. Ulmer
Screenplay: Michael Pertwee, Jack Davies
Producer: Edgar G. Ulmer
Cinematography: Gábor Pogány
Editor: Renato Cinquini
Music: Carlo Rustichelli
Script Supervisor: Shirley Ulmer

Cast: John Saxon, Rosanna Schiaffino, Larry Hagman, Peter Marshall, Brian Aherne, Nino Castelnuovo, Hans von Borsody

96 minutes / B&W

The Doris Day Show (Arwin Productions) U.S. 1968

DVD: MPI Home Video

Ulmer worked as unit production manager, primarily production planning, cost control and management of production.

Name Index

Title Index

Subject Index

About the Contributors

John Belton is professor of English and film at Rutgers University. He is the author of five books, including *Widescreen Cinema* (1992), winner of the 1993 Kraszna Krausz prize for books on the moving image, and *American Cinema/American Culture* (1994, 2004), a textbook written to accompany the PBS series *American Cinema*. He has edited three books, edits a series of books on film and culture for Columbia University Press, and serves as associate editor of the film journal *Film History*.

Peter Bogdanovich received two Oscar nominations for the small-town drama *The Last Picture Show*, the film that made him the hottest young director of 1971. More than thirty-five years later, with *Tom Petty and the Heartbreakers: Runnin' Down a Dream*, he's still hot. His other films include *What's Up Doc? Paper Moon*, *Mask*, and *The Cat's Meow*.

Vincent Brook has a Ph.D. in film and television from UCLA. He has been teaching media studies on the university level for more than twenty years, most recently at UCLA and USC. He has written dozens of journal articles, anthology essays, encyclopedia entries, and reviews; authored the book *Something Ain't Kosher Here: The Rise of the "Jewish" Sitcom* (2003); and edited the anthology *You Should See Yourself: Jewish Identity in Postmodern American Culture* (2006). He is currently working on a book about film noir from the standpoint of Jewish émigré directors.

Alec Charles is senior lecturer in media at the University of Bedfordshire. He is currently editing a collection of essays on *Media in the Enlarged Europe*.

His recent publications include chapters in *The Films of Tod Browning* (2006) and *Time and Relative Dissertations in Space* (2007).

Bernd Herzogenrath is professor of American studies and teaches American literature and culture at the University of Frankfurt and the University of Cologne, Germany. He is the author of *An Art of Desire: Reading Paul Auster* (1999), and the editor of *From Virgin Land to Disney World: Nature and Its Discontents in the USA of Yesterday and Today* (2001); *The Films of Tod Browning* (2006); *The Cinema of Tod Browning: Essays of the Macabre and Grotesque* (2008); and *Edgar G. Ulmer: Essays on the King of the Bs* (2008). His fields of interest are nineteenth- and twentieth-century American literature, critical theory, and cultural/media studies. He has just finished a project of a "Deleuzian History of the American Body/Politic"; future publications include a collection of essays on *Deleuze/Guattari & Ecology*, and an anthology on *Intermedia[lity]*. Bernd is also the organizer and "inventor" of the Ulmerfest, a biannual conference series on the work of Edgar G. Ulmer that takes place in Ulmer's hometown of Olomouc, Czech Republic. (See www.uni-koeln.de/phil-fak/englisch/abteilungen/berressem/herzogenrath/ulmer/index.htm.)

After years of digging through various archives, he also managed to locate Ulmer's birth home in Olomouc; there are now two memorial plaques on this house: one for Ulmer, one for Bernd.

Reynold Humphries was a student of Christian Metz and wrote his thesis on a corpus of Fritz Lang's American films into *Fritz Lang: Genre and Representation in His American Films* (1989). He has since specialized in the horror genre, publishing *The American Horror Film: An Introduction* (2002) and *The Hollywood Horror Film, 1931–1941: Madness in a Social Landscape* (2006). He has contributed to *Monstrous Adaptations* (2007), *The Cinema of Tod Browning* (2008), and *The Modern American Horror Film* (2009), as well as to special horror issues of *Post Script* and *Paradoxa*, and to the online journal *Kinoeye*. He has published essays on David Cronenberg and Michael Powell and has contributed to *101 Horror Movies* and *101 Science-Fiction Movies*. His other publications include essays in *Film Noir Reader 4, Gangster Film Reader*, *Docufictions*, and anthologies devoted to Kubrick and Huston, as well as articles on Hollywood, blacklisting, and the cold war in French publications; seven contributions to *501 Movie Directors*, and essays in French on Joseph Losey, Kenji Mizoguchi, and Jacques Tourneur. His latest book is *Hollywood's Blacklists: A Political and Cultural History* (2008).

Noah Isenberg is associate professor of university humanities at the New School, where he teaches literature, film, and intellectual history. He is the author, most recently, of a monograph on Edgar G. Ulmer's *Detour* and editor of *Weimar Cinema: An Essential Guide to Classic Films of the Era*. He is currently completing a full-scale critical study of Edgar G. Ulmer's life and career as a filmmaker. A recipient of fellowships from the National Endowment for the Humanities, Fulbright, the Alexander von Humboldt Foundation, and other grant agencies, his writing has appeared in such scholarly and non-scholarly publications as *Cinema Journal*, *New German Critique*, *Raritan*, *Partisan Review*, *Dissent*, *Bookforum*, *The Nation*, *The New Republic*, and the *New York Times*.

David Kalat is a film historian and motion picture preservationist. He has worked with such media companies as Turner Classic Movies, the Criterion Collection, Kino International, Film Preservation Associates, and Classic Media to promote film culture. He is the author of several well-regarded books on film history, including *The Strange Case of Dr. Mabuse* and *J-Horror*, and writes regularly for Video Watchdog and Turner Classic Movies Online. Through the auspices of his own company, All Day Entertainment, he has rediscovered and restored important works by such filmmakers as Harry Langdon, Jean Epstein, Edward Dmytryk, Fritz Lang, Claude Chabrol, and of course, Edgar G. Ulmer. He lives in La Grange Park, Illinois, with his wife and children.

Bill Krohn is the author of the award-winning *Hitchcock au travail* and of *Luis Bunuel: Chimera*, which have been published in several languages; and codirector/coproducer/cowriter of *It's All True: Based on an Unfinished Film By Orson Welles*. He has been the Los Angeles correspondent of *Cahiers du cinèma* for thirty years. He also reviews films for *The Economist*. He recently published French monographs on *Alfred Hitchcock* and *Stanley Kubrick* and is currently completing *Serial Killer Dreams* and translations of five "cine-poems" by Jean-Luc Godard, originally published by P.O.L., Paris.

Hugh S. Manon is an assistant professor in the screen studies program at Oklahoma State University, where he specializes in Lacanian theory and film noir. He has published in *Cinema Journal*, *Film Criticism*, and *International Journal of Žižek Studies*, as well as in several anthologies. He is currently completing a book project that links the rise and decline of classic American film noir with the advent of television. He recently led a graduate seminar entitled "Lacan and His Followers" and has taught courses on "Film Noir and the Classical Hollywood Crime Genres" at both the graduate and undergraduate level.

Andrew Repasky McElhinney is the maker of the films *The Scream* (1994), *Her Father's Expectancy* (1994), *A Maggot Tango* (1995), *Magdalen* (1998), *A Chronicle of Corpses* (2000), *Georges Bataille's Story of the Eye* (2003), and *Animal Husbandry* (2008). McElhinney is also a repertory film programmer, educator, journalist, burlesque performer, social-issue advocate, opera enthusiast, and multimedia video-installation performance artist who occasionally directs for the stage. Go to www.ARMcinema25.com.

Herbert Schwaab teaches literature, film and media studies in Dortmund and Lüneburg. He holds a Ph.D. in film studies from the Department of Media Studies at the Ruhr-University Bochum. His dissertation focused on the film philosophical works of Stanley Cavell and on concepts of popular culture, experience, and the ordinary. His main fields of research are television series, popular film, concepts of cinephilia, theory of criticism and interpretation, and film philosophy. He is currently working on an introduction to media philosophy based on readings of the sitcom *King of Queens*.

Robert Skotak has worked as a visual-effects supervisor and sequence director for motion pictures for over thirty years, with over eighty feature (primarily) and commercial credits to his name. He is the winner of two Academy Awards and two British Academy Awards for visual effects as supervisor of *Aliens* and co-supervisor of *Terminator 2*. He has worked creatively with Ridley Scott, Tim Burton, James Cameron, Sam Raimi, Woody Allen, Francis Ford Coppola, Gore Verbinski, and John Carpenter, among many others. Skotak has run his own visual effects company, *4-Ward Productions, Inc.*, since 1989, as a creator of models, matte paintings, digital composites, pyro, and other effects for numerous motion pictures. A person who was inspired to make motion pictures in the genre of the "fantastic" from the age of two, Skotak is a recognized film historian whose studies continue to add depth and insight to his own extensive experience.

Jonathan Skolnik teaches at the University of Massachusetts, Amherst. He is the author of articles on Berthold Auerbach, Paul Celan, Heinrich Heine, Arnold Zweig, and the image of the Wandering Jew. He was guest editor for special issues of *New German Critique* on "German-Jewish Religious Thought" (1999) and "Secularization and Disenchantment" (2005). He is at the moment working on a book entitled *"Two must have got hanged together . . .": German Jews and African Americans in Hollywood, 1932–1965*.

Alena Smiešková is an assistant professor at the Department of English and American Studies of University of Constantine the Philosopher in Nitra, Slovakia. In her Ph.D. work she examined the novels of Philip Roth in the light of contemporary postmodernist theories. She teaches American literature and American studies. Her research interests have been aimed at visual culture, the questions of artistic representation, and philosophy of art. The major theme that she has examined in a number of articles is recursive structures in the context of many artistic phenomena, such as street art, film, and fiction. She has been a nominee of the Fulbright Scholar Program, and during the academic year 2008/09 she is going to spend a semester at University of California Santa Cruz doing research on the impact of visual culture on American studies programs.

Miriam Strube is an associate professor in English and American studies at Paderborn University (Germany). She has received scholarships to do research at Princeton University, to participate in the Fulbright Summer School ("The Role of Media in American Society"), to be a visiting scholar at Columbia University, and to study at New York University. Her book on the sexual self-definition of women in literature, music, and visual culture will be published in the winter of 2008, and her textbook on American Philosophy in 2009. She has also written articles on hip-hop, *Sex and the City*, *The L Word*, and women and music, as well as on gender studies.

D. J. Turner has been a senior film archivist with the National Archives of Canada since 1974. A film historian and restorationist, Turner has supervised the restoration of numerous films, particularly titles involving Ernest Shipman (*Back to God's Country*) and Nell Shipman (*Something New* and *A Bear, a Boy and a Dog*). Other titles include *Carry on Sergeant!* (1928); *Lotos, Die Tempeltänzerin*; *The Night Riders*; *Tangled Trails*; and *The Arctic Patrol*, as well as *Damaged Lives* (in collaboration with Robert Gitt at UCLA) and *From Nine to Nine*. He participated in the Ulmer Conference organized by the New School University in New York in 2002. His work has appeared in many journals, including *Cinema Canada*, *Journal of the University Film Association*, *24 Images*, *Griffithiana*, *Journal of Film Preservation* (formerly *FIAF Bulletin*), and *Film History*. In 1987 he published *Canadian Feature Film Index, 1913–1985*. He has taught film history at Carleton University, Ottawa, and is working on a book about Canadian producer Ernest Shipman.

Arianné Ulmer Cipes is the daughter of Edgar G. Ulmer. She was an actress and has worked in the film business for many years. Today she runs the Edgar G. Ulmer Preservation Corp. in Sherman Oaks, California.

Tom Weaver, one of the "leading scholars in the horror field" (*New York Times*), is a Sleepy Hollow, New York–based film researcher and historian.

Since 1982, he has interviewed nearly six hundred actors, writers, producers, directors (etc.) for a variety of nationally distributed magazines. His books (nearly twenty) include *Universal Horrors*, an examination of the studio's classic chillers of the 1930s and '40s. Weaver has written liner notes, production histories, and cast bios for hundreds of laser discs and DVDs; provided DVD audio commentaries for *The Wolf Man*, *Bedlam*, *Creature from the Black Lagoon* and sequels, *Fiend without a Face*, *Devil Doll*, *The Haunted Strangler*, *The Atomic Submarine*, *It Came from Outer Space*, and many others; and guested on movie-related documentary series on American Movie Classics and E! An article cowritten by Weaver and Bob Burns appeared in the 2001 edition of *The Best American Movie Writing*, an annual publication that reprints important essays on film history. It was one of 26 pieces chosen from more than 320 books and magazines, including the *New Yorker* and the *New York Times*; previous volumes have featured articles by Steven Spielberg, Gore Vidal, Roger Ebert, and Martin Scorsese. Weaver is an eight-time winner of the Rondo Hatton Classic Horror Award, a fan-based award presented each year for the best in horror research and appreciation.